Deliberative
Arguing about Doing

Deliberative Rhetoric

Arguing about Doing

Windsor Studies in Argumentation Vol. 5

Christian Kock
University of Copenhagen

Edited by
Hans V. Hansen
University of Windsor

Windsor Studies
In Argumentation

University
of Windsor

Print Book: ISBN# 978-0-920233-80-1
E-Book: ISBN# 978-0-920233-81-8

Windsor Studies in Argumentation

Windsor Studies in Argumentation
Centre for Research in Reasoning, Argumentation and Rhetoric
University of Windsor
401 Sunset Avenue
Windsor, Ontario, Canada
N9B 3P4

Contents

Part 4: Rhetoric and Practice

Preface

I am glad to have the opportunity to recommend Christian Kock's book, *Deliberative Rhetoric: Arguing about Doing*, to argumentation theorists everywhere. The book is rich in detail and, as the table of contents indicates, broad in scope. It first considers rhetoric in relation to philosophy, then to argumentation, then to politics, and finally to education. In each section of the book we find substantial challenges to received opinion as well as provocations to pursue new avenues of research.

Three of the identifying characteristics of informal logic have been (i) its focus on public discourse rather than technical or scientific discourse, (ii) its rejection of formal methods, including formal logic, and (iii) its determination to offer approaches and methods that will be of value to students and the public. Christian Kock's work fits into this broad framework but he develops each of the characteristics in a specific way. First, he concentrates on discourse that has to do with deliberation and practical reasoning rather than the whole field of public discourse. Second, even though he shares with other argumentation theorists their rejection of formal logic, he criticizes informal logic's lack of attention to the distinction between theoretical and practical reasoning. And third, he takes a special interest in developing standards and directions for criticism of an important part of public discourse, deliberative political debate in democracies.

Kock's rhetorical theory is rooted in Aristotle's theory of deliberation and its reliance on practical reasoning. Practical reasoning is about what to do, not what to believe, and hence it is not subject to the same alethic standards as logical reasoning. When practical reasoning is done collectively, whether in the family circle or on the national stage, it is rhetorical argumentation that must carry the day. Rhetoric is, basically, for Kock, what one does by speech when deliberating with others about what to do. However, rhetoric as deliberation simply cannot operate without social values and this recognition presents a new set of problems for rhetorical argumentation: value subjectivity, value pluralism and value incommensurability, all of which encumber deliberation by putting up obstacles to a direct path to solutions. In as much as Kock is an advocate for the theory of deliberative argumentation, he lays out in some detail the difficulties that beset those actually engaged in this kind of rhetorical activity.

Contemporary political discourse is of special interest to Kock in the present book. He carries the same passion for deliberation that we imagine filled the Greek agoras forward to our time. This is evident, I think, when we consider his approach to debates. Our usual practice is that debaters will use an audience in their efforts to win a debate, and eventually an election. This they do by currying their audiences' favour. Yet often political arguers give no arguments at all for their views, sometimes they give weak arguments and sometimes they fail to respond relevantly to objections of which they are well aware. Kock's view, elaborated on the basis of his own critical studies of contemporary debates in Denmark and the European Union, is that we would be better served if we demanded that political debates be occasions for audiences to become more thoroughly acquainted with the details of the debaters' positions and their reasons for them. On this model it is the debaters that are being used: they are serving us, the public, making us better informed and ready for civic action.

I think this book, Professor Kock's *Deliberative Rhetoric*, is a very important publication in the Windsor Studies in Argumentation series. This is partly because it is an historically informed study of rhetorical theory and also because it engages and responds to alternative approaches to argumentation by some of the leading contemporary argumentation theorists, including Douglas Walton, Stephen Toulmin, and Frans van Eemeren. Mostly, however, Christian Kock's book will be appreciated for re-invigorating our thinking about the function and value of rhetoric in our modern democracies.

HVH
Windsor, Ontario
November 2017.

Acknowledgments

Windsor Studies in Argumentation gratefully acknowledges the assistance of Mr Luc Quenneville, typesetter in the University of Windsor Print Shop. We also thank Professor Kock for allowing us to use his variation of Raphael's School of Athens for the book's front cover. Most of all, we are extremely grateful to Mr Dave Johnston, Co-Director of the Centre for Digital Scholarship in the Leddy Library, University of Windsor, for patiently and persistently seeing the publication of this book through all the way to the finish line. Without Dave's dedication, skill, and energy, this book would not be.

Introduction

This volume brings together a selection of work done across a period of more than thirty years. I would like to offer this introduction as a help to readers who want to follow the thread of the papers in it and to explain the thinking behind them. I hope that these pieces will then together appear as a (somewhat) coherent effort centered on a unifying cluster of ideas.

The volume is called *Deliberative Rhetoric: Arguing about Doing* because I think this title and subtitle highlight the central ideas in that cluster. To start with the subtitle, this is not just a book focusing on argumentation and on arguing in general. It is a central feature of the book that I see arguing about *doing* as a distinctive category within the larger category of argumentation. I think that contemporary argumentation theory—a collective effort that I warmly applaud, by many excellent scholars who have done pioneering work—has, despite its advances, paid too little attention to the category of practical argumentation. Underlying this neglect is a failure to pay sufficient attention to a basic distinction, namely that between epistemic and practical reasoning—or, respectively, reasoning about what is *true* and reasoning about what to *do*. Several of the chapters in the volume address this distinction, arguing for it and seeking to tease out its implications. I have felt it necessary for a long time to insist on this distinction in publications and in talks, and readers of this volume may find passages here and there that sound pretty much like echoes of other passages. For this I apologize, but the reason is that I have found it hard to get a proper hearing for it. There seems to be a strong tendency among argumentation scholars—especially those whose background is in certain branches of philosophy—to fail to recognize that this distinction is valid and important. I object, for example, to textbooks and theories of argumentation that axiomatically state that the purpose of argumentation is to determine what is true. No, I say, in practical argument the ultimate purpose is to decide on a *choice*, and, to reiterate a quote from Aristotle that I have used many times, "choice is not either true or false."

My insistence on the difference between arguing about what is true and arguing about what to do has been taken as an assertion of a dichotomy; it has been pointed out, rightly, that there are many issues where a purported exclusive disjunction between arguing about truth and arguing about choice cannot be upheld. I completely accept this objection and have tried to accommodate it, e.g., in chapter 8. But as critics of unwarranted dichotomies should know well, one also implies an unwarranted dichotomy by asuming that if two things do not constitute a dichotomy, then they must be identical. There *are* important differences that do not constitute classic dichotomies, and the difference between epistemic and practical reasoning is an example of this. The two things are importantly different in many respects despite the fact that there are intermediary forms between them and also many hard or undecidable cases.

Moving from right to left in the title of this volume, we come to the word *deliberation*. I believe that precisely because of the differences between practical and epistemic reasoning, practical reasoning must always in principle be deliberative. This means—and here we may think of the etymology of the word *deliberate* and its cognates, which derive from *libra*, a scale for weighing—that in the standard case, there will be reasons (or "arguments") both for and against anything that one considers doing— that is to say, *valid* reasons. In this I deliberately use the term *valid* in a different sense from its use in formal logic. As will soon be clear, I believe that logically "valid" reasoning is in principle not available in practical reasoning, that is, reasoning for or against a given choice. This is because in practical reasoning there will be reasons of a certain *weight* on both sides. It follows from this that in practical reasoning a weighing or balancing must take place. If one accepts that, then one has to let go of any desire to see such reasoning as a deductive process. In practical reasoning there are in principle no reasons that deductively *entail* a certain decision as their conclusion. If there were, there could not be arguments of "some" weight on both sides. Why that is so I will try to explain, and many of the chapters make similar attempts.

In the model case of deductive argumentation, mathematics, there cannot be reasons of some weight on both sides. There is, for example, a deductively valid set of reasons, including a few axioms, that simply *entail* a theorem like that of Pythagoras. (In fact there are several proofs, i.e., sets of reasons or steps, that all *force* the conclusion that Pythagoras' theorem is true.) This fact entails that there could never be an argument "of some weight," or indeed of any weight, *against* the theorem. It is true, and any denial of it, or any alleged argument for doubting it, is false.

What about empirical sciences—like, e.g., cosmology, which involves theories like that of the "Big Bang"? Will my deep distinction between epistemic and practical reasoning not collapse because in such a domain (undeniably an epistemic domain) there will also be arguments of some weight both for and against a theory? Yes, there will no doubt, but in a different sense of the concept "weight." If some scientists believe that the universe began with a Big Bang and others believe it didn't, then they cannot both be right: both those claims cannot be true at the same time. If one of them is right, then the other is wrong. We may believe that the truth in the matter may never be conclusively found (which is what any Popperian theory of science tells us, since such a theory can never in principle be verified, only falsified). But even so, both parties in a possible debate between pro-Big-Bangers and anti-Big-Bangers are surely out on a quest for the truth. They both assume that there *is* a truth about the origin of the universe, and that it exists independently of us all, although they probably also agree that it can never be conclusively determined. All we can have in its stead, then, is probability. In *that* sense each of the parties in the dispute may have arguments of a certain weight: reasons that either add to or detract from the probability of their theory.

In practical reasoning, however, for example in political debate, things are not like that. Some people in a given society will want lower taxes and fewer public welfare programs. Others will want more welfare programs and will accept higher taxes as a means to it. There is no "truth" anywhere about what the correct level of taxation and welfare programs might be, and so there is no deductively binding (i.e., logically "valid") reasoning available to tell us which of the two disagreeing groups is right. There is not even such a thing as "cogent" or "sufficient" reasoning to this effect—if the words "cogent" or "sufficient" are to have any discernible meaning. I say this because I admit to being impatient with the use of these terms in discussions of what a "good" argument is. The accepted meanings of these words is that if a piece of reasoning has one of these qualities (which are often taken to be the same), then it deductively entails its conclusion. Then why not say that—if that is what one means? If that is *not* what one means, then I find the meanings of these words unclear, and I tend to see the use of them as an attempt to, on the one hand, reject deductivism and, on the other hand, have it too.

As for the political dispute between those who want a strong state with welfare programs and high taxation vs. those who want the opposite, their respective claims are not about what the world *is* like, but about what they want the world to *be* like. Both probably have reasons for their positions, and both might even, if they were to engage in deliberative debate, accept that there are certain reasons against their positions; but in that case they no doubt assign different *weights* to these reasons. Debater A will believe that the reason *x* speaks for his position, while the reason *y* speaks against it.

Conversely, debater B may believe that the reason *y* speaks for *his* position and the reason *x* against it. But they assign different weights to the reasons *x* and *y*—and that is where they disagree. There will be no deductive proof available to any of them, entailing the truth of his position—or even the "probability" of it. We are simply not talking about truth here, or about its more available substitute, probability; we are talking about choice or, if you will, "preference," "desire," or "will." And not only are the weights assigned to *x* and *y* different in the two debaters; also, the weights assigned by A and B to *x* and *y* may change, perhaps as a result of something that A and B say to each other—in short, as a result of rhetoric.

This shows that the "weight" of each reason should not be taken as completely analogous to the physical weight of an object (as argumentation scholars know, no analogies are complete anyway). The physical weight of an object is objectively determined by its mass and the gravitational force acting on the object. In contrast, the "weight" of reasons in practical reasoning is a metaphorical term; it may change by slow degrees or by discontinuous leaps, caused either by rhetoric, by personal experience or by some other factor. And as we saw, it may vary from one individual to the next. Moreover, to compound the complexity, this weight is in principle always relative: a reason has a certain weight (which is in fact an *un*certain weight) in *relation* to the aggregate weight of other reasons pertaining to the issue.

The fact that there are reasons on both sides of a disagreement with assigned "weights" that are variable in all these ways implies that practical reasoning is always in principle deliberation—i.e., an act of weighing on a pair of metaphorical scales. It is a process, always renewable, that in principle involves—or should involve—*all* relevant reasons pertaining to the issue.

This is a rather different image than the picture of argumentation underlying much traditional theory and pedagogy—where one typically assesses one argument at a time, and where, in the most traditional versions, each argument is assessed on a dichotomous scale as either valid (in which case the conclusion is deductively entailed) or invalid (in which case the argument is irrelevant and worthless).

Rather than this dichotomous, stop-go approach to the evaluation of argument I speak in these papers for something that could be called a "scale" model, which necessarily involves taking into account reasons on both pans of the scale. Another meaning of the term "scale" also applies, by the way: the "weight" of a reason should rather be seen as something that can be marked on a continuous scale or gradient, rather than as something that can have only two dichotomous values. The idea of "conductive reasoning" captures this kind of process, and so does the hallowed term "deliberation."

There is further a need to recognize that in this taking-into-account there will typically be reasons on the two sides that cannot be measured by the same unit or yardstick: reasons in practical reasoning are often what I call "multidimensional" in the sense that they belong to different dimensions. Philosophers have used terms like "value pluralism" and "incommensurability" for this complicating circumstance. Thus deliberation, i.e., the metaphorical weighing of the reasons relevant to an issue, is a process with no one authoritative answer, and there is no reason to assume that arguers in a dispute will necessarily find consensus, let alone the "truth." They may continue to disagree, in an enduring state of what John Rawls has called "reasonable disagreement."

This brings us to the last keyword in the book title: "rhetorical." Rhetoric, I argue, has from its first practical implementation by the sophists and its first theoretical conception by Aristotle been a social practice designed to deal with precisely the kind of reasoning circumscribed above. Aristotle, I argue, laid down a particularly strict and clearly demarcated conceptual definition of rhetoric, namely as public discussion of issues on which we may "deliberate" (*bouleuein*). Those issues are, as he repeatedly makes clear, only the sort of things we may decide to do or undertake—not all sorts of other issues where we can do nothing one way or the other. Rhetoric, by this definition, is precisely the public discussion of what we, as a collective, will decide to do.

This implies that traditional definitions of rhetoric as dealing with "the contingent," "the probable," etc., are not strict enough—at least not by Aristotle's standards. Rhetoric is the discussion of what we will do because we want things to be in certain ways; the "contingent" and the "probable" are terms whose core meaning is that they deny absolute certainty or necessity; but they still have to do with how things are, not how we want them to be.

I do not speak for a definition of rhetoric as strict as Aristotle's (I mean his "intensional" definition, which is the one I referred to above; his "extensional" definition is looser, genre-based and more empirical). But I think his narrow definition is worth highlighting because it identifies what

I consider to be the central domain of rhetorical argumentation: disagreement over proposed action. I would add, however, that in the rhetorical tradition this strict understanding has been supplemented, as with concentric circles around a core, with other domains of argument—and with other types of "speech acts" (or if you will, Wittgensteinian "language-games") that are not argumentation at all, having no strictly persuasive motive, but which are rather to seen as exemplifying the other two Ciceronian "offices" of the rhetor besides *movere*: *docere* and *delectare*. Common to all these functions are that in each of them a rhetor aims, through discourse, to have some kind of impact on his or her audience. Rhetors are out to affect people, not merely to prove propositions (which is something they cannot do anyway in rhetorical argument, since, as we have seen, no deductive *proof* is available there).

On the other hand, in order to perform all these functions, rhetoric disposes of a vast store of instruments and insights. They exist in order to help rhetors do things (or try to do them). As regards rhetorical argumentation, rhetorical arguers should openly admit that when they engage in it they are "strategic" in the sense that they want to persuade—that is, they want, if possible, to have their way.

These facts have, ever since Plato's *Gorgias*, cause a deep distrust of rhetoric and rhetors. So they are out to persuade? Persuade by any means—any whatsoever, regardless of truth and ethics? The reply to this concern is that some rhetors are indeed like that, that is, without regard for truth and ethics—but rhetoric and rhetors are not necessarily guilty of culpable disregard for the truth, or for ethics, for that matter. Rather, since rhetoric's central domain is deliberation about what we should do, it follows that there may in principle be legitimate but opposite courses of action to choose between—as for example in the choice between a neo-liberalist and a communitarian set of political values. (Or, for that matter, for a family that considers whether to spend their vacation in Spain or France.) No binding proof is available in any of these cases—but on the other hand a multitude of other means of impacting one's audience and its inclinations *are* available.

Despite the fact that in rhetoric one argues about decision, not about truth, and despite the fact that there are countless ways one can use discourse to argue for a decision, it is nevertheless an essential tenet in this book that there *is* such a thing as reasonable and responsible rhetoric, as well as its opposite: rhetoric that is unreasonable, irresponsible and socially pernicious. The foundational thinkers in the rhetorical tradition—figures like Aristotle, Cicero, Quintilian, Erasmus, Vico, Campbell, Kenneth Burke, Perelman—all take it for granted that on the one hand rhetoric can fulfill a constructive and necessary function in a polity; but on the other hand it can also do the opposite (and everything in between). This makes it meaningful to try to formulate what the criteria for socially constructive rhetoric are. What are rhetorical virtues, what are vices?

All of the thinkers just mentioned have—realistically—seen rhetoric as functioning on two levels: the personal and the social. A rhetor may speak strategically for his own cause, and in that there is nothing wrong *per se*; in fact it seems a plausible speculation that language arose among humans in order to perform various "strategic" functions. On the other hand one may also ask about the social functions and significance of a society's rhetorical practices.

Much of the work in this book circles around that issue. There is much to be said and much to be discussed when we ask what the criteria for socially desirable rhetoric are, precisely because rhetoric cannot be required to prove truths or be deductively valid. So what *can* we require? And if we have some idea of what sorts of rhetoric we wish to see and hear in a society, how can we encourage and nurture them, and how can we expose and discourage the less desirable kinds? What forms and venues of critical observation and commentary might have some kind of impact? What could be done in the educational system for a better argumentative dialogue on matters of shared concern, in the public sphere and among citizens? These are some of the issues that argumentation scholars, regardless of "school," should get together to address.

Some remarks to introduce the individual chapters in the book and establish a certain coherence between them might be in place. The chapters have been arranged in four parts.

Part 1, "Rhetoric and Philosophy," has three chapters that all address the relationship between these two humanistic disciplines, the oldest of all. I wish to suggest that they can learn from each other, rather than continue the mutual warfare that Plato began, and both make their distinctive contributions to a humanistic understanding of man in society.

Chapter 1, "Gorgias Reloaded. A New-Found Dialogue between Gorgias and Socrates," is not quite what the title asserts. It was originally a talk at the presentation of a new complete translation of Plato's writings into Danish. I happen to think that the criticism of rhetoric that Plato

7

launched through Socrates in *Gorgias* has enjoyed far too much unreflecting repetition by philosophers and other thinkers in later centuries. Reflection, however, is what it should bring about, so I playfully let Gorgias talk back instead of performing the part of the willing lamb-to-the-slaughter that Socrates' interlocutors have assigned to them in some of the dialogues. I let Gorgias enjoy the benefit of having learned from conversation with Aristotle in the Elysian fields, and I also let him expose what I consider an unfair, fallacious analogy argument in Socrates' comparison of the sophist/rhetorician and the harp-player in the *Protagoras*.

Chapter 2, "Choice Is Not True or False: The Domain of Rhetorical Argumentation," is a programmatic text in which I argue that leading contemporary argumentation theorists such as Johnson, van Eemeren and Houtlosser, and Tindale —all of whom I admire for many of their ideas, but not necessarily for all of them—have, in their attempts to address rhetoric, tended to define rhetorical argumentation with reference either to (a) the rhetorical arguer's goal (to persuade effectively), or (b) the means he employs to do so. However, a central strand in the rhetorical tradition itself, led by Aristotle, and arguably the dominant view in that tradition, sees rhetorical argumentation as defined with reference to the *domain of issues* discussed. On that view, the domain of rhetorical argumentation is centered on choice of action in the civic sphere, and the distinctive nature of issues in this domain is considered crucial. I argue that argumentation theories such as those discussed in the first part of the chapter promulgate an understanding of rhetoric that is historically inadequate. I further suggest that theories adopting this understanding of rhetoric risk ignoring important distinctive features of argumentation about action.

Chapter 3, "Aristotle on Deliberation: Its Place in Ethics, Politics and Rhetoric—Then and Now," is an attempt to highlight connections between Aristotle's thinking on rhetoric and on ethics and politics. Aristotle differs from most later philosophers in distinguishing clearly between epistemic reasoning, which aims for truth, and practical reasoning, which aims for choice. How can he posit this distinction and yet not dismiss practical reasoning as truth-neglecting flattery and manipulation, as Plato did? The question I try to answer here is one that many later rhetors and rhetoricians have also had to face. The answer lies in the concepts of deliberation (*boulē, bouleusis*) and deliberate choice (*proairesis*). They link Aristotle's rhetoric, ethics, and politics together and help provide interconnected definitions of all three. Ethics is about deliberate choices made by individuals. Politics and rhetoric are about the collective choices made by the polity: politics is about making such choices that the good life of all citizens is optimally secured; rhetoric is the principal means to do this. These links have not been much discussed by scholars, probably because few studies range across all three of these Aristotelian arts; a proper discussion of them should draw on modern work in ethics, political science, and rhetoric. The key concepts in Aristotle that the paper discusses offer inspiration for modern theories of "deliberative democracy," citizenship, argumentation, debate, and the public sphere.

Part 2, "Rhetoric and Argumentation," collects five chapters where I have done what I could to make clear how a rhetorical view can contribute to argumentation theory proper. I have great respect for what the leading figures in contemporary argumentation theory have done for this discipline that is fairly new in academe but no less necessary for that, but I also think rhetoric can bring useful new insights to the shared table. And the common denominator for those might be "pluralism." In all of these chapters there is a plea that significant distinctions should be made that much of the current theory is apt to neglect or downplay.

Chapter 4, "Multiple Warrants in Practical Reasoning," is one of two papers that discuss the lasting contribution of Stephen Toulmin to argumentation theory in light of the central ideas I wish to propose. The concept of "warrant," I argue, reflects Toulmin's general insights that argumentative validity in reasoning (which is not the same as logical "validity") comes in many forms, and that reasoning in most fields cannot possess the necessity and certainty that have attracted many thinkers to the "Rationalist" paradigm. However, there is a scarcity of concepts in one part of Toulmin's theory of argument. While pedagogical applications of his model offer a fine-grained system of warrant types for epistemic propositions ("sign" warrants, "causal" warrants, etc.), they lack categories of warrants for practical claims (i.e., proposals for action). One version of Toulmin-based pedagogy has only one such category—the "motivational" warrant. Ancient rhetorical thinking can help us correct this insufficiency. The author of the rhetorical textbook allegedly used by Alexander the Great proposed a broader typology of practical warrants. His approach highlights what I call the "multidimensionality," and hence what modern moral philosophers call the "incommensurability," of warrants—the absence of a common measure allowing for a "rational" balancing of conflicting warrants. The widespread occurrence of multidimensionality in practical argument lends support to Toulmin's general anti-rationalist view of reasoning. Moreover, while multidimensionality prevents a "rational" and binding balancing, I argue that it legitimizes and in fact necessitates the use of rhetoric in practical reasoning.

Chapter 5, "Is Practical Reasoning Presumptive?" addresses attempts by the most prolific contemporary argumentation theorist, Douglas Walton, to fit practical reasoning into a theoretical mold that in my view does not sufficiently recognize its distinctive features. Walton's model of practical reasoning as "presumptive" is, I argue, misleading. The notions of "inference" and of the "burden of proof" shifting back and forth between proponent and respondent lead to counterintuitive consequences. Because the issue in practical reasoning is a *proposal*, rather than a *proposition*, there are, in the standard case, several perfectly good reasons on both sides simultaneously, which implies that argument appraisal necessarily contains a subjective element—a fact that argumentation theory needs to conceptualize.

Chapter 6, "Multidimensionality and Non-Deductiveness in Deliberative Argumentation," argues that the focus in contemporary argumentation theory is too rarely on practical or deliberative argumentation as such. Many modern theorists mistakenly tend to see all argumentation as one homogeneous domain. Even so, there has recently been a tendency to differentiate more, for example in the work of Walton, who has defined different types of argumentative dialogue. However, to understand deliberative argumentation better, we also need to differentiate in another way, namely on the basis of argumentative issues (one might also say "domains," cf. above). When the issue is practical (i.e., action or choice), there will typically be multidimensionality among the reasons or warrants invoked, and this helps explain why deductive "validity" is not an option nor a meaningful evaluative criterion.

Chapter 7, "Constructive Controversy: Rhetoric as Dissensus-oriented Discourse," similarly suggests that current theories of argumentation underestimate the difference, emphasized by Aristotle, between theoretical and practical (action-oriented) argumentation. This is exemplified with the argument theories of Toulmin, Pragma-Dialectics, Habermas, Walton, and even Perelman and Olbrechts-Tyteca (whose fundamental views and insights I am otherwise strongly indebted to). Since antiquity, rhetoric has defined itself, not as argument designed to "win," but as action-oriented argument. What is perhaps most noticeable in this chapter is that it specifies some of the distinctive features of action-oriented argument. One is that its warrants include value concepts in audiences, implying an element of subjectivity in argument assessment. Between disagreeing individuals, but also inside each individual, several conflicting value dimensions are typically involved, not just the dimension of truth-falsity—and this makes sustained, reasonable dissensus inevitable.

Chapter 8, "Why Argumentation Theory Should Differentiate Types of Claim," further explores the distinction between epistemic reasoning (about the truth of propositions) and practical reasoning (about the adoption of proposals), emphasizing the depth of the differences. I use Aristotle's views of practical reasoning, as interpreted by the philosopher Anthony Kenny, to show that practical reasoning has a complex, "'backward" structure that does not allow for the predication of "truth" for the claims advanced, nor for a strict notion of "inference." Other features of practical reasoning such as multidimensionality and the role of subjectivity are discussed, and a spectrum of types of claim, ranging from the purely epistemic to the purely practical, is suggested.

Part 3, "Rhetoric and Democracy," widens the scope by bringing together seven chapters that all look at how argumentation and persuasion works, or should work, in the practical world of politics, ethics, and daily affairs.

Chapter 9, "Norms of Legitimate Dissensus," can be said to summarize much of what is said in this volume about the nature of deliberative debate and the consequent criteria for the assessment of it. I call for argumentation theory to learn from moral and political philosophy. Several thinkers in these fields help understand the occurrence of what we may call legitimate dissensus: enduring disagreement even between reasonable people arguing reasonably. It inevitably occurs over practical issues, e.g., issues of action rather than truth, because there will normally be legitimate arguments on both sides, and these tend to be incommensurable, i.e., they cannot be objectively weighed against each other. Accordingly, "inference," logical "validity," and "sufficiency" are inapplicable notions. Further distinctive features of pro and con arguments in practical argumentation are explored, and some corollaries are drawn regarding evaluative norms of legitimate dissensus. Examples from immigration-related public debates in Denmark are given.

Chapter 10, "Dialectical Obligations in Political Debate," zooms in on the crucial importance in public debate of not only arguing for one's own position, but also answering counter-arguments. Given the distinctive features of political debate, and of all practical reasoning, that have been asserted in this volume, it follows that political debaters have particularly stringent dialectical obligations: it becomes crucial, in the interest of the audience (i.e., all us citizens), that political debaters acknowledge good arguments on the opposite side and explain why, on balance, they deem the arguments favoring their own side to be weightier.

Chapter 11, "Virtue Reversed: Principal Argumentative Vices in Political Debate," summarizes, in a systematic overview, the principal "stultifying vices" that I have analyzed in a book whose title means "They Are Not Answering"—vices that I believe beset most public political debate in Western democracies. The conceptual hierarchy of these "vices" reflects a view of argumentative norms inspired by the "ARG" triad ("Acceptability—Relevance—Good Grounds") as well as by the concept of "dialectical obligations," both advanced by thinkers connected with the school of Informal Logic. The resultant typology presents, in negative, a bid for something that civic instruction might profitably teach students at all levels about deliberative democracy.

Chapter 12, "Rhetoric that Shifts Votes: A Large-Scale Exploratory Study of Persuasion in Issue-Oriented Public Debates," was written with two colleagues in the Rhetoric program at the University of Copenhagen, Charlotte Jørgensen and Lone Rørbech. It differs from all the preceding chapters in being a strictly empirical study—with a normative twist. It summarizes a study of 37 televised debates on political issues in Denmark, conducted live before representative audiences, with polls on the issues taken in the audience before and after each debate. These debates are of interest as research data because they were authentic, not experimental, and they suggest valuable insights about persuasive effects. Various rhetorical features were observed and related to debaters' success in attracting votes. In a qualitative interpretation of the observations, we suggest that debates such as these are likely to be won by debaters whose argumentation is fair and thoughtful. The debate format may enhance such a result, for the benefit of the democratic process. It was our study of these policy debates, I believe, that first alerted me to differences between epistemic and logical reasoning on the one hand and practical reasoning, including political debate, on the other.

Chapter 13, "The Rhetorical Audience in Public Debate and the Strategies of Vote-gathering and Vote-shifting," written with Charlotte Jørgensen, grew out of our work with the "Rhetoric that Shifts Votes" project, which generated the hypothesis that two different rhetorical strategies in issue-oriented debates will be apt to win votes from two different groups: what we call vote-gathering will be more likely to appeal to the Undecided voters, while the strategy we call vote-shifting is more likely to win votes from the opposite side. While vote-gathering tends to be "front-widening," vote-shifting tends to be "front-narrowing." We speak for debate formats that allow vote-shifting rhetoric to unfold and suggest that it would be strategically wise for debaters, as well as more useful for audiences, if debaters would focus on winning over shiftable voters from the opposite side.

Chapter 14, "Evaluation of Public Spokespersons," was written with the late Flemming Hansen, Professor of Marketing at the Copenhagen Business School. Like the preceding chapter, it is strictly empirical, aiming to find what properties ordinary people connect with the notion of "credibility"—a longtime pet subject of empirical communication research. The study uses factor analysis, as do many previous studies of the credibility construct, but with important modifications. Our findings suggest, essentially, that people tend to correlate credibility with some of the same qualities that were found to characterize "vote-shifters" in the "Rhetoric that Shifts Votes" study. To be credible, one need not be telegenic, spectacular or provocative (these attributes correlate more with a factor we call "charisma"), but should rather demonstrate the qualities one would hope to find in a judge: intelligence, competence, civility, respect for both sides of an issue.

Chapter 15, "Argumentation Democracy 101," is a sort of beginner's guide to the normative assessment of public debate, with proposals for its improvement. It builds on the opening chapter of my book in Danish, *De svarer ikke: Fordummende uskikke i den politiske debat* ("They Are Not Answering: Stultifying Vices in Political Debate," 2011, 2nd ed. 2013). I am pleased to report that for several weeks this book, aimed at a general audience, topped the Danish list of best-selling non-fiction. The chapter based on it sketches in broad strokes and accessible language a view of what deliberative debate in democracy could be, and ideally should be.

Part 4, "Rhetoric and Practice," widens the scope further. The chapters in this part overlap with other neighbor disciplines of rhetoric such as linguistics, pedagogy, and media studies.

Chapter 16, "Non-Truth-Conditional Quantification," is the earliest of the papers in the book. When I wrote it I didn't think of myself as either a rhetorician or an argumentation scholar, but more as a pragmatic linguist. The paper parallels, and is inspired by, Oswald Ducrot's thinking on language as more argumentative than referential, and I argue that an omnipresent element in everyday communication, namely the meanings of what I call "vague" adjectives and adverbials (elements that I later learned many linguists call "scalar") can only be understood if we see those meanings as argumentative. (Looking back, I would like to have said "rhetorical." As it happens, Ducrot himself went on to draw on terms and notions from the rhetorical tradition.) I polemically address a widespread view of how to account to for the meaning of linguistic items: the view that sees meaning as (almost) exhaustively describable in terms of "truth conditions." This stab at the "meaning-as-truth-conditions" theory anticipates my later claim that not all argument is about some proposition being true; lurking behind my stance here is a "rhetorical" theory of language to the effect that language is more fundamentally about inducing cooperation from others than about uttering true propositions.

Chapter 17, "Inception: How the Unsaid May Become Public Knowledge," opens a section featuring specific analyses of how language may function rhetorically—for better or worse. It uses H.P. Grice's concept of conversational implicature, and develops concepts based on Gricean thinking, in a rhetorical analysis of several passages in President George W. Bush's speeches prior to the 2003 invasion of Iraq. I propose that the passages in question, along with many others, were apt to suggest to audiences something that Bush never asserted (and ostensibly denied), namely that he believed Saddam Hussein to have been complicit in the 9/11 terrorist acts. Three types of suggestive mechanism are analyzed. They are offered as examples of rhetorical devices used in political communication that may create a kind of "public knowledge" that has neither been asserted, supported with reasons, or reflected upon. The intended relevance of this analysis for argumentation studies is that it cautions citizens in democracies about the views that political leaders will have us adopt underhandedly, without argument.

In Chapter 18, "A Good Paper Makes a Case: Teaching Academic Writing the Macro-Toulmin Way," my co-author Signe Hegelund and I contend that many of our students' problems in the writing of academic papers (including problems concerning typical rhetorical aspects like genre and task definition) may be addressed if we adapt Toulmin's argument model to explain the genre requirements regarding argumentation in academic papers, as opposed to everyday argumentation (including practical reasoning). Students, we say, should be encouraged to apply the model as an assessment criterion and, at the same time, as a heuristic tool while writing their papers. This involves a "macroscopic" or "top-down" approach to the evolving draft, not a "microscopic" analysis of individual passages. The paper suggests a number of class activities that will help students apply such a "Macro-Toulmin" view to their own work. I might add that I think this is what the "Toulmin model" is probably best at—because it was not in the first place conceived to model practical argument (i.e., argumentation about doing). I believe it is better seen as part of Toulmin's Wittgenstein-inspired campaign for a pluralism where different scholarly and scientific "fields" have, as it were, different "language-games" with different rules for what counts as data and, in particular, as warrants. This again reflects the fact that Toulmin, at the time when he wrote *The Uses of Argument*, was mainly interested in the theory of science. It is, indeed, striking that the book contains no examples of examples of arguments about doing, only examples of epistemic arguments (who can forget "Harry is a British subject"?). For these reasons I also believe that Toulmin's theory and model are in fact insufficient and potentially misleading as a theoretical basis for a study or pedagogy of practical argument.

In Chapter 19, "Generalizing Stasis Theory for Everyday Use," I propose a modernized version of ancient thinking about *stasis* (or *status*)—a topical system for argument invention used by defendants in court trials. Essentially, I suggest that, for purposes of pedagogy, criticism, and also argumentative practice, we may extend the use of *stasis* thinking to *all* practical disagreements, not just forensic cases, since all such disagreements invoke norms, formal or informal, that are functionally similar to the legal statutes in forensic reasoning. Furthermore, I suggest that we collapse the two main components of *stasis* theory—the *status rationales* and the *status legales*. The resulting systematic overview of argumentative strategies could, I argue, help focus political and social disagreements on the points where the essential disagreements remain. This might at the same time give more powerful persuasive tools to debaters and "more light, less heat" to their audiences.

Chapter 20, "Rhetoric in Media Studies: The Voice of Constructive Criticism," seeks to apply an idea of rhetoric as a socially constructive force to media criticism. With reference to studies in news reporting and political journalism and commentary, I suggest that various current program types and framing practices do not serve democracy and deliberation as well as they might.

On these pages I have underlined some of the central issues that weave through this book. Hopefully they will become more visible with the above remarks in mind. I have briefly summarized the individual chapters in a way that is meant to clarify how they relate to the recurrent themes. While I ask for the reader's attentiveness in recognizing these themes, I also apologize for having made the going bumpier than necessary. Most of the flaws of exposition that I am aware of have to do with the fact that these papers were produced over a long stretch of time, in an attempt to progressively clarify my own thoughts. This has made me repeat certain key ideas and examples more times than would have been fitting for a monograph. And the papers in this volume are reproduced in exactly the formulation they originally had. There would have been no point in trying to revise and update them—that task would inevitably lead to complete rethinking in monograph form (which is in fact a project I am engaged in). In addition to some unnecessary repetition, there is also on the other hand a certain lack of repetition and consistency in my use of key terms. I have tried out various wordings and key terms for key ideas and have at times, for example, spoken of reasoning, argumentation, or deliberation as more or less overlapping or synonymous notions. A list of other blemishes of expository rhetoric might be put together. I ask the reader's indulgence with this in the hope that the central ideas I speak for will crystallize and earn the reader's thoughtful consideration.

Part 1: Rhetoric and Philosophy

1.

Gorgias Reloaded: A New-Found Dialogue between Gorgias and Socrates

In the Elysian Fields, Socrates to his surprise meets his old rhetorical adversary Gorgias—who has, in the meantime, come to think twice about some of the alleged errors that Socrates made him admit to in the Platonic dialogue about their original encounter. Among other things, Gorgias has had the advantage of gathering a few points from a certain young thinker hailing "from up North" (he presumably means Stagira). Thus equipped, he takes Socrates to task about several of his anti-rhetorical pronouncements from back then that Gorgias now feels he is in a position to challenge.

SOCRATES Well, if *that* isn't—you can call me a sophist if that isn't— *Gorgias! Old boy!* Fancy meeting you here—in the Elysian Fields! The Island of the Blessed! The very man who brought that awful nuisance, rhetoric, to Athens! I'd never have thought I'd live to see that. In fact, I didn't.

GORGIAS No, you didn't see that one coming, did you, Socrates? And you know, it was only recently that they let us in, me and my gang—you know, the other sophists, Protagoras and Prodicus and Antisthenes and those guys.

And why do think *that* is? *You* did that to us. *You* did such a great job dragging our names through the mud, smearing me and the other sophists or rhetoricians, as you call us, and thanks to *you* most philosophers until this day have detested us.

Take a philosopher like John Locke, one of the bright lights who started the so-called Enlightenment—he said this in *An Essay on Human Understanding* (1690): "It is evident how much men love to deceive and be deceived, since rhetoric, that powerful instrument of error and deceit, has its established professors, is publicly taught, and has always been had in great reputation." He also said that rhetoric does nothing but "insinuate wrong ideas, move the passions, and thereby mislead the judgment"

(Book III, 34; 1841, 360). The great Immanuel Kant, a hundred years later, said that rhetoric "deserves no respect at all" —it is "gar keiner Achtung würdig" (Buch II, § 53; 1839, 192). And *you*, Socrates, taught them to say these things.

SOCRATES Okay, much of the stuff they said about you wasn't quite fair of you guys, I suppose.

GORGIAS But they got it from *you*, Socrates. *You* said, in the *Gorgias*, 463a, that rhetoric is "a practice that's not craftlike, but one that a mind given to making hunches takes to, a mind that's bold and naturally clever at dealing with people. I call it flattery, basically."

SOCRATES But then again, Gorgias, what you're quoting there does have *some* truth in it. You are the one who believes that words can act like a drug, and you wrote a speech in defence of Helen of Troy—who left her husband, damn it, to marry an enemy of Greece, because she couldn't help it: his sweet words had acted on her and seduced her with their flattery and their rhythm and their musical repetitions—acted like hypnotism. And you are fascinated by that! Admit it! Honestly, do you really think that speech is nothing but seduction?

GORGIAS Okay, Socrates, you are right, speech is not *just* seduction, but it *is* seduction among other things. I did say it's like a drug, and we all know that some drugs do good things and others do bad things, and sometimes they do a good thing and the next day they do a bad thing. You know what drugs are like: some put an end to disease and others to life, and that goes for discourses as well: "some give pain, others delight, others terrify, others rouse the hearers to courage, and yet others by a certain vile persuasion drug and trick the soul." *I* wrote that, in that speech you mention. Pretty persuasive, isn't it?

SOCRATES But it's terrible to use speech to do all those things, Gorgias.

GORGIAS Yes, I agree, sometimes it *is* terrible, but at least it's good to *know* that speech can do all these things—and to know how it's done. And *I* pointed that out, Socrates. A lot of it has to do with repetition and rhythm and variation and ambiguity and puns and parallelisms and with raising expectations and fulfilling them and circumventing them and surprising them, and things like that. With all this, words can work like music. You know, I can imagine how one day a huge crowd of people will be put into a state of rapture or frenzy by one person who speaks or sings. Imagine a thousand young girls screaming with joy—or a thousand young boys, for that matter, Socrates?

SOCRATES Now let's not get carried away, Gorgias. Better let's discuss what rhetoric really is. I asked you that when we last conversed, but I don't think you were able to answer.

GORGIAS Well, all this is *part* of what rhetoric is, Socrates. Words and sounds can do things to us, and carry us away, and it's better to know about it beforehand, so that we don't get carried away unless we really want to. It's a part of life, but you never seemed to really understand that. And the guy who wrote down everything you said, what's his name, he never understood it either. And that's strange because he wrote pretty beautifully himself—in fact, when I think about it, he wrote even better than I do, but did he want to be called a rhetorician? God forbid!

SOCRATES But you and your gang, Gorgias, you rhetoricians and sophists, you not only *told* people about these things, you also taught them to *do* these things.

GORGIAS You know, Socrates, nowadays there a quite a few wise people who think differently. We were not spin-doctors and manipulators, we were forerunners of democracy and the Open Society. Open discussion of everything! Nothing should be taken for granted! "The Open Society!"—do you know that the guy who wrote about that, he said that we were on the same side, you and I, fighting for human reason, on guard against dogmatism! *Now* what do say, Socrates?

SOCRATES *I* will ask the questions here, Gorgias. That's what makes it real, responsible dialectics. So now I ask again. What *is* rhetoric? And what is it *about*?

GORGIAS Well you know, Socrates, it's been nearly 2,500 years since I last tried to explain to all you Athenians what rhetoric is, and I've actually learned a great deal since then. Soon after I came to the Elysian Fields here I ran into another clever fellow, although he was not a real Athenian—he came from up North, he wrote books about rhetoric and all sorts of other things, and he put things in perspective for me. Did you not meet him when we were still down there, on earth?

SOCRATES There was a lot I didn't get around to, Gorgias. I was cut short.

GORGIAS Yeah, isn't that's too bad, Socrates, but come to think of it, you pretty much dug your own grave with that "apology" you came up with. You should have let *me* write that for you. But the way you handled that situation, you might as well have taken poison—I mean, taken it from the start.

SOCRATES You're trying to dodge my question again, Gorgias. So let me repeat the question I asked you 2,400 years ago: "What kind of persuasion, and of persuasion dealing with what, is rhetoric the art?" (*Gorgias*, 454a).

GORGIAS Well, that is something I have given a lot of thought since our last talk all those years ago, and I've found out that in that talk you really tricked me. You sometimes do that to people, you're no better than the rest of us. Take for example what you said about my colleague Protagoras. You compared a player of the harp or lyre [*kitharistēs*] to a sophist, such as me or Protagoras, and you said that the harp-player can teach us to talk about harp-playing; but what can the sophist teach us to talk about? Nothing in particular, you said—since his speeches can be about anything, or, in other words, nothing (*Protagoras*, 312d-e).

SOCRATES That's right, Gorgias.

GORGIAS But that's where you tricked us. You should have asked what *skill* each of them can teach. The harp-player can teach us the skill of harp-playing, and the sophist can teach the skill of public speaking. Instead you asked what the sophist's *speeches* are about. But then you should also have asked what the harp-player's *music* is about. If you want to compare two things, you should ask the same questions about them both. But you tricked us. You stacked the cards.

SOCRATES Very clever, Gorgias, it only took you 2,400 years to figure that out.

GORGIAS Well Socrates, this is just one example of how you pretend to be so honest and truth-seeking, but just like me you're simply out to persuade people. There are honest ways of doing that as well as less honest ways, and you know both kinds. Welcome in the club. I remember what you said about us sophists, it also applies to you: "there is no need to know the truth of the actual matters, but one merely needs to have discovered some device of persuasion which will make one appear to those who do not know to know better than those who know" (*Gorgias*, 459b-c).

SOCRATES Yes, and what did you answer, Gorgias? You walked right into my trap and said "is it not a great convenience, Socrates, to make oneself a match for the professionals by learning just this single art and omitting all the others?"

GORGIAS Honestly, Socrates, that's what I said according to that young man who wrote all those dialogues about you, just as Dr. Watson did about Sherlock Holmes! Would *I* actually have made such a stupid answer? What your young friend did there was to set up a "straw man" version of my opinion. Just like all the politicians are constantly doing to each other.

SOCRATES And it was you and your friends who taught the politicians and their spin-doctors all those underhanded tricks, Gorgias.

GORGIAS So did you, Socrates. But I think you philosophers and us rhetoricians, we should join forces to expose all the underhanded tricks we hear in political debate so that we can all deliberate about our common affairs in a reasonable manner.

SOCRATES So you are still dreaming about that silly idea, "democracy," Gorgias? I think it's not a dream, it's a nightmare.

GORGIAS Yes I do, Socrates, and let me tell what I learned after speaking to that guy from up North. He thinks rhetoric is a part of political science, and that political science is about securing the good life for everyone as far as possible, and he says that the most highly esteemed of the faculties in political science are strategy, domestic economy—and rhetoric! That's what he said in his *Politics*, 1094 b.

And what is rhetoric about? I agree with you, Socrates: it is very important to define what rhetoric is. I think it is about how we human beings can try to get each other to cooperate by using speech. If I were to come back to Athens today and set up as a teacher of rhetoric again, I would follow that guy's definition of what rhetoric is, and what its uses are. He says in his book about rhetoric, 1357a: "The duty of rhetoric is to deal with such matters as we deliberate upon without arts or systems to guide us." And he makes it very clear that what we can deliberate about is only that which we can decide to *do*. So rhetoric is the means we have in a democratic society to deliberate and make *decisions* together about our shared issues and problems. We can do that well or we can do it badly. Or we can let a dictator or the philosophers do it for us—that's what *you* want, right?

SOCRATES But what about the truth, Gorgias, should our first concern not be to find the truth? And that is where rhetoric fails us.

GORGIAS No, Socrates, I said that rhetoric should be our means for discussing what *to do*. Things like, should we wage war against the Spartans? Should we all use the same kind of money? Should we all form a large union, or should we stand alone? In these matters we do not discuss what the *truth* is, we discuss what we want to *do*. It's like when you discuss at home whether to buy a home, or when you discuss whether to see an exhibition of sculptures or a wrestling match, you and your wife Xanthippe—

SOCRATES You keep her out of it!

GORGIAS What I mean is that both you and your wife have a right to want what you want, and to win the discussion about it. You want to see the wrestlers, she wants to see the sculptures. Neither of your opinions is the "truth." My young Northern friend has said, in one of his books on ethics: "choice is not either true of false" (*Eudemian Ethics* 1226a). It's a matter of what you want, not of finding the truth.

SOCRATES If *I* want to see the wrestlers, and *she* wants to see the sculptures, then we discuss it in a civilized dialectical manner, and then we go to see the sculptures. That's dialectic. No rhetoric can help me there.

GORGIAS But without rhetoric, there's really no democracy, is there, Socrates?

SOCRATES There you go again with your "democracy." At the end of the day, what did *I* get out of it? They took a democratic vote and made me take poison.

GORGIAS But democracy is not just taking a vote, Socrates, it's having a reasonable public discussion where we deliberate on the choice we face, and *then* we take a vote. You know, our Greek word for "deliberate" is based on our word for "will." But the reasonable public discussion should be there first. As citizens we should all know rhetoric, not just so we can take part in public debates, but also so we can attend public debates with a critical ear and use what we hear, or the good parts of it, in our own deliberations. And *that's* where we can learn from you, Socrates, *you* know how to ask really penetrating questions, and insist on an answer to them. You really have a critical ear.

SOCRATES I have *two* critical ears, Gorgias.

GORGIAS Yes, but you also need to have an *appreciative* ear that can recognize a reasonable argument when you hear one. The citizens of Athens, for example, should be able to recognize both bad arguments and good ones when they hear them—even when the good arguments come from someone they disagree with. We should all learn to speak—but what good is that if no one listens to anyone else? Rhetoric can teach us that. It's not enough to have a big mouth that blabbers away. But it is not enough either to tear apart everything that other people say, the way you sometimes do. Look, *this* is *my* critical ear—and *this* is my *listening* ear.

SOCRATES I think what matters is what's between the ears, Gorgias. True wisdom, you know.

GORGIAS What use is it that we all have true wisdom between the ears if we don't also use it? I'd like to quote another Athenian, who happened to be my student. His name was Isocrates.

SOCRATES I knew him, Gorgias.

GORGIAS Well, then you also know that he wrote this: "because there has been implanted in us the power to persuade each other and to make clear to each other whatever we desire, not only have we escaped the life of wild beasts, but we have come together and founded cities and made laws and invented arts; and, generally speaking, there is no institution devised by man which the power of speech has not helped us to establish" (*Antidosis*, 254). What he's saying is that a city like Athens could never have existed without rhetoric.

SOCRATES But What use is rhetoric without wisdom, Gorgias?

GORGIAS Then again, what use is wisdom without rhetoric, Socrates? Here is something else that Isocrates said: "it behoves all men to want to have many of their youth engaged in training to become speakers, and you Athenians most of all. For you, yourselves, are pre-eminent and superior to the rest of the world, not in your application to the business of war, nor because you govern yourselves more excellently or preserve the laws handed down to you by your ancestors more faithfully than others, but in those qualities by which the nature of man rises above the other animals" (*Antidosis*, 293). He means speech, Socrates. He means rhetoric.

SOCRATES Honestly, Gorgias, I think I need to go home.

GORGIAS No, Socrates, we need you. And you know, the people of Athens still remember you. It's me that they've forgotten. But they need us both. I can teach them what words can do. You can teach them to be critical. We can both teach them to listen to each other.—Hey, are you listening?!

SOCRATES Sorry, what? Oh, right. I was just thinking that I don't know. In fact I have often thought that I know nothing, except one thing, which is that I don't know anything.

GORGIAS Well, isn't that's something, Socrates?

SOCRATES I don't know. Look, isn't it getting pretty hot here? Come on, let's go.

GORGIAS Sure, Socrates. You know, I think this is the beginning of a beautiful friendship.

REFERENCES

Aristotle. 1954. *The Rhetoric and the Poetics of Aristotle*. Translated by W. Rhys Roberts. New York: The Modem Library.

Aristotle. 1995. *The Complete Works of Aristotle. The Revised Oxford Translation*. I-II. 6th printing with corrections. Princeton: Princeton University Press.

Gorgias. 1990. *Encomium of Helen*. Tr. by Brian Donovan. Retrieved from http://www.classicpersuasion.org/pw/gorgias/helendonovan. htm#cite.

Isocrates. 1929. *Antidosis*. Tr. by George Norlin. Retrieved from http://www.loebclassics.com/view/isocrates-discourses_15_antidosis/1929/pb_LCL229.185.xml.

Kant, I. 1839 [1790]. *Kritik der Urtheilskraft*. Leipzig: Modes und Baumann.

Locke, J. 1841 [1690]. *An Essay Concerning Human Understanding*. London: Thomas Tegg.

Plato. 1987. *Gorgias*. Translated, with Introduction and Notes, by Donald J. Zeyl. Indianapolis/Cambridge: Hackett Publishing Company.

Plato. 1924. *Protagoras*. Tr. by W.R.M. Lamb. Retrieved from https://www.loebclassics.com/view/plato_philosopher-protagoras/1924/pb_LCL165.93.xml.

Popper, K. 2012 [1945]. *The Open Society and its Enemies*. London: Routledge.

2.

Choice is Not True or False:
The Domain of Rhetorical Argumentation[*]

Leading contemporary argumentation theories such as those of Ralph Johnson, Frans van Eemeren and Peter Houtlosser, and Christopher Tindale, in their attempts to address rhetoric, tend to define rhetorical argumentation with reference to (a) the rhetorical arguer's goal (to persuade effectively), and (b) the means he employs to do so. However, a central strand in the rhetorical tradition itself, led by Aristotle, and arguably the dominant view, sees rhetorical argumentation as defined with reference to the domain of issues discussed. On that view, the domain of rhetorical argumentation is centered on choice of action in the civic sphere, and the distinctive nature of issues in this domain is considered crucial. Hence, argumentation theories such as those discussed, insofar as they do not see rhetoric as defined by its distinctive domain, apply an understanding of rhetoric that is historically inadequate. It is further suggested that theories adopting this understanding of rhetoric risk ignoring important distinctive features of argumentation about action.

Since around the century's turn, leading argumentation theorists have been keen to address, even to integrate rhetoric—cf. Johnson (2000), van Eemeren and Houtlosser (1999, 2000, 2001, 2002), and Tindale (1999, 2004). These scholars are performing an important task. However, I aim to show that if they would pay attention to the way rhetoric has been defined by a lineage of important thinkers in the rhetorical tradition itself, they could enrich their understanding of the relationship between rhetoric and other approaches to argumentation, and important new insights about argumentation might ensue, in particular with regard to distinctive features of action-related argumentation.

---

[*] Originally published in *Argumentation* 23 (2009), 61-80. Reprinted with permission of Springer Publishers.

First we should acknowledge the fact that rhetorical thinking is about much more than argumentation. To George Campbell (1776, 1969), rhetoric is about "[t]hat art or talent by which the discourse is adapted to its end." Campbell goes on to explain that "[a]ll the ends of speaking are reducible to four; every speech being intended to enlighten the understanding, to please the imagination, to move the passions, or to influence the will." So the ends of discourse are multiple, and not all the discourse that Campbell would call rhetorical is argumentation, by any definition of that term; for example, poetry, in so far as it aims to "please the imagination", would not belong to the subject matter of argumentation theory. Clearly, then, argumentation theory does not cover the entire discipline that rhetoricians cultivate; argumentation and rhetoric intersect but are not coextensive. Not all of rhetoric is about argumentation; more importantly, not all argumentation is rhetorical.

The feature that several of the most important thinkers in the rhetorical tradition itself tend to emphasize in setting some argumentation apart as "rhetorical" is its subject matter. They see rhetorical argumentation as centered around a certain domain of issues—those concerning *choice of action*, typically in the civic sphere. However, many contemporary argumentation theorists who address the rhetorical tradition neglect this fact and instead apply a view of rhetorical argumentation based on its aims and means.

I shall support these claims by first looking at three important argumentation theories in our time which explicitly address rhetoric, but which define rhetorical argumentation without any reference to a domain of issues. Then I will show, by contrast, how a strong lineage of rhetorical thinking since Aristotle asserts a definition of rhetorical argumentation based on its domain: that of civic issues. Finally, I will discuss special characteristics of argumentation within this domain that remain undertheorized in modern argumentation theories as a result of this neglect.

I will comment on the three theories in ascending order of their "friendliness" towards rhetoric.

Ralph Johnson, whose theory is most coherently set forth in *Manifest Rationality* (2000), is one of the founders of the "Informal Logic" movement. Insisting on the dialectical nature of argumentation, he has proposed the notion of a "dialectical tier" in argumentation as separate from its "illative core" (1996, 2000, 2002), the dialectical tier being that level in argumentation where the arguer addresses argumentation presented by opponent(s). In general, Informal Logic has much in common with rhetorical thinking, in particular skepticism towards formalization and deductivism in argument description and evaluation. But Johnson lists three features that, in his view, distinguish the rhetorical view of argumentation from the conception he advocates.

First, rhetoric emphasizes "the need to take into account the role of Ethos and Pathos. To be effectively rational, rhetoric will insist that the argument takes account of the human environment and that it, as well, connects with human sentiment. Logic, on the other hand, sees the telos of rational persuasion as governed especially by Logos" (p. 269). Secondly, "Rhetoric will not generally require a dialectical tier in the argument" (p. 270). Thirdly, regarding the evaluation of argument, Johnson states: "Informal Logic should tend to favor the truth requirement over the acceptability requirement, whereas rhetoric will, I believe, take the reverse view" (p. 271). Rhetoricians might or might not embrace this formulation, depending on how it is read. The more likely reading is that, according to Johnson, rhetorical argumentation involves a willingness to set aside truth for the sake of acceptance by the audience, i.e., persuasive efficiency. On this view, rhetorical argumentation is defined by the arguer's attitude and is not seen as rooted in a distinctive domain.

Much the same is true of the second theoretical effort we will consider: the pragma-dialectical school. With a background in "speech act" philosophy, Popper's rationalism and a belief in the reasonable resolution of disputes that has much in common with Habermas, representatives of this school have taken an increasingly friendly and integrative stance towards rhetoric (van Eemeren and Houtlosser 1999, 2000, 2001, 2002). But essentially they represent the same view as in Johnson's third point, seeing rhetoric as persuasive efforts aimed at winning, i.e., at resolving a difference of opinion *in one's own favor*. As a result, rhetorical argumentation, in their view, involves "Strategic Manoeuvring", which manifests itself in three respects: (1) topical selectivity, (2) audience adaptation, and (3) presentational devices.

These three points undeniably capture important aspects of rhetoric. But in equating rhetorical argumentation with Strategic Manoeuvring, driven by a wish to win, van Eemeren and Houtlosser neglect the strong tradition in rhetorical thinking which defines rhetorical argumentation not only in terms of the arguer's attitude or resources, but also in terms of the issues discussed, i.e., in terms of its domain.

Defining rhetoric as they do, van Eemeren and Houtlosser risk being caught on the horns of a dilemma. What they envisage is, I contend, the peaceful coexistence of two ultimately irreconcilable motives. On the one hand, there is the dialectical assumption, built into their theory, that the purpose of argumentation is to resolve a difference of opinion, which may entail, among other things, the obligation for at least one of the debaters, possibly for both, to retract or modify their original standpoint. On the other hand, there is the motive, in the rhetorical arguer as defined by their theory, to resolve the difference of opinion in his own favor. It is obvious that if both parties in a discussion bring a rhetorical attitude, as thus defined, to their common enterprise, then in at least one of them the dialectical motive and the rhetorical motive will eventually clash; they cannot both "meet their dialectical obligations without sacrificing their rhetorical aims" (van Eemeren and Houtlosser 1999, p. 481). If, however, we define rhetorical argumentation with reference to a certain domain of issues, then we shall see this dilemma dissolve.[1]

The third of the argumentation theories we shall consider, and the one that most wholeheartedly embraces rhetoric, is that of Christopher Tindale (1999, 2004). Indeed, "Rhetorical Argumentation" is the title of a recent book of his. Yet, like Johnson and van Eemeren and Houtlosser, Tindale neglects many rhetoricians' domain-based definition of rhetorical argumentation; his view is that students of argumentation should approach the entirety of argumentation from a rhetorical point of view, incorporating

---

[1] Undoubtedly, van Eemeren and Houtlosser would deny that there is such a dilemma. Indeed, some of their formulations of how debaters could be rhetorical and dialectical at the same time are such that rhetoricians ought to give them their wholehearted endorsement, for example when they speak of "maintaining certain standards of reasonableness and expecting others to comply with the same critical standards", after which they go on to say that this commitment need not prevent debaters from "attempting to resolve the difference of opinion in their own favour" (2001, p. 151). This sounds like the position often articulated by the late Wayne Booth, and I agree with it completely. However, obeying standards of reasonableness is not the same as being committed to resolving the difference of opinion. It may be true that if debaters in politics and other spheres did obey such standards, they would reach consensus more often; but even with the severest standards upheld they often would not. Why? Some of the authentic debate examples that van Eemeren and Houtlosser have analyzed are actually about the kind of issues where consensus may never ensue, no matter how much reasonable discussion the discussants would have engaged in; this is also the kind of issue where rhetorical argumentation typically occurs. For instance, in the British debate about fox-hunting clearly no resolution of the difference occurs. Yet in most of the strategic manoeuvres on the two sides that van Eemeren and Houtlosser have discussed there is no unreasonableness, no "derailment" of strategic manoeuvring; but there is no consensus either. The pragma-dialectical theory, based on the ideal of the critical discussion and aiming at a resolution of the difference, predicts that if the rules are obeyed, consensus will occur. So why doesn't it? My answer is that legislation on fox-hunting is a typical example of an issue belonging to the rhetorical domain of issues—those ultimately concerned with choice of action, not truth.

logical and dialectical approaches in it. While Johnson and the pragma-dialecticians broadly agree to see argumentation in its entirety as a dialectical enterprise, Tindale sees argumentation, in its entirety, as a rhetorical pursuit: "as a central human activity, argumentation is essentially rhetorical in ways that far exceed methodology alone" (2004, p. 19). Only a rhetorical theory of argumentation, then, can be adequate. Central to what Tindale understands by a rhetorical theory is "addressivity", i.e., the notion that argumentation essentially relates to its audience; it is always "in audience", and similarly, it is always "in language", addressing and anticipating its audience in its every linguistic choice. This amounts to saying that all argumentation necessarily has (some of) the properties that van Eemeren and Houtlosser subsume under "Strategic Manoeuvring". Further, while the logical approach to argumentation, according to Tindale, sees argumentation as product, and the dialectical approach is concerned with procedure, the rhetorical approach that he favors sees it as a process in which arguer, audience, and argument are inextricably involved.[2]

To be sure, nearly everything in Tindale's approach recommends itself to rhetoricians. The features he highlights are indeed significant aspects of rhetorical argumentation which deserve illumination, and his work is full of valuable insights.

Johnson sees some argumentation as rhetorical by virtue of the strategic attitude held by the arguer; the pragma-dialecticians, we might perhaps say, see argumentation as rhetorical in varying degrees, depending on the amount and nature of the strategic manoeuvring present in it; Tindale sees all argumentation as essentially rhetorical.

Part of what this approach implies is seen in Tindale's view that truth should be replaced with acceptability in the assessment of premises. This move, in which Tindale chooses Johnson as his opponent, becomes less convincing for being completely general. Tindale questions the use of "truth" in argument evaluation across the entire front, regardless of what issues are being discussed. But this obscures the fact that even if his *general* objections against truth-based argument evaluation fall, there is still a domain of issues where truth would be a misplaced concept; to use a homespun formulation, there are some issues where the concept of "truth" is even more misplaced than in others. This domain is that of practical issues, as distinct from epistemic ones—that is, issues regarding choice of action rather than knowledge. Johnson and the pragma-dialecticians offer

---

[2] This division of labour was first suggested by Wenzel (1990).

no indication that a theory of argumentation in the practical domain would have to be in any way different from the general theory they present, for instance with regard to the availability of consensus or the possibility of determining the validity of arguments independently of audiences; neither does Tindale, despite his wholesale espousal of a rhetorical perspective.

Tindale does not distinguish between rhetorical argumentation and other types of argumentation that are not rhetorical. Johnson, as we saw, does makes this distinction by claiming, among other things, that rhetorical argumentation favors acceptability over truth. The pragma-dialecticians also make the distinction in the sense that argumentation using "Strategic Manoeuvring" is seen by them as rhetorical. However, the criteria we actually need to make the distinction do not have to do primarily with the arguers' attitude (as in Johnson), or with the strategies used by the arguers (as in the pragma-dialecticians). Instead, the rhetorical attitude that arguers sometimes take, and the rhetorical strategies they employ, are corollaries of the domain of issues about which they argue. As stated at the outset, the rhetorical nature of an argument or an argumentative exchange has to do with the domain to which the issue in question belongs.

So what is this domain? The domain of rhetorical argumentation centrally includes *decisions about specific actions*. The action may be a political one, e.g., laying down a law or declaring a war; or it may be a forensic action, i.e., one that responds under the law to a past act. Traditionally, rhetoric also includes epideictic, which is not directly tied to action; however, Perelman and Olbrechts-Tyteca (1969) see the main function of epideictic as underpinning the social values invoked in argumentation over actions.

This domain-based view of rhetorical argumentation, which sees it as centrally concerned with choice of action, rather than with any issue at all, can also help us realize that argumentation about actions has characteristics that differ significantly from argumentation over the other main type of issues: those concerned with how something "is".

Another way of marking the same distinction would be to recall the distinction between, on the one hand, "Directive" and "Commissive" speech act types and, on the other, "Assertive" speech act types in regard to "direction of fit". As Searle has it, "the Assertive class has the word-to-world direction of fit and the Commissive and Directive classes have the world-to-word direction of fit" (1979a, p. 76; see also Searle 1979b, 1983). The term "direction of fit" originates in Austin (1953) and was explored in Anscombe (1957). What it pinpoints is that what matters in assertives is that the word (statement) should fit the world; what matters in commissives and directives is that the world should be made to fit the word. The issue in public argumentation over choice of action is a commissive, not an assertive.

It is crucial to realize that in argumentation about actions, such as political debates, the issue cannot necessarily be dialectically or philosophically resolved. About some issues arguers may legitimately entertain, *and* uphold, divergent standpoints.

The claim that some issues are like that superficially resembles the "Protagorean" position in epistemology. To put it simply, Protagoras believed *all* issues were like that, while Plato's believed that *no* issues were like that. Since Aristotle, however, a long line of rhetorical thinkers have realized that *some* issues are essentially like that, namely those concerning choice of action; here, reasonable and legitimate disagreement is common, so a difference of opinion between debaters may not be resolvable, no matter how much reasonable discussion they engage in.

The distinction between those issues that are essentially resolvable and those that are not, together with the very existence of these latter issues, is often bypassed, or explicitly denied, in philosophical thinking. However, to understand rhetoric, and to understand practical argumentation in the political sphere and elsewhere, one must accept this distinction. Further, to understand the distinction one must understand that issues relating to specific actions, or to the evaluation of them, are essentially non-resolvable. In discussing essentially non-resolvable issues arguers may legitimately wish to win *and* persist in this wish, resorting to "Strategic Manoeuvring" all the way. No amount of reasonable dialectical discussion will necessarily compel an arguer to retract or modify his standpoint (although he is sometimes persuaded to do so). Instead, ethos and pathos will often be involved in debates over such issues. The existence of these kinds of issues underlies Perelman's insistence on the distinction between "demonstration" and "argumentation", where argumentation, unlike demonstration, is inevitably audience-relative.

In the following section, I take a closer look at how an important tradition in rhetoric itself has seen rhetorical argumentation as defined by a distinctive domain: issues of civic action. The first and foremost representative of this view, I contend, is Aristotle, but the view of rhetorical argumentation as crucially concerned with civic action dominates rhetorical thinking throughout antiquity. In later epochs too it remains continually present, sometimes dominant, sometimes standing alongside other views which see "rhetoric" as primarily defined by the rhetor's aim: to persuade. Yet the original conception of rhetoric as a discipline that deals with argumentation, as hammered out by ancient theorists from Aristotle onwards, is centered around the notion of rhetoric as argumentation about civic action.[3] Consequently, an argumentation theory that defines "rhetoric" (and its derivatives) primarily with reference to the arguer's aim to persuade has a seriously truncated view of what rhetoric means in the rhetorical tradition itself. Further, I argue that theorists who accept this aim-based, truncated view of rhetoric do so at a cost, since the domain-based conception of rhetorical argumentation as concerned with civic action could have helped them understand crucial features of argumentation in this domain that otherwise tend to be overlooked.

The focus on civic issues as central to the classical conception of rhetoric is well expressed in George Kennedy's unequivocal statement: "Rhetoric in Greece was specifically the civic art of public speaking as it developed under constitutional government, especially in Athenian democracy of the fifth and fourth centuries" (1999, p. 1). The emphasis on civic issues was there from the beginning.

Aristotle has a twofold definition of rhetoric: an intensional and an extensional. As for the intensional approach, the *locus classicus* is this: "Let rhetoric be [defined as] an ability, in each [particular] case, to see the available means of persuasion" (1355b; Kennedy's translation (1991)). This statement, when read in isolation, does not in itself imply that rhetoric has a particular domain of its own, but Aristotle has more to say. Other arts, such as medicine and geometry, have their particular domains; the

---

[3] Jeffrey Walker seems to make a strong case against such a claim. He sees rhetoric as rooted in the poetic/epideictic kind of discourse performed by "singers", aiodoi, according to Hesiod (c. 700 BC.); the "pragmatic discourse" of later age is, to Walker, a "'secondary' projection of that rhetoric into the particular forums and dispute occasions of civic life" (2000, p. 10). I have no need to contradict Walker's genealogy; as I noted initially, rhetoric is a wider concept than rhetorical argumentation. Yet it remains true that most ancient theorists of rhetorical argumentation from Aristotle onwards see it as rooted in civic issues. And in fact, there is a reason why poetic and epideictic features of the discourse of the aiodoi may be "projected" into the domain of civic debate. As will be discussed below, such debate is about choosing action, not about the truth of propositions. In debate about choice of action, two opposite standpoints may both be legitimate and reasonable; it is not the case that one is "true" while the other is "false". Hence neither debater may be compelled by dialectical argument to retract his standpoint and agree with the other. Instead, debaters must seek to win the free adherence of their opponents and audience by including, among other arguments and appeals, features known poetic and epideictic discourse.

doubt that this raises is whether rhetorical argumentation may then deal with these domains (since no demarcation as to domain has so far been implied), or whether they are off limits to rhetorical argumentation. But a few pages later, in the discussion of the function of rhetoric, Aristotle effectively cancels out the idea that rhetorical argumentation may be about any subject whatever: "Its function is concerned with the sort of thing we debate [*bouleuometha*] and for which we do not have [other] arts" (1357a).[4] Here the domain of rhetorical argumentation is expressly limited to things about which we "*bouleuometha*", that is, "deliberate, take counsel or make a decision" (Liddell and Scott's counterparts for *bouleuein/ bouleuesthai*). The stem of this verb (of which *bouleuometha* is the middle voice, first person plural) is *boulē*: will, determination, plan, design, decree; it is genetically related to words in later languages such as *volontas* or, indeed, "will". So *bouleuometha* means that we resolve with ourselves (hence the middle voice) what is our will on an issue.[5] Hence rhetoric is not a generic name for any kind of argument that aims to persuade, regardless of what it is about.

The next phrase further limits the range of rhetorical argumentation: "…and among such listeners as are not able to see many things all together or to reason from a distant starting point". This may imply that arguing is only rhetoric when it occurs before such an audience; but another plausible reading is that this specifies the usual context of rhetorical argumentation, rather than an essential feature. The following passage adds a further limitation: "And we debate [*bouleuometha*] about things that seem to be capable of admitting two possibilities". This implies that *bouleuein/ bouleuesthai* only makes sense in relation to certain issues—on my interpretation those where we may *decide* to effectuate either one or the other possibility. Aristotle could not here, I suggest, be referring to all those issues on which people may have different views, for that would hardly imply any limitation at all, thus making the statement vacuous. For example, the question of whether matter is composed of atoms was never an issue on which it would be meaningful to *bouleuein*.[6] To be sure,

---

[4] This follows Kennedy's translation (1991). The translation in the complete English edition of Aristotle's works, by J.H. Freese (Aristotle 1926), consistently uses "deliberate", as does Kennedy some of the time; it is a word which, like the Greek *bouleuein*, is tied more closely than "debate" to discussions of what we will.

[5] Long notes that Aristotle uses the middle voice of *bouleuein* throughout the *Ethics*, giving the word the self-reflexive meaning "to take council with oneself", and thereby underlining the importance of this self-reflexivity to his concept of *phronēsis* (2002, p. 52).

[6] This example will probably raise objections to the effect that, as Alan Gross (1990),

generations of physicists argued over the existence of atoms; but (to set up a pointed contrast) atoms cannot be "willed" into existence (or out of it), so one cannot *bouleuein* about their existence. An atomic bomb, on the other hand, can be willed into existence, so there is every reason to *bouleuein* about doing just that. By contrast, Aristotle's next sentence again insists that some issues are unsuitable for rhetorical argument: "no one debates [*bouleuetai*] things incapable of being different either in past or future or present, at least not if they suppose that to be the case" (1359a makes an almost identical stipulation).

So much for Aristotle's attempt to define rhetorical argumentation intensionally, i.e., with reference to its essential properties; we see that his definition crucially involves *domain*, i.e., the type of issues discussed. Aristotle "extensional" definition of rhetoric enumerates its three constituting *genres*: the deliberative, the forensic and the epideictic. This too clearly restricts the domain of rhetoric. Eugene Garver, in a commentary on van Eemeren and Houtlosser, has put it simply enough: "rhetoric is restricted to the subjects of deliberation, judicial disputes and epideictic situations" (2000, p. 311).

Some would ask whether (and how) the epideictic genre shares all the features Aristotle saw as essential to rhetoric. It clearly shares some features with he other two genres, including their context (speeches in front of a public audience) and all their linguistic resources; but it is not

---

Jeanne Fahnestock (2003) and others have shown, argumentation in the natural sciences is full of rhetoric. However, while features of rhetorical argumentation may, unavoidably, show up even in domains like science, there remains a difference of principle between arguments over truth and arguments over action. To be sure, a scientist may have been influenced in part by the rhetoric of, e.g., Einstein's writing, to opt for atomic theory in the sense that he chooses to believe in the existence of atoms and to propagate this belief in his teaching, etc.; but he may not decide to bring about the existence of atoms, any more than he may decide to bring about anything else in the fundamental constitution of nature. He may, however, as any other human being, decide to bring about any number of changes or events in his own life, e.g., to marry, to quit smoking, to eat a hamburger, to kill himself; or he may decide to help bring about events and changes in the social world he inhabits, e.g., by voting for a given presidential candidate. Similarly, he may argue for the truth of atomic theory, but not for atoms coming into existence; conversely, he may argue for the election of the candidate of his choice, but that argument is not an argument for the "truth" of that choice. Of course, an argument for someone's election may be (and usually is) supported by assertions whose truth the arguer argues for, e.g., that the candidate is well qualified, that his policies are wise, etc. But what we argue for in deliberation, such a the election of a given candidate, is not a proposition that may have a truth value; by contrast, what we argue for in science is precisely a proposition that may have a truth value, even though the philosophy of science tells us that we will never be able conclusively to determine that truth value.

immediately clear that what we do in epideictic speeches is *bouleuein* in the sense just discussed. In the other two genres we clearly do that: in the deliberative genre we argue about a future action in order to reach a decision together (hence *genos SUM-bouleutikon*); this does not imply that we all *agree* on that decision, but, to apply a distinction suggested by Rescher (1993), those who do not *agree* with it *acquiesce* to it. In the forensic genre, we argue in order to decide on our action in response to a fact in the past (a crime or other legal issue, to which we may decide to respond with a certain punishment or other legal action). So both these genres fit the description of the domain of rhetorical argumentation given above: we argue about what action it is our will to take. The epideictic only fits that description more indirectly; as noted above, Perelman (1969) sees epideictic speeches as consolidating the values on which all debate about actions and judgments must rest (for a related view, see Hauser 1999). Arguably, however, Aristotle's intensional definition of rhetoric (based on the nature of its domain) is not completely coextensive with his extensional definition; but both agree on defining rhetoric and rhetorical argumentation with reference not to a motive or a set of resources, but to a certain domain.

In Chapters 4–8 of the *Rhetoric*, Book I, Aristotle goes on to discuss what he clearly sees as the first and foremost of the three genres: the deliberative. He uses the same words (primarily *bouleuein/bouleuesthai*) and makes many of the same stipulations as he did about rhetoric in general in the first chapters, thus in effect elevating the deliberative to the quintessence of rhetoric, and reiterating how deliberation is restricted to a certain domain of issues, i.e., things that we may decide to *do*:

> As to whatever necessarily exists or will exist or is impossible to be or to have come about, on these matters there is no deliberation…the subjects of deliberation [*peri hosōn estin to bouleuesthai*] are clear; and these are whatever, by their nature, are within our power and of which the inception lies with us (1359a).

This domain-based notion of rhetorical argumentation is also manifest in the following reproach: "much more than its proper area of consideration has currently been assigned to rhetoric" (1359b). There could hardly be a "proper area" if rhetorical argumentation is persuasive argument on anything. But who is the target of criticism here? A likely answer is: sophists who have taught that all issues belong to the domain of rhetoric.

The remarks in the *Rhetoric* on the restricted domain of *bouleuein* do not stand alone. Again and again in Aristotle's other writings on ethics, politics, and related subjects, we find similar, emphatic stipulations. *The Nicomachean Ethics* is quite insistent:

> ... nobody deliberates about things eternal, such as the order of the universe, or the incommensurability of the diagonal and the side, of a square. Nor yet about things that change but follow a regular process, whether from necessity or by nature or through some other cause: such phenomena for instance as the solstices and the sunrise. Nor about irregular occurrences, such as droughts and rains. Nor about the results of chance, such as finding a hidden treasure. The reason why we do not deliberate about these things is that none of them can be effected by our agency. We deliberate about things that are in our control and are attainable by action...we do not deliberate about all human affairs without exception either: for example, no Lacedaemonian deliberates about the best form of government for Scythia; but any particular set of men deliberates about the things attainable by their own actions (1112a; this is Rackham's translation, which, unlike Kennedy's translation of the *Rhetoric*, is consistent in translating *bouleuein* as "deliberate").

Likewise, the *Eudemian Ethics* has several pointed formulations insisting that we can only *bouleuein* about things we may choose to do because they "rest with us": "we do not deliberate about affairs in India, or about how to square the circle; for affairs in India do not rest with us, whereas the objects of choice and things practicable are among things resting with us" (1226a).

To sum up, *bouleuein/bouleuesthai* is what we do in rhetorical argumentation; moreover, it is a central concept in Aristotle's ethical and political thinking, as is witnessed by the dozens of occurrences of it, many with careful discussion, not only in the *Rhetoric*, but also in the ethical books, the *Politics*, the *Athenian Constitution*, the *Virtues and Vices*, the *Metaphysics*, and others. These passages embody a notion of *bouleuein* as applicable only to debate over actions within the debaters' agency. In brief, the domain of rhetorical argumentation is, for Aristotle, civic action, that is, issues concerning how a body of humans will choose to act.

This exegesis of course comes with the qualification that Aristotle's text is complex and often appears to contradict itself. The scope of Aristotle's theory of rhetoric remains contested—see, for example, the variety of positions in Gross and Walzer's volume (2000). Even so, the point that "deliberation" is about actions *within our own agency* stands out so strongly in the Aristotelian corpus that commentators should pay more attention to it than they have.

Certainly the notion that rhetorical argumentation is about civic action is asserted again and again by later Hellenistic rhetoricians. According to Kennedy (1994, p. 97, citing Sextus Empiricus' *Against the Professors*, 2.62), Hermagoras of Temnos defined the duty of the orator as "to treat the proposed political question (*politikon zētēma*) as persuasively as possible". Although his writings are lost, we know from the many references to him in Cicero, Quintilian, and others, that for Hermagoras rhetoric was rooted in civic life (this is the meaning of "political"); forensic and deliberative debate were its two pillars.

Much of the Hermagorean thinking is reproduced in the earliest Latin book of rhetoric, the anonymous *Rhetorica ad Herennium*, and in Cicero's *De inventione*. The *Rhetorica ad Herennium* (Anon 1964; c. 90 BC) defines the function of the orator as follows (in Caplan's translation): "The task of the public speaker is to discuss capably those matters which law and custom have fixed for the uses of citizenship [*ad usum civilem*], and to secure as far as possible the agreement of his hearers" (I.II.2). Notice how the definition of the domain of rhetoric given here goes hand in hand with the understanding that the object sought in rhetoric is the agreement [*adsensio*] of hearers (or as Perelman would say: their *adherence*); further, that the adherence of one's hearers is a matter of *degree* in the sense that one should seek to secure it *as far as possible*—a phrase echoing Aristotle's *endechomenon*.

Cicero's youthful work *De inventione* (Cicero 1968; c. 85 BC) endorses Aristotle's extensional circumscription of rhetoric to the three genres, and agrees that the domain of rhetorical argumentation is indeed circumscribed; he proposes to classify "oratorical ability as a part of political science" (I, vi, 6). Accordingly, Hermagoras is criticized for including too much in the "material of the orator", namely both "special cases" [*causae*] and "general questions" [*quaestiones*] like "Is there any good except honor?" This dichotomy appears also under the names definite vs. infinite questions. Rhetorical argumentation has no business dealing with the latter, whereas the former constitute its distinctive domain: "It seems the height of folly to assign to an orator as if they were trifles these subjects in which we know that the sublime genius of philosophers has spent so much labour" (I, vi, 8).

Cicero may later have felt that he limited the domain of rhetorical argumentation unduly by assigning only the finite issues to its domain. Some of his later writings on rhetoric further dichotomize the "infinite" issues into questions about cognition and questions about action. *De partitione oratoria* (c. 45 BC) distinguishes between a "propositum cognitionis", whose object is a *scientia*, and a "propositum actionis, quod refertur ad faciendum quid". While the former, we may assume, is still the domain of philosophers and "far removed from the business of an orator", it is debatable whether the latter category of issues should be seen as philosophical, rhetorical, or something in between, a "rhetoric of the philosophers", as it were—a term actually used by Cicero in *De finibus* 2.6.17, as discussed by Remer (1999, p. 46). (Today many would call such thinking "practical philosophy".) What remains clear is that rhetorical argumentation is still defined by the social and practical nature of the issues discussed. A statement to that effect from Cicero's fullest work of rhetorical thinking is these words of the statesman and lawyer Antonius in *De oratore* (Cicero 1967; c. 55 BC):

> ... to return to our starting point, let us take the orator to be someone who, as Crassus described him, is able to speak in a manner that is suited to persuasion. Moreover, let his sphere be restricted to the ordinary practice of public life in communities; let him put aside all other pursuits, however magnificent and splendid they may be, and, so to speak, be hard pressed day and night in performing this one labor. (Book I, 260)

Here the broader, motive-based definition ("to speak in a manner that is suited to persuasion") is narrowed and thus becomes the "classical", domain-based definition of rhetoric as speaking about "the ordinary practice of public life in communities". Cicero lets Scaevola take a similar view (Book I, 35–44). It is true that Crassus—whose views are usually taken to coincide with Cicero's own mature position—represents the more expansive conception of rhetoric, where rhetors are in effect defined as practical philosophers; this is most clearly seen in his famous eulogy of oratory as the founder and upholder of human societies. The others object to the breadth of the scope of rhetoric as Crassus sees it, or rather, they question the comprehensiveness of the wisdom and knowledge attributed to the rhetor. The fact remains that all three interlocutors, including Crassus, firmly link the function of rhetoric to the practical and social sphere; in the words of Crassus, rhetoric pertains to the "humanum cultum civilem" and the establishment of "leges iudicia iura" (Book I, 33).

In some of the rhetorical thinkers who build on Aristotle and Cicero we see a broad, "general" definition and a narrow, "civic" definition either alternate or coexist. Quintilian's *Institutio oratoria* (Quintilian 2001; c. 90 AD), conceived in a time of absolute imperial power where citizens had little room for debate and less for decision on the practice of public life, leans toward the broad view, making rhetoric the centerpiece of the education of the "good man"; yet Quintilian too, echoing Isocrates and Cicero's Crassus, emphasizes the indispensability of rhetoric in the domain of civic action: "I cannot imagine how the founders of cities would have made a homeless multitude come together to form a people, had they not moved them by their skilful speech, or how legislators would have succeeded in restraining mankind in the servitude of the law had they not had the highest gifts of oratory" (II.xvi.9). So even if, to Quintilian, rhetoric does not necessarily concern communal civic action, the intimate bond between the two still holds in the sense that communal civic action necessarily involves rhetoric; and despite the broadness of his definition, action is still at its center: "in the main, rhetoric is concerned with action; for in action it accomplishes that which it is its duty to do … it is with action that its practice is chiefly and most frequently concerned" (II.xviii.2).

To Greek rhetoricians in the following centuries, the domain of rhetoric was even more sharply defined, as Malcolm Heath makes clear: "The premise that rhetoric was concerned with speech on civic questions is something on which Zeno, Minucianus, and Hermogenes still agreed in the second century AD" (2004, p. 299). Hermogenes (c. 150 AD), who was to become for centuries the authoritative rhetorician in the Byzantine world, gives no explicit definition of rhetoric, but in the opening of his treatise on stasis simply declares: "The present discussion deals with the division of political questions into what are known as heads"; he goes on to stipulate that a political question (*politikon zētēma*) is "a rational dispute on a particular matter, based on the established laws or customs of any given people, concerned with what is considered just, honourable, advantageous, or all or some of all these things together. It is not the function of rhetoric to investigate what is really and universally just, honourable, etc." (Quoted from Heath 1995, p. 14). A similar assumption that rhetoric is argumentation about political issues is evident in the two Greek treatises of the third century edited by Dilts and Kennedy (1997), the "Art of Political Speech" by Anonymous Seguerianus and the "Art of Rhetoric" by Apsines of Gadara.

A string of rhetoricians writing in Latin under Christian emperors continue to assert the civic/political definition. In the *De rhetorica* formerly attributed to St. Augustine the rhetor undertakes his task "proposita quaestione civili" (Halm 1863, p. 137). Sulpicius Victor (c. 400

AD) expressly rejects the broad "bene dicendi scientia" as his definition of rhetoric in favor of "bene dicendi scientia in quaestione civili", noting that in such questions it is asked "whether something should be done or not done, whether it is just or unjust, expedient or inexpedient" (Halm 1863, p. 313). To C. Chirius Fortunatianus (c. 450 AD) the function of the orator is "[t]o speak well on civil questions. To what end? In order to persuade, insofar as the state of affairs and the attitude of the audience permits, in civil questions" (Halm 1863, p. 81; translated in Miller *et al*. 1973, p. 25). Boethius (c. 457–526), in *De topicis differentiis* (Boethius 1978), aims to effect a grand synthesis of argumentative topics into a single art. While the dialectical discipline "examines the thesis only" (1205C), the subject matter of rhetoric is "the political question" (1207C); it is concerned with "hypotheses, that is, questions hedged in a multitude of circumstances" (1205D). He notes another difference not often attended to by modern argumentation theorists, namely that the rhetorician "has as judge someone other than his opponent, someone who decides between them" (1206C). So, according to Boethius, rhetorical argumentation addresses audiences, not opponents, and is defined by its domain: that of civic/political issues. It may be said of Boethius as of many of the other thinkers we are enumerating here: all the distinctive properties of rhetorical argumentation, including its general aim, persuasiveness, and its specific topics and resources, follow as corollaries of its domain. As I shall discuss in more detail shortly, when a debate is about choosing action, not about the truth of propositions, two opposite standpoints may both be legitimate and reasonable; it is not the case that one is "true" while the other is "false". Hence neither debater may be dialectically compelled to retract his standpoint and agree with the other. Debaters must instead try to persuade their opponents (or audiences) to give their adherence freely; this they do by employing a broader range of (noncompelling) topics and resources than the limited range of resources through which, in dialectics, agreement may be compelled. The domain-based definition is upheld throughout the Middle Ages even by thinkers aiming to apply ancient teachings to the purposes of the church, such as Isidore of Seville (c. 630): "Rhetoric is the science of speaking well: it is a flow of eloquence on civil questions whose purpose is to persuade men to do what is just and good" (Miller *et al*. 1973, p. 80); and Rabanus Maurus (c. 820): "Rhetoric is, as the ancients have told us, skill in speaking well concerning secular matters in civil cases" (Miller *et al*., 1973, p. 125). Honorius of Autin (12th Century) describes rhetoric as "the second city through which the road toward home passes" and declares: "The gate of the city is civil responsibility, and the highway is the three ways of exercising that responsibility: demonstrative oratory, deliberative, and judicial" (Miller *et al*. 1973, p. 201). For encyclopedists of the 13th Century such as Vincent de Beauvais and Brunetto Latini rhetoric is indisputably the science of speaking well on civil questions; for the latter, it "is under the science of governing the city just as the art of making bits and saddles is included under the art of cavalry" (Robert 1960, p. 110).

Renaissance culture in Italy sees a resurgence of rhetorical thinking with a decisive emphasis on the civic definition. Fumaroli states that "rhetoric appears as the connective tissue peculiar to civil society and to its proper finalities, happiness and political peace *hic et nunc*" (1983, pp. 253–254). According to Cox (2003), rhetoric in Quattrocento Italy "positioned itself, as it had done in Cicero's Rome, as an essential component of the science of government, teaching as it did the skills of rational persuasion through which collective decisions were reached... Practical utility, and specifically utility to civic life, is patently the governing criterion of the genre" (p. 671). The first and perhaps the most comprehensive renaissance textbook of rhetoric, George of Trebizond's *Rhetoricorum libri quinque* (c. 1430), drawing on the *Rhetorica ad Herennium* and other classical sources, consistently affirms the domain-based view of rhetoric as "a science of civic life in which, with the agreement of the audience insofar as possible, we speak on civil questions" (quoted from Kennedy 1999, p. 235). Thomas Wilson's *Art of Rhetoric*, as one of many Renaissance rhetoric texts in the vernacular, squarely identifies the "Matter Whereupon an Orator Must Speak" as civic issues, i.e., as "all those questions which by law and man's ordinance are enacted and appointed for the use and profit of man" (1994 [1560], p. 45)—a close paraphrase of the *Rhetorica ad Herennium*.

While the lineage of politically-based definitions of rhetoric thus remains unbroken from antiquity until the Renaissance, it is true that there are also, most of that time, thinkers asserting the broader, persuasion-based definition. In fact, this tradition gains strength in the following centuries—an epoch where rhetoric falls into academic and philosophical disrepute, branded as verbal trickery by leading thinkers such as Locke and, a century later, Kant.[7] Giambattista Vico's is a lonely voice speaking up for rhetoric; characteristically, his *Institutiones oratoriae* (1711–1741) reasserts the

---

[7] For Locke rhetoric is a "powerful instrument of error and deceit" (1959 [1690], II, p. 146; Book III, X, p. 34); for Kant it is "gar keiner Achtung würdig" (1914 [1790], p. 404; Sect. 53, footnote).

action-centred definition: "The task of rhetoric is to persuade or bend the will of others. The will is the arbiter of what is to be done and what is to be avoided. Therefore, the subject matter of rhetoric is whatever is that which falls under deliberation of whether it is to be done or not to be done" (1996, 9). Perhaps the most influential 18th Century rhetorician, Hugh Blair (1783), leans towards the broader definition but, like Quintilian, maintains that "the most important subject of discourse is Action, or Conduct, the power of Eloquence chiefly appears when it is employed to influence Conduct, and persuade to Action" (2004, p. 265).

The 20th and 21st Centuries have seen the gradual return of rhetoric to academic respectability. It is true that the term itself has meant a variety of things to different modern thinkers, but the notion that rhetoric is defined primarily by its domain of issues is common to a series of the most important ones. To Perelman and Olbrechts-Tyteca that domain is generally defined as those issues where arguers seek the adherence of audiences rather than the demonstration of truths; but from the start they treat "deliberation and argumentation" as synonyms (1969, p. 1) and describe their aim as "a theory of argumentation that will acknowledge the use of reason in directing our own actions and influencing those of others" (3). The view of rhetorical argumentation as crucially concerned with action seems to become clearer in later writings by Perelman, such as the long article which summarizes his theory (1970), significantly titled "The New Rhetoric: A Theory of Practical Reasoning". Other seminal thinkers on rhetoric in our time who have maintained the same connection include Lloyd Bitzer: "a work of rhetoric is pragmatic; it comes into existence for the sake of something beyond itself; it functions ultimately to produce action or change in the world" (1968, p. 4) and Gerard Hauser: "rhetorical communication, at least implicitly and often explicitly, attempts to coordinate social action" (2002, p. 3).

To sum up, it seems fair on this background to say that when contemporary argumentation theorists such as those discussed in the first section, in their attempt to address or integrate rhetoric, adopt a view of it as defined primarily by a motive to persuade, without considering the domain-based view of rhetoric as deliberation about civic action, then they neglect what is arguably the dominant notion in the rhetorical tradition itself of its identity.

But what makes this oversight important? Why does an argumentation theory guilty of this oversight—even a theory that integrates rhetoric or professes to be rhetorical—run the risk of seriously underestimating important insights and distinctions?

The answer is that argumentation which is concerned with proposals for action has distinctive properties setting it apart from argumentation over propositions; these are the properties that are easily overlooked by argumentation theories, such as the three we have discussed, which see argumentation as concerned with the truth or falsity of propositions and inferences. Whenever a debater argues for a certain action and/or an opponent argues against it, neither of these two standpoints can ever be predicated to be "true". As Aristotle points out in the *Eudemian Ethics*, in deliberation we argue about choice; and a choice is not a proposition that can be true or false:

> ... it is manifest that purposive choice is not opinion either, nor something that one simply thinks; for we saw that a thing chosen is something in one's own power, but we have opinions as to many things that do not depend on us, for instance that the diagonal of a square is incommensurable with the side; and again, choice is not true or false. (1226a)

One way to explain why this is so is the following. When a human (or a collective of humans, such as a legislative body) deliberates about a choice, several values may be invoked both pro and con, and several desirable "ends" will be variously affected by whatever choice is eventually made. Friends, wealth, health, honor, security are some of them (Aristotle has enumerated these in Book I, Chapter 5 of the *Rhetoric*). Normally, a given proposal cannot serve all these ends equally; if it is designed to serve one of them, the consideration of one at least of the other ends may speak against it. For example, the introduction in public hospitals of a new treatment which can help some patients may be so costly that it hinders the attainment of other worthy ends; any decision that has a cost by the same token precludes the use of the same financial means for some other proposal. However, there is no generally agreed and intersubjective way to calculate and balance benefits in one area against costs in another; for example, most people would agree that not all the important considerations relevant to political actions can (or should) be converted into economic terms. In addition to economic cost there are all sorts of other accounts on which a proposal may be either recommended or opposed. For example, national security considerations that may arguably be served by, e.g., the indefinite detainment of suspected terrorists might be contradicted by counterconsiderations of ethics, legality, honor, or the friendship of other countries. In such situations, some individuals in the governing body and the electorate usually judge that the considerations speaking for the proposal or policy outweigh those against, while other individuals judge just as decisively that those speaking against it are weightier.

So in principle, deliberation will always have to recognize the relevance of several ends, several kinds of considerations, and several dimensions to the choice that has to be made. Moreover, individuals will differ in regard to the relative weight they assign to them. It may be that for each consideration in itself—such as the economic cost of a war, or its cost in human lives—debaters may have views that may be more or less true (or at least probable). But the fact remains that the relevant considerations in such a case belong to different dimensions, so that none of these considerations, e.g., cost in human lives, can be reduced or converted to one of the others, or to a "common denominator" or "covering" unit for all the relevant considerations. What lacks is, in a phrase from John Stuart Mill, a "common umpire" (1969, p. 226) to which all the considerations may be referred, yielding an objective calculation of how to balance the pros and the cons.

This is where we may see the importance of insisting that the central domain of rhetoric is debate over proposals for action, and of setting this domain apart from that of propositions. Proposals and choices cannot be "true", and do not aspire to it. The problem is not that it is hard to assess the truth value of a political proposal, or that "probability" will have to do; more radically, it is a categorical mistake to speak of truth (or probability, for that matter) in regard to a proposal as such. It may be *supported* by propositions that can be true (or probable); but in principle, none of the opposing standpoints in a deliberation can ever possess truth. Hence, debaters representing opposite courses of action may legitimately do so, and continue to do so. Because of the inherent multi-dimensional structure of deliberation over proposals (i.e., the fact that several competing ends or considerations may be invoked), debaters may assess the aggregate weight of the pros and the cons differently, and continue to do so; the same holds for the individuals who listen to them and whose adherence they seek.

Looking back, we may now see why it is that the dilemma faced by van Eemeren and Houtlosser dissolves when we realize that rhetorical argumentation is rooted in the domain of proposals and action, not in that of propositions and truth. The dilemma was that arguers cannot "meet their dialectical obligations without sacrificing their rhetorical aims" (1999, p. 481), where the arguers' "rhetorical aims" refer to their intention to "win" (have the difference of opinion resolved in their own favor). There is no dilemma because arguers debating proposals are *not* dialectically obliged to resolve their difference of opinion. In debating choice of action there is no truth to be attained, and unlike what happens in Socratic dialectic, or in pragma-dialectical "critical discussion", opponents arguing reasonably will not necessarily move towards consensus. The opposing standpoints represented by the two debaters are *not* contradictory propositions that cannot both be true, and of which at least one has accordingly to be retracted or modified; they are about choice, and, in the words of Aristotle, "choice is not true or false". Arguing for a given choice and arguing against it are in principle equally legitimate standpoints, and it is not the case that, as a result of reasonable discussion between the two arguers, one of the standpoints must necessarily be retracted. So it is not unreasonable for both arguers, when the issue is choice of action, to wish to win (and hence to resort to "Strategic Manoeuvring"): it would only be unreasonable for an arguer to persist in his wish to win if his standpoint had to be retracted as a result of the discussion— which is not necessarily the case.

The fact that, in matters of choice, none of the arguers will necessarily be forced to retract his standpoint, and, conversely, that none can conclusively "prove" his standpoint, is also the reason why all the resources of rhetorical argumentation: ethos and pathos, topical selectivity, audience adaptation, presentational devices, and more, will usually be mustered. Even if arguers cannot demonstrate the "truth" of their standpoints, they may try to win the adherence of the individuals in the audience, or even of their opponent, for them. The pros and the cons in a given issue of choice cannot be aggregated or balanced in an intersubjective manner, since no common measure exists; individuals must assess the relative weights of the pros and cons by their own lights, but arguers have all the resources of rhetoric at their disposal to win their adherence.

As we have seen, a strong and unbroken tradition of rhetorical thinking from Aristotle until the present sees rhetoric as defined by its domain: issues of choice in the civic sphere, where the adherence of other individuals may be worked upon and perhaps gained. But doing just that is also an important concern for arguers discoursing on issues outside the circumscribed domain of civic action; most proponents of, e.g., scientific or philosophical theories naturally wish to be persuasive. So the resources of rhetorical argumentation also play a part outside its central domain; indeed, many thinkers in the rhetorical tradition itself lean towards the "broad" definition. Nevertheless it is problematic when theorists of argumentation see rhetoric as primarily or even exclusively defined by the arguer's wish to persuade. Such a truncated definition allows theorists to forget what most rhetorical thinkers have always known, namely that argumentation concerning choice of action is a distinct domain with distinctive features.

To reiterate, some of these distinctive features of rhetorical argumentation are the following: in argumentation about choice of action reasonable disagreement may exist *and* persist indefinitely[8]; in that domain it is not the case that one of two opposed arguers may conclusively prove his standpoint, or be forced to retract it; but it is a domain rich in resources by which arguers may influence other individuals' adherence. When an issue is truly a matter of choice, as in political deliberation and the civic sphere generally, rhetorical argumentation plays a central and indispensable part, precisely because "choice is not true or false". Every individual, legislator or voter regularly has choices to face; rhetoric is a social practice that helps us choose. In the words of the *Nicomachean Ethics* (1112b), quoted by Garver (2000, p. 310): "On any important decision we deliberate together because we do not trust ourselves".

REFERENCES

Anon. 1964. *Ad C. Herennium: De ratione dicendi (Rhetorica ad Herennium)*, with an English translation by H. Caplan (Loeb Classical Library, 403). Cambridge: Harvard University Press.

Anscombe, G.E.M. 1957. *Intention*. Oxford: Basil Blackwell.

Aristotle. 1995. *The Complete Works of Aristotle. The Revised Oxford Translation*, I-II. 6th printing with corrections. Princeton: Princeton University Press.

Aristotle. 1926. *The Works of Aristotle Translated into English under the Editorship of W. D. Ross*, Vol. xxii. Oxford: Clarendon Press.

Aristotle. 1926. *The 'Art' of Rhetoric*, J.H. Freese, trans. Cambridge: Harvard University Press. (Loeb Classical Library, 193).

---

[8] The notion of reasonable disagreement and its inevitability on political, ethical and other practical issues there is a large body of thinking by contemporary philosophers that argumentation theory might do well to address; see, e.g., Rawls (1989, 1993), Larmore (1996); Kock (2007).

Austin, J.L. 1953. How to talk–some simple ways. *Proceedings of the Aristotelian Society* 53: 227–246.

Bitzer, L.F. 1968. The rhetorical situation. *Philosophy and Rhetoric* 1, 1–14.

Blair, H. 2004 [1783]. *Lectures on Rhetoric and Belles Lettres*, Linda Ferreira-Buckley and S. Michael Halloran (Eds.). Carbondale, IL: Southern Illinois University Press.

Boethius, A.M.S. 1978. *Boethius's De Topicis Differentiis*. Translated, with notes and essays on the text, by Eleonore Stump. Ithaca: Cornell University Press.

Campbell, G. 1969 [1776]. *The Philosophy of Rhetoric,* L.F. Bitzer (Ed.). Carbondale IL: Southern Illinois University Press.

Cicero, M.T. 1967. *De Oratore; De fato; Paradoxa Stoicorum; De partitione oratoria,* E.W. Sutton and H. Rackham (Eds.). London: Heinemann.). (Loeb Classical Library, 368.)

Cicero, M.T. 1968. *De Inventione; De Optimo Genere Oratorum; Topica.* With an English translation by H.M. Hubell (Loeb Classical Library, 386). London: Heinemann.

Cox, V. 2003. Rhetoric and humanism in Quattrocento Venice. *Renaissance Quarterly* 56, 652–694.

Dilts, M.R., and G.A. Kennedy. 1997. *Two Greek Rhetorical Treatises from the Roman Empire: Introduction, Text and Translation of the Arts of Rhetoric Attributed to Anonymous Seguerianus and to Apsines of Gadara.* Leiden: Brill.

van Eemeren, F.H., and P. Houtlosser. 1999. Strategic manoeuvring in argumentative discourse. *Discourse Studies* 1, 479–497.

_____. 2000. Rhetorical analysis within a pragma-dialectical framework: The case of R. J. Reynolds. *Argumentation* 14, 293–305.

_____. 2001. Managing disagreement: Rhetorical analysis within a dialectical framework. *Argumentation and Advocacy* 37, 150–157.

_____. 2002. Strategic manoeuvring: Maintaining a delicate balance. In *The Warp and Woof of Argumentation Analysis*, ed. F.H. van Eemeren and P. Houtlosser (Eds.). Dordrecht: Kluwer Academic Publishers, 131–160.

Fahnestock, J. 2003. *Rhetorical Figures in Science.* New York: Oxford University Press.

Fumaroli, M. 1983. Rhetoric, politics, and society: From Italian Ciceronianism to French Classicism. In *Renaissance Eloquence*, J.J. Murphy (Ed.). Berkeley CA: University of California Press, 253–273.

Garver, E. 2000. Comments on "Rhetorical analysis within a pragma-dialectical framework: The case of R.J. Reynolds". *Argumentation* 14, 307–314.

Gross, A.G. 1990. *The Rhetoric of Science*. Cambridge, MA: Harvard University Press.

Gross, A.G., and A.E. Walzer (Eds.). 2000. *Rereading Aristotle's* Rhetoric. Carbondale IL: Southern Illinois University Press.

Halm, K. 1863. *Rhetores Latini Minores: Ex Codicibus Maximam Partem primum Adhibitis Emendabat Carolus Halm*. Teubner: Lipsiae [Leipzig].

Hauser, G.A. 1999. Aristotle on epideictic: The formation of public morality. *Rhetoric Society Quarterly* 29, 5–23.

_____. 2002. *Introduction to Rhetorical Theory*, 2nd ed. Prospect Heights, IL: Waveland.

Heath, M. 1995. *Hermogenes on Issues: Strategies of Argument in Later Greek Rhetoric*. Oxford: Clarendon Press.

_____. 2004. *Menander: A Rhetor in Context*. Oxford: Oxford University Press.

Johnson, R.H. 1996. The need for a dialectical tier in arguments. In *Proceedings of the International Conference on Formal and Applied Practical Reasoning*, D.M. Gabbay and H.J. Ohlbach (Ed.). Berlin: Springer, 349–360.

_____. 2000. *Manifest Rationality: A Pragmatic Theory of Argument*. Mahwah, N.J: Lawrence Erlbaum Associates.

_____. 2002. Manifest rationality reconsidered: Reply to my fellow symposiasts. *Argumentation* 16, 311–331.

Kant, I. 1914 [1790]. *Kritik der Urteilskraft*. In *Werke*, Vol. V., Ernst Cassirer and Hermann Cohen (Eds.). Berlin: Bruno Cassirer.

Kennedy, G.A. (trans.). 1991. *Aristotle on Rhetoric: A Theory of Civic Discourse*. New York: Oxford University Press.

_____. 1994. *A New History of Classical Rhetoric*. Princeton, NJ: Princeton University Press.

_____. 1999. *Classical Rhetoric and its Christian and Secular Tradition from ancient to modern times*, 2nd ed.. Chapel Hill NC: The University of North Carolina Press.

Kock, C. 2007. Norms of legitimate dissensus. *Informal Logic* 27: 179–196. (This volume, Chapter 9.)

Larmore, C. 1996. *The Morals of Modernity*. Cambridge: Cambridge University Press.

Locke, J. 1959 [1690]. *An Essay Concerning Human Understanding*. Collated and annotated, with prolegomena, biographical, critical, and historical by A.C. Fraser, Vol. I–II. New York: Dover.

Long, C.P. 2002. The ontological reappropriation of phronēsis. *Continental Philosophy Review* 35, 35–60.

Mill, J.S. 1969 [1863]. Utilitarianism. In *The Collected Works of John Stuart Mill*, Vol. X. Toronto: University of Toronto Press.

Miller, J.M., M.H. Prosser, and T.W. Benson. 1973. *Readings in Medieval Rhetoric*. Bloomington, IN: Indiana University Press.

Perelman, C. 1970. The new rhetoric: A theory of practical reasoning. In *The Great Ideas Today*, 272–312. Chicago: Encyclopedia Britannica Press.

Perelman, C., and L. Olbrechts-Tyteca. 1969 [1958]. *The New Rhetoric. A Treatise on Argumentation*. Notre Dame IN: University of Notre Dame Press.

Quintillian. 2001. *The Orator's Education, vol. II*. D.A. Russell (Ed. And trans.). Cambridge: Harvard University Press. (Loeb Classical Library 124.)

Rawls, J. 1989. The domain of the political and overlapping consensus. *New York University Law Review* 64, 233–255.

_____. 1993. *Political Liberalism*. New York: Columbia University Press.

Remer, G. 1999. Political oratory and conversation: Cicero versus deliberative democracy. *Political Theory* 27: 39–64.

Rescher, N. 1993. *Pluralism: Against the Demand for Consensus*. Oxford: Clarendon Press.

Robert, J.E. 1960. *Book Three of Brunetto Latini's Tresor: An English Translation and Assessment of its Contribution to Rhetorical Theory*. Diss. Stanford: Stanford University.

Searle, J.R. 1979a. What is an intentional state? *Mind* 88: 74–92. New Series.

Searle, J.R. 1979b. *Expression and Meaning*. Cambridge: Cambridge University Press.

Searle, J.R. 1983. *Intentionality: An Essay in the Philosophy of Mind.* Cambridge: Cambridge University Press.

Tindale, C. 1999. *Acts of Arguing: A Rhetorical Model of Argument.* Albany, NY: State University of New York Press.

Tindale, C. 2004. *Rhetorical Argumentation: Principles of Theory and Practice*. Thousand Oaks, CA: Sage.

Vico, G. 1996. *The Art of Rhetoric* (*Institutiones Oratoriae*, 1711–1741). G. A. Pinton, A. Giorgio and A.W. Shippee (trans. and ed.). Amsterdam: Rodopi.

Walker, J. 2000. *Rhetoric and Poetics in Antiquity*. New York: Oxford University Press.

Wenzel, J.W. 1990. Three perspectives on argument: Rhetoric, dialectic, logic". In *Perspectives on Argumentation: Essays in the Honor of Wayne Brockriede*, R. Trapp and J. Schuetz (Eds.). Prospect Heights, IL: Waveland Press, 9–26.

Wilson, T. 1994 [1590]. *The Art of Rhetoric*. P.E. Medine (Ed.). University Park, PA: Pennsylvania State University Press.

3.

Aristotle on Deliberation:
Its Place in Ethics, Politics and Rhetoric*

Aristotle differs from most later philosophers in distinguishing clearly between epistemic reasoning, which aims for truth, and practical reasoning, which does not. How can he posit this distinction and yet not dismiss practical reasoning as flattery and manipulation, as Plato did? The answer lies in the concepts of deliberation (boulē, bouleusis) and deliberate choice (proairesis). They link Aristotle's rhetoric, ethics, and politics together and help provide definitions of all three: ethics is about deliberate choices by individuals. Politics and rhetoric are about the collective deliberate choices by the polity: politics is about making these choices well so that the good life of all citizens is optimally secured; rhetoric is the principal means to do this. These links have not been much discussed by scholars, probably because few studies range across these three Aristotelian "arts"; a proper discussion of them should draw on modern work in ethics, political science, and rhetoric. These key concepts and Aristotle's discussions of them offer inspiration for modern theories of "deliberative democracy," citizenship, argumentation, debate, and the public sphere.

One important difference emphasized by Aristotle which Plato had sought to downplay concerns reasoning in different realms. Aristotle differs from his master, and from many later philosophers, in seeing *epistemic* reasoning and *practical* reasoning as distinct domains. In the former, the concern is to find truth, or, failing that, the nearest we can come to it: probability. In the latter, what we are ultimately concerned with is not truth but decisions on action.

* Originally published in *Let's Talk Politics. New Essays on Deliberative Rhetoric*, H. Van Belle, P. Gillaerts, B. Van Gorp, D. Van De Mieroop, and K. Rutten (Eds.). Amsterdam: John Benjamins 2014, 13-26. Reprinted with permission of the publisher.

By insisting on this as an essential feature of practical reasoning, and more specifically, of that subspecies of it which he calls rhetoric, Aristotle bared a flank to a charge that has ever since been leveled against rhetoric, most forcefully by Plato: that it is truth-neglecting flattery and manipulation.

It is well known that Aristotle did not agree with this charge. It is less clearly realized that the reason why has to do with his concepts of *deliberation* and *deliberate choice*. Not only do they help furnish a reply to the charge, they also link together Aristotle's theories of rhetoric, ethics, and politics together and help provide definitions of all three: ethics is about deliberate choices by individuals. Politics and rhetoric are about the collective deliberate choices by the polity: politics is about making these choices well so that the good life of all citizens is optimally secured; rhetoric is one of the principal means to do this.

These links have not been much discussed by scholars, probably because few scholars have had interests ranging across all the three Aristotelian "arts" just mentioned. Moreover, if we want to have the full benefit of Aristotle's cross-disciplinary thinking in this area, it will be useful also to connect it with modern work in ethics, political science, and rhetoric. These key concepts and Aristotle's discussions of them offer inspiration for modern theories of "deliberative democracy," citizenship, argumentation, debate, and the public sphere.

The original terms in Aristotle usually translated as "deliberation" are *boulē* and *bouleusis*. The core meaning of *boulē* is usually given as "will, determination"; there is probably a genetic relation between *boulē* in Greek, *voluntas* in Latin, and modern equivalents like *will* in English, *Wille* in German, etc. The corresponding verb, *bouleuein*, is usually translated in Aristotle's writings as "to deliberate".[9]

This term is crucially important in several of Aristotle's writings, primarily in the ethical works. In all of them, he specifically insists that we

---

[9] It is striking that the modern translation of the *Rhetoric* most frequently quoted, that of George Kennedy, unlike older translations like that of Freese and others, is inconsistent in its renderings of this word and its derivatives; for example, in a crucial passage where Aristotle states the function of rhetoric, using the medial first person plural of *bouleuein*, i.e., *bouleuometha*, Kennedy's translation says that rhetoric is "concerned with the sort of things we *debate*" (1357a; Kennedy, p. 41; my emphasis). As will be clear below, Aristotle is insistent that what we "deliberate" upon is a clearly defined subcategory of that which we "debate". There seems to be no reason for Kennedy's choice here other than carelessness— but he is not alone among modern scholars in overlooking how Aristotle makes a crucial distinction and sharply demarcates the scope of rhetoric.

can only deliberate about what we can undertake ourselves. "We deliberate about things that are in our power and can be done" (*Nicomachean Ethics* 1112a) is one of many statements. Another is: "we do not deliberate about the affairs of the Indians nor how the circle may be squared; for the first are not in *our* power, the second is wholly beyond the power of action" (*Eudemian Ethics* 1226a). So, for example, "no one deliberates about what cannot be otherwise" (*Nicomachean Ethics* 1139b, with an almost identical formulation at 1140a); "since it is impossible to deliberate about things that are of necessity, practical wisdom cannot be knowledge nor art" (ibid., 1140b); "about things that could not have been, and cannot now or in the future be, other than they are, nobody who takes them to be of this nature wastes his time in deliberation" (*Rhetoric* 1357a).

Deliberation is the kind of reasoning that precedes deliberate choice, for which Aristotle's term is *proairesis* (some translate it "purposive choice", e.g., Kenny 1979). *Proairesis* literally means "taking something rather than (something else)".

What makes these concepts so important to Aristotle's ethical thinking is that the individual's deliberate choices are what primarily determines that individual's ethical worth. Rhetoric, however, is also about deliberate choice, but of a different kind, i.e., collective choices by people organized in groups like the *polis*.

The identity of rhetoric is closely bound up with deliberation, inasmuch as the function of rhetoric (its *ergon*) is "to deal with such matters as we deliberate upon without arts or systems to guide us, in the hearing of persons who cannot take in at a glance a complicated argument, or follow a long chain of reasoning" (1357a). In most references to Aristotle's definition(s) of rhetoric it tends to be forgotten that rhetoric is thus rooted in "such matters as we deliberate upon"; instead, all the attention is given to terms like "the available means of persuasion" (1355b), "present us with alternative possibilities" (1357a), the presence of hearers, the lack of systematic rules, and other features. However, the restriction of rhetoric to dealing with "such matters as we deliberate upon," in the understanding just stated, is a crucial element in Aristotle's intensional definition of rhetoric; indeed most leading rhetorical thinkers since Aristotle follow him in thus defining rhetoric as argument concerned with social decision or action, "civic issues," etc., as documented in Kock (2009).

This demarcation of rhetoric, I contend, is more to the point—historically and theoretically—than the many current demarcations that emphasize the "contingent," the "probable," etc., as for example in

Brockriede & Ehninger (1960), the paper that initiated the use of Toulmin's theory in the teaching of argument:

> Whereas in traditional logic arguments are specifically designed to produce universal propositions, Toulmin's second triad of backing, rebuttal, and qualifier provide, within the framework of his basic structural model, for the establishment of claims that are no more than probable. (p. 46)

To be sure, there are "broader" definitions of rhetoric which do not see rhetoric as rooted in any particular domain of issues, e.g., in Quintilian and in Campbell's *Philosophy of Rhetoric* (1776); the latter defines rhetoric (or rather, eloquence) as "that art or talent by which the discourse is adapted to its end." This is also a meaningful demarcation and aligns well with how rhetoric is defined in many academic programs (including the one this writer is affiliated with at the University of Copenhagen). So my insistence that Aristotle defines rhetoric as linked to "things on which we deliberate" is not an endorsement of this definition, which is indeed quite restrictive; rather, I point to it because it is often overlooked, and mainly because it brings out Aristotle's insistence on the differences between epistemic and practical reasoning—to which I think we should pay more attention.

It is worth repeating that what Aristotle does is to distinguish between the domain where we *ultimately* discuss truth, and the domain where we *ultimately* discuss choice. In his view, there is a domain where there is no "truth" to find, but there are also domains where truth does exist and can either be found, or where at least the best attainable degrees of probability may serve in its stead.

So, if we follow Aristotle, it is clear that we should not theorize about argumentation as if all claims people may argue about are claims about something being true. Some claims, for example, are claims for a deliberate choice, a *proairesis*. And a *proairesis* is not a proposition expressing a belief or an opinion (*doxa*). *The Eudemian Ethics* in particular makes that clear:

> Choice is not an opinion either, nor, generally, what one thinks; for the object of choice was something in one's power and many things may be thought that are not in our power, e.g. that the diagonal is commensurable. Further, choice is not either true or false [*eti ouk esti proairesis alēthēs ē pseudēs*]. Nor yet is choice identical with our opinion about matters of practice which are in our own power, as when we think that we ought to do or not to do something. This argument applies to wish as well as to opinion. (1226a)

Once this is clear, it seems to me to terminate the old dispute between what we might call hardcore "Platonists" and other thinkers we might call hardcore "Protagoreans": both are wrong. Hardcore Platonists are wrong in thinking that a truth exists and can be found (through dialectical/pseudo-mathematical reasoning) on *any* kind of issue. Hardcore "Protagoreans" (and many contemporary thinkers, including some "discourse" theorists and some "social constructivists") are wrong in thinking that on *no* kinds of issue does a truth exist.

Aristotle's distinction might also help "solve" (or dissolve) the old antagonism between (some) champions of rhetoric and philosophy, respectively: since rhetoric is (centrally, "ultimately") not concerned with "truth," but with (social) choice, there is no reason why philosophers should suspect rhetoric *per se* of subverting, or unconscionably disregarding, truth; rhetoric is not *about* truth. To be sure, it relies on the giving of reasons that may be true or false, or at least probable or improbable; but that for which the reasons are given is not an assertion that may be true or false. Incidentally, rhetoricians should realize that not all philosophers believe, in Platonic fashion, that *every* issue is about the truth of some assertion.

But why is it that choice is neither true nor false? This question may be elucidated with reference to a few distinctive features of the way we reason about deliberate choice. Not all of these features, I should add, are discussed by Aristotle; some of the insights I am going to cite are drawn from other thinkers, and some nuances I wish to add on my own.

1) Although deliberate choice of some action is based partly on epistemic beliefs (as we just saw), it is never based *only* on epistemic beliefs, i.e., beliefs about what is true or probable, but also on inner attitudes in the choosing individual; these attitudes, since they are located in the individual, may in that sense be termed "subjective." Some of them are ethical and are discussed by Aristotle in the pertinent works on ethics; others are emotions, *pathē*, discussed primarily in the second book of the *Rhetoric*. It is worth recalling here that the theory of emotions set forth there sees an emotion as having two components: (a) an affective one *and* (b) an epistemic one (cf. Fortenbaugh 1970 and later writings). The second book of the *Rhetoric* defines a series of emotions (*pathē*) in such a manner; for example, anger is defined as follows: "Anger may be defined as (a) a desire accompanied by pain, for a conspicuous revenge for (b) a conspicuous slight at the hand of men who have no call to slight oneself or one's friends" (1378a).

2) These "attitudes" of both kinds, besides being individual, are *graded*, i.e., they come in any number of degrees. That is to say, someone's allegiance to a certain ethical value may be more or less strong, by any number of degrees, compared to his or her allegiance to other values that may, in a given case, contradict it. Similarly, the emotion, e.g., anger, that motivates an individual to a certain action, may be more or less strong compared to the factors that prompt that individual to desist from the action.

3) As the previous point indicates, *plural* values are involved, even for an individual: each of us believes in a *plurality* of values that often collide, that is to say, speak for contradictory decisions on specific issues. This recognition is tantamount to the meta-ethical belief often named "value pluralism," associated with thinkers like Isaiah Berlin.

Aristotle's account of practical reasoning as interpreted by Anthony Kenny (1979) may help us further understand this plurality/pluralism that makes it impossible to infer the "true" answer to a question of choice. Put in simple terms: an action that promotes one value or good probably counteracts another.

Kenny explains how in all practical reasoning, as Aristotle sees it, we argue as it were backwards; that is, we start with a certain goal, value or end that we want to promote, for example, health; given that the end is good, we look for a means to bring about that end, because that means will also, in that respect, be good. Thus, if health is the end, it follows that what brings health is also good, and since exercise is something that brings health, it follows that exercise is good. So, to speak generally, we look for steps in reasoning that will transfer or *preserve goodness* from the end to the means.

If we compare this kind of reasoning with reasoning about propositions, we see that there we look for steps in reasoning that will *preserve truth*. For that purpose we need truth-preserving rules, whereas in practical reasoning we need "goodness-preserving" rules. But these two kinds of rules are quite different. Kenny points out that whereas Aristotle himself managed to formulate truth-preserving rules for propositions, he did not even try to formulate a parallel set of goodness-preserving rules for practical reasoning; nor has anyone else attempted to do so. The reason is that practical reasoning is much more complicated, and so are the goodness-preserving rules that would be required to codify it. Because practical reasoning works as it were backwards from the desired end or effect or good to an available means, whereas reasoning about propositions works forward from the truth of one proposition to the truth of another that follows, the following applies:

> If a proposition is true, then it is not also false; but if a project or proposal or decision is good, that does not exclude its being also, from another point of view, bad. Hence, while truth-preserving rules will exclude falsehood, goodness-preserving rules will not exclude badness. (Kenny 1979, p. 146)

This explains why, for a given choice we face that asks us to either undertake a given action or desist from it, there usually is no one "true" choice. For example, we may consider undertaking a given action because we believe it will promote a certain ethical good that we wish to promote; but any action that promotes one good or value tends to counteract others. This state of affairs is brought out in figure 1—a diagrammatic rendition of certain aspects of Aristotle's theory of the will, relying in part on Kenny.

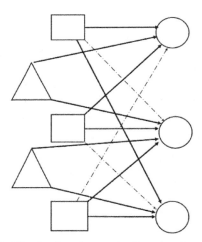

Figure 1. The logic of practical reasoning illustrtated
Circles illustrate goals
Rectagles illustrate available means
Triangles illustrate unavailable means
A bold arrow means: promotes a goal
A dotted arrow means: counteracts a goal

What we see here is, first, that we all endorse a *plural* set of values or ends (the circles). Certain actions might be imagined that would simply promote one or more of these goods without counteracting any; but such actions are generally unavailable. As a banal illustration of this, no state can decide to spend some of its wealth on building a beautiful opera house and yet retain the same amount of wealth to spend for other worthy purposes. Wealth that does not diminish when spent is, alas, not available. But a certain amount of wealth of the ordinary kind is often available, besides other means for achieving the ends we endorse. Another means available to most states is warfare; it might bring about some benefit, but it certainly has costs, e.g., in human lives, thus counteracting the common end of preserving human lives. Thus any action will have good and bad (presumptive) effects, or in different terms, advantages and drawbacks. And that just accounts for the foreseen *consequences* of that action. A different set of considerations might concern *deontic* principles that it might either embody or violate, e.g., a principle that the taking of human lives is *per se* wrong.

Thus it is clear that any action has any number of straight as well as dotted arrows emanating from it towards goods (values, goals) that it is seen either to promote or counteract. The facts that any individual's set of these values/goals is (1) in principle subjective (although to a large extent shared), (2) graded, and (3) plural, together ensure that, as a standard case, no one incontrovertible choice presents itself, nor does anything that we might, even in a derived sense, call the "truth."

The main theme in what I have said so far is what we might call the inevitable plurality and, indeed, *multidimensionality* of the ends, goods, or values (in Toulmin's terms it would be "warrants") that are potentially relevant in deliberation (and hence in its subdivisions: ethical and rhetorical reasoning). There is not just one kind of value that should be attended to, as is the case in epistemic reasoning, where that value is truth value (substitutable, if need be, with probability value).

Before moving on to how Aristotle might illuminate the interrelations between rhetoric, ethics, and politics, we may pause to comment on the question of whether Aristotle himself is a "value pluralist." There has been much debate on this between philosophers, with, among others, Martha Nussbaum (1986) on the "pluralist" side and Charles Larmore (1996) on the "monist" side. Aristotle does not declare himself a pluralist, in fact he says that there is a supreme ethical value that dominates all others, namely philosophical contemplation (*Nicomachean Ethics* 1177b); but on the other hand his ethical theory does analyze *several* distinct ethical qualities, and his famous theory of the golden mean (*to meson*) can be seen as a theory where two potentially contradictory values must be balanced. For example, courage is analyzed as a mean between bravery that sets aside fear and prudence that seeks self-preservation (1115a ff.); both are ethically good if not driven to excess, so true courage is a mean between them. Another instance of Aristotle reasoning in a way that arguably is *de facto* pluralist occurs at the opening of the *Politics*; there he suggests a plurality of (intrinsic) values that humans, unlike animals, are committed to:

> ... whereas mere voice is but an indication of pleasure or pain, and is therefore found in other animals (for their nature attends to the perception of pleasure and pain and the intimation of them to one another, and no further), the power of speech is intended to set forth the expedient and inexpedient, and therefore likewise the just and the unjust. And it is a characteristic of man that he alone has any sense of good and evil, of just or unjust, and the like, and the association of living beings who have this sense makes a family and a state. (1253a)

Since, as humans, we both understand what is beneficial vs. harmful, and also what is just and unjust, we can indeed be said to have at least two mutually independent goals or ends to guide us in our choice of action; and then the argument made above on the multidimensional and pluralistic nature of our practical reasonings will apply.

So there is in Aristotle, as in ancient rhetoric generally, a realization that in deliberation about choice several heterogeneous (or we might say, incommensurable) values or ends will inevitably be intertwined. That goes for reasoning in ethics as well as in rhetoric, where (as we saw above) we reason together about the collective decisions of the polity.

Christopher Lyle Johnstone is one of the first, and still one of the few, philosophers who have tried to relate the *Ethics*, the *Rhetoric* and the *Politics* to each other. He would have it that in these reasonings in the polity, ethical values are somehow supreme; "moral truths" of a communal kind, he argues, are amalgamated out of individual moral visions through the agency of rhetoric:

> The deliberative functions of rhetoric identify it as the instrument whereby individual moral visions are shared, modified, and fused into the communal moral principles that regulate our shared undertakings. Out of individual knowings we create communal moral truths; rhetoric is the instrument of that creation. (1980, p. 17)

I would argue that Johnstone's view of the workings of rhetoric in society, as expressed here, is too idealistic. Aristotle is more of a realist, some would say more of a believer in *Realpolitik*. To be sure, he has succinctly defined and comprehensively analyzed ethical reasoning; but he has not said that rhetorical reasoning is identical with ethical reasoning. On the other hand, nor has he said that ethical reasoning has no place in rhetorical reasoning. Rather, the broad picture of his thought on rhetoric, ethics and politics is that rhetorical deliberation in the polity is, and has to be, a jumble of individuals' self-interest, the collective self-interest of the polity, considered in terms of presumptive consequences, ethical and legal (deontic) principles, and all sorts of other considerations. It is, to use the terms employed above, pluralistic and multidimensional.

The few scholars who, after Johnstone, have attempted to correlate in a more systematic way Aristotle's theories of rhetoric, ethics, and society, have been less prone than he was to equate rhetoric with the creation of "moral truths." One of these scholars is the political theorist Mary P. Nichols, who emphasizes how public deliberation, i.e., rhetoric, fuses private interests with considerations of the collectively advantageous as well as the just:

> By recognizing the heterogeneity of common opinion and trying to incorporate that heterogeneity into a consistent whole, the rhetorician arrives at a comprehensive position that is both rooted in common opinion and able to go beyond common opinion. He is restrained by the individuals whom he addresses at the same time that he is able to educate them. … It is the existence of a public realm of discourse that makes man's political life more than the conflict of private interests and passions, that allows cities that come into existence for the sake of mere life to become associations in which men share speech about the advantageous and the just. (1987, pp. 661-662)

Nichols cites, at this point, the same passage from the opening of the *Politics* that was quoted above about *logos* as man's prerogative; and she goes on to argue that the obligation of the deliberative rhetor to integrate and absorb self-interest in fact makes it a noble pursuit: "Paradoxically, deliberative rhetoric is nobler and more statesmanlike than forensic not only because it aims at a general or public end but also because it must address a greater variety of private interests and concerns" (1987, p. 663).

Public rhetoric, Nichols also observes, which allows self-interest a chance to appeal to the population at large, contains in itself a safeguard against precisely the kind of selfish manipulation that Platonic critics expect from it; that safeguard is the fact that any instance of public rhetoric is revelatory of the *ethos* of the speaker from the very first word. Thus ethotic effects constitute a reason to cultivate public rhetoric rather than to suspect it:

> Addressing the popular fear that the speech of a clever rhetorician might hide his ends, Aristotle calls attention to the extent that a man reveals himself in his speech. If a rhetorician is to be persuasive, he must show that his advice is advantageous to his audience, that what he is praising is noble, or that he has justice on his side. In such cases, his premises, his conclusions, and his examples all reveal his character. (1987, p. 665)

Above and elsewhere, I have emphasized the inevitability of plural values, and, as a corollary of that, of dissensus (cf. Kock 2007). So does the political scientist Triadafilos Triadafilopoulos: "Aristotle argues that political speech should bridge the gaps between the public and private spheres, passions and reason, individual interests and the common good, equity and law" (1999, p. 742). That is to say, Aristotle shows us how to steer a middle course, find a *meson* as it were, between rival conceptions of the public sphere, namely those which see it, respectively, as all-out rivalry between entrenched interests, and as Habermasian communicative rationality:

> Aristotle's fusion of reason, emotion, and performance also provides us with a unique alternative to both agonistic and rational/deliberative conceptions of the public sphere ... Deliberative rhetoric is unique in that it appeals both to the listener's private interests and the business of the community. ... Orators on either side of a debate use persuasive speech to influence their audience's decision. ... Unlike Habermas, he rejects the claim that truly universalizable norms can be apprehended intersubjectively through rational discourse. (1999, pp. 744ff.)

Going a step further, the political theorist Bernard Yack argues that the obligation of public deliberative rhetors to integrate appeals to advantage and self-interest with communal considerations is ennobling rather than demeaning. For one thing, "it rules out explicitly self-serving arguments" (2006, p. 422). Other recent political theorists, including John Dryzek (2000, 2010), have argued along similar lines for the place of deliberation and rhetoric in democracy. That is, although we all have our own interests at heart as one strong motivating force, we still know and expect that in *public* rhetoric the appeal should be to the *public* interest.

Such a mixed, pluralist, multidimensional view of political deliberation goes against certain influential paradigms in political science and economics. Among these are the so-called "Rational Choice" theories, and similarly a close relative of these, namely the "economic theory of democracy" of Anthony Downs (1957). Regarding the forces that motivate politicians and citizens alike, Downs (like the Rational Choice theorists, among whom he may or may not be counted) holds one-track, pseudo-physical theories. As to what motivates political parties this theory claims:

> ... political parties in a democracy formulate policy strictly as a means of gaining votes. They do not seek to gain office in order to carry out certain preconceived policies or to serve any particular interest groups; rather they formulate policies and serve interest groups in order to gain office. Thus their social function—which is to formulate and carry out policies when in power as the government—is accomplished as a by-product of their private motive—which is to attain the income, power, and prestige of being in office. (1957a, p. 137)

As to what motivates citizens (voters), Downs's theory in its original pure form is equally categorical in its reliance on just one factor:

> Because the citizens of our model democracy are rational, each of them views elections strictly as means of selecting the government most beneficial to him. Each citizen estimates the utility income from government action he expects each party would provide him if it were in power in the forthcoming election period, that is, he first estimates the utility income Party A would provide him, then the income Party B would provide, and so on. He votes for whatever party he believes would provide him with the highest utility income from government action. (1957a, p. 138)

This attitude in citizens is what Downs and like-minded theorists see as "rational": "Whenever we speak of rational behavior, we always mean rational behavior directed primarily to selfish ends" (1957b, p. 27).

What we can safely say is that Aristotle's thinking on rhetoric, ethics and politics presents a more complex picture than this, and one that I would argue is more realistic. He neither postulates the supremacy in public deliberation of "moral truth" nor that of crass self-interest, but explains how both these kinds of motive, and the full spectrum in between, have roles to play.

As for the role of self-interest and considerations of advantage as against ethics, Yack makes clear that, unlike what is ideally the case in forensic reasoning (namely that *only* justice should determine any decision, as symbolized by the blindfolded Lady Justice), deliberation on political decisions has no right to completely disregard the interest of the members of the polity in the name of blind justice. Indeed, total abnegation of self-interest on behalf of the collective would undercut a rhetor's ethos: "Impartiality and disinterestedness recommend individuals to us as judges but not as political deliberators, since deliberators are supposed to be pondering our fate and theirs, not the disputes and interests of others" (2006, pp. 423-424).

The function of a state according to Aristotle, as the opening of the *Nicomachean Ethics* makes clear, is to secure for all its citizens the "Supreme Good," and that is why the science of politics is the master-craft, "the most authoritative of the sciences." This also is why Aristotle lists rhetoric, along with "domestic economic and strategy," as "one of the most highly esteemed of the faculties" in the state (1094a): rhetoric enables the political community to perform its essential function, which also provides its definition. In the words of Bernard Yack, the function of political communities is to serve "our shared interest in establishing the conditions—laws, moral habituation, opportunities for the exercise of prudence, and the other virtues—that make it possible to lead the Aristotelian good life" (p. 424).

It may be in place to sum up the main insights that we may gain by pulling together Aristotle's thoughts on deliberation as expressed in his ethical, political and rhetorical writings.

From the ethical works, students of rhetoric may learn that if rhetoric is concerned with such matters as we deliberate upon, then its central subject matter is not the truth or probability of propositions, but actions that we may choose to undertake. From Aristotle's *Politics*, rhetoricians may learn that politics is the noble art of statecraft and that rhetoric should be proud to be an integral and necessary part of it.

Ethics, in turn, might learn from rhetoric and politics that rhetorical deliberation in the state is a distinctive human activity that is just as necessary and worthy as the individual's deliberation over ethical choice, as well as being more complex.

Politics, finally, might learn from ethics about the essential nature of deliberation. From rhetoric it might learn about the specific workings and resources of this verbal *praxis*, so essential to the state's endeavor to secure the good life for all.

REFERENCES

Aristotle. 1991. *On Rhetoric: A Theory of Civic Discourse.* G.A. Kennedy (trans.). New York: Oxford UP, 1991.

Aristotle. 1995. *The Complete Works of Aristotle. The Revised Oxford Translation.* I-II. 6th printing with corrections. Princeton: Princeton University Press.

Brockriede, W., and D. Ehninger. 1960. Toulmin on argument: An interpretation and application. *Quarterly Journal of Speech* 46, 44-53.

Downs, A. 1957a. An economic theory of political action in a democracy. *Journal of Political Economy* 65, 135-150.

_____. 1957b. *An Economic Theory of Democracy.* New York: Harper and Row.

Dryzek, J. 2000. *Deliberative Democracy and Beyond: Liberals, Critics, Contestations.* Oxford: Oxford University Press.

_____. 2010. Rhetoric in democracy: A systemic appreciation. *Political Theory* 38, 319-339.

Fortenbaugh, W.W. 1975. *Aristotle on Emotion: A Contribution to Philosophical Psychology, Rhetoric, Poetics, Politics and Ethics.* New York: Barnes & Noble.

Habermas, J. 1997. *The Theory of Communicative Action,* vol. 1: *Reason and the Rationalization of Society.* T. McCarthy (trans.). Cambridge: Polity Press.

Johnstone, C. L. 1980. An Aristotelian trilogy: Ethics, rhetoric, politics, and the search for moral truth. *Philosophy Rhetoric* 13, 1-24.

Kenny, A. 1966. Practical inference. *Analysis* 26, 65-75.

_____. 1979. *Aristotle's Theory of the Will.* London: Duckworth.

Kock, C. 2003. Multidimensionality and non-deductiveness in deliberative argumentation. In F. H. van Eemeren, J. A. Blair, C. A. Willard, and A. F. S. Henkemans (Eds.), *Anyone Who has a View: Theoretical Contributions to the Study of Argumentation.* Dordrecht: Kluwer Academic Publishers. 155-171. (This volume, Chapter 6.)

_____. 2007. Norms of legitimate dissensus. *Informal Logic* 27, 179-196. (This volume, Chapter 9.)

_____. 2009. Choice is not true or false: The domain of rhetorical argumentation. *Argumentation 23,* 61-80. (This volume, Chapter 2.)

Larmore, C. 1996. Pluralism and reasonable disagreement. In *The Morals of Modernity*. Cambridge: Cambridge University Press, 152-173.

Nichols, M.P. 1987. Aristotle's defense of rhetoric. *The Journal of Politics* 49, 657-677.

Nussbaum, M. 1986. *The Fragility of Goodness*. Cambridge: Cambridge University Press.

Triadafilopoulos, T. 1999. Politics, speech, and the art of persuasion: Toward an Aristotelian conception of the public sphere. *The Journal of Politics* 61, 741-757.

Yack, B. 2006. Rhetoric and public reasoning: An Aristotelian understanding of political deliberation. *Political Theory* 34, 417-438.

Part 2: Rhetoric and Argumentation

4.

Multiple Warrants in Practical Reasoning[*]

The concept of warrant reflects Toulmin's general insights that validity in reasoning comes in many forms, and that reasoning in most fields cannot possess the necessity and certainty that attract many thinkers to the 'Rationalist' paradigm. However, there is a scarcity of concepts in one part of Toulmin's theory of argument. While the pedagogical applications of Toulmin's model offer a fine-grained system of warrant types for propositions (sign warrants, causal warrants, etc.), they have only one category of warrant for practical claims (proposals for action)—the 'motivational' warrant. Fortunately, ancient rhetorical thinking can help us correct this insufficiency. For example, the author of the rhetorical textbook used by Alexander the Great proposed a typology of practical warrants. His approach highlights what I propose to call the 'multidimensionality', and hence what modern moral philosophers call the 'incommensurability' of warrants—the absence of a common measure allowing for a 'rational' balancing of conflicting warrants. The widespread occurrence of multidimensionality in practical argument lends support to Toulmin's general anti-rationalist view of reasoning. Moreover, while multidimensionality prevents 'rational' balancing, it legitimizes and even necessitates the use of rhetoric in practical reasoning.

For over 50 years, Stephen Toulmin has consistently argued that validity in reasoning comes in many forms dependent on field, function, and context. Just as energetically, he has argued that most of all these forms of validity are different, each in its own way, from the paradigm set up in the 17th Century in the wake of Descartes' rationalism and Newton's universal mechanics—the paradigm in which validity in reasoning meant geometrical certainty, universality, and necessity. Toulmin's first book, *An Examination of the Place of Reason in Ethics* from 1950, was also his first

[*] Originally published in *Arguing on the Toulmin Model: New Essays on Argument Analysis and Evaluation*, D. Hitchcock and B. Verheij (Eds.). Dordrecht: Springer 2006, 247-259. Reprinted with permission of the Publisher.

to strike this theme. Here, he argued that what constitutes good reasoning in the field of ethics follows different rules than good reasoning in other fields, e.g., mathematics, physics, or aesthetics. Indeed, reasoning in ethics is at least two separate things, both distinct in function and form.

Toulmin's fundamental insight into the multiform, non-universal and non-necessary nature of validity in reasoning was inspired, no doubt, by the later Wittgenstein's teaching at Cambridge. This insight, at any rate, is bound up with an unmistakably Wittgensteinian view of language, several years before the actual publication of the later Wittgenstein's thinking, as in this statement: "Speech is no single-purpose tool. It is, in fact, more like a Boy Scout's knife" (Toulmin 1950, p. 83).

The idea that good reasons are many kinds of things, while anticipated in 1950 and reiterated to this day, was stated in its most explicit form in *The Uses of Argument* in 1958. The idea underlies the famous 'argument model,' whose centerpiece is the notion of 'warrant.' The main difference between Toulmin's model and traditional formal models, beginning with the Aristotelian syllogism, is that warrants are not premises about the issue in question but assumptions we rely on about the kind and degree of argumentative weight we may assign to the grounds offered. And the underlying insight here is precisely that there are, depending on field and context, many kinds and degrees of argumentative weight.

So Toulmin's main point in introducing the notion of warrant is to highlight the variety of ways and degrees in which the step from grounds to claim may be justified. There is no one universal and timeless way in which reasoning takes place. From first to last, the main thrust of Toulmin's thinking about reasoning is against the assumed uniformity of warrants, and against the idea that reasoning in all fields of human reasoning proceeds from premises to conclusions in a certain, deductive, and universal manner. The relations between grounds and claims in human reasoning may be warranted to varying degrees and in any number of ways; and, to adopt a phrase from Toulmin's latest book, *Return to Reason*, this is why we now need to abandon the dream which ties "certainty, necessity, and rationality into one single philosophical package" (2001, pp. 205-206). This entrancing dream, the intellectual program of Modernity, as Toulmin calls it, sprang from seeds planted in the 17th Century in reaction against the rampant irrationality of the religious wars and in exultation over the triumphs of universalist, geometrical reasoning as demonstrated by Newton. Only in the last decades, Toulmin argues, are Western intellectuals waking up from this dream.

Further, one might say that Toulmin is above all concerned with the epistemology and history of science, and his master insight is that even science is not describable by the mathematical paradigm of certainty, necessity, and rationality. There is no unitary Royal Road to certain knowledge of what is the case.

The centrality of this concern in Toulmin's thinking perhaps explains the curiously subdued part played by practical reasoning, i.e., argumentation over political and social *action*, in most of his theoretical work. As shown by all his examples in *The Uses of Argument* (including the classic assertion "Harry is a British subject"), Toulmin's theory of argumentation tends to dwell on arguments over propositions, i.e., claims about what is the case, and it rarely looks at claims regarding policy, i.e., proposals for action, whether in the political or the personal sphere. Toulmin's main concern is with the epistemology of reasoning and hence with those fields primarily where the Rationalist paradigm has in particular made its seductive bid for supremacy—e.g., the sciences, economics, and philosophical ethics. That a geometrical or Rationalist account of political argumentation is illusory is far more obvious to most, even philosophers.

The fact that Toulmin in *The Uses of Argument* dealt so cursorily with practical reasoning may explain why the pedagogical applications of Toulmin's model also have had little to say about it. Wayne Brockriede and Douglas Ehninger (1960) were the pioneers in using Toulmin's model as a pedagogical tool. It is from them that we have the most common typology of warrants. They base it on the Aristotelian concepts of *logos*, *ethos*, and *pathos*, respectively:

(1) an arguer may carry data to claim by means of an assumption concerning the relationship existing among phenomena in the external world, (2) by means of an assumption concerning the quality of the source from which the data are derived; and (3) by means of an assumption concerning the inner drives, values, or aspirations which impel the behavior of those persons to whom the argument is addressed. (1960, p. 48)

Arguments of type (1) are called *substantive*, of type (2) *authoritative*, and of type (3) *motivational*. Of these main types, only substantive arguments are further subdivided—by means of a "commonly recognized," six-fold ordering that includes arguments based on *cause*, *sign*, *generalization*, *parallel case*, *analogy*, and *classification*. No further distinctions are introduced concerning "authoritative" or "motivational" arguments. Instead, Brockriede and Ehninger cross-tabulate the types they have defined with a typology of claims based on the ancient *stasis* system, which renders four categories: *designative claims* (whether something is), *definitive claims* (what something is), *evaluative claims* (of what worth it is), and *advocative claims* (what course of action should be pursued). The resulting table shows, among other things, that "motivational" arguments are applicable only to evaluative and advocative claims. Conversely, about the warrants that may be invoked in support of advocative claims, we only learn that they are motivational.

The net result is that in the applications of Toulmin's model to the teaching of argument there is a surprising shortage of concepts to describe warrants relevant to advocative claims, i.e., practical reasoning. The solitary term "motivational" is little help, in fact it might mislead us into thinking that only *pathos* appeals have a role here, or even that their only role is here.

This omission is serious not only because it keeps us from understanding that there are different types of "motivational" warrant. Even more, it is serious because if we do not understand and consider the variety of warrant types invoked in arguments about action, neither do we understand why these arguments so often involve the amount of controversy that they do, and why they necessarily involve rhetoric rather than geometrical demonstration.

This neglected reason for the 'rhetorical' rather than demonstrative or rational nature of practical argument has to do with what I have proposed to call the *multidimensionality* of such arguments (Kock, 2003). The main reason why we should distinguish between types of motivational warrants is that these belong to different *dimensions*; and this fact again explains why practical arguments are the province of rhetoric, not demonstration.

The point in choosing the term "dimensions" for different types of warrant is that dimensions are not reducible or translatable to one another; for the understanding of a multidimensional complex, each dimension is necessary.

The issues that cluster around the notion of multidimensionality have been discussed by philosophers for the last 25 years or so under other headings such as *incommensurability* and *incomparability*.

Perhaps the most articulate and convincing spokesman for the notion of incommensurability in recent years has been Joseph Raz. He defines the condition of two reasons for action being 'incommensurate' in the following way:

> Two competing reasons (for specific actions on specific occasions) are incommensurate if and only if it is not true that one defeats the other, nor that they are of equal strength or stringency. They are incommensurate in strength, that is, reason does not determine which of them should be followed, not even that there is equal reason to follow either. When reasons are incommensurate, they are rendered optional, not because it is equally good (or right or reasonable) to choose the option supported by either reason, but because it is reasonable to choose either option (for both are supported by an undefeated reason) and it is not unreasonable or wrong to refrain from pursuing either option (for both are opposed by an undefeated reason). (2000, pp. 102-103)

Raz sees his position, including his belief in the widespread occurrence of incommensurate reasons, as an instantiation of what he calls a "classical" stance, as against a "rationalist" one. Interestingly, then, Raz joins Toulmin in the ranks of the self-styled anti-rationalists. There are, according to Raz, three crucial differences between the two conceptions:

> First, the rationalist conception regards reasons as requiring action, whereas the classical conception regards reasons as rendering options eligible. Second, the rationalist conception regards the agent's own desire as a reason, whereas the classical conception regards the will as an independent factor. Third, the classical conception presupposes the existence of widespread incommensurabilities of reasons for action, whereas the rationalist conception, if not committed to complete commensurability, is committed to the view that incommensurabilities are relatively rare anomalies. The three differences come down to a contrast between the rationalist view that generally rational choices and rational actions are determined by one's reasons or one's belief in reasons and are explained by them, as against the classical conception that regards typical choices and actions as determined by a will that is informed and constrained by reason but plays an autonomous role in action. (2000, pp. 47-48)

To simplify, what characterizes the "rationalist" is his belief that reasons for one action are necessarily stronger than those for another, and hence "require" or "determine" that particular action. Raz, like Toulmin, is sceptical of such determinism. As we saw, the crucial insight in Toulmin is his rejection of necessity and certainty in human reasoning. And that, in

Toulmin, goes for human reasoning of all kinds, not just for moral or practical reasoning.

But Raz, I suggest, has insights that might supplement Toulmin's. This is because he is more consistently concerned than Toulmin with the particular complexity inherent in practical reasoning as a result of the simultaneous presence of incommensurate reasons. To go a step further, I suggest that the main reason to reject necessity in practical reasoning is not the epistemic complexity of any individual single warrant (this is the issue that has always been Toulmin's central concern), but the multidimensionality and hence incommensurability (Raz's main concern) of the *set* of warrants that may be invoked in each case.

It should be noted here that the multidimensionality and incommensurability we are talking about here is not the same concept as the incommensurability that Thomas Kuhn pointed to in *The Structure of Scientific Revolutions* in 1962. What Kuhn meant was the inability of two competing epistemic paradigms to accommodate each other's viewpoints—the kind of incompatibility that, according to Kuhn, would precede a scientific revolution. Instead, what we are talking about here is the issue that has been a constant concern of moral philosophers at least since it was highlighted by James Griffin in the article "Are There Incommensurable Values?" (Griffin, 1977). It is the problem that may arise for anyone facing a practical decision because a certain value or warrant argues for a certain action A, whereas another value or warrant, incommensurate with the first, argues against A. As a paradigmatic example, we might cite the British debate over fox-hunting, where the "cruelty to animals" argument against this practice relies on a bio-ethical warrant, whereas pro-fox-hunting arguments rely on economic and social warrants about livelihood and "hallowed traditions." Or again, there is the ongoing debate in many countries over criminal legislation; here left-wingers rely on a social utility warrant when they point out that severe punishments are costly and do not prevent crime, whereas right-wingers tend to rely, among other things, on a "justice" warrant in demanding that victims' sentiments be respected.

In each of these two exemplary issues, incommensurate warrants are at play. In both cases, both sides have arguments that carry *some* weight. The problem is one of deliberation—a word that etymologically means the weighing of alternatives against each other on a scale. To decide which alternative has the weightier arguments in its favour, one would seem to need one common measure or warrant that could put the grounds arguing for the two alternatives on a common denominator and calculate the net result in a deductive, i.e., necessary way. No such common denominator exists, and, as I have tried to show elsewhere (Kock, 2003), no matter how one would try to define it, it would involve arbitrariness and hence not be necessary.

Yet numerous philosophers beginning with Plato have felt the need for such a common measure and have suggested what it might be. Martha Nussbaum in *Love's Knowledge* has discussed the Greeks' need for such a 'value monism' that reduces all values, whether physical beauty, scientific truth or moral goodness, to one and the same, thus saving humans from facing the disturbing complexities of ethical and practical decisions. Toulmin himself has pointed to the distinctly mathematical inspiration behind Plato's epistemology and ethics (2001, 18-19). Against the Platonic monism Nussbaum sets Aristotle's belief that each virtue and good is a particular thing, so that in regard to "honor, wisdom, and pleasure, just in respect of their goodness, the accounts are distinct and diverse" (*Nicomachean Ethics*, 1096b). But the monistic urge in philosophy has been strong, as witness, e.g., John Stuart Mill's belief in the necessity of setting up utility as an "umpire" in the clashes between incompatible moral demands:

If utility is the ultimate source of moral obligations, utility may be invoked to decide between them when their demands are incompatible. Though the application of the standard may be difficult, it is better than none at all: while in other systems, the moral laws all claiming independent authority, there is no common umpire entitled to interfere between them; their claims to precedence one over another rest on little better than sophistry, and unless determined, as they generally are, by the unacknowledged influence of considerations of utility, afford a free scope for the action of personal desires and partialities. (*Utilitarianism*, Ch. 2)

However, in spite of all such attempts, a growing number of moral philosophers nowadays are convinced, like Raz, that incommensurability and hence optional choices, rather than required choices, are a condition of our moral and practical life.

But what that means is only that there is no necessary, deductive and certain algorithm telling us what is required when a moral or practical choice has grounds that argue for different actions and invoke different warrants or values. However, the existence of incommensurability and optional choices does *not* mean that we do not weigh alternatives and make choices. We do make choices, and we do so because we have debated reasons and weighed them against each other. Only we do not have a common measure or umpire that will render an indisputable, algorithmic verdict, in the way that a pair of scales renders an objective, physical verdict as to which scale has most weight on it.

This description of the situation for anyone faced with a choice between incommensurate reasons is similar to the description faced by Chaïm Perelman when, in concluding his project *De la justice* in 1945, he realized that he could find no rationally binding justification of the values underlying human laws. When Perelman found that such a value rationalism was not viable, he did not, as is well known, opt for complete scepticism or relativism. Instead, he acknowledged that people do in fact argue about the values they cannot prove. And he decided to investigate *how* they argue.

This, as is also well known, led to his "re-discovery" of rhetoric. Perelman and Toulmin, in the same year, both made a pioneering case for the claim that in most human matters no necessity or certainty is achievable, yet for precisely that reason argumentation is possible and indeed necessary. But they both concentrated on the uncertainty of our reliance on any single warrant or value on which we wish to step from grounds to claim; neither of them gave their full attention to the particular difficulty caused by the simultaneous presence of several incommensurate values or warrants.

It is a fact not often remarked upon that 1958, the year which saw the publication of both Perelman's and Toulmin's groundbreaking works on argumentation, was also the year in which Isaiah Berlin's thinking on value pluralism was first fully articulated in his inaugural lecture at Oxford, "Two Concepts of Liberty." As in the case of Toulmin, Berlin's seminal idea springs from a view that there is no single and universal criterion of meaningfulness for all domains of human knowledge or science. But more explicitly than Toulmin, Berlin takes his pluralist reasoning into the realm of ethics and politics, shaping (if not inventing) the notion of incommensurability.

Toulmin, of course, was not unaware of it. He had commented on the type of quandary it presents as early as in *Reason in Ethics*:

> Given two conflicting claims ... one has to weigh up, as well as one can, the risks involved in ignoring either, and choose 'the lesser of two evils.' Appeal to a single current principle, though the primary test of

the rightness of an action, cannot therefore be relied upon as a universal test: where this fails, we are driven back upon our estimate of the probable consequences. (1950, p. 147)

Here we have Toulmin's characteristic rejection of the universal supremacy of any single principle, and we also have the understanding that a weighing must take place. The appeal to a principle and the estimate of consequences, by the way, are the two different types of reasoning in ethics that may both be valid, depending on the situation. But what Toulmin does not go into is the fact that the weighing of consequences will lack determinacy when the conflicting claims rest on warrants belonging to different dimensions, e.g., honour and utility in the guises of, respectively, bio-ethics and livelihood.

Many years later, Jonsen and Toulmin in *The Abuse of Casuistry* were acutely aware that humans may face moral problems "beyond the reach of universal principles and general theories, and require them to strike equitable balances between varied considerations in ways relevant to the details of each particular set of circumstances" (1988, p. 306). "At any stage in the development of a people and culture, experience brings them to adopt certain general opinions about the *scope, force*, and *relative priority* of different kinds of moral considerations" (p. 325). The crucial terms here, seen from our angle, are "equitable balances" and "relative priority." Similarly, as one of the main reasons for the difficulty of applying concepts "outwardly" to the world of concrete objects, Jonsen and Toulmin mention that "parallel arguments often point to different presumptions the practical implications of which have to be reconciled" (p. 327). However, even in this work of practical ethics, by far the most attention is given to the other main reason that mere principles are insufficient, the epistemic reason, i.e., the consideration that "presumptive conclusions can have 'certitude' only when the relevance of the concepts or terms involved is not in doubt" (p. 327).

This epistemic difficulty militating against determinism in reasoning clearly is and always was Toulmin's main concern. The paradoxical requirement in practical decisions to strike a balance between warrants lacking a common measure is one that he does not explore in similar depth. In *An Introduction to Reasoning*, the textbook that Toulmin co-authored with Rieke and Janik (1979), we find fine-grained distinctions between warrant types for factual propositions, very similar to those in Brockriede and Ehninger (sign warrants, causal warrants, etc.), but again there is no comparable attempt to distinguish between warrants for practical (advocative) claims.

Ancient rhetoric, however, had more to offer here. From its beginning in so-called sophistic teaching, rhetoric was centrally concerned with argument about action. We need only go to what is probably the very oldest extant textbook on rhetoric in the West, the *Rhetorica ad Alexandrum*, a work whose author—one Anaximenes—we do not know, but which is believed to have been written for the rhetorical training of the young Alexander the Great.

This book has had a strange fortune in the history of rhetoric. We do not know whether young Alexander actually used it, but we know that it has been either ignored or roundly condemned by commentators ever since. The classicist Manfred Fuhrmann, for one, who edited a modern text of this work, has also written an introduction to classical rhetoric in which he calls it "radically relativistic," condemning its "barefaced opportunism" and "eely routine" (1984, 29). The kind of teaching that brings down this abuse on the author's head is exemplified in the following enumeration:

> … he who persuades must show that those things to which he exhorts are just, lawful, expedient, honourable, pleasant, and easy of accomplishment. Failing that, when he is exhorting to that which is difficult, he must show that it is practicable and that its execution is necessary … It is for these qualities … that those who seek to persuade or dissuade must look. (1421b)

What hostile critics appear to feel about such advice is that the author is telling us to claim indiscriminately that any proposal we advocate is *all* these things. However, we may also read "Anaximenes" as saying that the following are the warrants which are in fact invoked in arguing about actions. Such actions—so arguments might go—should be executed because they are one or more of the following:

- just (dikaia)
- lawful (nomima)
- expedient (sympheronta)
- honourable (kala) (a better translation than Rackham's might be 'noble')
- pleasant (hēdea)
- easy of accomplishment (rhaidia)

Where difficult actions are concerned, we may further invoke the warrants that are:

- practicable (dynata) and
- necessary (anankaia)

Suddenly, it becomes clear that what "Anaximenes" presents is an inventory of the warrants available for practical reasoning. In arguing over practical issues, people essentially invoke warrants found in this list. They do so because they have to. What alternatives can we cite that do not really fall under one of these headings? On the other hand, can any items be stricken from the list? Even if we did made minor corrections of that kind, we still have here a helpful synopsis of the *dimensions* of practical reasoning. The point about dimensions, please recall, is that they are all necessary; they are not reducible or translatable to one another. An action may be "honourable" but not very "expedient;" it may be "just," but not "lawful;" etc. Even disregarding the epistemic uncertainty of applying these attributes "outwardly" to the world of concrete objects, we are still faced with the second difficulty: that of weighing incommensurate warrants on the same scale, for example, just so much "honour" against so much "expediency." We lack the common measure that will enable us to do this with "certainty, necessity, and rationality."

This second difficulty undercutting rationality in practical reasoning has, I suggest, only had passing attention in Toulmin's work. It is this kind of incommensurability that Raz and other moral philosophers have explored. But while Raz can thus be said to take his analysis a step further than Toulmin, he too stops short. It is not enough to say that two competing courses of action, relying on incommensurate reasons, are optional. It is true that we cannot weigh them with certainty and necessity, as the rationalist would; but we humans *do* weigh such options and make choices anyway.

Perelman and "Anaximenes" are among the thinkers who have realized how we do that. Since a number of incommensurate warrants may be invoked, and since there is no logical or philosophical way to measure which one carries most weight in any given case, we are left with the resources of rhetoric to help us decide, or—if that is our aim—to win the adherence of others for a given choice. We cannot measure. "Demonstration," to use Perelman's term, is not applicable; but rhetoric is.

Among the resources we can use to help us weigh alternatives whose weight cannot be measured are, according to "Anaximenes," *analogies*, *opposites*, and *examples*. By emphasizing likenesses and/or differences between the action under consideration and other, paradigmatic ones, we may bring ourselves and others to decide that the reasons arguing for that action are weightier than those arguing against.

Essentially, the resources we are directed to here are the same that Perelman and Olbrechts-Tyteca found in the empirical project which became *The New Rhetoric*. Moreover, these resources constitute the method of "casuistry" which Jonsen and Toulmin explored in their book, and which Toulmin has in effect advocated from the start of his career. Instead of universal principles, casuistry deals in analogy or "parallel arguments": Practical arguments, they state,

> draw on the outcomes of previous experience, carrying over the procedures used to resolve earlier problems and reapplying them in new problematic situations ... the facts of the present case define the *grounds* on which any resolution must be based; the general considerations that carried weight in similar situations provide the *warrants* that help settle future cases...[and] so the resolution of any problem holds good *presumptively*; its strength depends on the *similarities* between the present case and the precedents; and its soundness can be challenged in situations that are recognized as *exceptional*. (1988, p. 35)

By 1988, Jonsen and Toulmin had realized that argumentation as they see it and rhetoric are largely synonymous terms: "Practical moral reasoning today still fits the patterns of topical (or 'rhetorical') argumentation better than it does those of formal (or 'geometrical') demonstration" (p. 326). But this was not always Toulmin's understanding of what the term "rhetoric" means. As a philosopher, he seems to have been taught that rhetoric is the strategic effort to win compliance in one's audience by any means; in *Reason in Ethics* the phrase "rhetorical force" refers to properties which are "useful in forwarding ... particular policies" (1950, p. 195). Only later does the insight gradually develop in Toulmin's writings that rhetoric is more than the strategic promotion of one's interests; that in fact rhetoric is legitimate and necessary in debating ethical and deliberative issues.

One important reason why this is so, and one which—had he considered it—might have led Toulmin to embrace the term "rhetoric" and the rhetorical tradition earlier, is precisely the multidimensionality of the warrants invoked in practical argumentation and the resultant lack of a common measure to help us decide which is the weightiest. Since no logical inference or calculation can tell us how incommensurate dimensions should be weighted in deliberation, the result is that two opposite standpoints on a deliberative issue may both be legitimate (or "optional," as Raz has it); and this again implies that the use of rhetoric to win adherence for one's standpoint becomes not only legitimate but necessary.

Rhetoric comes into the picture not just because people want to sway and persuade each other but because people may legitimately have different views of the same matter and prefer different courses of action. When people use rhetoric to try to win each other's adherence, they do so not just because they want others to comply at any cost (this is the "strategic" definition of rhetoric), but because they may be legitimately convinced that the view they represent is not only an *optional* one but the *preferable* one; and their opponents may have the same legitimacy in thinking likewise of *their* standpoint. So rhetoric exists because it may be legitimate to hold several different views on a matter and because those holding each of these views may legitimately wish to win the adherence of the others.

Philosophers have been slow to acknowledge, let alone explain, that this is so. Why it is so has to do, as I have tried to show, with multidimensionality. This concept implies 1) that different warrants may be invoked in a debate which are incommensurate with each other; and 2) that different people, or the same person at different times, may assign different weights to arguments belonging to different dimensions.

Both these facts, again, have to do with the fact that on the one hand there is no rational, necessary and certain way to weigh arguments invoking incommensurate warrants on the same scale; on the other hand people who have to make practical decisions have to weigh them on the same scale somehow. Rhetoric helps them do this, but not in a rational way, i.e., not in a way that can pretend to be necessary and certain. So the existence of rhetoric helps explain how there can be, on the one hand, choices where no one alternative is mandatory, yet where some people, on reasoning, find one alternative preferable and some the other.

This kind of situation is well known to us all, and the more thoughtful textbooks on argumentation are aware of it as well:

In many ethical judgments, you and your audience might agree on certain values, but not necessarily rank them in the same way. ... most of the time weighting will be the crucial issue for your audience. People are quite likely to agree about the relevance of a set of criteria, but they often disagree about which particular ones are most important in a given situation. (Fahnestock and Secor, 2004, p. 249)

Rhetorical theory and textbooks ever since antiquity have been acutely aware of the same fact. As the *Rhetorica ad Alexandrum* exemplifies, they have been aware of the incommensurate warrants in practical argumentation, so that they can help us correct this scarcity of concepts in one part of Toulmin's system. Also, they are aware of the means we still have of weighing alternatives, including the topical tools of similarities, differences, and paradigmatic examples, as well as the numerous devices of amplification and diminution, with the aid of which we may add to or detract from the weight of any given argument.

Such a sophistic argumentation theory antagonized Plato and is still by many seen as cynical, relativist and opportunist. Indeed, some of the major classical rhetoricians, including Aristotle, did what they could to reduce the warrants invoked in practical argumentation to one single dimension (that of expediency, *sympheron*, cf. *Rhetoric*, 1358b).

However, the earliest rhetorical theorists, I suggest, had it right. They knew that practical reasoning has several dimensions, which is why decisions cannot be found on a merely rationalist basis. For example, they would have dismissed current pretensions to prioritize objectively between policies for the improvement of the world's predicament on the basis of the single warrant of economic cost-benefit. Yet they did point to resources for reason to use where rationality fails. The type of multidimensional theory represented by the *Rhetorica ad Alexandrum* has, even now, a realism and practical applicability which argumentation theory, along Toulmin's lines or otherwise, would do well to attend to.

So, practical reasoning in situations characterized by multidimensionality and incommensurability becomes the realm of rhetoric. Some might object here that while the displacement of the rationalist paradigm with its demand for universal and necessary forms of argument does open space for a conception of rhetoric as a legitimate mode of ethical and political inquiry, it also tempts rhetoricians to rush too quickly into this space and lay claim to occupy more of it than they can justify. Instead of making the strong claims that the practical reason is the province of rhetoric and that rhetoric is necessary to it, should we not make the more modest and more easily sustained claim that rhetoric is one legitimate dimension of practical reason? Ethics, for one, would certainly seem to be another.

A reply to this concern would be that while ethical considerations and arguments undeniably are and should be involved in practical reasoning, including policy debates, that still does not imply that the part played by rhetoric is, by the same token, diminished. The two categories are not mutually exclusive. That is to say, we might perhaps define them so that they are; but such a definition would be, as far as rhetoric is concerned, misleading. Rhetoric, I suggest, should be understood as the totality of resources at the disposal of arguers who wish to increase adherence to their standpoint in debates where choices are, as Raz has it, optional'. They are optional because individuals may legitimately opt for one or the other.

Philosophy ends here, because philosophy is, by its very nature, about finding solutions that hold with equal validity for all. Ethics, as a branch of philosophy, is about answering ethical questions in ways that hold equally for all.

Rhetoric, by contrast, is not about finding answers that hold equally for all. And rhetoric is not complementary to ethics (which would make the two mutually exclusive). Rather, rhetoric can be defined as the means we have to influence the standpoints of *individuals* on optional issues. They are usually optional because there is incommensurability involved. Ethical considerations may indeed enter into the rhetorical efforts of one individual to win the adherence of others, perhaps in conflict with other ethical considerations, or with considerations of, say, expediency. The point is that on optional issues, individuals may opt differently, and be differently influenced, and even be moved to change their minds—individually. All this is what rhetoric is there to do. Philosophy can only state that incommensurability and the resultant optional issues exist—a rather recent philosophical insight that many philosophers still hotly deny, possibly because it seems to leave them at a dead end.

But the dead end is only apparent, an appearance caused by the philosophical presumption to find solutions holding equally for all. The road sign at this point might read, "Incommensurability ahead." Beyond is the realm of rhetoric. We can bring all our reasonings there, including ethics. Thanks to rhetoric, we are not, even in that realm, stuck with unsolvable dilemmas. We may actually find solutions to the quandaries we meet, and with rhetoric we can perhaps win the adherence of other individuals for those solutions; but because of incommensurability, the adherence of individuals is all that our reasoning may achieve.

References

Aristotle. 1926. *The Works of Aristotle Translated into English under the Editorship of W. D. Ross*. Volume xxii.

_____. *The Art of Rhetoric*. Translated by J.H. Freese. (Loeb Classical Library, 193.) Harvard University Press, Cambridge, MA.

_____. Aristotle. 1937, *The Works of Aristotle Translated into English under the Editorship of W. D. Ross*. Volume xvi. *Problems*, Books 22-38.

_____. 1937. *Rhetorica ad Alexandrum*. Translated by W. S. Hett, H. Rackham. (Loeb Classical Library, 317.) Cambridge, MA.: Harvard University Press.

Berlin, I. 2002. Two concepts of liberty. In *Liberty, Incorporating Four Essays on Liberty*. Oxford: Oxford University Press, 166-217.

Brockriede, W., and D. Ehninger. 1960, Toulmin on argument: An interpretation and application, *Quarterly Journal of Speech* 46, 44-53.

Fahnestock, J., and M. Secor. 2004. *Rhetoric of Argument*, 3rd ed. Boston: McGraw-Hill.

Fuhrmann, M. 1984. *Die antike Rhetorik: eine Einführung*. München: Artemis-Verlag,

Griffin, J. 1977. Are there incommensurable values? *Philosophy and Public Affairs* 7, 39-59.

Jonsen, A., and S.E. Toulmin. 1988. *The Abuse of Casuistry: A History of Moral Reasoning*. Los Angeles: University of California Press.

Kock, C. 2003. Multidimensionality and non-deductiveness in deliberative argumentation. In F.H. van Eemeren, J.A. Blair, C.A. Willard and A.F. Snoeck Henkemans (Eds.), *Anyone Who Has a View: Theoretical Contributions to the Study of Argumentation*. Dordrecht/Boston/London: Kluwer Academic Publishers, 157-171. (This volume, Chapter 6.)

Kuhn, T.S. 1962. *The Structure of Scientific Revolutions*, Chicago: University of Chicago Press.

Nussbaum, M. 1991. *Love's Knowledge: Essays on Philosophy and Literature*, New York: Oxford University Press.

Perelman, C., and L. Olbrechts-Tyteca. 1969. *The New Rhetoric: A Treatise on Argumentation*. J. Wilkinson and Purcell Weaver (trans.). Notre Dame: University of Notre Dame Press.

Raz, J. 2000. *Engaging Reason: On the Theory of Value and Action*, Oxford: Oxford University Press.

Toulmin, S.E. 1950. *An Examination of the Place of Reason in Ethics.* Cambridge: Cambridge University Press,

Toulmin, S.E. 1958 *The Uses of Argument*, Cambridge: Cambridge University Press.

Toulmin, S.E., R. Rieke, and A. Janik. 1979. *An Introduction to Reasoning.* New York: Macmillan.

Toulmin, S.E. 2001. *Return to Reason*, Cambridge, MA.: Harvard University Press.

5.

Is Practical Reasoning Presumptive?[*]

Douglas Walton has done extensive and valuable work on the concepts of presumption and practical reasoning. However, Walton's attempt to model practical reasoning as presumptive is misguided. The notions of "inference" and of the burden of proof shifting back and forth between proponent and respondent are misleading and lead to counterintuitive consequences. Because the issue in practical reasoning is a proposal, not a proposition, there are, in the standard case, several perfectly good reasons on both sides simultaneously, which implies that argument appraisal necessarily contains a subjective element—a fact argumentation theory needs to conceptualize.

One of many notions in argumentation theory that have received deserved recognition thanks to the work of Douglas Walton is presumptive reasoning. Several items on his impressive list of publications deal with it (among them 1991, 1993, 1996a, 1997a, 2001). It means, as is well known, a type of argumentation midway between assertion and assumption: in its basic form, a proponent offers an argument for a claim, and this argument is seen as sufficient to shift the burden of proof to those who want to question the claim: "With presumption then, the burden of (dis)proof lies on the respondent, not on the proponent" (Walton 1996, xii). The opponent/respondent must either (presumptively) accept the claim or rebut the argument. Presumptive reasoning, thus conceived, creates a special kind of inference, different from both deductive and inductive inference, and characterized in particular by the shifting of the burden of proof. It is "nonmonotonic" and can be modeled with the calculus for "plausible reasoning" suggested by Rescher (1976). Other related concepts are "default reasoning" (as in Reiter 1980) and "defeasibility." Walton has

[*] Originally published in *Informal Logic* 27 (2007), 91-108. Reprinted with permission of the Editors.

shown that presumptive reasoning is widespread in real-life argumentation of any kind.

Beside the burden-of-proof criterion, the other crucial component of Walton's theory of presumptive reasoning is the notion of *argumentation schemes*, with associated lists of "Critical Questions," one list for each scheme. In presumptive reasoning a proponent basically advances a claim by using a certain recognized argumentation scheme; this shifts the burden of proof to the opponent, who should then take it upon himself to rebut or criticize the argument by raising questions of the types specified for each argument scheme.

Walton's work on presumptive reasoning is valuable, first, by highlighting this notion itself and by demonstrating how widespread it is in real-life discourse, and second, by compiling and exemplifying argumentation schemes. However, as Blair has argued, both the "provenance" and the classification of Walton's schemes remain unaccounted for; "Walton's list of schemes seems to drop from out of the blue" (Blair 2001, p. 379). Third but not least, Walton's lists of "associated" critical questions constitute an immensely helpful resource for reasoning in several domains.

1. Practical Reasoning

The point where I wish to challenge Walton's theory of presumptive reasoning is where its application to practical reasoning is concerned.

Walton defines practical reasoning as "a goal-driven, knowledge-based, action-guiding species of reasoning that coordinates goals with possible alternative courses of action that are means to carry out these goals, in relation to an agent's given situation as he/she/it sees it, and concludes in a proposition that recommends a prudent course of action" (1997b, p. 160). Furthermore, Walton repeatedly refers to "the two basic types of practical inferences," which are "the *necessary condition scheme* and the *sufficient condition scheme*" (1996a, p. 11; emphases in the original). In more recent versions, though, the "sufficient condition scheme" (where the argument that an action is a sufficient reason to carry out a goal creates the inference that the action should be undertaken) seems to disappear, and the assumption seems to be that there is only one argumentation scheme of practical reasoning (e.g., Walton and Godden 2005, who repeatedly refer to "the practical reasoning scheme", as if there was only one, and meaning by this the scheme where, if something is a necessary condition for realizing a goal, it creates a presumptive inference that this action should be undertaken).

While doubting parts of the basic definition, I believe to be in harmony with Walton in understanding practical reasoning as concerning *action*— either about *whether* a given action (or policy) is to be undertaken by an agent, or about *what* action is to be undertaken. Practical reasoning concerns decisions about actions that an agent contemplates, and which are in his or her power to undertake.

My claim is that for practical reasoning the presumptive model is misleading. To put it in provisional terms, it is just not the case in practical argumentation that any argument for an action creates a presumptive inference that the action it supports should *either* be undertaken, *or* has something "wrong" with it. It is wrong to suggest that if not rebutted, such an argument is strong enough to immediately mandate the decision (albeit in a presumptive way); and it is just as wrong to suggest that if a pertinent critical question is raised about the argument, then it is rebutted and as it were dealt with.

An objection reminiscent of this has been made by Robert Pinto (2001, 2003). Essentially, he claims that many of the "critical questions" attached to the argumentation schemes have a purely heuristic, rather than a normative force. Hence they "cannot be used, as Walton says they can, to shift the burden of proof back to a proponent" (Pinto 2001, p. 112). For example, in the case of an Argument from Sign, when the critical question "Are there any other events that would more reliably account for the sign?" is raised by the respondent, then there is, according to Pinto, no burden on the proponent to show that there are no such events; instead there is a burden on the respondent to identify one.

I agree that critical questions do not automatically have the force to initiate this tennis-like back-and-forth-volleying of the burden of proof. In fact, Walton has recently modified (and mollified) his earlier conception to accommodate this insight; in regard to whether a critical question is sufficient to make the argument default, or whether the burden is on the questioner, he now finds that "this may be different for different critical questions of a scheme" (Walton, Prakken, and Reed 2004, p. 86; cf. also Walton and Godden 2005). However, my criticism is more fundamental. I reject the underlying notion introduced by the very idea of presumption: the purely "binary" view where a party *either* carries a burden of proof *or* does not, and where that burden is *either* incurred *or* shifted through presumption.

Is Practical Reasoning Presumptive?

Such an implicit binarism is particularly misleading where arguments in practical reasoning are concerned. As I shall try to demonstrate with an extended example, in practical reasoning it is often legitimate, indeed necessary, to speak of *degrees* of strength in arguments (or "premises"); and furthermore it is necessary to recognize that in practical reasoning the degree of strength of premises is, in the nature of the case, often assessed *subjectively* and hence differently by individuals involved in the decision process.

A first reply to this criticism could be that Walton recognizes practical reasoning as a distinct domain, and that the theory of presumptive reasoning accounts for counterarguments precisely by specifying appropriate critical questions to be raised (1996a, p. 12).

Indeed Walton, almost alone among the argumentation theorists today who come from a philosophical background, does recognize practical argumentation as a separate domain (1990; 1996a, pp. 11-13, 176-180; 1996b; 1997b). What many overlook is the simple fact that in practical reasoning people argue about an action, not about a proposition or assertion. Yet Walton too, while alert to this difference, has often tended to blur it even while stating it. Commenting on a distinction between practical and "theoretical or discursive" reasoning, he states: "In the action type of critical discussion, the proposition is a practical ought-proposition that contains an imperative" (1996a, p. 177). This phrase is puzzling. Evidently, Walton senses that the issue in practical reasoning is not merely an "ought-proposition," and so he adds that it "contains an imperative"— thereby inventing a new hybrid. But is a proposition that "contains" an imperative still a proposition? Is an imperative not a wholly different kind of speech act? Apparently Walton, at this stage, cannot abandon the ingrained idea that reasoning, and hence also practical reasoning, is about propositions. But that for which we argue in practical reasoning is not a proposition about what we "ought" to do, nor about what is "prudent," although both these considerations (which are far from identical) may enter into the reasoning as premises. The issue in practical reasoning is a *proposal* about what to do (a point I have contended, and whose implications I have tried to explore, in Kock 2003a, 2003b, this volume, Chapter 6).

For the sake of clarity, let me state clearly that one of the distinctive features of proposals *vis-à-vis* propositions is that proposals are not cognitive and hence do not have truth-values. Although not everyone shares that view, I will not belabor it here, beyond an example that, in my estimate, makes it obvious. Let us take the case of a president making a proposal for his country to invade another country, say, Iraq. I do not see how what he proposes, invading Iraq, could possibly be true or false. It is an *act*, and acts do not have truth-values; propositions do (or some of them). However, the premisses for the proposal (e.g., that Iraq has WMD's) may have truth-values. Also, the claim that the invasion will promote democracy in the Middle East (another premiss) may have (or acquire) a truth-value. As for the value-claim that democracy in the Middle East is a highly valuable good it is a moot point whether and how such statements may have truth-values. My point is not dependent on how this question is answered. What I do claim, among other things, is that acts, and proposals to undertake acts, cannot have truth-values; that instead they have a large and open-ended range of *properties*, about all of which we may make propositions that may have truth-values; that about all of these properties we may make value-judgments; that these may legitimately differ across individuals; and that for all these reasons decisions about acts and proposals cannot be "inferred" from the truth of any single proposition relating to them.

Hence, even to conclude that a proposed act would be "prudent," however debatable that judgment itself might be, licences no "inference" to the act itself. We may decide to do the "prudent" thing, but on the other hand we might not, for example because considerations of ethics, duty or honor override "mere" prudence. Or again, prudent decisions may be overridden by motives such as desire for glory, thrills, or sexual pleasure. What this shows is the categorical difference between a proposition, which is the issue in theoretical/discursive reasoning, and a proposal, which is the issue in practical reasoning. This distinction Walton, while aware of practical reasoning as a separate domain, has repeatedly failed to formulate with any clarity.

It should be said, in all justice, that recent work by Walton on practical argumentation (2006) does much to dissipate the fog generated by earlier formulations. He now recognizes that the issue in what he calls "deliberation dialogue" is indeed a proposal, not a proposition, and that a proposal is a distinctive kind of speech act. He further presents a valuable overview of the criteria and critical questions that may be invoked in deliberation dialogue and in the appraisal of it, and he discusses other hallmarks of deliberation or practical reasoning, such as its dependence on values and the simultaneous presence in it of relevant pro and con arguments. But the fundamental notions of inference and presumption are still not questioned, the implied binarism is still extant in them, and the misleading and counterintuitive features of his "presumptive" account of practical reasoning which I shall discuss below, remain.

2. Walton's Inference Model

Although Walton has moved towards clarity in accepting that deliberation/practical reasoning is about proposals, not propositions, he still assumes that what we argue for in practical reasoning follows as a *conclusion* or *inference* from a properly applied argument scheme, the way a proposition follows from its premises by inference. In practice his revised account does not contradict formulations found in the earlier versions such as these: "In a practical inference, the conclusion is an imperative that directs the agent to a prudent course of action" (1996a, p. 11); "it concludes in an imperative that directs the agent to a course of action" (1990, p. xi). Here we have, besides the notions of "inference" and "conclusion," two additional residues from propositional logic, suggesting the binding nature of this conclusion: it is an *imperative*, and it *directs*. Walton's model of practical reasoning, and hence also of how to evaluate arguments in that domain, is still a wholehearted inference model.

Inference models of argumentation and argument evaluation (whether deductive, inductive, presumptive or otherwise) may be likened to an electrical circuit. In deductive inference, validity turns the switch on, and it stays on; if validity is absent, the switch is off and stays off. In non-monotonic inference, there is a toggle switch which can turn the inference on and off again. In the presumptive inference model the toggle switch turns a *presumption* of the inference on and off, while at the same time shifting the burden of proof back and forth. In all inference models, a given argument is evaluated in terms of whether it turns the inference on or not, and the switch only has two positions: on and off. This is tantamount to saying that when you accept an argument in such a model, you are bound to accept the conclusion. There is a two-way bind between argument and conclusion, even when, as in presumption, it is possible to become unbound again.

In such a model, in order for an argument *not* to turn the inference (or inference presumption) on, there has to be something "wrong" with the argument, and the critical questions associated with the argument schemes are there to help identify what may be "wrong." Blair, in his critique of Walton's presumptive reasoning model, explicitly aligns presumptive inference with the deductive and inductive varieties; he refers to its "probative force" and "cogency" as if these terms were synonymous, and states that for presumptive inference, "to accept the premises and grant the validity of the inference using that scheme yet deny the plausibility of the conclusion, under the circumstances—without suggesting that any conditions of rebuttal exist—is pragmatically inconsistent" (2001, p. 376). Blair criticizes Walton for not providing rationales explaining why each argumentation scheme is cogent, but implicitly accepts that what we should expect of any argumentation is "cogency."

3. Why the Inference Model is Misleading

The inference model of practical reasoning is misleading because it is *not* necessarily a defect in an argument used in practical reasoning that it does not authorize an inference. Walton's model, unquestioned in this respect by Blair, rests on the erroneous assumption that in practical reasoning (as in any other kind of presumptive reasoning), an argument *either* turns the (presumptive) inference on, or it can be rebutted. Accordingly, the critical questions which form a central part of Walton's theory are designed to rebut presumptive arguments, i.e., to throw the burden of proof back on the proponent. However, in practical reasoning an opponent of a proposal will not and should not necessarily doubt or rebut an argument proffered by the proponent; instead, he may fully acknowledge the proponent's argument, but then present a counterargument which, in his view, speaks even more strongly against the proposal than the proponent's argument speaks for it.

It might be objected here that Walton's model anticipates the existence of such counterarguments, and it does so precisely in the form of critical questions. The book version (1996, p. 13) lists the following kinds of critical questions to be asked in practical reasoning about a proposed action, A, aimed by an agent, *a*, at realizing a goal, G:

Q1: Are there alternative ways (other than A) of realizing G?

Q2: Is it possible for *a* to do A?

Q3: Does *a* have goals other than G that should be taken into account?

Q4: Are there other consequences of bringing about A that should be taken into account?

The first version of this list (in 1990, p. 85) makes no mention of "other goals." In a later, shorter version Walton gives a slightly expanded list (1997, p. 610; *A* is now the goal and *B* the action):

Are there alternatives to *B*?

Is *B* an acceptable (or the best) alternative?

Is it possible to bring about *B*?

Does *B* have bad side effects?

Are there goals other than *A* that need to be considered?

There is no denying that these are relevant questions to raise about any proposal, and they seem to categorize possible counterarguments against it well. However, the problem is with the fundamental structure of the model, not with the questions as such.

4. Unreasonable Implications of the Inference Model

In the inference model, to adduce possible alternatives, other consequences, and other goals serves to rebut the original argument and thus turn the "practical inference" off. On this analysis, any argument for which any of the critical questions has an affirmative answer is relegated to the "off" category, along with arguments that are palpably absurd and worthless.

But any practical argument for which, e.g., one of the questions Q1-Q4 can be answered affirmatively, is certainly not by that token worthless. In practical reasoning affirmative answers to several of the questions would be the standard case. If nothing else, there will always, no matter what goal a proposal aims to promote, be "other goals" to take into account, since any person in any society will entertain multiple other wishes, purposes or values which he wants promoted. Any proposal has costs in relation to some of these other goals. For example, nearly every political action costs money, thus counteracting the "goal" of preserving our common wealth (and also counteracting all the other goals we might spend money on). So at least one of the critical questions Q1-Q4 has an affirmative answer even for arguments that most people would find highly relevant, acceptable, and strong.

Also, generally there would be no way to rebut these critical questions. Proponents would have to admit, "Yes, there *are* other consequences; yes, there *are* goals other than G to take into account." And there would probably be alternative actions that might serve the same goal. So every single argument for any practical proposal would find itself relegated to the "off" category. Strangely, Walton seems to think this would be the exception, e.g.: "Presumptive inferences ... are subject to withdrawal or rebuttal *in exceptional cases*" (1996a, p. xi; emphasis added). Nevertheless, what the presumption model implies is, absurdly, that any proposal to do anything for the promotion of any goal should, by the lights of state-of-the-art argumentation theory, be abandoned.

Clearly, an appropriate model for practical reasoning should instead recognize it as a characteristic feature of practical reasoning that there may be legitimate, non-rebuttable arguments both for and against a proposal— arguments which would not necessarily contradict or refute each other. A pro-argument, A, might be perfectly true, acceptable, and relevant, and at the same time a con argument, B, might be so too; and yet they might not contradict each other at all. The contradiction would only be between the proposals they were used to support.

In other words, an argument in practical reasoning may have nothing at all wrong with it, in the sense that there is nothing to criticize or rebut, and yet it may not create any natural presumption, directive or imperative to embrace the proposal it is used to support; conversely, in order to escape the burden of proof regarding a proposal, an opponent of it does not have to criticize or rebut every argument supporting it.

But even for its unnaturalness, might not the presumptive model be defended as a handy way of stating the standard argument types in practical reasoning? No, the model is not only awkward and unrealistic when applied to practical reasoning; it also has pernicious consequences, one of which is the following:

Because the presumptive model implies that in order for a discussant to be entitled to reject a proposal for which an argument is presented, he must rebut the argument, it follows that he must either give that proposal presumptive acceptance, or else rebut *every single* argument presented in its favour.

Such compulsive refusal of recognition to opposing arguments is in fact what we witness daily in public debates or interviews with politicians as participants. Politicians and other public discussants routinely behave as if recognizing any argument or any critical question from the opposite side would create a cogent inference to the opponent's proposal; hence such recognition must be avoided by any available means, including evasion, distortion or blank denial. The social harm of this practice is that the public audience gets much less of a chance to critically assess the relative strengths of the case for, respectively against, the proposal under discussion.

5. An Alternative Model

A theory of political and other practical argumentation which recognizes that there may be legitimate arguments on both sides of an issue would counteract this tendency. It would make clear that there need not be anything wrong or questionable about an argument in practical reasoning, but even so respondents (or voters) may be entitled to reject the proposal for which the argument is presented in support. On such a model, one may recognize the merit of a (counter-) argument without underwriting a presumptive inference to the proposal for which it argues; one would not necessarily reject the truth of the opponent's argument as such, nor its acceptability or relevance in support of the proposal, but the forced presumptive inference from recognition of the argument to acceptance of the proposal.

The presumptive model, in contrast, instantiates the same misleading binarism that inheres in other inference-based models of argumentation and argument evaluation. Either one accepts the argument and gets the inference to the proposal in the bargain; or, if one wants to reject the proposal, one is compelled to reject the argument, together with any other conceivable argument for the proposal as well.

Rather than institutionalizing this dilemma, argumentation theory should stop basing argument appraisal in practical reasoning on the recognition of an inference from argument to "conclusion" —deductive, inductive, presumptive or otherwise. In practical argumentation, even legitimate arguments legitimate no inference to the proposal; instead they provide *an impact of a certain strength* to a decision-maker's decision about that proposal.

The phrase "a certain strength" is crucial. A theory which is adequately to reflect practical reasoning must conceptualize the fact that in such reasoning the strength of arguments is a matter of *degrees*.

In present-day argumentation theory there is a certain consensus that the criteria to be applied in argument evaluation can be formulated as *acceptability*, *relevance*, and *sufficiency*. This is the case in Informal Logic (see, e.g., Blair & Johnson 1987, Blair 1992, 1995; Johnson 2000 has acceptability, truth, relevance, and sufficiency); but the same trio is also found in theory based on the pragma-dialectical framework (e.g., Henkemans 2003) and in textbook literature, (e.g., Trapp, Driscoll *et al.* 2005). We may speak of these three as the recognized *dimensions* of argument evaluation.

If argumentation theory is to conceptualize degrees of strength in arguments, which of these dimensions would it affect, and how?

Acceptability (and/or "truth") is, as it were, the epistemic dimension. As for relevance, it has to do with the argument's conceptual or qualitative correctness, its having an appropriate application to the issue at hand. For both of these dimensions, it is debatable whether and how a concept of degrees might be applicable to them. Sufficiency, however, is by its nature a quantitative, not a qualitative concept; it is about there being *enough* of something. In argument evaluation it says that there is enough acceptable, relevant argumentation to cross a certain threshold. But "sufficiency," like the other concepts in the triad, is a *binary* criterion. This is how it is used in mathematics, where, e.g., a condition is either sufficient, or it is not; there is no such thing as it being "somewhat" sufficient, or "more" sufficient than another condition. However, in practical reasoning arguments differ along the quantitative dimension not just in a binary (on-off) way, but by degrees; we have just seen the counterintuitive consequences of insisting on a purely binary conception. Yet most philosophical argumentation theory lacks theoretical tools to deal with degrees along the quantitative dimension.

6. Degrees of Argument Strength and Subjectivity

Arguments are sometimes referred to as having a certain *weight*. "Premiss weight" has been suggested as a concept to be used in deductive logic for uncertain premises (e.g., Adams *et al.*, 1975). "Fuzzy logic" (or models inspired by it) has spawned many attempts to conceptualize reasoning about concepts that "do not have crisp boundaries" (Zadeh 1965, p. 141).

Another precedent for using "weight" about arguments in practical reasoning is the "set of scales" metaphor, where arguments are seen as weights of varying mass, placed in the two scales. This metaphor has served the judicial system in Western countries since the Romans. The idea is that any weight in one scale is merely one element in a larger act of deliberation (a word which means "weighing on scales"). Crucial to this metaphor is the feature so characteristic of weight: it has *degrees*— the notion that is excluded by inference models.

The notions of gradualism and of the aggregate totality of arguments are well embodied by the "scales" image. But another implication of that image is less appropriate. Weight/mass, as a purely physical parameter, suggests that there is an objective, physically determinable mass to any single argument—and hence a possibility of determining, with precision and objectivity, which scale outweighs the other.

Trudy Govier makes just this point in a note on the idea of "weighing" reasons in the chapter on "Conductive Arguments and Counterconsiderations" in her widely used text, *A Practical Study of Argument*:

> No implication that we can mathematically measure or judge the relevance and comparative strength of various reasons or counterconsiderations is intended at this point. The metaphor of 'weighing' could be deemed misleading; however, it does not seem possible to eliminate it save by substituting another metaphor. (2004, p. 415, n. 5)

Precisely the wish to make well-defined, intersubjectively valid inferences and calculations even with fuzzy premises drives the attempts to use "weight" and related physical concepts in theories inspired by Fuzzy Logic and related conceptions. But just as a binary quantitative argument evaluation cannot be upheld in practical reasoning, intersubjectivity too cannot be fully upheld.

The need to recognize degrees of premiss strength is only the first necessary step. In addition, we must recognize that individuals may evaluate a given premiss *differently* along the quantitative dimension. The lack of intersubjectivity in this respect is the reason why "weight" is a questionable metaphor. Instead, we might simply refer to the quantitative dimension of arguments in practical reasoning as "strength."

Are we driven, then, to the conclusion that the appraisal of argument strength in practical reasoning inherently involves a subjective element? My answer is yes.

Govier, however, presents a "method for appraising conductive arguments" that some might see as aiming at objective appraisal of conductive arguments—defined, following Wellman (1971), as cases where are several separately relevant premises both on the pro and the con side, which is precisely the category where practical reasoning belongs. The method involves determining the acceptability and relevance of all premises that may be adduced on both sides and then judging which side outweighs the other. Cautiously, Govier neither claims nor denies that this (rather commonsensical) procedure will yield "objective" appraisal. But she does say this: "To reflect on what the pros and cons are, and how you would evaluate them or 'weigh up' the reasons requires good judgment, which you have to supply for yourself" (2004, 404). An earlier version of the text had formulations like this: "Answers, however, especially for issues as profound as that of euthanasia, will emerge from individual judgment about the significance of the various factors" (1992, p. 311).

All in all, the denial of "mathematical" weighing, the use of the second person pronoun, and the reference to "individual" judgment which "you have to supply for yourself" make it clear that Govier does not see her method as yielding objective or intersubjective appraisal, but rather as involving a subjective element, at least in the "weighing" of the factors— although she seems reluctant to say so. This reluctance might have to do with the fact that she does not set off practical reasoning as a separate domain within conductive argument, and/or with her background as a philosopher. Other texts by writers with a rhetorical background are less hesitant to acknowledge this subjective element explicitly, as in this statement:

> In many ethical judgments, you and your audience might agree on certain values, but not necessarily rank them in the same way. ... most of the time weighting will be the crucial issue for your audience. People are quite likely to agree about the relevance of a set of criteria, but they often disagree about which particular one are most important in a given situation. (Fahnestock and Secor, 2004, p. 249)

I concur. To reiterate the two claims I make about argument "strength" in practical reasoning, they are: 1) We must conceptualize argument strength as a non-binary, that is, gradualistic ("scalar") notion. 2) We must conceptualize the fact that the strength assigned to arguments in practical reasoning may legitimately differ from one individual to another.

I will support these claims, which together also provide my main reasons for questioning Walton's presumptive model of practical reasoning, by discussing an authentic, paradigmatic example.

6. An Example of Practical Reasoning: the Euro Debate

A practical political issue in many European countries in the 'nineties was the adoption of a common currency, the Euro. In most countries this issue was decided by Parliament; some countries had referendums (Denmark, 2000; result: rejection. Sweden, 2003; result: rejection). Other countries are currently deliberating the issue.

In these debates, several macroeconomic arguments have been proffered, mainly predictions of likely consequences of either adoption or rejection of the Euro. Some arguments have turned on microeconomics and simple convenience: e.g., it is easier to travel between countries if one does not have to change one's cash. Arguments of yet another nature have had to do with the political implications, in a broader sense, of Europe (or most of it) going together on one single currency. Other arguments invoke feelings of national identity, or the symbolic significance of a national currency. As is well known, many people in Germany were reluctant to abandon the Deutschmark, but most German skeptics have now apparently acquiesced. On the other hand, there is a continuing wish among Britons to retain Sterling for reasons that have to do, at least in part, with national identity, and these feelings are strong enough to make the Government move with extreme caution on the issue.

We have here a paradigm case of an issue in practical reasoning. It illustrates a number of significant facts, stated above, about practical reasoning in general.

First, let us consider the argument that if a country joins the Euro, its citizens will not have to change their money nearly as often when traveling between European countries. There is no doubt that this is a true ("acceptable") argument: all else equal, international travel will undeniably be easier with the Euro. Also, this argument is undoubtedly relevant; greater ease of international travel is an irrefutable advantage of adopting the Euro. However, it would be hard to find many who feel that this premiss alone—we may call it the *convenience argument*—is "sufficient" to trigger adoption of the Euro as an inference. On the other hand, it is also clear that there is nothing "wrong" or defective at all about the convenience argument. Even if one does not see it as reason enough to join the Euro, it is undeniably an argument of *some* strength. Notice that this strength, such as it is, cannot be rebutted or annulled; it *counts* (although most people would probably agree that it does not have "a lot of" strength).

So, clearly, in practical reasoning arguments may have a certain degree of strength which may not, however, be considered sufficient to trigger what Walton calls a directive inference, but which still counts.

Moreover, given that an argument has *some* degree of strength, it will not necessarily have the *same* degree of strength for everyone. This formulation is of course of a rather intuitive nature; what "the same" means in this context is so far unclear. We might imagine an empirical definition, by which individuals would have to mark the perceived strength of the argument on a 1-7 Likert scale; a fair prediction is that not all marks would hit the same point on the scale, although most marks would probably cluster at the lower end.

Again, we might think of two different types of people, e.g., a person living in a rural inland area who rarely travels abroad, and a businessperson who does so regularly. It is entirely plausible that to the latter person the convenience argument would have more strength than it would to the former. We might say that to both these people the convenience of a common currency would be an advantage of some value, but that to one of them this value is greater than it is to the other. Furthermore, we should recognize that this difference between the two people regarding the respective strength they assign to the convenience argument is completely "legitimate." It matters less to the first person than it does to the second. This undeniable circumstance shows that in practical argumentation at least, there is such a thing as argument strength which *legitimately* varies from one person to the next.

It might be objected to this example that it is somehow "wrong" for a given voter, in deciding whether to vote for the Euro, to think merely of his or her own subjective convenience. Arguably what both our individuals ought to do would be to consider what is best for the country, since they are presumably both going to be involved in a collective decision for the country as a whole.

Let us accept this premiss for the sake of the argument. Still, regarding the *relative* strengths of the arguments that we have enumerated, we would find legitimate individual differences which could not be delegitimized or explained away by theory. The convenience argument has not been the only one to play a part in the Euro debates. (If it had been the only relevant one—but only in that unnatural case—then we might have had a presumptive inference in favor of joining the Euro.) On any such issue there are, as a matter of course, countless other considerations: the macro- and microeconomic ones, political goals, and considerations relating to national identity, symbolic significance, etc. The simultaneous existence of all these explains why no single argument on such an issue can be sufficient to trigger a directive inference, even though a number of these considerations might all be acceptable, relevant and endowed with *some* strength.

What concerns us just now is that to some people a given consideration, e.g., Sterling's "national-symbolic" value, may have more *relative* strength than it does to others. As a matter of fact, it appears that in Britain national-symbolic arguments have sufficient strength for many people to override arguments relating to convenience or economics. If we agree that this divergent assignment of argument strength across individuals is an empirical fact, then the question is whether argumentation theory should recognize it as legitimate—or whether such a recognition should be condemned as relativistic. Of course it *is* legitimate, and a fact argumentation theory should describe and account for, not try to legislate out of existence. For example, to some Britons the status of the Sterling as a symbol of national identity has sufficient strength as an argument to determine their stand against the Euro. To other Britons, the "national identity" argument may also be a strong anti-Euro argument, but they may not perceive it as quite strong enough to override the economic or political arguments they believe speak for the Euro. To still another group of Britons, the "national identity" argument is perhaps of utterly negligible strength; to them, it may even have what we might call negative strength, in the sense that traditional feelings of British national identity are so unappealing to them that they would be more than willing to give up any tokens of such feelings the sooner the better.

7. What the Example Demonstrates

We may define "degrees of strength" in some absolute sense or in a relative sense (as describing how strong a given argument is perceived to be by a given person in relation to *other* arguments). What the example of the "national identity" argument demonstrates is, again, that in practical reasoning an argument may legitimately have different degrees of strength to different people; and it would demonstrate this no matter which absolute or relative definition of strength we might devise.

Our example has also shown a fundamental yet curiously under-theorized circumstance: in practical reasoning arguers appeal to a multiplicity of goals to which those who are to decide are committed. Walton is aware of this when he describes practical reasoning as "a goal-driven, knowledge-based, action-guiding species of reasoning that coordinates goals with possible alternative courses of action that are means to carry out these goals" (1997, p. 608). This formulation captures much of the complexity of practical reasoning. It is precisely true that there are always *several* goals which must be coordinated; and that is the primary reason why practical reasoning is unfit to be modeled as presumptive. Unfortunately, however, Walton forgets this insight when he repeatedly refers to "the local inference used in practical reasoning," in which "*A* is the goal," and, since "*B* is necessary to bring about *A*, therefore, it is required to bring about *B*" (1997, p. 608). Such a conception, where there is only one goal and one argument scheme in view, and where anything that is necessary to bring that goal about is then "required," is inadvertently suggestive of a closed mindset utterly alien to all that Walton stands for.

Instead of speaking about "goals," a terminology which perhaps encourages narrowing "one-goal-at-a-time" conception of practical reasoning, we might speak about *values*. Any "goal" implies that one assigns a *value* to a certain state of affairs that one wishes to promote. In practical deliberation, several values are involved for each participating individual. A proposal may be seen, by each individual, as promoting some of his or her values and at the same time as counteracting others. It then becomes a question, for that individual, of *how strongly* the decision is seen as promoting or counteracting the values involved. Further, the decision depends on the *strength of the individual's commitment* to each of the pertinent values. Whether we want to define the "strength" of these values, for each individual, in absolute terms or in relative terms, the fact remains that not all individuals, not even all individuals in a circumscribed cultural group (such as "all Britons"), can legitimately be expected to hold identical sets of values, arranged in the same relative order—or "hierarchy," to use Perelman's and Olbrechts-Tyteca's term (1969, pp. 80-84). So, when facing a practical proposal, such as adopting the Euro, each individual who is to decide and, possibly, participate in the debate, will, in principle, consider the arguments proffered in it from the vantage point of his or her own hierarchical set of values.

8. The Charge of Relativism

A claim such as this runs the risk of being branded by some argumentation theorists as "relativism." The charge of relativism against other theories has been made repeatedly in writings by the Pragma-Dialectical school (most recently in van Eemeren & Grootendorst 2004, p. 130, with reference to Perelman & Olbrechts-Tyteca, 1969). A similar criticism has recently been made, in very sweeping fashion, by Boger (2005).

The attack on relativism, but also much of the theory that is under attack for alleged relativism, is based on the tacit but faulty assumption that this scholarly issue is about audience relativity ("relativism") in *all* argumentation and in *all* compartments of argument evaluation. In other words, the mistake on all sides is a failure to distinguish between those domains and types of argumentation where audience relativity is inherently present, and those where it is not. Proponents of audience relativity tend to write as if their claims have reference to *all* argumentation; their critics make the same mistake. Consequently, the scholarly discussion becomes a rather pointless quarrel where one party is perceived as saying that *all* evaluation criteria in argumentation are audience-relative, and the other party counters this perceived claim by saying, indignantly, that their opponents are perniciously relativistic and that *all* evaluation criteria should certainly be audience-independent. What I argue is *not* that all evaluation criteria are audience-relative, but that *some* are, more specifically those pertaining to the degree of relative strength of value-based arguments in practical reasoning.

Thus, if argument strength, in value-based practical reasoning, *legitimately* varies from one person to the next, it does not deserve to be called "relativism" or the like, if this term implies that argumentation theory ought not to recognize such a thing. The convenience of not having to change currency when traveling will matter in different degrees to people who deliberate the Euro issue. A theory which refuses to conceptualize facts such as this commits a grave error of omission; a proper theory should describe them and find proper places for them.

Calling such a theory "relativistic" does not make the facts it describes less true or more avoidable. What alternative description could a "non-relativistic" argumentation offer? Would it venture to assess objectively precisely *how* strong the various arguments in, e.g., the Euro debate, are? Will argumentation scholars tell voters just how much strength they *ought* to assign to the convenience argument, to the "national identity" argument, and to the economic and political arguments, respectively? Or would argumentation theorists, to evade recognition of this alleged relativism, fall back on the time-worn denial strategy of postulating that all arguments, in practical reasoning as in logic, are either valid or invalid? While many argumentation theorists, including Douglas Walton, have abandoned deductive validity as the sole criterion of argument evaluation, and while the new concepts and categorizations which they have suggested have indeed deepened our insight into the workings of real-life argument, still when it comes to argument appraisal they have largely remained transfixed by the linear and binary mode of thinking characteristic of deductive logic. The few exceptions, such as Wellman's notion of "conduction" (1971), have received too little attention. Theorists have been afraid of opening the door to gradualism in the appraisal of argument strength, perhaps because they see that they will then have no way of avoiding what they abhor as "relativism." Thus, newer concepts to substitute traditional "validity" have not managed to (or even sought to) escape binarism; that is equally true whether the criterion suggested is "sufficiency," or, as in Walton's presumptive reasoning, correct use of argumentation schemes.

True enough, there are many aspects of everyday argumentation on which argumentation scholars can and should pronounce evaluative assessments in binary terms. In the public sphere we may every day hear moves which are unequivocally fallacious or dishonest and deserve exposure. Yet, as Walton has repeatedly shown, there are just as many points where argumentation scholars have been overzealous to pronounce generalized, categorical judgment. Walton has added countless welcome nuances to the appraisal of real-life argumentation. However, where practical reasoning is concerned—and the Euro debate is just one instance of that—his presumptive model fails to capture some of the central features. Because practical reasoning deals with actions and with the multiple values which provide warrants for them, it works in a way that argumentation scholars should study rather than be uncomfortable with: there are degrees of argument strength; the appraisal of degrees of argument strength may be inherently subjective; and this is legitimately so.

REFERENCES

Adams, E.W., and H.P. Levine. 1975. On the uncertainties transmitted from premises to conclusions in deductive inferences. *Synthese* 30, 429-460.

Blair, J.A. 1992. Premissary relevance. *Argumentation,* 6, 203-217.

_____. 1995. Informal logic and reasoning in evaluation. *New Directions for Program Evaluation* 68, 71-80.

_____. 2001. Walton's argumentation schemes for presumptive reasoning: A critique and development. *Argumentation,* 15, 365-379.

Blair, J.A., and R. Johnson. 1987. Argumentation as dialectical. *Argumentation* 1, 41-56.

Boger, G. 2005. Subordinating truth–is *acceptability* acceptable? *Argumentation* 19, 187-238.

van Eemeren, F. H., and R. Grootendorst. 2004. *A Systematic Theory of Argumentation: The Pragma-dialectical Approach.* Cambridge: Cambridge University Press.

Fahnestock, J., and M. Secor, 2004. *A Rhetoric of Argument*, 3rd ed. Boston: McGraw-Hill.

Henkemans, A. F. S. 2003. Complex argumentation in a critical discussion. *Argumentation,* 17, 405-419.

Kock, C. 2003a. Gravity too is relative: On the logic of deliberative debate. In F.H. van Eemeren, J.A. Blair, C.A. Willard, and A.F.S. Henkemans, (Eds.), *Proceedings of the Fifth Conference of the International Society for the Study of Argumentation.* Amsterdam: Sic Sat, 627-632.

Kock, C. 2003b. Multidimensionality and non-deductiveness in deliberative argumentation. In van F.H. van Eemeren and P. Houtlosser (Eds.), *Anyone Who Has a View: Theoretical Contributions to the Study of Argumentation.* Dordrecht: Kluwer, 157-171. (This volume, Chapter 6.)

Perelman, C.L., and Olbrechts-Tyteca, L. (1969). *The New Rhetoric: A Treatise on Argumentation.* Notre Dame: University of Notre Dame Press.

Pinto, R.C. 2001. *Argument, Inference and Dialectic: Collected Papers on Informal Logic.* Dordrecht: Kluwer.

Pinto, R.C. 2003. Commentary on C. Reed & D. Walton's "Argumentation Schemes in Argument-as-Process and Argument-as-Product". In J.A. Blair, D. Farr, H.V. Hansen, R.H. Johnson and C.W. Tindale (Eds.), *Informal Logic at 25: Proceedings of the Ontario Society for the Study of Argumentation.* Windsor: OSSA.

Reiter, R. 1980. A logic for default reasoning. *Artificial Intelligence* 13, 81-132.

Rescher, N. 1976. *Plausible Reasoning: An Introduction to the Theory and Practice of Plausibilistic Inference.* Assen-Amsterdam: Van Gorcum.

Trapp, R., W. Driscoll and J.P. Zompetti. 2005. *Discovering the World Through Debate: A Practical Guide to Educational Debate for Debaters, Coaches and Judges.* New York: Central European University Press.

Walton, D.N. 1990. *Practical Reasoning: Goal-driven, Knowledge-based, Action-guiding Argumentation.* Savage, MD: Rowman and Littlefield.

_____. 1991. Rules for plausible reasoning. *Informal Logic* 14, 33-51.

_____. 1993. The speech act of presumption. *Pragmatics and Cognition* 1, 125-148.

_____. 1996a. *Argumentation Schemes for Presumptive Reasoning.* Mahwah, N.J.: Lawrence Erlbaum Associates.

_____. 1996b. Practical reasoning and the structure of fear appeal arguments. *Philosophy and Rhetoric* 29, 301-313.

_____. 1997a. How can logic best be applied to arguments? *Logic Journal of the IGPL* 5, 603-614.

_____. 1997b. Actions and inconsistency: The closure problem of practical reasoning. In G. Holmstrom-Hintikka and R. Tuomela (Eds.). *Contemporary Action Theory, Vol. 1.* Dordrecht: Kluwer, 159-175.

_____. 2001. Abductive, presumptive and plausible arguments. *Informal Logic* 21, 141-169.

_____. 2006. How to make and defend a proposal in a deliberation dialogue. *Artificial Intelligence and Law.* DOI 10.1007/s10506-006-9025-x. 63 pp.

Walton, D.N., H. Prakken and C. Reed. 2004. Argumentation schemes and burden of proof. In F. Grasso, C. Reed and G. Carenini (Eds.). *Working Notes of the 4th International Workshop on Computational Models of Natural Argument* (CMNA2004) ECAI: Valencia, 81-86.

Walton, D.N., and D. Godden. 2005. The nature and status of critical questions in argumentation schemes. In *The Uses of Argument: Proceedings of the Ontario Society for the Study of Argumentation, 2005, D. Hitchcock (Ed.).* Hamilton, Ontario: OSSA, 476-484.

Wellman, C. 1971. *Challenge and Response: Justification in Ethics.* Carbondale IL: Southern Illinois University Press.

Zadeh, L.A. (1965). Fuzzy sets. *Information and Control* 8, 338-353.

6.

Multidimensionality and Non-Deductiveness in Deliberative Argumentation*

In current argumentation theory, the focus is not often on deliberative argumentation as such. Many modern theorists tend to see argumentation as a homogeneous phenomenon. Even so, there has recently been a tendency to differentiate more, for example in the works of Douglas Walton, who has defined different types of argumentative dialogue. However, to understand deliberative argumentation better, we also need to differentiate in another way, namely on the basis of argumentative issues. Aristotle did this when he defined the three main genres of rhetoric. And if we take a closer look at the nature of the issues in deliberative argumentation, several interesting implications will ensue. Deliberative argumentation will turn out to be at odds with assumptions widely accepted in current theories, such as pragma-dialectics and the model of "presumptive" reasoning advocated by Walton.

The essential fact about deliberative argumentation is that it is not about truth, but action. This fact has been cursorily acknowledged by some theorists, but hardly explored. Toulmin (1958), who makes a strong case for distinguishing between argumentative fields, nevertheless only considers arguments for claims like "Harry is a British citizen" and other constative propositions. Even Perelman and Olbrechts-Tyteca fail to make a consistent distinction between arguments about action and arguments about truth. On the one hand, they emphasize that deliberative argumentation is "oriented toward the future" and "sets out to bring about some action or to prepare for it by acting, by discursive methods, on the

* Originally published in *Anyone Who Has a View: Theoretical Contributions to the Study of Argumentation*, F.H. van Eemeren, J.A. Blair, C.A. Willard & A.F. Snoeck Henkemans (Eds.). Dordrecht: Kluwer Academic Publishers 2003, 157-171. Reprinted with permission of Springer Publishers.

minds of the hearers" (1969, p. 47); on the other hand, they cloud the distinction by repeatedly speaking of "theses" presented for the audience's assent. Characteristically, to find acknowledgement that the issues in deliberative argumentation are not propositions or theses, we must go to the textbook literature, including the work that Toulmin co-authored (1979). Educators remember what theorists like to forget: deliberative argumentation is ultimately not about what is true, but about what to do.

A typical deliberative issue is (for the United States, at the time of writing), "starting a war on Iraq." Those who propose this action are making a proposal. It would be a categorical mistake to predicate truth, or for that matter falsehood, of a proposal. Proposals are not propositions (assertions, constative statements); they do not predicate that anything is the case.

Walton comes close to saying just that in his distinction between "practical" and "discursive" reasoning, when he states: "In the action type of critical discussion, the proposition is a practical ought-proposition that contains an imperative" (1996, p. 177). However, he blurs the distinction again by describing the deliberative issue as a proposition about what is "prudential." The issue in deliberative argumentation is not a proposition; it is a proposal. It does not predicate a state of affairs, nor what ought to be the case; it proposes an action. It is like proposing a toast, or proposing marriage to someone. Proposals cannot be true or false.

All this is not to deny that deliberative argumentation usually involves a great deal of constative propositions, e.g., "Iraq supports Al-Qaeda terrorists." Such a claim may indeed be used as an argument in favour of starting a war; but the ultimate issue at the top of the argumentative hierarchy is the decision on whether to take action in the form of war. Similarly, the issues of recent referendums in Europe have not been propositions, but proposals to adopt the common currency, or to accept the treaty of Nice. Such issues cannot be formulated as constative statements, and they cannot have truth-values. What we vote about is not the truth of a proposition, but the acceptance of a proposal.

It may seem formalistic to insist on this distinction. But it has important implications. One of them is that, strictly speaking, there cannot be any logic of deliberative argumentation. This is because "logic" is about propositions, whereas deliberative argumentation is about proposals. And this accounts for another essential feature of deliberative argumentation, namely what we may call its multidimensionality.

This term means that arguments for or against a proposal may belong to a number of separate dimensions. If I propose marriage to someone, she might find me a prudential choice; but she might not love me. And even if she did love me, there would still be the fact that to marry her, I would have to break up my current family, which would be ethically questionable. So in deliberating upon my proposal of marriage, the chosen woman would have to do some mental juggling of arguments belonging to three dimensions: prudence, inclination, and ethics—and perhaps even more.

As we know from experience as well as from countless fictional narratives in literature, drama, or film, no logical rules can tell us how to put such heterogeneous arguments on a common denominator and calculate the net result. They lack commensurability. On the war against Iraq, too, there are many arguments on both sides, representing many dimensions. Some believe it will stabilize the region; others, that it will not. Both these arguments belong to the dimension of the socially advantageous, or, in Walton's term, the "prudential." But other arguments in the same debate belong to an ethical or religious dimension. Some argue that a pre-emptive attack on another country is an indefensible infringement of international law; others, that murderous dictators like Saddam Hussein must be deposed. Again, the dimensions that the various arguments belong to lack commensurability.

By contrast, in a discussion of whether a certain proposition is true— that is, whether a certain predicate can be truthfully predicated of a certain subject—we only have to consider one dimension, namely the one represented by that predicate.

The insight that deliberative rhetoric is multidimensional is as old as rhetoric itself, and it remains standard doctrine throughout antiquity. A brief overview of classical thinking on this theme may be in order here.

We find the multidimensional view of deliberation full-fledged in early Sophistic rhetoric, as in the *Rhetorica ad Alexandrum*, probably the oldest extant book on rhetoric, once thought to be by Aristotle. This text, which may antedate Aristotle's by a few years, offers a list of dimensions in deliberative argument: "he who persuades must show that those things to which he exhorts are just, lawful, expedient, honourable, pleasant, and easy of accomplishment" (1421b).

This type of advice has always struck some commentators as cynical or opportunistic in the way it suggests a battery of alternative lines of argument; it has an air of "try anything that works" or even "anything goes." But this seeming opportunism represents the fundamental insight that when we have to decide about contested actions, more than one general premise may come into play.

Aristotle, Plato's student, who saw his task as that of turning rhetorical textbook lore into a *tekhnē*, went out of his way to make deliberative debate neatly one-dimensional by declaring that "[t]he end of the deliberative speaker is the expedient or harmful [*to sympheron kai blaberon*] … all other considerations, such as justice and injustice, honour and disgrace, are included as accessory to this [*symparalambanei*]" (*Rhetoric*, I, iii, 5; 1358b).

Subsequent classical theory, however, continues to recognise at least two mutually independent dimensions in deliberative argument. The anonymous author of the influential *Rhetorica ad Herennium* (c. 90 B.C.) pays only a token tribute to one-dimensionality but effectually comes down on the side of the multidimensional view (1954, 3.3.):

> The orator who gives counsel will throughout his speech set up Advantage (*utilitas*) as his aim, so that the complete economy of his entire speech may be directed to it.
>
> Advantage in political deliberation has two aspects: Security (*tuta*) and Honour (*honesta*).

He goes on to subdivide each of these two, establishing a multi-layered hierarchy of values. However, the governing notion that Advantage is one notion is hard to see as more than a fudge when is has two "aspects" (*partes*) as potentially antagonistic as Security and Honour.

Young Cicero, writing his *De inventione* perhaps a few years later, explicitly recognizes that deliberative argument has two dimensions, *honestas* and *utilitas*, whereas for each of the other two main genres there is only one: *aequitas* for the forensic genre, *honestas* for the epideictic. As also done in the *ad Herennium*, each of these is then subdivided into several component parts, and further complications are introduced in the form of feasibility, ease of accomplishment, necessity, and *affectio* (meaning a temporary change in the way some specific situation is evaluated) (*De inventione*, 2, pp. 156-176).

Roughly similar analyses appear in Cicero's mature works. In the *De oratore* (written 55 B.C.) the experienced Antonius explains how, in deliberative matters, some debaters will emphasize aspects of *utilitas*, such as peace, wealth, power, or revenue, while others will talk about aspects of *honestas*, notably *immortalis memoria* and *laus*. Whichever of these one prefers, considerations of feasibility and necessity are always paramount (II, 334ff.). The shorter and more technical work *De partitione oratoria* (written towards 50 B.C.) presents a somewhat more complex analysis. Further considerations introduced here include the assessment of how important a course of action is (*quam sit magnum*), a factor which may argue for it although it may be hard of accomplishment. Also, Cicero points out that the hearers who are to decide on deliberative issues are of two classes: one which in all matters prefers *dignitas* (a term also used in *De oratore*, which may or may not be synonymous with *honestas*), and another which always looks for gain and for *voluptas* (*De partitione*, 83-89).

Quintilian devotes the whole of book III, chapter 8, of his *Institutio* to a discussion of the deliberative genre, declaring at the outset disagreement with those rhetoricians who see *utilitas* as its sole end. If one criterion were sufficient in deliberative debate, he would opt for Cicero's *dignitas*; however, we must recognize the fact that deliberative audiences will often consist mainly of uneducated people, and this implies that we should distinguish between *utile* and *honestum*. In another respect, too, deliberative argument is multidimensional: it is not, as some claim, restricted to questions belonging to the qualitative status; issues of conjecture and definition, and issues belonging to the various legal status are involved as well.

In the so-called "second sophistic" during the centuries following Quintilian, we find, as in the early sophistic reflected in the *Ad Alexandrum*, an unabashed recognition that deliberative rhetoric has a diversity of equal, incommensurable dimensions, and no attempt is made to make one of them the master dimension or common denominator of all. The meticulous systematizer of Hellenistic rhetoric, *Hermogenes* (c. 150 A.D.), has included deliberative argumentation in his stasis system under the name "the practical issue"(*stasis pragmatikos*), and he simply states that its "divisions" are the following: "legality; justice; advantage; feasibility; honour; consequence" (1995, p. 52). His work on invention gives a highly technical account of how any line of argument that one chooses may be systematically structured and "worked up" (*ergasia*). Conley rightly says of the Hermogenean system: "This is clearly a long way from the syllogism-based notion of rhetoric familiar from, say, Aristotle's Rhetoric" (1990, p. 56).

What is important to gather from this overview of classical thinking about deliberation is primarily the insight that unites all these thinkers, with the possible exception of Aristotle himself: deliberative argumentation has more than one dimension. How many dimensions or "topics" each thinker recognizes, how they are named, and what exactly is the structure of the conceptual hierarchy in which they are arranged, is not the issue here. Instead I wish to highlight the fact that with as soon as we have more than one dimension, we have, in principle, incommensurability.

We might add that even in a model which recognises only one master dimension, such as Aristotle's with its *sympheron-blaberon* axis, we find that the explication of what this implies takes us back to Aristotle's ethical key concept of *eudaimonia*—which he then proceeds to analyse in chapters 5 and 6 of his Book I. Chapter 7 presents a list of *topoi* for deciding which of two goods is the greater one. But even in such a system, incommensurability is inevitable. The very fact that there is a list of *topoi* for deciding which is the greater or lesser good implies that an action A may involve a greater good than B in relation to one *topos*— but at the same time a lesser good in relation to another *topos*. At the end of the day, the master rule that allows us to calculate objectively which good is the greater one eludes us.

A further important observation is that gradual differences in regard to a given dimension are recognized by all the classical rhetoricians. The dimensions they deal in are not exclusive dichotomies, like the true vs. false opposition. Not only in to regard to importance, as we saw in Cicero, but for all relevant dimensions it is clearly possible that a given action may have more or less of the quality designated by that dimension. The advantage that will accrue from a given action may be greater or lesser; it may be honourable, or dishonourable, to a greater or lesser degree; it may be more or less feasible.

Finally, both Cicero and Quintilian emphatically note that people differ in regard to the weight they will ascribe to each of the dimensions. So not only are there separate dimensions, on each of which the proposed action will be assigned a graduated evaluation; also, each of the individuals who are to evaluate will do their separate and subjective evaluations.

All in all, the kind of multi-dimensional theory typified by Hermogenes' list, or that of the *Ad Alexandrum*, which is practically the same, is, as we have now seen, mainstream thinking in ancient rhetoric. The diversity of such lists, and the absence of "truth" from them, were no doubt some of the aspects of sophistic doctrine that made Plato and others see rhetoric as opportunistic flattery and a method for turning black into white. We may compare this sophistic recognition of multidimensionality with the disillusioning discovery by the Pythagorean mathematicians of irrational numbers. (For example, the relation between the diagonal and the sides of a square is irrational. No mathematical calculation can find a common denominator, or "commensurability," between them.)

By contrast, economic cost and benefit, for example, are commensurable entities. Both have the same denomination: money; they may therefore be reduced to one coefficient. Not so with the various arguments that are advanced about deliberative proposals such as starting a war, adopting the Euro, banning abortion or capital punishment. In such matters, there is no algorithm for tallying up the pros and cons.

This is why the distinction between and propositions and proposals is important. With propositions, we may, in principle, have deductive validity. A proposition is one-dimensional in that it asserts one predicate, and that is why the truth of that predication may follow from the truth of the premises. A proposal does not assert anything, although several propositions representing separate dimensions may be asserted as premises for or against the decision to accept a given proposal.

As a consequence, in deliberative issues there can be no deductive inference from premises to acceptance. This point is central to Perelman's entire thinking about argumentation; indeed, he sees the defining feature of "argumentation," as opposed to "demonstration," in the fact that argumentation is "noncompulsive," i.e., that deductive inference is not possible. The following statement of this principle from one of Perelman's later writings squarely aligns "truth," as in propositions, with "demonstration," and "argumentation with "decision," as in proposals.

In argumentation, it is not a matter of showing (as it is in demonstration) that an objective quality (such as truth) moves from the premises towards the conclusion, but rather it is a matter of showing that one can convince others of the reasonable and acceptable character of a decision, based on what the audience already assumes and based on the theses to which it adheres with sufficient intensity. (1989, p. 11)

By contrast, in arguing for a proposition we may in principle make a deductive inference, i.e., make the truth of the premises "move towards the conclusion," and this proposition may then be used in deliberative debate as an argument for adopting a given proposal. But at that stage there is no deductive inference. There will always be other arguments in the matter, pertaining to other dimensions, and there is no deductive way to reduce the multiple, multidimensional arguments to one common denominator and deduce a net result.

Perelman and Olbrechts-Tyteca anticipated this characteristic of deliberative argumentation. They pointed out that "the possibility of arguing in such a way as to reach opposite conclusions" will always exist "when the argumentation aims at bringing about an action which is the result of a deliberate choice among several possibilities" (1969, p. 46).

However, much current theory has failed to follow this lead. In pragma-dialectics, for example, some form of deductivism is central, i.e., a belief in a normative rule demanding that the conclusion should follow in a valid manner from the premises. One of the ten basic rules of pragma-dialectics states: "A party may use only arguments in its argumentation that are logically valid or capable of being validated by making explicit one or more unexpressed premises" (Rule 8 in van Eemeren *et al.*, 1996, p. 284). But as we have just seen, because deliberative argumentation is about proposals and hence multidimensional, it does not allow for logical validity.

Pragma-dialecticians are aware of a difficulty here. A footnote to the passage just quoted states that "valid" is used in "a broader sense," so that there is no "dogmatic commitment" to deductivism. However, it never becomes quite clear in what broader sense "valid" is to be taken. There are sporadic comments, but they all deal with the kind of reservations about the validity concept that are internal to the purely formal definition, e.g., how to avoid granting "validity" to an inference where the conclusion tautologically repeats a premise. What we generally do not find in pragma-dialectics, however, is a clear recognition that arguments in, e.g., ethical or political debate may be perfectly good and legitimate, and yet not be valid in any sense resembling deductive validity.

The qualification that arguments, if not logically valid, should be "capable of being validated by making explicit one or more unexpressed premises" does not fix this hole in the theory. The unexpressed premises thus imputed to arguers so that their arguments may be "validated" are, in many cases, premises that these people themselves would undoubtedly reject. For example, a British opponent of the Euro may believe in the argument that Sterling, as a symbol of national identity, should be preserved. But that person is not thereby committed to the premise that any symbol of national identity should always be preserved in any country or context. And only such a general premise would serve to "validate" his argument against the Euro. So the notion of "validating" arguments by reconstructing their unexpressed premises does not do justice to the way many people actually use arguments on deliberative issues.

Another example of a premise where this kind of validation would misrepresent the arguer's own standpoint may be cited from a televised debate discussed in Jørgensen, Kock and Rørbech (1998). The issue was whether to ban surrogate motherhood arrangements. The opponent of this proposal was Ms. Pia Kjærsgaard (later to become leader of the anti-immigrant Danish People's Party, which has recently generated international attention). Her main argument was that a ban on surrogate motherhood would be a curtailment of personal freedom. Interestingly, this charismatic and powerful political leader lost the debate to a soft-spoken academic who argued that babies born by surrogate mothers might become merchandise. But what is more relevant in the present context is the fact Ms. Kjærsgaard would never accept a general premise rejecting every curtailment of personal freedom. After all, any law curtails personal freedom. For example, her party has recently helped introducing new laws severely restricting citizens' rights to bring foreign spouses to the country.

Several theorists who sympathize with pragma-dialectics have sensed that its deductivist position is in need of qualification or defence. One such theorist is Leo Groarke, who states, with praiseworthy explicitness, "natural language arguments should be understood as attempts to formulate deductive arguments" (1999, p. 2). He points out, amongst other things, that validity in the relation between premises and conclusion only means that the conclusion preserves any certainty inherent in the premises, not that a certain conclusion can be drawn from uncertain premises. But even with this—perhaps rather obvious—qualification, deductivism is still at odds with the kind of arguments found in deliberative debate. And the way Groarke speaks of "inductivism" as the only alternative to deductivism indicates that in fact he only has argumentation about propositions, i.e., constatives, in mind. The fact is that in deliberative debates we often hear arguments that are quite certain and legitimate, for example that if we adopt the Euro, we will not need to change our money when travelling to another member country; but in spite of such unassailable arguments, the conclusion, namely the adoption of the Euro, does not follow deductively (as a majority of Danish voters demonstrated when they rejected the Euro in a referendum in September 2000).

Another attempt to preserve some version of the normative validity requirement is based on the idea of arguments being presumptive or defeasible. Douglas Walton is the foremost exponent of this approach.

However, the notion of presumptiveness is slippery. It is clear that presumptive reasoning is non-monotonic, in the sense that new arguments may come up so that debaters are no longer committed to the presumed conclusion. But what is the nature of this commitment to the presumed conclusion—as long as it lasts? It seems that there are two versions of this commitment, one weaker and one stronger. In the weak version, when an arguer offers an argument in support of a conclusion, then a burden of proof is shifted onto the respondent, who then has to question or attack the argument. By doing that, he can shift the burden back onto the other side. In the strong version of what presumption means, the respondent is committed to accepting the conclusion, in a presumptive way, unless he can find fault with the argument.

This latter meaning of presumption seems to be understood in the following statement by Walton, summarizing the views of van Eemeren and Grootendorst (1992): "If the hearer accepts the premises of the speaker's argument, and the argument is an instance of a genuine and appropriate argumentation scheme (for the type of dialogue they are engaged in), then the hearer must or should (in some binding way) accept the conclusion" (Walton 1996, p. 10). Walton goes on to say that this "does not appear to be 'validity' in the same sense in which the word is familiarly used in deductive (or even inductive) logic." But still we find here the same general tendency as in the deductive model of argumentation: if an argument is "valid," then the hearer is in some way "bound" to accept the conclusion. Validity, even if it does not mean deductive or monotonic validity, means "bindingness"—although the precise nature of the binding commitment or burden is often hard to pin down.

I suggest that argumentation theory, at least as far as deliberative argumentation is concerned, needs to abandon the notion that the validity of an argument has to do with the conclusion being in some way binding. Plain deductivism, reconstructionism, and presumptionism are all versions of the deductivist way of thinking about argumentation. But for deliberative argumentation at least, this way of thinking is false. A look at any deliberative debate will show that the arguments used there may be perfectly good and legitimate, indeed that they may fully deserve the term "valid"—and yet the conclusion they support does not follow in any binding way. In most cases, not even the debater who uses a given argument in deliberation believes that the hearer should be bound by the conclusion. Moreover, respondents in deliberative argumentation often do not feel obliged to raise critical questions about their opponents' arguments, lest they should become bound to accepting their conclusion. This is not because they abandon their standpoint or shirk their duties as debaters. Just as often, it is because they acknowledge that the opponent has a legitimate argument; but, on the other hand, they believe they have arguments for their own standpoint that have greater weight.

The reason that deliberative debaters may think so is precisely that deliberative argumentation is multidimensional. This property implies that arguments may be perfectly good and yet not binding.

In a recent paper by van Eemeren himself, with Peter Houtlosser (2000), we find an excellent example of deliberative argumentation, illustrative of many of its central features. They quote a heated British debate on fox-hunting, which can be seen as illustration of how each side, precisely because of the multidimensionality of such debates, has legitimate arguments which carry some weight, but which cannot in themselves entail a conclusion.

The anti-hunters argue that foxhunting is cruel, and they draw an analogy to cock-fighting and bear-baiting—both of which were banned long ago. The pro-hunters argue that a ban would unsettle popular rural traditions and have a divisive effect, "setting town against country." Both these arguments are legitimate and carry some weight, yet neither of them is sufficient in itself to entail a conclusion. Even many of those who would use one of these arguments in a debate over this issue are probably not ready to accept a "reconstructed" general premise that would make their argument deductively valid; even die-hard foxhunters hardly believe that any socially divisive policy should necessarily be rejected. The abolitionist campaign in the United States 150 years ago was socially divisive and did set town against country; and even for an abolitionist like Lincoln himself, this argument no doubt was legitimate and had a certain weight. However, in the particular situation it was outweighed, for him and for many other Americans, by other considerations. Similarly, the cruelty argument is legitimate and yet not deductively valid. There are many cruel practices in our society, some of them traditional and some modern, but recognizing that they are cruel does not entail a commitment to having them all banned. Neither does the analogy to other cruel practices that have been banned entail such a commitment. One debater in van Eemeren and Houtlosser's article offers further analogies such as horse races and "the far larger cruelty of factory farming." However, many people who feel that there is indeed an amount of cruelty in horse racing and factory farming probably do not believe that they should *eo ipso* be banned. Thus, when theorists impute such an unexpressed belief to them in order to "validate" their argument, the theorists are at odds with how people actually think.

The example questions not only the deductivist account of argumentation, but also the presumptionist theory. That theory would hold that if a debater points out that foxhunting is cruel and argues that it should therefore be banned, then that presumption stands, and the opponent should then carry the burden of proof and refute the argument. But none of the pro-fox-hunters in the debate seem to have tried to refute the cruelty argument, in fact they may tacitly have recognized its legitimacy; instead, they meet it with an argument belonging to another dimension, i.e., the social good of hallowed traditions and the avoidance of divisive laws. Thus an ethical argument is countered, not cancelled, with social arguments. One may see all these arguments as acceptable and having at least some weight—and many people probably do. This is tantamount to saying that none of them is logically valid or "binding," not even in the "presumptive" way.

A final, paradigmatic example may be in order. In an article titled "The right to live vs. the right to die: No single yardstick," columnist Ellen Goodman (1986) describes two cases of people who wished to be allowed to die by starvation. One was an 85-year-old man in Syracuse, N.Y., who had recently had a stroke, and who had deliberately stopped eating. The administrators of the nursing home where he lived wanted to force-feed him, and took the case to court. However, Justice Miller of the State Supreme Court ruled against them, writing in his ruling, "I will not, against his wishes, order this man to be operated upon and/or to be force-fed." Goodman comments that she approves of this ruling. The fact that the man wished to die of starvation was indeed a legitimate reason in favour of letting him die—but even so, it was not a reason that deductively entailed the decision.

Here Groarke's point about deductive validity being only certainty-preserving, not certainty-establishing, is irrelevant: the man certainly wished to die, and this was undoubtedly a legitimate argument, yet the decision did not follow deductively. It would obviously be false to "reconstruct" a general unexpressed premise underlying the Justice's decision (and Goodman's approval of it) to the effect that "all persons who wish to die of starvation should be allowed to do so." The premise we may reconstruct is rather that a person's wish to die of starvation is a reason in favour of letting that person do so. No more, no less.

That this is so is brought out explicitly by Goodman's second example: a 26-year old woman in California, severely handicapped by cerebral palsy, wanted to be allowed to starve herself to death. Yet here the judge denied her request. And Goodman agrees with this decision too. But there is no inconsistency. It is much more reasonable to say that in both cases, she (like the judges handling the cases) holds the premise, stated before, that a person's wish to die of starvation is a reason in favour of letting that person do so. No more, no less. It is a premise with some weight in both cases, but in neither case does this premise, however true and certain, deductively entail the conclusion. In one case, this reason is on the "winning" side of the argument; in the other case, on the losing side. In both cases, it is legitimate and has a certain weight.

In defence of the deductivist account, one might rightly point out that the patient's own wish is not the only premise in either of the two cases. The deductivist might then argue that when this premise is added to the other pertinent premises in each of the cases, then the conclusion in each of the two cases follows deductively. In other words, for the old man one would say something like this: his own wish, his advanced age and the nature of his illness together entail the conclusion that he should be allowed to die. For the young woman, her youth would be one of the premises that, in spite of her own wish, deductively entail the opposite conclusion.

It is easy to see how artificial such an account would be. How does one add up the premises favouring a certain conclusion, and how does one subtract the ones favouring the opposite conclusion? How old does one have to be to be allowed to starve oneself to death? How ill? We would need an algorithm assigning a specific weight to each premise, using the same common denominator for all the premises, and we would need a rule defining just how much weight on one side would be needed to constitute a deductively valid inference. The two cases in question were both brought to court and decided there, but obviously no such formula exists in the laws of the two states. Even if it did, it is obvious that a rule stating just how much weight is needed to make a conclusion deductively "valid" would be quite arbitrary; a different threshold value might just as well have been chosen.

For Goodman too, a whole set of considerations explain why she thinks differently of the two cases. But that is precisely the nature of making decisions, whether in court, in politics, in ethics or in everyday life. In a situation where several considerations or premises simultaneously play legitimate parts, the demand that conclusions follow deductively from their premises is doomed to failure, or forced to resort to artificial *ad hoc* constructions. The only natural way to account for argumentation in such situations is to say that a number of arguments or premises are all legitimate and relevant, but that there is no deductively valid link from the relevant premises to any conclusion.

Indeed, we might argue that the use of the term "valid" in logic is a misnomer, and that the term might be much better employed for precisely those arguments that are legitimate without being deductively valid or cogent. Instead, "valid" arguments would be those that speak with some weight for the conclusion.

If one follows Walton's account, one might object that these cases still allow of a semi-deductivist or "presumptionist" interpretation. A patient's own wish to die of starvation, we might say, creates a presumption that the patient be allowed to do so—unless there are other factors that negate this presumption. Thus we have a valid inference of the "presumptive" or "defeasible" kind.

The answer to this account is that there are always other factors. They do not arrive out of the blue; they are always there already. But in neither of the two cases do these other factors that may plead for the opposite decision negate the legitimacy of the patient's own wish. That wish remains a legitimate argument of some weight, even if we decide that there are other arguments of greater weight that plead for the opposite decision. The idea that we either have to negate and demolish an argument, or else accept the conclusion for which it pleads, is false.

The attentive reader will not have missed the fact that the two contrasted examples cited by Goodman do not strictly belong to the deliberative genre, but are in fact cases of judicial reasoning. However, this circumstance might actually be seen as an *a fortiori* argument for the thesis presented here: we see that even in legal argumentation, which is of course much more constrained than deliberative argumentation by the existence of explicit and binding rules (such as laws and other provisions), we find that decisions with deductive force are (often) not possible; even here we often find an array of arguments on both sides, belonging to several dimensions, so that there is no objective or deductive way of calculating the relative strength of the opposite cases. This fact has long been central to the thinking of leading theorists of legal reasoning, including Joseph Raz, Robert Alexy, and Aleksander Peczenik (cf., e.g., Alexy 1978, Raz 1986, Peczenik 1995). Essentially, it implies that "[a] reasonable legal argumentation is a special case of a reasonable moral argumentation" (Peczenik, p. 747). Accordingly, the "incommensurability" of values or dimensions entering into ethical, political and legal decisions has been the object of sustained theoretical reflection in recent years (cf., notably, the writers contributing to Chang 1998).

The two cases described by Goodman are thus telling examples of how the making of decisions in politics, ethics or law is better described by the term "casuistry," as defined by Jonsen and Toulmin (1988), than by a model based on the deductive application of general principles.

It seems that we need an alternative metaphor for thinking not only about deliberative argumentation, but more broadly about how we discuss decisions—instead of the old metaphors that have to do with "chains" of reasoning or lines of argument that "bind" the opponent.

The ancient forensic image of the scales in which opposing arguments are weighed is a good starting point, emphasizing as it does that deliberation is related to *libra*, the Latin word for scales. However, while this image is illustrative of some features of deliberative debate, it is misleading about others.

Some interesting aspects well illustrated by the "scales" image are:

(1) In deliberative debate there is no deductive or "valid" demonstration of the claim, in the sense of "valid" defined by logic. Indeed, deliberative debaters often do not proceed from "premises" to "conclusion," as logicians do, but the other way around, i.e., they begin with a standpoint for which they then try to find arguments. To apply the scales image, people generally have a preconceived wish to tip the scales one way or the other, and they look for weights to throw into one of the two pans.

(2) Arguments used by deliberative debaters defy evaluation by binary standards such as valid/invalid, or sound/unsound; in deliberative debate there will generally be some arguments on both sides that have some weight. The assessment of the relative merit of arguments will typically be a matter of degrees.

(3) Although deliberative debaters sometimes pretend that their arguments make their proposals deductively valid or "binding," just as often they do not and would not pretend any such thing. This calls into question the way argumentation theorists "reconstruct" deliberative arguments by introducing "validating" premises.

(4) Deliberative debate is usually not linear, i.e., it is usually not limited to the establishment or refutation of one "clinching" argument. This is

because there are no clinching arguments in deliberative debate, which again is why there are often several arguments on each side. Staking all on one line of argument in the belief that if the opponent accepts that, he must also accept the conclusion, is illusory.

The renaissance thinker Lorenzo Valla, a harsh critic of the medieval mode of thinking that aimed at logical proof in human or theological matters, made this point eloquently, if perhaps with off-putting belligerence, when he wrote, in a commentary on the medieval philosopher Boethius:

> What is more inept than arguing the way the philosophers do, where, if one word is wrong, the whole case falls? The orator, on the other hand, uses many reasons of various kinds, he brings in opposites, he cites examples, he compares similar phenomena and forces even the hidden truth to appear. How miserable and inept is the general who lets the entire outcome of the war depend on the life of one single soldier! The fight should be conducted across the whole front, and if one soldier falls, or if one squadron is destroyed, others and still others are at hand. This is what Boethius should have done, but like so many others he was too deep in love with dialectics. (Valla, 1970, p. 113).[10]

All this is well illustrated by the "scales" image. However, even more interesting are certain features of deliberative argumentation that this image misrepresents:

(5) The decision on a deliberative issue cannot be deductively inferred by adding and subtracting the respective weights on the two sides. Arguments in deliberative debate may lack commensurability, i.e., they cannot be put on a common denominator in any binding way. Attempts to tally up the relative merits of alternative proposals in an objective fashion, e.g., in terms of economic cost and benefit, are thus illusory.

(6) This is because the weight of each argument is a subjective or "phenomenological" property relative to each member of the audience. As we saw, one may acknowledge that fox-hunting has some social value, and at the same time feel that the suffering inflicted on the foxes argues against

---

[10] Quid enim ineptius philosophorum more ut si uno verbo sit erratum tota causa periclitemur? At orator multis et variis rationibus utitur, affert contraria, exempla repetit, similitudines comparat et cogit etiam latitantem prodire veritatem. Quam miser ac pauper imperator est qui omnem fortunam belli in anima in unius militis ponit! Universitate pugnandum est et si quis miles concidit aut si qua turma profligata est, alia subinde atque alia sufficienda. Hoc modo agendum Boethio erat, qui ut plurimi alii nimio amore dialectice deceptus est.

foxhunting with greater weight. But for the person sitting next to you it might be the other way around.

(7) However, even if there is no binding or formal way to define a "common denominator" for the pros and cons on a given deliberative issue, people nevertheless may have to decide between the two sides. And somehow they manage. Sometimes they even change sides after listening to argumentation. Apparently they do find a way to put the arguments on the same scales and assess which side has more weight. But this cannot be done formally; which way the scale tips is, for each person, a "phenomenological" property, resulting from the total impact of all the rhetorical *stimuli* which that person has received. In deliberative argumentation gravity, too, is relative. Weight in deliberative argumentation is a matter of degrees: deliberative arguments are not either valid or invalid, but have more or less weight. Moreover, that weight is relative to the person who judges it, and that person's judgment is influenced by the rhetoric that is used to either enhance or reduce that weight. Enhancing the weight of an argument is what Aristotle called *auxēsis* and Latin rhetoricians *amplificatio*; reduction is *meiosis*. The insight that the weight of an argument may be enhanced or reduced by degrees, and for each member of the audience individually, is one of the defining features of rhetoric; the insight that arguments belong to many dimensions is another.

The very fact of multidimensionality in deliberation, which prevents deduction in any form, also necessitates rhetoric. Deliberative argumentation is full of arguments on both sides that all have a certain weight—except that their weight is anything but certain or definite, but changeable and relative.

An important qualification is in place here. The present account of the "logic" of deliberative argumentation does not include the view that any argument proffered in any deliberative debate has some weight. The account given here has as its central tenet that arguments in deliberation belong to several dimensions and that this is one reason why deductive validity is not a relevant yardstick in the evaluation of such arguments. However, it does not follow from this that no concept of validity should be applied, nor that no arguments are ever "invalid." An account with such implications would be not only counter-intuitive but also pernicious. Pragma-dialectics is right in insisting that there is a need for a set of rules stating which speech acts are permissible and which are more or less blameworthy in a critical exchange. My point of departure has been that at least one of the standard rules of pragma-dialectics, and probably some of the others, must be rewritten if we are to have an adequate and useful tool for modelling deliberative debates. But the normative thrust of the pragma-dialectical account must be preserved. Argumentation specialists critically need conceptual tools for the normative monitoring of, and critical intervention in, ongoing political and social debates.

Construction of a conceptual basis for such practically oriented monitoring and intervention is well under way among argumentation specialists belonging to many orientations, such as pragma-dialectics, informal logic, and others. These efforts ought to be coordinated and strengthened. However, theoretical views which overlook the multidimensionality of social and political debate and which hold, e.g., that some form of deductive validity is an applicable value criterion, impede the effort to build a platform for the normative criticism of public debate.

Indeed, I believe that one of the main categories of blameworthy debate behaviour is the tendency on the part of politicians and other debaters to suggest that an argument of theirs entails a certain policy with deductive validity; or, in a looser formulation, a tendency to say or suggest that their own arguments have stronger force than is warranted. Typically we find debaters behaving as if it was the case that because the policy they propose may have this or that advantage, it therefore follows that it should be adopted. The point in such cases is precisely what has been the main point of this article: that an argument for a policy may be perfectly good, yet this is not equivalent to saying that the adoption of that policy follows deductively. This distinction is overlooked by theories committed to deductive validity in any form.

Similarly, the idea that the other side may have legitimate arguments of some weight seems abhorrent to many politicians. This might be the common denominator for another main category of blameworthy debate behaviour: the tendency to ignore, misrepresent or offhandedly dismiss any argument that can be made against one's own policies, or in favour of those of the opponent. Many citizens, by contrast, probably believe that on most contested issues, there is in fact something to be said on both sides. Such voters will want to know what it is and to get a chance to evaluate the relative merits of all reasonable arguments. Politicians who flatly deny or ignore that the opposition may have a point, maintaining that their own policies are unassailable, are not credible in such citizens' eyes, and they probably help promote the kind of democratic cynicism reflected in, e.g., dwindling election turnouts.

Argumentation theory should teach would-be deliberative debaters to acknowledge legitimate arguments on the opposite side. They would probably be more willing to do so if it were also made clear that the acceptance of some of the opponent's arguments does not deductively entail a commitment to the opponent's proposals or policies. In accordance with this principle, argumentation specialists should keep a vigilant eye on debaters who tend to suppress or misrepresent arguments made by the opponent; this is something pragma-dialectics has always emphasized, and rightly so. And they should show that the necessary function of deliberative debate is to identify, in Aristotle's phrase, "the available means of persuasion" (cf. Rhetoric 1355b) on both sides, thereby helping audiences form their own individual assessments of their relative weight. This would in turn help democracies sustain the credibility of political processes currently threatened by polarization, non-participation, and cynicism.

REFERENCES

Alexy, R. 1978. *Theorie der Juristischen Argumentation*. Frankfurt a.m.: Suhrkamp.

Conley, T.M. 1990. *Rhetoric in the European Tradition*. Chicago: The University of Chicago Press.

Aristotle 1926. *The Art of Rhetoric*. J.H. Freese (trans.). Cambridge, MA: Harvard University Press. (Loeb Classical Library, 193.)

Aristotle (1937). *Problems, Books 22-38,* and *Rhetorica ad Alexandrum.* W.S. Hett, and H. Rackham (trans.). Cambridge, MA: Harvard University Press. (Loeb Classical Library, 317.)

Chang, R. (Ed.). 1998. *Incommensurability, Incomparability and Practical Reason*. Cambridge: Harvard University Press.

Eemeren, F.H. van, and R. Grootendorst. 1992. *Argumentation, Communication, and Fallacies*. Mahwah, NJ: Lawrence Erlbaum Associates.

Eemeren, F.H. van, R. Grootendorst, F. Snoeck Henkemans. 1996. *Fundamentals of Argumentation Theory: A Handbook of Historical Backgrounds and Contemporary Developments*. Mahwah, NJ: Lawrence Erlbaum Associates.

Eemeren, F.H. van, and P. Houtlosser. 2000. Argumentation, interpretation, rhetoric. http://www.argumentation.spb.ru/2000 1/papers/1 2000p1.htm.

Fuhrmann. M. 1984. *Die Antike Rhetorik: Eine Einführung*. München: Artemis-Verlag.

Goodman, E. 1986. The right to live vs. the right to die: no single yardstick. In *From Thought to Theme: A Rhetoric and Reader for College English*, 8th ed. W.F. Smith and R.D. Liedlich (Eds.). San Diego CA: Harcourt Brace Jovanovich, 386-388.

Groarke, L. 1999. Deductivism within pragma-dialectics. *Argumentation* 13, 1-16.

Heath, M. 1995. *Hermogenes on Issues: Strategies of Arguments in Later Greek Rhetoric*. Oxford: Oxford University Press.

Jonsen, A., and S.E. Toulmin. 1988. *The Abuse of Casuistry: A History of Moral Reasoning*. Los Angeles: University of California Press.

Jørgensen, C., C. Kock, and L. Rørbech. 1998. Rhetoric that shifts votes: An exploratory study of persuasion in issue-oriented public debates. *Political Communication* 15, 283-299. (This volume, Chapter 12.)

Peczenik, A. 1995. Argumentation in ethics, legal dogmatics and legal practice. *Argumentation* 9, 747-756.

Perelman, C., and L. Olbrechts-Tyteca. 1969. *The New Rhetoric: A Treatise on Argumentation*. J. Wilkinson and P. Weaver (trans.). Notre Dame, IN: University of Notre Dame Press.

Perelman, C. 1989. Formal logic and informal logic. (French original written 1981.) In M. Meyer (Ed.), *From Metaphysics to Rhetoric*. Dordrecht: Kluwer Academic Publishers, 9-14.

Raz, J. 1986. *The Morality of Freedom*. Oxford: Clarendon Press.

Toulmin, S.E. 1958. *The Uses of Argument*. Cambridge: Cambridge University Press.

Toulmin, S.E., R. Rieke, and A. Janik. 1979. *An Introduction to Reasoning*. New York: Macmillan.

Valla, L. 1970. *De Vero Falsoque Bono*. Critical edition by Maristella de Panizza Lorch. Bari: Adriatica Editrice.

Walton, D.N. 1996. *Argumentation Schemes for Presumptive Reasoning*. Mahwah, NJ: Lawrence Erlbaum Associates.

7.

Constructive Controversy—Rhetoric as Dissensus-oriented Discourse[*]

Current theories of argumentation underestimate the difference, emphasized already by Aristotle, between theoretical and practical (action-oriented) argumentation. This is exemplified with the argument theories of Toulmin, pragma-dialectics, Habermas, Walton, and Perelman. Since antiquity, rhetoric has defined itself, not as argument designed to "win," but as action-oriented argument. Several distinctive features of action-oriented argument are identified. One is that its warrants include value concepts in audiences, implying an element of subjectivity in argument assessment. Between individuals, but also inside each individual, several conflicting value dimensions are typically involved, not just the dimension of truth-falsity, which makes sustained, reasonable dissensus inevitable.

All those of us who are interested in the theory of argumentation cannot and should not try to describe all kinds of argumentation with one model or one theory. I believe that numerous misunderstandings and mistakes which argumentation theorists have been guilty of, in the past as well as today, can be put down to a misguided attempt to develop one great theory that is supposed to account for all the essential characteristics of all argumentation.

It is not that there is anything wrong *per se* with such strong and comprehensive theories of an entire domain. It would be wonderful to have one if it worked. But such theories rarely do; nevertheless we often let them mislead us into making naive initial assumptions which we cling to and do not really question or investigate because we are too busy working on our theory so that it may be thought to cover the entire domain.

---

[*] Originally published in *Cogency* 1 (2009), 89-112. Reprinted with permission of the publisher.

To be more specific, I will claim that there are certain fundamental differences between argumentation about what is true, on the one hand, and on the other hand, argumentation about what to do. Philosophers since Aristotle have designated this same difference with the terms theoretical reasoning vs. practical reasoning. Historically, philosophers have been predominantly concerned with theoretical reason, but at least many of them have been aware of this difference. Arguably, however, many thinkers and educators who have made argumentation their chief interest have tended to forget this difference in their eagerness to cover the whole domain of argumentation with one theory.

I will first comment briefly on a few of the leading theories and theorists of argumentation. My view is that what each of these has given us is essentially *either* a theory that applies well to theoretical argumentation, *or* a theory that applies well to practical argumentation. But all of them have believed that one grand theory could encompass the essential features of argumentation as such; none have thought that here were fundamental differences between theoretical and practical argumentation. Hence, they have done little to explore these differences. I will try to do a little more.

The argumentation theory of Stephen Toulmin, centered on the famous argument model (Toulmin 1958), is a case in point. The model has been used to map and to teach all kinds of argumentation, whether theoretical or practical, and perhaps especially practical argumentation, since that is what students in schools and colleges most call for and need. This has been done, also by Toulmin himself (cf. Toulmin *et al.*, 1979), despite the fact that Toulmin's theory and model were primarily meant to elucidate argumentation as it occurs in science and scholarship. That becomes clear when we read *The Uses of Argument* in the context of those of Toulmin's other writings (e.g., 1961, 1985, 1990, 2001), whose focus is his campaign against the Cartesian idea of deductive certainty and universality as criteria for reasoning in all scientific fields. Instead, Toulmin argues that each science, each field, has its own rules and warrants; hence there are many different *kinds and degrees* of validity in reasoning, depending on field. On the other hand, it is arguably a common feature of scientific and scholarly reasoning in any field that its basic building blocks are those found in Toulmin's famous model: claims, grounds, warrants, backing, qualifiers and rebuttals. If so, the model captures essential features of any true piece of academic reasoning, including those attempted by students in papers and theses, etc. And thus the most natural educational use of the model is in the teaching of academic writing.

This claim (which has been developed in Hegelund and Kock, 2000, 2003) may be supported with a few examples of how the model usefully illustrates, on the one hand, the way academic writing in a given field, in order to qualify as such, ought to contain instantiations of the six elementary components of argument; on the other hand, for each theoretical field, how the instantiations of them will be different. For instance, in historical scholarship an argument will typically use so-called sources as grounds to argue for a claim about the past. The warrant here will typically be what historians call source criticism (*Quellenkritik*, as Leopold von Ranke called it). Warranted by proper source criticism, historical data will give a certain kind and degree of validity to a claim. The theoretical backing for these warrants has been formulated by Ranke and other thinkers who have theorized about historical method.

Another example: in quantitative fields where statistical tests and the like are used as grounds for a claim, the warrants that confer a specific kind and degree of validity on them consist in statements about the internal and external validity of the samples and other aspects of study design, about the appropriateness of the tests used, etc. Backing for these warrants is supplied by theoretical thinking, much of it developed by Sir Ronald Fisher and later scholars in statistics. In all scholarly fields, we must also have qualifiers, rebuttals and other types of discussion of reasonable objections, etc. So the Toulmin model well reflects what is expected of scholarly argument in a given field, while also allowing for the differences between concepts and norms of validity across fields.

But by the same token it is also clear that Toulmin's model is less well fit to represent what we call practical argumentation, i.e., arguments about what to do. For one thing, such reasoning typically does not discuss its own warrants; the explicit discussion of warrants, possibly with backing and all the rest, is precisely what sets academic reasoning apart. Students given the Toulmin model in order to analyze a piece of everyday practical reasoning will often look in vain for these typically academic elements, and they may then, in frustration, endow a more or less arbitrary sentence in the text with the status of "warrant." This illustrates our general thesis: theoretical reasoning is a species apart; taking a model meant to capture the essential features of theoretical reasoning in science and scholarship and expecting it to perform as well in practical and everyday argumentation is problematic.

It may be objected that much of Toulmin's later thinking (in particular in Jonsen & Toulmin, 1988, as well as several smaller works, such as

1981) does focus on a distinction between theoretical and practical reason. This is particularly so where Toulmin engages questions of medical ethics; here, theoretical and practical reason are described as "two very different accounts of ethics and morality: one that seeks eternal, invariable principles, the practical implications of which can be free of exception or qualifications, and another which pays closest attention to the specific details of particular moral cases and circumstances" (Jonsen & Toulmin, 1988, p. 2). Notice again Toulmin's persistent anti-universalist stance in the rejection of "invariable principles" and his respect for "particular moral cases" and "casuistry" (a term that inspired the book's title); but where the emphasis in *The Uses of Argument* was on the distinctness of warrants in each cognitive field, the distinction that he and Jonsen now draw accentuates the individual case where action must be decided on. Warrants according to the 1958 model, while field-dependent, are general and cannot provide decisions in the hard cases that, e.g., medical ethics encounters. One reason why this is so is that specific cases cannot always be subsumed with certainty under any given principle (or warrant): "presumptive conclusions can have 'certitude' only when the relevance of the concepts or terms involved is not in doubt" (1988, p. 327). Another difficulty is that in any given case, several principles (warrants) may be relevant simultaneously, requiring reasoners to "strike equitable balances between varied considerations in ways relevant to the details of each particular set of circumstances" (1988, p. 306). The existence, in practical reasoning, of conflicting considerations that are simultaneously valid is, as we shall see below, a major difference between practical and theoretical reasoning. In fact Toulmin had been aware of these kinds of difficulties ever since his first book, *An Examination of the Place of Reason in Ethics* (1950), which has, for example, the following statement: "Given two conflicting claims … one has to weigh up, as well as one can, the risks involved in ignoring either, and choose 'the lesser of two evils.' Appeal to a single current principle, though the primary test of the rightness of an action, cannot therefore be relied upon as a universal test: where this fails, we are driven back upon our estimate of the probable consequences" (1950, p. 147). But the fact remains that the theory and model for which he is most famous belong to a line of thought and a segment of his career where his overriding concern was the field-dependency of warrants in theoretical reasoning.

Pragma-dialectics (most recently and authoritatively set forth in van Eemeren and Grootendorst, 2004) is another influential theory in our time which has the advantage of capturing features (or rather: norms) of theoretical argument—yet I argue that it too has problems with practical argument. One of its main tenets is that argumentation is always in principle a critical discussion between a protagonist and an antagonist, where the protagonist seeks to defend a thesis against the antagonist's objections and critical questions. This view is inspired by the critical rationalism of Karl Popper and provides a useful model of the way academic argumentation *ought* to proceed. Another tenet is that the goal of critical discussion is always to resolve a difference of opinion between protagonist and antagonist, i.e., to reach consensus. This too reflects the way things ought ideally to be in scholarly discussion, because scholarly discussion is essentially theoretical argumentation. But for practical argumentation this model does not hold, as we shall see.

An important thinker about argumentation who has received too little attention from argumentation theorists is Jürgen Habermas. He, unlike the pragma-dialecticians, is strongly aware of differences between various types of claims that people may argue for. In what we call practical argumentation we do not argue, as Habermas makes clear, about the truth of propositions, but about actions, and so the warrants that we appeal to are not propositions that we hold to be true, but norms of action that we hold to be *right*. The rightness of certain norms is a very different kind of validity claim (*Gültigkeitsbedingung*, as Habermas calls it) from the truth that validates constative speech acts. And both are different from the sincerity that validates expressive self-representations and from the adequacy of value standards that validates evaluative expressions.

Argumentation theorists would do well to heed the distinctions that Habermas lays down here. Of particular importance in this context is Habermas' insistence that the validity claim of a proposal for action is not the truth of a premiss but *rightness* according to some norm. However, his main thrust is to say that even though a proposal for action makes a different kind of validity claim, it is still subject to a "communicative rationality" whose goal is for the discussants to reach consensus on right action thanks to the paradoxical "unforced force of the better argument." So, regarding the orientation towards consensus, Habermas essentially holds the same view as the pragma-dialecticians and sees no difference between the various types of speech act that he has defined. He sums up his theory as follows:

> ... actions regulated by norms, expressive self-representations, and also evaluative expressions, supplement constative speech acts in

constituting a communicative practice which, against the background of a lifeworld, is oriented to achieving, sustaining, and renewing consensus—and indeed a consensus that rests on the intersubjective recognition of criticizable validity claims. (1997, p. 17).

Habermas, in his thinking about communicative action, anticipated the pragma-dialecticians by insisting that argumentation should be guided by certain procedural rules of reasonableness or rational communication; these rules exist to ensure that the speech acts performed by discussants do not obstruct the inherent goal of the argumentative dialogue: consensus; and they primarily require that discussants are under no force or constraint except the paradoxical "unforced force of the better argument."

According to Habermas all this should equally be the case in theoretical argumentation *and* in practical argumentation. But while there is certainly a need for norms of reasonableness in practical argumentation, for example in public political debate, it does not follow that the goal of such debates is or should be consensus, nor that the compliance with such norms will lead towards consensus. In taking this view, one confronts formidable opposition among present-day thinkers. Not only is there the pragma-dialectical school and the many argumentation theorists who tend to go along with it; in addition, a broad range of political, philosophical and rhetorical thinkers in our time who have attempted to ground the legitimacy of democracy in deliberation and debate have assumed that the inherent aim of deliberation is consensus. Besides Habermas, this includes, in various ways, political theorists like Joshua Cohen (e.g., 1989, 1993, 1998), Joseph Bessette (1994), and Seyla Benhabib (e.g., 1994, 1996), or a rhetorician like Thomas Goodnight (e.g., 1993).

What unites all these theories is the idea that in practical argumentation as well as in theoretical argumentation, if we have a truly rational, critical discussion, we will eventually or at least tendentially approach a resolution to our difference of opinion; in these theories, the right action exists as a potential inference from the accepted premises and the agreed rules of reasonable discussion.

Another version of a theory that sees practical argumentation as merely a special kind of inference has been proposed by Douglas Walton. As one of the few philosophical argumentation theorists today, Walton recognizes practical argumentation as a separate domain (Walton, 1990; 1996a, pp. 11-13, 176-180; 1996b; 1997b). What many other theorists have overlooked is the simple fact that in practical reasoning people argue about an action, not about a proposition or assertion. But my objection to

Walton's analysis is that he never decisively abandons the assumption that practical reasoning is about propositions, and so he never questions the assumption that what we argue for in practical reasoning follows as a conclusion or inference from a properly applied argument scheme, the way a proposition follows from its premises by inference. Consider the following formulations: "In a practical inference, the conclusion is an imperative that directs the agent to a prudent course of action" (1996a, p. 11); "it concludes in an imperative that directs the agent to a course of action" (1990, p. xi). Here we have, as in propositional logic, the notions of "inference" and of a "conclusion," as well as two additional indications of the binding nature of this conclusion: it is an *imperative* which *directs*. Walton's model of practical reasoning, and hence also of how to evaluate arguments in that domain, is an inference model: what to do follows as an inference. However, as Walton has emphasized in many contexts, the inference in practical argumentation is *presumptive* or *defeasible*. If there is a good argument for doing something, it follows that we should do it—*unless* there are other considerations which then cancel out the argument. It is, as he would say, subject to defeat; what was a valid argument becomes defeated or invalid. In other words, a good argument in practical argumentation is good if the conclusion follows from it—presumptively, that is.

Although Walton has done much to elucidate practical argumentation, this is a serious problem in his theory: arguments in practical argumentation *either* trigger an inference, *or* they are invalidated. I shall argue that practical argumentation is not like that (for a fuller version of this critique, see Kock 2007).

To be sure, a recent development in Walton's work on practical argumentation (see, e.g., Walton 2006) takes a long step towards repairing the shortcomings of his earlier conception. In particular, he now clearly recognizes that the conclusion in what he calls "deliberation dialogue" is a *proposal*, not a proposition, and that a proposal is a distinctive kind of speech act, of which he then presents a careful analysis. Also, the same paper contains, among other things, a valuable overview of the criteria and critical questions that may be invoked in deliberation dialogue and in the evaluation of it. The dependence of deliberation on values is theorized, and so is the existence of simultaneous pro and con arguments. However, the paper does not recognize that the notions of inference and presumption in deliberation are called into question by this new approach, and most of the distinctive features of argumentation in deliberation dialogue which will be discussed below, and all of which are corollaries of the basic properties just mentioned, remain largely unaddressed.

The last leading theorist I will mention in this overview is Chaïm Perelman. He differs from all the others in the sense that what his theory is really about is practical argumentation. This is not quite clear in *The New Rhetoric* (Perelman & Olbrechts-Tyteca 1969), which often claims to be a theory of *all* argumentation. This work is somewhat vague on the distinction between argumentation for truth and argumentation for action, and hence it repeatedly describes argumentation, the domain of rhetoric, as what we do to gain "adherence to a thesis." But in Perelman's later writings (e.g., 1979, which is titled "The New Rhetoric: A Theory of Practical Reasoning") he is more explicit that what he is concerned with is indeed "practical reason" – defined as "the actual process of deliberation that leads to decision making in practical fields such as politics, law, and morals" (1083) or as "finding good reasons to justify a decision" (1099). He even states explicitly that "it is highly unlikely that any reasoning from which we could draw reasons for acting could be conducted under the sign of truth" (1086).

When Perelman defines rhetoric or argumentation as reasoning about actions decisions, he is in unison with the dominant rhetorical tradition itself. For Aristotle, what we do in rhetoric is to deliberate, βουλεύειν, and he makes it clear that "the subjects of deliberation are clear; and these are whatever, by their nature, are within our power and of which the inception lies with us," in other words, what we may decide to do. The same idea is stated repeatedly in his ethical writings: "We deliberate about things that are in our control and are attainable by action" (1112a). A similar demarcation of the realm of rhetoric occurs in most of the later sources, such as the *Rhetorica ad Herennium*, which states: "The task of the public speaker is to discuss capably those matters which law and custom have fixed for the uses of citizenship," or Boethius, to whom the subject matter of rhetoric is explicitly "the political question." (A fuller discussion of the action-based definition of rhetorical argument in the rhetorical tradition itself is found in Kock 2009.)

We may note here that most modern argumentation theorists who have discussed rhetoric have misunderstood what the classical conception of rhetoric is. They see rhetoric as that kind of argumentation where the main object is to win the discussion, not to find the truth. But rhetoricians primarily define their discipline as concerned with argument about actions;

and that is why, in a sense, rhetorical argumentation is unconcerned with truth, since actions are neither true nor false.

What we have seen now is that a series of leading thinkers in the field of argumentation are all guilty of a hasty generalization: they all believe *either* that all argumentation works pretty much along the lines of theoretical argumentation, *or* (in the case of Perelman in *The New Rhetoric*) the other way around. I will now try to point out some deep differences between these two basic domains.

We may start with the well-known observation that practical argumentation so often leaves out explicit statements of the warrant and its backing. This is because the grounds we give in practical reasoning for a proposed action are typically different from those used in theoretical argumentation. These grounds are generally alleged *advantages* of doing the action or alleged *drawbacks* of not doing it. And an advantage relies for its warrant on something we assume is already present in our audience: a *value concept* we believe we share with that audience. If we say that a given plan will bring peace to the Middle East, we take for granted that our audience values peace in the Middle East, and peace generally. If a friend or family member suggests that we watch a DVD of the film *American Pie* tonight, we might argue against this by saying that *American Pie* is vulgar, thereby taking for granted that the circle of friends or family members share a negative valuation of vulgarity. In other words, the ultimate warrants in practical argumentation are value concepts, and these we often assume are already present in our interlocutors, so that we do not have to establish them, not even make them explicit.

This is why practical reasoning about worldly concerns is full of *enthymemes.* That is Aristotle's term for a premiss which is assumed to be present in the hearer's mind—and just that is the original meaning of the word. The feature that an enthymeme is often left unexpressed is not essential (for an authoritative statement of this view, see Burnyeat 1996). An enthymeme is something which is already in the *thymos*, i.e., "in the soul," of the hearer.

So warrants in practical argumentation are value concepts located in audiences. From this follows another fact which some theorists find scandalous (notably the pragma-dialecticians, in several statements), namely that these warrants are *subjective*: they vary across individuals. Some individuals might think that vulgarity, although quite bad, is not *such* a bad thing, so they might agree to watch a film which has some vulgarity in it if it also has other, redeeming qualities. Others again might actually find that the kind of vulgarity to be found in *American Pie* is in fact appealing, not appalling.

Another example illustrating the same point, but this time on the level of national policy, might be laws which curtail people's right to privacy in order to promote security against terrorism. Some individuals might resent such laws, feeling that their loss of privacy far outweighs the alleged gain in security; but others might have it the other way around. This shows that different individuals may not endorse the warrants invoked in practical argumentation with the same *degree of strength*. The strength of the value concepts on which practical argumentation relies for its warrants is subjective; in a slightly less provocative term, it is audience-relative. This is a fundamental fact in practical argumentation, yet several leading thinkers in state-of-the-art argumentation theory have failed to recognize it and have roundly condemned those theorists, notably Perelman, who have provided a place of honour in their theories for this fact. (We can now see that the reason Perelman provided a place for it is that his theory is really about practical argumentation, whereas the theory of his harshest critics— the pragma-dialecticians—is really about theoretical argumentation.) The failure to recognize this is one instance of the grave misunderstandings caused by an underlying failure to respect the distinction between theoretical and practical reasoning.

Although value concepts are not held with equal strength by all individuals, it is probably true that most people in a culture do have most of their value concepts in common. Yet each individual probably also holds some values *not* shared by a majority. And just as importantly, we have seen that they do not agree on the *relative* priorities between the values that they do share.

Yet another complication is that the set of values held by a given individual, and even that subset of these values which is shared by practically everyone in the culture, are not necessarily in harmony with each other. The philosopher Isaiah Berlin has talked about the "pluralism" of values, meaning that "not all good things are compatible, still less all the ideals of mankind." For example, he points out "that neither political equality nor efficient organization nor social justice is compatible with more than a modicum of individual liberty, and certainly not with unrestricted *laissez-faire*; that justice and generosity, public and private loyalties, the demands of genius and the claims of society can conflict violently with each other" (1958, repr. 1998, p. 238).

Of course this is something that ordinary human beings have always known in an intuitive way. Practical philosophers, such as Cicero, who was a rhetorician as well, have known it too. He writes:

> … between those very actions which are morally right, a conflict and comparison may frequently arise, as to which of two actions is morally better—a point overlooked by Panaetius. For, since all moral rectitude springs from four sources (one of which is prudence; the second, social instinct; the third, courage; the fourth, temperance), it is often necessary in deciding a question of duty that these virtues be weighed against one another. (*De officiis* 1.63.152.)

But philosophers, beginning with Plato and including many in recent decades who have become argumentation theorists, tend to theorize as if all values *were* compatible and did *not* clash. Or at least as if the lack of compatibility between them was no real problem. They tend to think, for example, that if we can agree that something is good, then it follows that we must have it, or do it. Philosophers have concentrated on figuring out what it meant for a thing to be good, and on arguing about what things are truly good in a general sense, and have given less thought to situations where many different things are indeed good, but where we cannot have them all at the same time. However, this is a kind of situation we face every day in our lives.

True enough, some philosophers have indeed worked on this issue, but their thinking has either run along the lines of Plato's insistence that virtue and well-being are in fact one and the same value, or they have, like Jeremy Bentham and John Stuart Mill, believed that they could order all human action by applying the rule of the greatest happiness for the greatest possible number. That would indeed be convenient, but it would require what Mill calls a "common umpire" to settle the claims between the incompatible values. In other words, there would have to be a universally agreed common unit or denominator so that the advantages a given action might have in regard to a certain value might be objectively converted into happiness and weighed against the unhappiness caused by the drawbacks the action might have in regard to another value; for example, for legislation involving an invasion of privacy, that drawback would have be objectively measured against the alleged advantage of reducing the risk of terrorist acts, and increasing the chance of solving terrorist crimes to a certain unknown degree. Unfortunately, and obviously, such a common denominator does not exist and could never be constructed; the very construction of it would be just as controversial as the debatable legislation itself. What we cannot do is what the philosopher John Finnis describes in the following words: "Aggregate the pluses, subtract the minuses, and pursue the option with the highest balance" (1998, p. 216). It is impossible because the relevant arguments in any practical issue usually belong to different *dimensions*. There *is* no common denominator or unit by which they can all be objectively compared and computed. They are, to use a mathematical term, incommensurable.

So we have at least three fundamental reasons why practical argumentation works in a different way from theoretical argumentation: There is, first, the *subjectivity* of the value concepts which are the necessary warrants when we discuss what actions to take; secondly, there is the *incompatibility* of all human values, and thirdly, we now also face what some recent philosophers have recently called their ultimate *incommensurability* (see, e.g., Griffin 1977, Raz 1998, Finnis 1998). There *is* no objective or philosophical way to compute the advantages and drawbacks of proposed human actions and weigh them up against each other.

This does not mean that all possible actions are equally good, or that there is no point in discussing what to do, or in choosing one action over another. What it means is merely that we have no *objective* method of *calculating* what to choose. In fact, if we had such a method, we would have no choice; our "choices" would be made for us beforehand. Choice means precisely that we may legitimately elect to do either one thing *or* another. But that there is choice surely does not mean that we might as well not choose anything, or that there is no reason to debate our upcoming choices. The point is that each individual has the right to choose, and that no one has the right or the authority to choose on everyone's behalf. Nor is there any way for philosophy to determine in a compelling manner (i.e., by inference) what the right policy is.

Yet individuals must choose, and choice makes it desirable that they have in fact balanced or weighed the advantages and drawbacks of the possible decisions facing them or their society. Now this "weighing" process, while it is not possible in an objective or inter-subjective way, is still necessary *and* possible for the individual. The balancing process in matters where a body of individuals must choose between actions within their power is called deliberation. This is an appropriate term, since it comes from the Latin word *libra*, meaning a pair of scales. Given the individual's value concepts (which we remember are in principle subjective) and the choices as they appear to him, one of the alternatives may eventually, after weighing the advantages and drawbacks, appear preferable to him. The same alternative may not appear preferable to his neighbour, or to the majority of citizens. But then the individual is free to try to influence his neighbours so that they may eventually come around and see things his way. This kind of influence is usually exerted by means of language and is called rhetoric.

The three distinctive features of practical argumentation just enumerated: the subjectivity of the values on which it depends, their incompatibility, and their incommensurability, as well as the approach to these notions taken in the rhetorical tradition, have been more fully discussed in Kock (2003) and Kock (2007).

We may now look at some distinctive features of practical argumentation not captured by models or theories designed for theoretical argumentation. Let us remember the categorical difference between what we argue about in the two domains. Theoretical argumentation is about propositions that may be true or false. Practical argumentation is about what to do, and whatever we do does not have the property of being true or false. We argue about proposals, not propositions.

First, the status of reasons is different in the two domains. Practical pro and con reasons, as we saw, represent advantages and drawbacks of competing policies; they remain valid and are not made invalid even if one policy is chosen over another. We choose a given policy because we place a high value on its alleged advantages, but the possible drawbacks inherent in that policy do not lose their validity or cease to exist.

Let us take one simple example drawn from the micro-politics of family life. One family member, let us call him F, wants to buy a large Chesterfield armchair for the family room. He argues that such a chair is highly comfortable and suitable for TV watching and generally chilling out. Another family member, let us call her M, strongly opposes the plan. She agrees that such a chair is comfortable, but argues that it is ugly, heavy and very expensive indeed. F happens to acknowledge these drawbacks but thinks that the expected comfort to be had in the chair outweighs them. M thinks they do not.

The example shows how the primary pro and con reasons in deliberative argumentation have the status of advantages and drawbacks as perceived by the arguers. Notice that both F and M may well agree on all the advantages and drawbacks of the chair. For both of them, they are inherent in the plan to buy the chair. However, they disagree on *how much weight* to assign to them. And no advantages or drawbacks are refuted even if one plan conclusively defeats the other. If the scheme is conclusively abandoned, the armchair does not cease to be comfortable. If the family actually buys the chair, it remains heavy and expensive. (It is a little different with the alleged ugliness of the chair. Ugliness is an aesthetic quality, and aesthetic argumentation is a category in itself with intricacies which we will not get involved with at the moment.)

In theoretical argumentation, by contrast, pro and con reasons are only important by virtue of their probative or inferential force (or, with a word used by informal logicians and derived from the same verb as "inferential": their *illative* force); that is, they are important for what may perhaps be *inferred* from them, i.e., what they point to, signify or suggest, not for what they *are*. Once the issue has been decided one way or the other, the reasons supporting the discarded position lose their relevance. For example, until a few years ago doctors used to believe that ulcers were caused by stress and acidity; when two Australian doctors, Marshall and Warren, in papers in the early 1980's, suggested that ulcers were caused by bacteria (later named *Heliobacter pylori*), they were generally disbelieved. The bacteria known around 1980 could not survive in the acidic environment of the stomach; this seemed to suggest that *no* bacteria could survive there, hence ulcers could not be caused by bacteria. However, it was soon found that certain bacteria, including the *heliobacter*, could indeed survive in the stomach. Thus the illative force of the original reasons was simply cancelled; it lost its validity. Marshall and Warren's theory is now generally accepted; they received the Nobel Prize in 2005, and millions of patients have been cured of their ulcers. This example shows how the relevance of facts used as reasons in theoretical reasoning resides in what these facts point to, signify or suggest, that is, in their illative force, not in those facts themselves.

Second, we see that in practical argumentation both pro and con reasons may be relevant simultaneously. In other words, the advantages and drawbacks indicated by the pro and con reasons may be real and remain so. In theoretical argumentation the pro and con reasons may also be real in themselves, but the two opposite states of affairs supported by the pro reasons and the con reasons, respectively, may not both be real simultaneously.

Third, this means that in practical argumentation no party can be logically *proven* to be either right or wrong. This is tantamount to saying that reasons in practical argumentation can never in principle be "valid" in the traditional sense of *entailing* their conclusion, nor can they be "sufficient" to entail a conclusion. No reasons in practical argumentation *entail* the proposals for which they argue. No reasons are "sufficient." No matter how many reasons you may muster for your proposal, your opponent is never *compelled* by those reasons to accept it. Put another way, in practical argumentation all reasons are, in principle, weights among other weights on a pair of scales. This means that in practical argumentation a set of reasons $P1$ through Pn may very well be both true, relevant and weighty, and yet the conclusion (i.e., the proposal for which they argue) is not "true" (as we have noted, proposals cannot be true or false), nor does it follow by any kind of inference or entailment. Whether or not to accept the proposal is a matter of choice for each individual audience member. In theoretical argumentation, conclusive inferences do exist, and scholars and scientists are trying to find them all the time. The theory that no bacteria can live for long in an acidic environment like our stomach has been conclusively refuted.

Fourth, the strength or weight of reasons in practical argumentation is a matter of degrees. Advantages and drawbacks come in all sizes. Along with this comes the fact that practical argumentation typically persuades by degrees. An individual may gradually attribute more weight to a given reason, so he or she may gradually become more favorably disposed towards the proposal. Not so in theoretical argumentation. A medical scientist is not free to say that the existence of *heliobacter* in the stomach carries little weight in regard to whether bacteria can live in that kind of environment.

Fifth, in practical argumentation arguers should have no problem in granting that their opponents may have relevant reasons. The drawbacks that my opponent sees in my proposal may in fact be relevant, just as the advantages that I see in it, and the ones that my opponent sees in *his* proposal. Arguers may be more prone to adopt this attitude when they realize that just because you acknowledge the relevance of an opponent's reasons, this does not entail that you adopt his proposal. In theoretical argumentation one reason against a thesis may defeat it. Unfortunately public debaters seem to believe this is also the case in practical argumentation, and so they tend to deny that their opponents have any relevant reasons at all, even when they patently do.

Sixth, this brings us to a crucial difference between practical argumentation and theoretical argumentation. As the armchair example shows, two opponents in practical argumentation will not necessarily tend towards consensus, let alone reach it, even if they follow all the rules we may devise for responsible and rational discussion. They may legitimately support contradictory proposals, and continue to do so even after prolonged discussion.

In theoretical argumentation, prolonged and rule-obeying discussion must eventually or tendentially lead to consensus. Doctors who believe that bacteria cause the majority of ulcers and doctors who believe that they don't cannot both be right. But one of the parties has to be right. There is a truth somewhere about the matter, and the goal is to find it. So prolonged disagreement in, e.g., medical science over an issue like that is an unstable and unsatisfactory state.

Rules of critical discussion, as we find them in particular in pragma-dialectics, are devised to ensure that discussions proceed toward the goal which pragma-dialecticians as well as Habermas and his followers postulate for them: a resolution of the difference of opinion, or in another word: consensus.

We should have such rules by all means. We all know the depths to which public political argumentation often descends. But again, individuals may legitimately differ over some practical proposal, and *continue* to do so, even after a prolonged discussion that follows all the rules. This is due to the fact that although most norms in a culture are shared by most of its members, not all their norms are the same, and furthermore everyone does not subscribe to the same *hierarchy* of norms. In other words, as we saw in the armchair example, for some people an appeal to one norm carries more weight than an appeal to another norm, whereas for another individual it is the other way around—even when they in fact share both norms. Hence they may never reach consensus on what to do, no matter how reasonably they argue.

So in practical argumentation consensus is not the inherent goal, and it becomes legitimate, in a sense not accounted for by Habermas, for both individuals in such a discussion to argue in order to achieve success for his or her proposal, rather than consensus. In deliberation, dissensus is not an anomaly to be corrected. Instead of trying to prove the opponent wrong the wise deliberative debater will often acknowledge that the opponent has some relevant reasons, but nevertheless try to make his own reasons outweigh them in the view of those who are to judge. This kind of discourse is the essence of rhetoric.

Seventh: The last characteristic of practical argumentation we shall look at has to do with what we just saw. In practical argumentation arguers argue in order to persuade individually. The weight of each reason is assessed subjectively by each individual arguer and spectator, and each individual must also subjectively assess the aggregate weight of all the relevant reasons; it follows from this that what will persuade one individual will not necessarily persuade another. In theoretical argumentation, by contrast, there is an underlying presumption that whatever is valid for one is valid for all. Admittedly, it is also a fact that a theoretical proposition will only be accepted by some, not by all; but the presumption of any philosophical theory is that it is presents a truth which is valid for all. Practical arguers make no such presumption, but hope to persuade *some* individuals to adopt the proposal they support. That is also why we tend to have a vote on practical proposals, but not on propositions. A majority cannot decide what the truth is; but it can decide what a body of people will do.

So the nature of practical argumentation is controversy, not consensus. It is good if antagonists can find a way to what John Rawls (1993) calls an overlapping consensus, but they might not, and it is legitimate that they remain at odds. In theoretical argumentation continued dissensus means that uncertainty still prevails, and debate must continue until consensus is reached. In practical argumentation dissensus may persist indefinitely because values differ, and this is legitimate.

But why have argumentation at all if not in order to find consensus or at least move toward it? What other purpose could argumentation between two antagonists possibly have? And how could it have such a function, whatever it is?

To answer these questions one has only to think of a factor that is curiously left out of most current theories of argumentation as well as theories of the public sphere and deliberative democracy: the audience. It is primarily for the sake of the audience that debates between opponents in practical argumentation make sense. A public sphere consists not only of participants, but also, and primarily, of spectators. They are individuals who are all, in principle, entitled to choose freely which of two or more alternative policies they find preferable. In order to choose they need information on their alleged advantages and drawbacks, on how real, relevant, and weighty they appear in the light of their respective value systems.

A crucial factor in this assessment is that both debaters must always answer what their opponent has to say. Any reason either pro or con offered by one debater must have a reply from the opponent, who should either acknowledge its relevance and weight or give reasons why its relevance and/or weight should be downgraded. Listening to this kind of exchange will help each audience member form his own assessment of how relevant and weighty the reasons on both sides are. This is how continued dissensus and controversy may be constructive without ever approaching consensus.

It is an old assumption in rhetorical thinking that rhetorical debate is constructive not only in helping debaters motivate and perhaps propagate their views, and not only in helping audience members build an informed opinion, but also in building society. Isocrates and Cicero are among the chief exponents of this vision. We cannot all agree on everything, but we can build a cohesive society through constructive controversy.

It is worth noting, in conclusion, that in political science and philosophy there is a growing body of scholarship and opinion arguing for a conception of democracy based on a recognition of dissensus rather than consensus. For example, Rescher (1993) is resolutely pluralist and anti-consensus, in theoretical as well as practical reasoning. There are determined "agonists" such as Honig (1993) and Mouffe (e.g., 1999, 2000, 2005), as well as thinkers who emphasize the centrality of "difference" in democracy (such as Young, e.g., 1997). Gutmann & Thompson take a balanced view, emphasizing deliberation as well as pluralism: "A democracy can govern effectively and prosper morally if its citizens seek to clarify and narrow their deliberative disagreements without giving up their core moral commitments. This is the pluralist hope. It is, in our view, both more charitable and more realistic than the pursuit of the comprehensive common good that consensus democrats favor" (2004, p. 29). Dryzek too is cautiously balanced in arguing that the ideal of deliberative democracy must recognize dissensus: "Discursive democracy should be pluralistic in embracing the necessity to communicate across difference without erasing difference" (2002, p. 3). All these thinkers acknowledge the need for continued exchange among citizens of views and reasons, despite the impossibility (or undesirability) of deliberative consensus.

Few seem to realize that rhetoric has always existed in this democratic tension: we cannot force agreement, but we can and should present reasons to each other for the free choices we all have to make. As Eugene Garver has said: "The more we take disagreement to be a permanent part of the situation of practical reasoning, and not something soon to be overcome by appropriate theory or universal enlightenment, the more rhetorical facility becomes a central part of practical reason" (2004, p. 175).

Continuing dissensus is an inherent characteristic of practical argumentation. In the rhetorical tradition this insight has always been a given. In contemporary political philosophy it is by now perhaps the dominant view. Argumentation theory should not be so specialized that it remains ignorant of these facts.

REFERENCES

Benhabib, S. 1994. Deliberative rationality and models of democratic legitimacy. *Constellations* 1, 26-52.

Benhabib, S. 1996. Toward a deliberative model of democratic legitimacy. In *Democracy and Difference: Contesting the Boundaries of the Political*. Princeton NJ: Princeton University Press,67-94.

Berlin, I. 1958. *Two Concepts of Liberty*. Oxford: Clarendon Press. Reprinted in H. Hardy and R. Hausheer (eds.), *The Proper Study of Mankind: An Anthology of Essays*. London: Pimlico, 1998.

Bessette, J. M. 1994. *The Mild Voice of Reason: Deliberative Democracy and American National Government*. Chicago: University of Chicago Press.

Burnyeat, M.F. 1996. Enthymeme: Aristotle on the rationality of rhetoric. In Amelie Oksenberg Rorty (ed.), *Essays on Aristotle's Rhetoric*. Berkeley: University of California Press, 88-115.

Cohen, J. 1989. Deliberative democracy and democratic legitimacy. In A. Hamlinand P. Pettit, P. (eds.), *The Good Polity*. Oxford: Blackwell, 17-34

Cohen, J. 1989. Moral pluralism and political consensus. *New York University Law Review* 64: 233-55. Reprinted in D. Copp, J. Hampton, and J. Roemer (eds.), *The Idea of Democracy*, Cambrid-ge: Cambridge University Press, 1993. 270-291.

Cohen, J. 1998. Democracy and liberty. In J. Elster & A. Przeworski (eds.), *Deliberative Democracy*, Cambridge: Cambridge University Press. 185-231.

Dryzek, J. S. 2002. *Deliberative Democracy and Beyond: Liberals, Critics, Contestations*. Oxford: Oxford University Press.

van Eemeren, F.H., & Grootendorst, R. 2004. *A Systematic Theory of Argumentation: The Pragma-dialectical Approach*. New York: Cambridge University Press.

Finnis, J. 1998. Commensuration and public reason. In Ruth Chang (ed.), *Incommensurability, Incomparability, and Practical Reason*. Cambridge, MA.: Harvard University Press, 1998. 215-233.

Garver, E. 2004. *For the Sake of Argument: Practical Reasoning, Character, and the Ethics of Belief*. Chicago: University of Chicago Press.

Goodnight, T. 1993, A "New Rhetoric" for a "New Dialectic": Prolegomena to a responsible public argument. *Argumentation* 7, 329-342.

Griffin, J. 1977. Are there incommensurable values. *Philosophy and Public Affairs* 7, 39-59.

Gutmann, A., and D. Thompson. 1990. Moral conflict and political consensus. *Ethics* 101, 64-88. Reprinted in R. B. Douglass, G. Mara, and H. Richardson (eds.), *Liberalism and the Good*, New York: Routledge. 125-47.

Gutmann, A., and D. Thompson. 2004. *Why Deliberative Democracy?* Princeton: Princeton University Press.

Habermas, J. 1997. *The Theory of Communicative Action. Vol. 1: Reason and the Rationalization of Society*. Thomas McCarthy (Trans.). Cambridge: Polity Press.

Honig, B. 1993. *Political Theory and the Displacement of Politics*. Ithaca: Cornell University Press.

Ivie, R.L. 2002. Rhetorical deliberation and democratic politics in the Here and Now". *Rhetoric & Public Affairs* 5, 277-285.

Jonsen, A., and S. E. Toulmin. 1988. *The Abuse of Casuistry: A History of Moral Reasoning*. Los Angeles: University of California Press.

Kock, C. 2003. "Multidimensionality and non-deductiveness in deliberative argumentation". In F.H. van Eemeren, J. A. Blair, C. A. Willard & A. F. Snoeck Henkemans (eds.), *Anyone Who Has a View: Theoretical Contributions to the Study of Argumentation*. Dordrecht/Boston/London: Kluwer Academic Publishers, 157-171. (This volume, Chapter 6.)

Kock, C. 2006. Multiple warrants in practical reasoning. In D. Hitchcock and B. Verheij (eds.), *Arguing on the Toulmin Model: New Essays on Argument Analysis and Evaluation*. Dordrecht: Springer, 269-280. (This volume, Chapter 4.)

Kock, C. 2007. Is practical reasoning presumptive?" *Informal Logic* 27, 1, 1-18. (This volume, Chapter 5.)

Kock, C. 2009. Choice is not true or false: The domain of rhetorical argumentation. *Argumentation* 23, 61-80. (This volume, Chapter 2.)

Kock, C., and S. Hegelund. 2000. Macro-Toulmin: The argument model as structural guideline in academic writing. In C.W. Tindale, H.V. Hansen, and Elmer Sveda (eds.), *Argumentation at the Century's Turn*. St Catharines: The Ontario Society for the Study Of Argumentation. (CD-ROM. ISBN: 0-9683461-1-1.)

Kock, C., and S. Hegelund. 2003. A good paper makes a case: Teaching academic writing the macro-Toulmin way. In L. Björk, G. Bräuer, L. Rienecker & P. S. Jörgensen (eds.), *Teaching Academic Writing in European Higher Education*. Dordrecht: Kluwer Academic Publishers, 75-85. (This volume, Chapter 18.)

Mouffe, C. 1999. "Deliberative Democracy or Agonistic Pluralism?" *Social Research* 66: 745-58.

Mouffe, C. 2000. *The Democratic Paradox*. London: Verso.

Mouffe, C. 2005. *On the Political*. London: Routledge.

Perelman, C. 1979. The new Rhetoric: A theory of practical reasoning. In E. Griffin-Collart and O. Bird (eds.), *The New Rhetoric and the Humanities: Essays on Rhetoric and Its Applications*, Dordrecht: D. Reidel, 1–42. Reprinted in P. Bizzell and B. Herzberg (eds.), *The Rhetorical Tradition: Readings from Classical Times to the Present*, New York: St. Martin's Press, 1990, 1077-1103.

Perelman, C., and L. Olbrechts-Tyteca. 1958. *La Nouvelle Rhétorique: Traité de l'Argumentation*. Paris: Presses Universitaires de France. Translated by J. Wilkinson and P. Weaver as *The New Rhetoric: A Treatise on Argumentation*. Notre Dame: University of Notre Dame Press, 1969.

Rawls, J. 1993. *Political Liberalism*. New York: Columbia University Press.

Raz, J. 1998. Incommensurability and agency. In R. Chang (ed.). *Incommensurability, Incomparability, and Practical Reason*. Cambridge, MA.: Harvard University Press, 1998. 110-128.

Rescher, N. 1993. *Pluralism: Against the Demand for Consensus*. Oxford Clarendon Press.

Toulmin, S.E. 1950. *An Examination of the Place of Reason in Ethics*. Cambridge: Cambridge University Press.

Toulmin, S.E. 1958, *The Uses of Argument*, Cambridge University Press, Cambridge.

Toulmin, S.E. 1961. *Foresight and Understanding: An Enquiry into the Aims of Science*. New York: Harper & Row.

Toulmin, S.E. 1981. *The Tyranny of Principles. Hastings Center Report* 11, 31-39.

Toulmin, S.E. 1990. *Cosmopolis: The Hidden Agenda of Modernity* NY: Free Press.

Toulmin, S.E. 2001. *Return to Reason*. Cambridge, MA.: Harvard University Press.

Toulmin, S.E., R. Rieke and A. Janik. 1979. *An Introduction to Reasoning*. New York: Macmillan.

Walton, D.N. 1990. *Practical Reasoning: Goal-driven, Knowledge-based, Action-guiding Argumentation*. Savage, MD: Rowman and Littlefield.

Walton, D.N. 1996a. *Argumentation Schemes for Presumptive Reasoning*. Mahwah, N.J.: Lawrence Erlbaum Associates.

Walton, D.N. 1996b. Practical reasoning and the structure of fear appeal arguments. *Philosophy and Rhetoric* 29, 301-313.

Walton, D.N. 1997. Actions and inconsistency: The closure problem of practical reasoning." In G. Holmstrom-Hintikka and R. Tuomela (eds.), *Contemporary Action Theory*, Vol. 1, Dordrecht: Kluwer. 159-175.

Walton, D.N. 2006. How to make and defend a proposal in a deliberation dialogue. *Artificial Intelligence and Law* 14, 177-239.

Young, I. M. 1997. Communication and the other: Beyond deliberative democracy. In *Intersecting Voices: Dilemmas of Gender, Political Philosophy, and Policy*. Princeton, N.J.: Princeton University Press. 60-74.

8.

Why Argumentation Theory Should Differentiate Between Types of Claim*

This paper argues that argumentation theory should see the various claims that arguers may disagree and argue about as representing a spectrum of types. Not all claims that people may disagree about concern the truth of some proposition. Some claims, for example, are proposals for doing something. The distinction between propositions and proposals equals that between epistemic and practical reasoning, and the article leans on Aristotle's thinking about these concepts, as interpreted by Anthony Kenny. Also, the essential kinship of the notions of deliberation, rhetoric and conductive reasoning is asserted, as is the inalienable role of subjectivity in practical reasoning. The proposed spectrum of types of claim ranges from epistemic (factual) claims at one end to practical claims at the other—with, e.g., evaluative, interpretive, and stipulative claims in between.

1. Introduction

Argumentation theory needs a typology of *types of claim* (where "claim" means that for which an arguer argues). This view is in line with the Wittgensteinian idea of multiple "Sprachspiele" and with the notion of different fields with different types of warrant, etc., in Toulmin (who was, incidentally, Wittgenstein's student).

The main reason that necessitates such a typology is that much which can be said theoretically about argument for one type of claim is misleading when said about argument for claims of other types; neglecting the differences between these types is a pernicious Platonic fallacy, against which philosophical argumentation scholars should be warned.

One important type distinction, as I have argued repeatedly elsewhere, is that between theoretical or epistemic reasoning (i.e., arguing for truth of propositions) and practical reasoning (i.e., arguing for the adoption of proposals); although some argumentation theorists have recognized this

* Originally published in *Conductive Argument: An Overlooked Type of Defeasible Reasoning*, J.A. Blair, and R.H. Johnson, (Eds.). London: College Publications, 2011, 62-73. Reprinted with permission of the publisher.

distinction, they have not, I believe, fully understood the amount and the depth of the differences it implies.

In general, there is no lack of recognition that not all the claims we argue about in real-life argument are about philosophical truth. But the distinctions most often applied are, I suggest, either too vague or directly misleading. For example, we often hear a distinction between necessary and contingent propositions, where a contingent proposition is one that is neither necessarily true nor necessarily false. But as this definition makes clear, all claims are still seen as propositions which are to be assessed with regard to their truth or falsity. Another related, insufficient distinction depends on the concept of probability: some claims, it says, are about something being true, others about something being merely probable. This distinction, for example, is seen by Brockriede and Ehninger as an important reason to adopt Toulmin's argument theory for the teaching of practical argument:

> Whereas in traditional logic arguments are specifically designed to produce universal propositions, Toulmin's second triad of backing, rebuttal, and qualifier provide, within the framework of his basic structural model, for the establishment of claims that are no more than probable (1960, p. 46).

However, I would argue that the concept of probability misleads us regarding the nature of the claims we argue about in practical reasoning. To say that something is probably the case is an epistemic claim just like the claim that something is definitely the case. To say that the ongoing global warming is probably to a large extent man-made is such a claim. But to say that the EU should reduce its CO_2 emissions by 30 per cent is not a claim or proposition about what is "no more than probable"; it is not a proposition at all, but a proposal to the EU to make a decision and implement it.

Just as the concepts of contingency and probability are insufficient to identify the differences between the types of claim that we may argue about, they are also insufficient for another task, namely that of demarcating what rhetoric is about. Although rhetoric has been defined, at least since Aristotle, as argument centered on issues in a certain domain, that domain is not properly defined by means of concepts like the contingent or the probable, nor is that what Aristotle did, as we shall see below.

Jeanne Fahnestock and Marie Secor are rhetoricians who, in a number of papers and textbooks over several years, have made a proposal for a typology of claims or arguments, based on a reinterpretation of ancient *stasis* theory. One recent version of their proposal (Fahnestock and Secor, 2003) distinguishes between the following types of argument: What is it? (definition arguments); how did it get that way? (causal arguments); is it good or bad? (evaluation arguments); what should we do about it? (proposal arguments). An earlier version (Fahnestock and Secor, 1988) proposed that what they call the stasis of an argument could belong to five types, according to whether it concerns an issue of fact, definition, cause, value, or action.

Basically, my proposal in this paper is not new and adds nothing to such an approach as far as the notion of different types of claim is concerned. Rather, my intention is to point to the necessity of making this kind of typological distinction at all, and to show that the differences between types are deeper than generally assumed by most contemporary theorists of argumentation. As a consequence, we will find that many irreducible theoretical differences emerge, in particular between "theoretical," truth-oriented argument on the one hand and practical, action-oriented argument on the other.

2. A spectrum of types

However, I do not wish to set up what might be a misleading dichotomy. Nor am I eager to commit myself to a fixed number of distinguishable "types," whether four or five or another number, as in Fahnestock and Secor's theory and pedagogy. Rather, I suggest that we need to think about the relevant differences in terms of a spectrum. It would have purely theoretical (truth-oriented, "alethic") claims at one end and purely practical ones at the other. In between, and probably with intermediary areas separating the "types," should, at least, be types like interpretive claims (next to theoretical claims) and value claims of different kinds (next to practical claims). My basic concern is to heighten an awareness of differences.

I believe the point I want to make here is highly apposite because contemporary argumentation theorists, in my view, give far too little attention to these differences, assuming too blithely that argumentation is about one homogeneous kind of thing, and that, for instance, all argumentation is basically about showing the truth of something. As the example of Fahnestock and Secor shows, scholars with strong practical and pedagogical leanings are far more aware of the usefulness of making these distinctions.

What this has to do with conductive argument is that the closer you move toward the "practical" end of this spectrum, the more will conductive argument be the natural and inevitable order of the day. Some of the corollaries of this are these: at this end of the spectrum, good arguments are rarely, if ever, logically valid; the "goodness" of arguments is gradual, multidimensional, and in certain respects relative to individuals; and inference, in the strict, traditional sense of that term, does not exist.

It should be added that rhetoricians such as Aristotle, Cicero, and many others, have always, in some form or other, recognized these views (or most of them), although not many rhetoricians after Aristotle have theorized them. However, philosophically trained argumentation scholars have, at best, only recognized them very reluctantly, or not at all. So I am also trying to add the weight of an "authority" argument to my case when I base it, in particular, on Aristotle. To spell out one important difference between the two ends of the spectrum I turn to Aristotle's theory of the will and related subjects, including his theory of practical reasoning, i.e., reasoning about what to do, as propounded by the British philosopher Anthony Kenny (1979).

3. The logic of practical reasoning

One important insight in Aristotle that Kenny has helped clarify is that in practical reasoning we argue as it were backwards; that is, we start with the valuable goal or result that we want to bring about, for example, health; thus, if health is a good thing, it follows that what brings health is also good, and since exercise is something which brings health, it follows that exercise is good; moreover, if I bicycle to work rather than drive, I get exercise, so bicycling to work is good. Bicycling to work is an available means to this good, i.e., it is in my powers to do. So I may decide to do it. Before I decide to do it I may engage in deliberation (with myself and possibly with my family) on whether that is what I will do.

What we see here is that in practical reasoning, and hence in practical argumentation (we leave aside for the moment the relation between these two terms) we begin with the goal or the end, i.e., the value we wish to promote. Given that the end is good, we look for a means to bring about that end, because that means will also, in that respect, be good. So we look for steps in reasoning that will transfer or *preserve goodness* from the end to the means.

If we compare this kind of reasoning with reasoning about propositions, we see that there we look for steps in reasoning that will *preserve truth*. For that purpose we need truth-preserving rules, whereas in practical reasoning what we need is something that could be called goodness-preserving rules. But these two kinds of rules are quite different. Kenny makes clear that whereas Aristotle himself managed to formulate truth-preserving rules for propositions, he did not even try to formulate a parallel set of goodness-preserving rules for practical reasoning, nor has anyone else attempted to do so, let alone succeeded. The reason is that practical reasoning is much more complicated, and so are the goodness-preserving rules that would be required to codify it. Because practical reasoning works as it were backwards from the desired effect or good to an available means, whereas reasoning about propositions works forward from the truth of one to proposition to the truth of another that follows, we may notice the following:

> If a proposition is true, then it is not also false; but if a project or proposal or decision is good, that does not exclude its being also, from another point of view, bad. Hence, while truth-preserving rules will exclude falsehood, goodness-preserving rules will not exclude badness. (Kenny 1979, p. 146)

As an example of this "backwardness", we might take the following piece of reasoning:

"More nuclear power means reduced CO_2 emission" ($p => q$).

$=>$

"Reduced CO_2 emission is good" $=>$ More nuclear power is good" (q *good* $=> p$ *good*).

Notice the backward, goodness-preserving reasoning from the desired goal to an available means. What should be remembered, however, is that more nuclear power may be good *from this point of view*—but possibly bad from other points of view. So it does not simply follow deductively that we should have more nuclear power because we want reduced CO_2 emission, i.e., no such "inference" is valid. The notion "practical inference," if understood as a piece of reasoning on which a certain purposive choice follows as a deduction or entailment from the recognition of a certain goal, is a phantom; other means to the same goal might be available and indeed preferable, and there might be other goals that might be interfered with if we chose to aim for this particular goal. It is no improvement on the notion of "practical inference" to speculate that practical inference is an entailment that is "presumptive"; what this amounts to is essentially to say that when a good reason for a given choice has been offered, the inference is accepted, but as soon as a counter consideration is brought forward, it is cancelled—and so on *ad infinitum* (cf. this volume, Chapter 4).

This state of affairs is illustrated in Figure 1. The rectangles are available means or courses of action, while the circles are the goals or ends, that is to say, the goods that we wish to promote. Triangles are means that happen to be unavailable. A straight arrow between a means and a goal indicates that this means will promote this goal, while a dotted arrow indicates that the means will counteract the goal. The point is that for any goal there is more than one available means; but any means that promotes some goal will at the same time counteract at least one other goal. As for the means represented by triangles, all their effects are desirable, i.e., they promote several of our goals and counteract none; sadly, however, these means are unavailable.

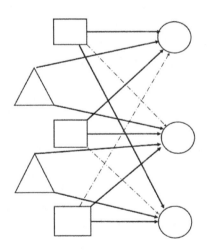

Figure 1: Practical reasoning illustrated.

The rectangles are available means or courses of action, while the circles are goals (goods that we wish to promote). Triangles are unavailable means. A bold arrow between a means and a goal indicates that this means will promote this goal, while a dotted arrow indicates that the means will counteract the goal.

To this complicated structure is added the further complication that when we are engaged in practical reasoning, what we have to do first is consider a goal we want to promote, and then look backwards along the straight arrows at the various means that might promote it. Some of these, as we saw, happen to be unavailable, and among the ones that are available we find that they also have dotted arrows leading towards other goals; that is, although they may be good from the point of view of the goal we began our reasoning with, they counteract other goals and are thus bad from other points of view.

The backward logic by which we reason from ends to means is called by Kenny, in an early paper (1966), a "logic of satisfactoriness," as opposed to the "logic of satisfaction." The former is concerned with the way a satisfactory end or goal transfers its satisfactoriness backwards to the choices that will promote it, while the latter is concerned with the way a proposition's state of satisfaction, i.e., of being satisfied, is transferred forwards to another proposition.

If we could reduce practical reasoning to inferences from the truth of certain propositions to the truth of others that follow, things would be simpler; but we are not reasoning about truth. If I want to stay healthy and therefore choose, in light of that premiss, to pursue the habit of bicycling to work, then that decision cannot be called true, nor is it false. It may be true that this kind of exercise may enhance my health, but that is not the same thing as saying that the decision to pursue it is a "true" decision. Kenny, interpreting Aristotle, says: "if the conclusion of a piece of practical reasoning has the imperative form 'Pursue this' or 'Avoid that' it is not something which can itself be straightforwardly described as true or false." (Kenny 1979, p. 94)

Another way of stating the same difference is this: Truth is a one-dimensional thing, perhaps even a dichotomous thing; for many propositions it is indeed the case that they are either true or false. Goodness, by contrast, is a multi-dimensional thing (cf. this volume, Chapters 6 and 5). That is why there is no goodness-preserving rule that excludes badness. My decision to bicycle the twelve miles to work may be good from the point of view of my personal fitness; but it may be bad from another point of view: it might imply that I cannot find the time or energy to do my work properly, or to walk my dog in due time after work, or maybe I risk being run over by cars or mugged on the way, or catching pneumonia in the rain, or over-exercising and thereby permanently damaging my weak knee. Also, there is the fact that I may find exercise of any kind, including bicycling, so dreadfully boring that is significantly reduces my quality of life.

Thus it is clear that we must stop theorizing as if all claims people may argue about are claims about something being true. Some claims are claims for a purposive choice, or in Aristotle's term, for a προαίρεσις. And a προαίρεσις is not a proposition expressing a belief or an opinion (a δόξα). The *Eudemian Ethics* in particular makes that very clear:

> ... it is manifest that purposive choice is not opinion either, nor something that one simply thinks; for we saw that a thing chosen is something in one's own power, but we have opinions as to many things that do not depend on us, for instance that the diagonal of a square is incommensurable with the side; and again, choice is not true or false [ἔτι οὐκ ἔστι προαίρεσις ἀληθὴς ἢ ψευδής]. Nor yet is purposive choice an opinion about practicable things within one's own power that makes us think that we ought to do or not to do something; but this characteristic is common to opinion and to wish. (1226a)

Carl Wellman, the originator of the concept of conductive reasoning, seems to take an ambiguous position on the question of whether what we argue for in practical reasoning can be true or false. In several of his ethical writings he declares himself an ethical objectivist, in the sense that ethical judgments in his view can indeed be true or false; but on the other hand a statement like the following seems to accept that truth or falsity is not what we argue about in practical reasoning:

> Too often reasoning is conceived of as a logical operation upon propositions, statements, sentences, or beliefs only. Reasoning must be so restricted, it is alleged, because the validity of an argument is tied to the truth-value of the premises and the conclusion. Where there is no truth or falsity, as in the case of exclamations or imperatives, there can be no reasoning. But if this were so, there could be no such thing as practical reasoning; reasoning that does not arrive at practice or action in the end is not genuinely practical. (1976, p. 545)

So practical reasoning is ultimately about action, not about beliefs that may have truth or falsity. But could we not say that after all purposive choice is a kind of belief, namely to the effect that one *should* do something? Aristotle specifically addresses this question and answers it in the negative. His reasons include the following: The object of such a belief is a goal, e.g., to be healthy; by contrast, the object of purposive choice is a means, e.g., exercise. Moreover, one can believe that one should do something without acting on that belief or even intending to. Other observations in Aristotle that refute the identification of a purposive choice with a belief are these: We choose *to* do something or avoid it; we believe *that* something; a choice is judged as good because its object is good, i.e., it is a choice of the right object, whereas a good belief is judged as good because is the right kind of belief, i.e., a *true* belief; and finally, belief has gradations, whereas purposive choice is dichotomous: you either choose to do a thing or you don't (*Nicomachean Ethics* 1112a2-14; Kenny 1979, p. 72).

4. Deliberation, rhetoric and conductive reasoning

In Aristotle's thinking on practical reasoning, the concept of purposive choice is wedded to that of deliberation. The domain of deliberation is demarcated in exactly the same way as that of purposive choice. A purposive choice is one that is preceded by deliberation on the object of that choice. This is where we may notice a link in Aristotle's thinking that has not been properly pointed out yet, not even by experts like Kenny, namely the link between his ethical thinking and his rhetoric. It is precisely the concept of deliberation that connects them. Deliberation (βούλη; verb: βουλεύειν) is the kind of reasoning that concerns our ethically relevant choices; but it is also the kind of reasoning that rhetoric is made of. What distinguishes rhetoric from ethical reasoning is the fact that rhetoric is speech in front of audiences about the things on which we deliberate in public, i.e., the purposive, collective choices of the polity; moreover, the function of such reasoning is not to achieve consensus between the discussants but to influence the members of the audience, whose role (as Aristotle makes clear) is to act as judges.

Let me add that the expression "influence the members of the audience" reflects the function of rhetoric from the point of view of the public speaker; from the point of view of the polity as such, the function of rhetoric is to supply the available reasons for the decisions being considered. (There is more on social deliberation as the domain of rhetoric in this volume Chapter 2; more on the social function of rhetoric in Chapters 5 and 9.)

Moreover, it is clear that as soon as we are looking at claims for something being the best choice, we are dealing with conductive reasoning. This is precisely because any purposive choice, although it may be good from some point of view, might still be bad from another point of view. In fact these other points of view are always relevant—or shall we say, in the standard case they are. Admittedly, it is also true that Aristotle in his discussions of practical reasoning and practical inference has pretty consistently limited himself to cases where only one end is taken into consideration and only one available means to bring it about is considered;

thus one might get the false impression that in practical reasoning, as in deductive reasoning, the normal case is that we are able to establish a chain of reasoning which necessarily leads us to a conclusion, namely a claim regarding what one should do. That is to say, we might get the false impression that there is something we might call practical inference which is structurally very similar to deductive inference, and we might be tempted to introduce the term "practical syllogism," although there is no such expression in Aristotle, and although the examples of practical reasoning we find in him are hardly ever syllogisms in form, but are much more complex.

Two further claims that I made at the outset should also be explained, namely these: "goodness" of arguments is gradual, and it is, in certain respects, relative to individuals. Both of these claims are based on the multiplex structure of practical reasoning. Nuclear power plants may help us reduce CO_2 emission, and that is a good reason for building them—but *how* good? That of course depends on what can be said against building them, i.e., it depends on what other goals might be adversely affected, and what alternative means might also be available to promote the same goal. For example, the risk connected with radioactive waste from nuclear power plants is a well-known reason that speaks against them, and so is the cost of building them, running them, demolishing them, etc.

What we have here is clearly a case of conductive reasoning, insofar as there are, in Govier's terms, "separately relevant non-sufficient factors" as well as "counter considerations" (Govier, p. 69). But once we recognize the presence of separately relevant factors and counter considerations, we must necessarily ask how strong these factors and considerations are, i.e., "how much support they give to the conclusion" (Govier 1987, p. 70)—in other words, we must recognize that their strength is a matter of degrees. And along with that insight also goes the insight that the strength of the reasons and counter considerations is, at least in some respect, relative to individuals. How could it be otherwise? If we recognize that the weight of reasons and counter considerations is assessed by individuals along continuous scales, how likely would it be that all individuals would assign exactly the same weight along these scales to all these reasons and counter considerations?

In the example of the nuclear plants this problem of indeterminate degrees is obvious: just *how* strong is the counter consideration about radioactive waste disposal? Experts can give us figures about radioactive decay and the likelihood of accidents now and in the future—but how much weight these considerations will have in our deliberations on whether we to choose to build more nuclear power plants is still, and unavoidably will be, relative to individuals. Some will decide that the counter considerations outweigh the pro considerations, others that they do not. There is no objective answer to the question—which amounts to saying that the answer is relative to the individuals who have to decide.

This is so not only because of the fact that individuals must be assumed to assign weight to any given factor along a continuous scale, but also because of the fact that there is no inter-subjectively recognized *commensurability* between the scales that will be involved. For example, just how much weight will risks affecting future generations have in relation to risks affecting the present generation? What part should be played here by ethical considerations? And how much weight will risks as such have when held against the putative benefits in regard to the prevention of climate change, especially when these benefits are also putative and of uncertain magnitude—just as are the predicted climate changes? Moreover, what about the financial costs of making certain choices now, held against the putative future costs of not making them? And what about risks and costs held against benefits?

My point is not that we should not try to hold all these considerations together and against each other, because we have to, and that is what deliberation is all about; but the point is that there is not and cannot be any authoritative and inter-subjectively demonstrable way or doing so.

5. The vexed subjectivity issue

The issue I have just addressed is one that, in my view, constitutes a sore point in philosophy and philosophically based argumentation theory. It is an issue that you had better not touch, or you risk an outcry of pain and rage. Philosophers, at least those coming from logic and epistemology, seem so wary of being associated with any sort of "subjectivism" or "relativism" that they, as I see it, will blithely deny the testimony of an overwhelming bulk of everyday experience. Even those few philosophers, such as Wellman, Govier, and other informal logicians who have been bold enough to reject deductive validity as the one criterion of good argument, and who have given us a three-dimensional method of assessing arguments (e.g., Govier's "ARG": Acceptability, Relevance, and Good Grounds/weight)—even these thinkers have been extremely wary, or blankly unwilling, to concede the property that seems to me to follow with necessity from the admission of relevance and weight as aspects of a good argument: namely the fact that both of these aspects, and in particular weight, are subject to legitimate individual judgment.

Wellman's position on this issue is representative. He insists that the "validity" of arguments in conductive reasoning is not governed by rules or criteria—where, we should remember, the "validity" of an argument does not mean deductive validity, but simply that it offers "good reasons for its conclusion" (Wellman 1971, p. 21). Yet both in *Challenge and Response* and elsewhere he professes ethical objectivism and says, e.g., "that there can be one and only one correct answer to any ethical question and that which answer is correct is independent of anyone's acceptance or rejection" (Wellman 1968, p. 98). Although he insists that no objective weighing can take place, as in an actual pair of scales, his basic position is that "we" will weigh the arguments in conductive reasoning as if we were one person; the way to find the "correct" answer is to continue our discussion, because such "disagreement can be overcome by further reasoning" (Wellman 1975, p. 220). His view of validity "projects an ideal of universal agreement" (Wellman 1971, p. 96) —with one restriction "built into the claim": "a valid argument will, through the process of criticism, remain or become persuasive *for everyone who thinks in the normal way*" (ibid.).

We may remark, in passing, that this "restricted" view of validity would seem to place Wellman in the company of Perelman and his "universal audience." But in any case, I suggest that even if we accept the claim that valid arguments in ethics (and other instances of conductive argument) will be persuasive for anyone who thinks "in the normal way," this does not prove the stronger claim that "there can be one and only one correct answer to any ethical question" (or similar claims in different phrasings). For what is a "valid" argument to Wellman? It is simply a good one; but it is not one that *entails* its conclusion. And even if we all (or at least all those of us who are "normal") were to agree that an argument is "good," this may not lead to the same conclusion for us all, for it does not *entail* its conclusion.

There is, for one thing, the matter of just *how* good the argument is, i.e., the matter of its *weight*, and even more importantly, of its *relative* weight when held against the counter considerations. Of these "weights" Wellman, Govier, and others have clearly said (and I could not agree more) that they *cannot* be "calculated," "measured" or the like. In fact, Wellman himself, almost inadvertently as it appears, concedes that the "weighing" may not lead to the same result for everyone; the whole "calculation" idea "suggests too mechanical a process as well as the possibility of everyone reading off the result in the same way"; so assuming that everyone would do that is apparently erroneous, and furthermore we should avoid "suggesting any automatic procedure that would dispense with individual judgment" (Wellman 1971, p. 58).

This is possibly the only reference to individual judgment in the book, but it represents, I would say, an inevitable insight that many philosophers have sought to repress because they feel about it the same way one feels about a sore tooth. In ethical assessment, there *is* individual judgment involved, certainly in the sense that the relative *weight* of a consideration when "weighed" against other considerations, pro and con, is subject to individual judgment. As I said, even if we do admit that we may have universal agreement among all normal people that an argument is "valid" (i.e., good)—and we may admit that for the sake of the argument—we would still, to reach the one "correct" answer together, also have to agree on the *relative* weight on this consideration when "hefted" against all the others (to use the term Wellman suggests). And why and how would we assume that this quasi-universal agreement on the relative weight of all relevant considerations would come about? To claim that it would is an empirical hypothesis that, as I see it, is challenged by a massive amount of daily experience. Do disagreements of this nature generally get resolved by prolonged discussion between people holding different ethical and political views? Have recurring disagreements of this kind generally been settled by centuries of discussion among philosophers? These, obviously, are "rhetorical" questions: they answer themselves.

Most of those who happen to read this paper are probably academics who routinely serve as examiners in their institutions. In my own country, many exams are graded by two examiners—one "internal" (the instructor who has taught the course) and one "external" (an experienced expert in the field, coming from outside the institution). Often in grading a paper or an oral presentation these two will disagree on the "conclusion," i.e., the grade to be given. Both may agree on all the noteworthy properties of the student's effort, the good ones as well as the not so good ones; so there will be agreement on which considerations are acceptable and relevant to the assessment. Yet we may still disagree on the relative weight of these considerations, and often do; for example, the fact that the student does not spell very well will undoubtedly count as a "negative" factor for both of us, but in the eyes of the external examiner this shortcoming is perhaps weighty enough to cause the grade to be a C, all things considered, whereas to me it is not quite as weighty as that, given the "positive" considerations, to which I assign more relative weight.

In such cases we naturally discuss things for a while, but let us say that this does not bring agreement. We also look at rules and regulations, but although there is a clause about "formal" factors such as spelling having some weight in assessment, there is no rule to help us decide whether this degree of bad spilling is enough to land this effort in the C category, or whether it should still be a B. Yet rules dictate that we should find agreement.

What I believe this example shows, along with countless others in everyday disagreements in the domains of ethics, politics, education, etc., is that there *is* no "one and only one correct answer" as to the merit of the student's paper. The external examiner and I both disapprove of bad spelling; it just happens that, in this particular case, he disapproves more strongly than I do. To generalize, the circumstance that different individuals may legitimately differ as to how much relative weight they assign to relevant considerations when making practical decisions such as this one, is an undeniable and ineradicable fact of life, and moreover, I suggest, one that no one could really *wish* would go away.

6. The problem of many dimensions

Moreover, while this example highlights a problem that could hardly be seen as ethical, the argument I have made could be made in an analogous manner for issues with clear ethical considerations involved. Let us imagine a student who does rather badly at an exam. The external examiner wants to fail her; I lean towards letting her scrape through. I now point out that she is eight and half months pregnant and poor as well; in fact, she comes from a disrupted family with a history of drug abuse, crime, sexual abuse, etc. The external examiner seems unmoved. I now change tactics and point out that the department depends for its survival on the number of graduates we turn out, and every "pass" grade counts. Silence. I further inform my co-examiner that the young woman, if she passes this exam, will have finished her final degree, and incidentally that her whole family, or what is left of it, is eagerly waiting at home to start the celebrations, but also she already has a been offered a rather nice job, provided she gets her degree; however, if she fails to get it, and thus the job, her residence permit will expire, and she will be expelled from the country, to which she came as a fugitive from Afghanistan, and where she worked her way up through the educational system, studying at day and washing floors at night. Back in Afghanistan, by the way, there's a good chance that she will be caught by fundamentalist thugs and killed.

What would you say if you were the external examiner in this case? Would you say that *all* these considerations are absolutely irrelevant and should not have been cited, and we should simply assess the young woman's performance at its merit and fail her? Or would you say that one or two of these considerations, especially the last one, might after all fact be relevant to what you decide, and if relevant, it is also weighty enough for you to let her pass? (In any case, you would probably say that the internal examiner—that is, me— "doth protest too much.") Or would you say that the first considerations I mentioned are perhaps relevant, but surely not weighty enough to let her pass, but the last ones are?

What I believe the example shows is a number of things: 1) It is also true of *ethical* considerations that they may legitimately be assigned different relative weights by different individuals. 2) Moreover, it is quite possible that also the *relevance* of given considerations in ethical and other practical issues may legitimately be differently assessed by different individuals. 3) In relation to a given decision, such as grading an exam, there may be considerations belonging to different *dimensions* of judgment—considerations which are not compatible because they are incommensurable. In academic exams, grading is supposed to be determined only by professional (i.e., scholarly) considerations; but who can deny that, at least in extreme cases, other considerations, such as ethical and humanitarian ones, to say nothing of economic ones, may legitimately be cited.

Even if, in deliberating on a given choice, we did not have multiple and incommensurable factors to deal with, and even if we could have some kind of objective quantification of just how much good that choice would do in relation to a given goal or value, and even if that choice could objectively be said to do a lot of good, it would still be categorially wrong to call it a "true" choice. Truth value is one thing, but the kind of value that a good choice brings is another.

7. The spectrum of claims

I have now tried to show that argumentation scholars should distinguish between claims about beliefs and claims about choices. But instead of advocating a dichotomy I wish to suggest that our typology of claim types should probably be more like a spectrum. It would have purely theoretical (truth-functional or alethic) claims at one end and purely practical ones (choices) at the other. In between, and probably with intermediary areas separating the "types", should, at least, be types like interpretive claims and value claims of different kinds.

A hasty version of such a spectrum or continuum might look like the chart on page 165.

Some of the points I wish to make are these:

There are intermediary gradations between pure factual (alethic) claims and pure claims of choice. Norms and values are in a third position in between; they are not facts about the world as such, nor are they pure arbitrary choices. Aristotle sees them as intuitions underlying claims of choice.

Carl Wellman, it might be added, is another philosopher who thinks that practical claims are distinct from epistemic ones, and also that there are additional subtypes and intermediary types of claim or argument that ought to be distinguished. Some claims or arguments are more practical than others: "The most practical arguments, I suppose, are those that conclude with judgments of what ought to be done or ought not to be done; only one step more remote from practice are those which conclude with value judgments setting up goals worthy of pursuit or evils to be avoided" (Wellman 1976, p. 531). So Wellman too sees value judgments in some intermediary position between epistemic claims and "real" practical arguments.

Specific evaluations are more like choices than abstract values are; using abstract values as warrants, we make specific evaluations of acts or objects in our world.

Interpretive claims as a category seem to me to resemble choices even more. We choose a paradigm or a theory in scholarship not simply because we think it is truer but because it addresses other issues, generates more valuable insight, more interesting discussions, more perspectives—in short, we think it yields more value along several dimensions. (For example, I think it generates more value to look at practical argumentation as conductive rather than as presumptive, deductive, abductive, or what other alternatives there might be.)

Stipulative claims are almost like interpretive claims; they are purposive choices, and as such they cannot have truth value, but we make them because we think they bring other kinds of value, such as being more practical.

Finally, the purely *practical claims* about purposive choices are similarly made by people who think that on balance the values, purposes or goals they subscribe to are more strongly promoted by a certain choice than by others (for example, by *not* making the choice they consider)—but as we saw, because of the complexities of practical choices, including their irreducible relativity to individuals, it is categorially misleading to describe them as either true or false.

In conclusion, my aim has been to demonstrate that argumentation theory should abandon all attempts to look at all claims as if they were of one and the same type, namely propositions which may be true or false. Instead of seeing truth value as the only kind of value that is relevant for argumentation theory, we should recognize that there are many values—in fact, an open set of them—that are relevant in argumentation, and that it ought also to be so in argumentation theory.

The difference I have highlighted between propositions and proposals for purposive choice is basically a reflection of distinctions recognized not only in Aristotle but in modern philosophy as well, notably in the distinction in speech act philosophy between assertives on the one hand and directives, commissives, etc., on the other (Searle 1975, 1983), or he distinction set up by Austin (1953), Anscombe (1957), and others between utterances with a word-to-world "direction of fit" and those with a world-to-word direction of fit (such as directives and commissives).

Understanding the importance of this difference will make the need for a developed theory of conductive argument more obvious, for argumentation for purposive choice is necessarily conductive. If argumentation theory insists on neglecting these insights, it makes a bad choice.

	Factual (alethic, theoretical) claims	Claims about social facts, such as norms	Claims about values	Evaluations / Claims about interpretive claims	Stipulative claims / Claims about choice of interpretive claims	Practical claims (i.e., about purposive choice of action)
Claim type	Factual (alethic, theoretical) claims	Claims about social facts, such as norms	Claims about values	Evaluations / Claims about interpretive claims	Stipulative claims / Claims about choice of interpretive claims	Practical claims (i.e., about purposive choice of action)
Examples of claims	There is water on Mars; "Look, Sire, the peasants are revolting!"	This nation is a multicultural one	Multiculturalism is good; Charity is the greatest good	Hubble was the greatest astronomer in the 20th Century; Picasso sucks; "Yuck! The peasants are *revolting!*"	Let's do Deconstructionism rather than mainstream literary history	Pluto is henceforth not a 'planet', but a 'dwarf planet'	Let us send an expedition to Mars
Examples of reasons given	The channels we see could not be caused by anything but water	Everyone keeps saying it	Multiculturalism makes for a more peaceful world	Hubble's discovery of the expanding universe is mind-blowing	It's more interesting and will get us more graduate students	It is more practical that way	It will make us top nation again and generate a lot of great technology

REFERENCES

Anscombe, G.E.M. 1957. *Intention*. Oxford: Basil Blackwell.

Austin, J.L. 1953. How to talk—some simple ways. *Proceedings of the Aristotelian Society* 53, 227-46.

Brockriede, W., and D. Ehninger. 1960. Toulmin on argument: an interpretation and application. *Quarterly Journal of Speech* 46, 44-53.

Fahnestock, J. and M. Secor 1985. Toward a modem version of stasis. In: C.W. Kneupper (Ed.), *Newspeak: Rhetorical Transformations*. Arlington, TX: Rhetoric Society of America, 217-226.

_____. 1988. The stases in scientific and literary argument. *Written Communication* 5, 427-443.

_____. 2003. *A Rhetoric of Argument: Text and Reader*. 3rd ed. New York: McGraw-Hill Higher Education.

Govier, T. 1987. *Problems in Argument Analysis and Evaluation*. Dordrecht: Foris.

Kenny, A. 1966. Practical inference. *Analysis* 26, 65-75.

_____. 1979. *Aristotle's Theory of the Will*. London: Duckworth.

Kock, C. 2003. Multidimensionality and non-deductiveness in deliberative argumentation. In F.H. van Eemeren, J.A. Blair, C.A. Willard, A.F. Snoeck Henkemans (Eds.), *Anyone Who Has a View: Theoretical Contributions to the Study of Argumentation*. Dordrecht: Kluwer Academic Publishers, 155-171. (This volume, Chapter 6.)

_____. 2006. Multiple warrants in practical reasoning. In D. Hitchcock and B. Verheij (Eds.), *Arguing on the Toulmin Model: New Essays on Argument Analysis and Evaluation*. Dordrecht: Springer Verlag, 247-259. (This volume, Chapter 4.)

_____. 2007a. Is practical reasoning presumptive? *Informal Logic* 27, 1-18. (This volume, Chapter 5.)

_____. 2007b. Norms of legitimate dissensus. *Informal Logic* 27, 179-196. (This volume, Chapter 9.)

_____. 2007c. Dialectical obligations in political debate. *Informal Logic* 27, 233-247. (This volume, Chapter 10.)

_____. 2009. Choice is not true or false: the domain of rhetorical argumentation. *Argumentation* 23, 61-80. (This volume, Chapter 2.)

Searle, J.R. 1975. A taxonomy of illocutionary acts. In K. Gunderson (Ed.), *Language, Mind and Knowledge*. Minneapolis: University of Minnesota Press, 344–369. Reprinted in Searle (1979), *Expression and Meaning*. Cambridge: Cambridge University Press, 1-29.

_____. 1983. *Intentionality: An Essay in the Philosophy of Mind*. Cambridge: Cambridge University Press.

Wellman, C. 1963. The ethical implications of cultural relativity. *The Journal of Philosophy* 60, 169-184.

_____. 1964. Judgments of value and obligation. *Ethics* 74, 143-149.

_____. 1968. Emotivism and ethical objectivity. *American Philosophical Quarterly* 5, 90-99.

_____. 1971. *Challenge and Response: Justification in Ethics*. Carbondale, IL: Southern Illinois University Press.

_____. 1975. Ethical disagreement and objective Truth. *American Philosophical Quarterly* 12, 211-221.

_____. 1976. The justification of practical reason. *Philosophy and Phenomenological Research* 36, 531-546.

_____. 1999. Relative moral duties. *American Philosophical Quarterly* 36, 209-223.

Part 3: Rhetoric and Democracy

9.

Norms of Legitimate Dissensus[*]

The paper calls for argumentation theory to learn from moral and political philosophy. Several thinkers in these fields help understand the occurrence of what we may call legitimate dissensus: enduring disagreement even between reasonable people arguing reasonably. It inevitably occurs over practical issues, e.g., issues of action rather than truth, because there will normally be legitimate arguments on both sides, and these will be incommensurable, i.e., they cannot be objectively weighed against each other. Accordingly, "inference," "validity," and "sufficiency" are inapplicable notions. Further distinctive features of pro and con arguments in practical argumentation are explored, and some corollaries are drawn regarding evaluative norms of legitimate dissensus. Examples from immigration-related public debates in Denmark are given.

This paper makes a call for argumentation theory to open up towards disciplines such as moral and political philosophy. As argumentation scholars, we have much to learn from them and their emphasis on human *action*, as an individual as well as a social phenomenon. They, on the other hand, have something to learn from scholars who scrutinize words, texts, and utterances to see how people use them to act.

I suggest that, on the whole, contemporary argumentation theory has been too narrowly allied to one or two branches of philosophy—logic and epistemology—to the neglect of those other traditions which see humans as moral and political *agents*. This narrow perspective has allowed theorists in our field to work on the tacit assumption that argumentation is largely about how the truth of certain statements (called conclusions) may be inferred from the truth of other statements; and how people proceed, or should proceed, when arguing over such matters.

If argumentation theory would open up more towards moral and political philosophy, it would attain a widened perspective—one where not

---

[*] Originally published in *Informal Logic* 27 (2007), 179-96. Reprinted with permission of the Editors.

all argumentation is about whether statements are true, because some argumentation is about what to do.

These two categories of argumentation ought really, I suggest, to be seen as two separate domains. Aristotle saw them that way and named the two domains *episteme* and *praxis*. Also, as we shall see, he believed that argumentation in one of these domains is in many respects very different from argumentation in the other. To Plato, on the other hand, truth was the issue in any serious discussion, and he would have considered the Aristotelian distinction false. Unfortunately, modern argumentation theory has largely walked tacitly in Plato's footsteps in this respect, not in Aristotle's.

One of the perspectives that get left by the wayside when argumentation theory takes this line is what I tentatively label *legitimate dissensus*.

But isn't this a near-tautology? After all, *any* discussion begins with dissensus; argumentation itself is based on it. So of course dissensus is legitimate. In the argumentation business it is our daily bread.

I am not talking about that kind of dissensus, though. The kind of dissensus I mean is the kind that will not go away, even after prolonged discussion. This kind of dissensus I call legitimate because it may not only exist but also endure. Even while using our best tools for the sake of common understanding, we do not reach consensus. At the end of our mutual engagement, we may still not have resolved our dispute, that is, we do not even agree as to who has won the argument; each of us may have played by the rules, yet there is no objective state of affairs as to the outcome of the game. Very likely we have also disagreed along the way as to the validity, or legitimacy, of some of the individual moves made by the discussants.

By contrast, in a game like for example chess there can be no such dissensus. Either both agree who has won, or both agree that the game is drawn. To have dissensus over the result of a chess game is just not chess. Board games are based on unanimity as to the legitimacy of the moves and the outcome of the game. A player who disputes the legitimacy of my moves or claims he has won when he is in fact checkmate is not being reasonable, and no one should play chess with such a person. For chess players to dissent on such matters is not legitimate.

Since Plato, it has been a prevalent idea among philosophers that when we discuss any matter, the discussion works the same way as in chess, or at least it should if we are reasonable. We may have a dispute at the beginning of the discussion and we may both wish to prevail in it, but the idea is that we discuss by a set of rules that are agreed between us; that way we will always be in agreement as to the legitimacy of any move made by any of us, and we move from dissensus toward consensus in the sense that either I prevail, or you prevail, or we both agree to assume a third position; but whichever result ensues none of us disputes it. In that sense we move hand in hand from dispute to its resolution.

Plato himself dramatized this method in many of his dialogues, most tellingly in the *Meno*, where Socrates questions a slave on how to construct a square twice as big as another square. Through their question-answer dialogue they come to the common understanding that the right way to do that is not to draw a square with sides twice the length of the original, but to use the diagonal of the original square as the side of the new one. And no one has questioned that insight since. In the *Gorgias*, Socrates describes the method explicitly by explaining that the two discussants are each other's only witnesses: "if on my part I fail to produce yourself as my one witness to confirm what I say, I consider I have achieved nothing of any account towards the matter of our discussion, whatever it may be; nor have you either, I conceive, unless I act alone as your one witness, and you have nothing to do with all these others" (472b). "See therefore," he goes on, "if you will consent to be put to the proof in your turn by answering my questions" (474a).

The basic assumption here, and the basic warranty for the epistemic value of the method, is the same as the basic assumption in chess: both players agree on the rules, both agree on the legitimacy of each move, and both in consensus vouch for the outcome.

A similar view underlies the modern notion of "logical dialogue games." It has played an important role in the work of Douglas Walton (1984 and many other publications), and it underlies the idea of the "critical discussion" in Pragma-dialectics (most recently codified in van Eemeren and Grootendorst 2004). In all of these conceptions—chess and other board games, the Platonic dialectic, logical dialogue games, and Pragma-dialectics—we find the same belief in commonly agreed rules securing unanimity as to the legitimacy of every move, resulting in a movement towards resolution of the original dispute, that is, consensus.

Outside of argumentation theory proper, there is yet another school of thought which has central notions in common with all these. The political philosophy of Jürgen Habermas and many who are inspired by him is centered around the ideal of a public discourse where participants obey "den zwanglosen Zwang des besseren Arguments" ("the unforced force of the better argument") (1972, 161), reaching (or approximating) consensus along this road.

However, Habermas, unlike Plato and unlike the pragma-dialecticians, explicitly recognizes important differences between the two domains of argument that we began with, those of *episteme* and *praxis*, respectively. Arguing about actions is not like arguing about the truth of propositions, in that the warrants we appeal to will not be other propositions we hold to be true, but *norms of action* that we hold to be "right." This rightness is a different kind of validity claim (*Gültigkeitsbedingung*) from the truth that validates constative (i.e., epistemic) speech acts; and both are again different from the sincerity that validates expressive self-representations or from the adequacy of value standards that validates evaluative expressions.

Argumentation theorists might pay more attention to the distinctions that Habermas lays down here. Nevertheless, as far as the main thrust of Habermas's argumentation theory is concerned, he joins the other thinkers who conceptualize argumentation as analogous to chess. Even though a proposal for action does make a distinctive kind of validity claim which is not truth, it is still just one form of a communicative practice which "is oriented to achieving, sustaining, and renewing consensus—and indeed a consensus that rests on the intersubjective recognition of criticizable validity claims" (1997, 17).

Central to all these conceptions is the idea that discussants in a dispute are as it were collaborators in a quest for consensus; they start from dissensus, but using regulated and reasonable discussion as their tool they collaborate towards a common understanding, which may either be identical with what one of them began with, or an understanding new to both.

In opposition to all of these, my claim is precisely that because of the difference Habermas has seen (while the others, from Plato onwards, have either denied or underestimated it), namely the difference between epistemic and practical reasoning, we should understand that whereas consensus may be a meaningful theoretical ideal in the epistemic domain, it is not so in that of *praxis*. In the domain of *praxis*, enduring dissensus is inevitable and legitimate in a way that it is not in the epistemic domain, and it is high time that argumentation theory comes to a full and unabashed understanding of this.

On this point some of the leading figures in the moral and political philosophy of our time have something to teach us argumentation theorists. On the other hand, we may have something to tell them about how people actually argue about such matters, and how it is still meaningful for them to so argue, even though it is legitimate for them to dissent. But we cannot teach them much about actual argumentation until we, on our part, have fully accepted *their* insight, namely that on practical issues people may find themselves in legitimate and enduring dissensus.

Just why is that?

Perhaps the simplest way to answer that question is to say that practical issues are essentially about choice, not truth, and the notion of choice implies the legitimacy of enduring dissensus. Aristotle said it succinctly in the Eudemian Ethics: "choice is not true or false" (1226a).

Another kind of answer to the question has been attempted by John Rawls (perhaps, with Habermas, the most influential social and political philosopher of our time). His statement of the question is interesting in itself: "Why does our sincere and conscientious attempt to reason with one another fail to lead us to agreement? It seems to lead to agreement in science, or if disagreement in social theory and economics often seems intractable, at least—in the long run—in natural science" (1989, 236). Notice that Rawls accepts the distinction between the epistemic and practical domains: in natural science consensus is, at least in the long run, an ideal and an actual achievement; in social theory and economics, given their inevitable overlap with practical politics, it is less so, and in practical politics proper: not at all. Rawls disregards answers to the effect that people are driven by narrow interests or that they are irrational or stupid; we want to know why *reasonable* people disagree. Assuming that they "share a common human reason, similar powers of thought and judgment, a capacity to draw inferences and to weigh evidence and to balance competing considerations," then what could the sources of disagreement be? Whatever they are, Rawls calls them "the burdens of reason," or "the burdens of judgment" in the version appearing four years later in *Political Liberalism* (1993). His tentative list of them includes the following points (emphases are mine):

(a) The *evidence*—empirical and scientific—bearing on the case may be *conflicting and complex*, and hence hard to assess and evaluate.

(b) Even where we agree fully about the kinds of considerations that are relevant, *we may disagree about their weight*, and so arrive at different judgments.

(c) To some extent *all of our concepts, not only our moral and political concepts, are vague and subject to hard cases*; this indeterminacy means that we must rely on judgment and interpretation (and on judgments about interpretations) within some range (not itself sharply specifiable) wherein reasonable persons may differ.

(d) ... *our total experience, our whole course of life up to now, shapes the way we assess evidence and weigh moral and political values*, and our total experiences surely differ ... in a modern society ... the total experiences of citizens are disparate enough for their judgments to diverge.

(e) Often *there are different kinds of normative considerations of different force on both sides of a question and it is difficult to make an overall assessment.*

(f) ... *In being forced to select among cherished values, we face great difficulties in setting priorities*, and other hard decisions that may seem to have no clear answer.

With all due respect for Rawls I believe we may further reduce and arrange this list as follows.

1) First on the list of sources of reasonable disagreement is still the complexity of evidence (a). This difficulty is found in epistemic as well as practical discussions.

2) Second on the list I put the vagueness or disputability of the concepts we use to subsume the cases we discuss (c).

3) The third source of reasonable disagreement is the disputability of the weight we assign to relevant considerations. This is Rawls's item (b).

Looking at our revised list so far, anyone familiar with the history of rhetoric will perhaps recognize a reformulation of the ancient system of *stasis* or *status* (lucidly explained in Heath 1995). (1) corresponds to the *conjectural* status of fact. (2) is the *definitional* status: under what concept are we to subsume the fact? (3) is the *qualitative* status where we discuss the *circumstances* of the fact because they may influence the weight or gravity we assign to the fact.

Furthermore, it may be argued not only that the first three of Rawls's burdens of reason match the three main *status* in ancient argumentation theory, but also that both these sets match the three types of evaluation criteria set up by many modern theorists, such as Govier's "ARG" conditions as defined in her well-known textbook (2005, 63ff.): the *acceptability* condition, the *relevance* condition, and the *good grounds* condition. An argument is acceptable if we take it as referring to a fact; it is relevant if the concept it invokes is indeed instantiated by the matter at issue; and the judgment that is represents good grounds is an assessment of its weight or gravity.

As for Rawls's point (d), it actually provides part of the empirical explanation of (b) and (c) and is thus not a separate point in itself. Now for (e) and (f). Rawls remarks that the first four are not peculiar to reasoning about values (1989, 236), or as he says in the later version, they are "not peculiar to the reasonable and the rational in their moral and practical use" (1993, 56); but the last two are. This is a crucial observation.

I suggest that (f) logically comes first. It means that our values may conflict. It is not just that two different individuals or groups in a society may believe in conflicting values; it is also that the set of values held by a given individual (as well as that subset of these values which are shared by practically everyone in the culture) are not fully in harmony with each other. The philosopher Isaiah Berlin has talked about the "pluralism" of values, meaning that "not all good things are compatible, still less all the ideals of mankind." For example, he points out "that neither political equality nor efficient organization nor social justice is compatible with more than a modicum of individual liberty, and certainly not with unrestricted *laissez-faire*; that justice and generosity, public and private loyalties, the demands of genius and the claims of society can conflict violently with each other" (1958, repr. 1998, 238).

Of course this is something that ordinary human beings have always known in an intuitive way. Practical philosophers, such as Cicero, who was a rhetorician as well, have also known it. He writes:

between those very actions which are morally right, a conflict and comparison may frequently arise, as to which of two actions is morally better ... For, since all moral rectitude springs from four sources (one of which is prudence; the second, social instinct; the third, courage; the fourth, temperance), it is often necessary in deciding a question of duty that these virtues be weighed against one another. (*De officiis* 1.63.152)

The everyday reality of moral conflict between the values in which an individual or a social group believes has in our time been asserted by a wide range of moral philosophers. Walter Sinnott-Armstrong (1988) has argued in depth that moral conflict is indeed possible. Rawls himself cites Thomas Nagel (1979) for the view that "there are basic conflicts of value in which there seem to be decisive and sufficient (normative) reasons for two or more incompatible courses of action; and yet some decision must be made" (237, footnote 7).

To understand why this may be so, I believe we should look at item (e), where Rawls talks about "*different* kinds of normative considerations ... on both sides of a question" (237). The fact that considerations may be of different *kinds* is the reason why we often cannot just calculate which side has the stronger case. Cicero cites four different sources of moral rectitude; others might be added. Because they are qualitatively different, there is no intersubjective, algorithmic way of measuring them on the same scale. They are *incommensurable*. And we are not just talking about the sort of incommensurability first identified by the ancient mathematicians who found that, e.g., the side of a square and its diagonal are incommensurable. After all, they still belong to the same dimension: length; hence they are objectively comparable, and it is easy to demonstrate that the diagonal is longer than the side (cf. Stocker 1990, p. 176). But considerations involved in moral and other practical decisions often do not have "lengths" that can be objectively compared, nor do they have objective "weights," although we often use that term about them. Neither are we talking about situations like a business investment that has involved a certain cost and brought a certain return. Cost and return belong to the same dimension (money); deduct one from the other, and you have the net result: profit.

Not so when we consider the pros and cons of a practical decision. As Trudy Govier has emphasized, "there is no formula or rule that we can apply to determine whether reasons for the conclusion outweigh reasons against it" (2005, 399), and in a footnote commenting on the term "outweigh" she says: "No implication that we can mathematically measure or judge the relevance and comparative strength of various reasons or counterconsiderations is intended at this point" (p. 415). When for example we discuss whether it was right to let a certain number of lives be sacrificed in an attempt to bring democracy to a foreign country, then the cost on one dimension is not as it were restored on the other dimension; instead a qualitatively different benefit is appealed to (cf. Stocker 1990, pp. 272-277). We may refer to this circumstance as the irreducible *multidimensionality* of deliberative argumentation (Kock 2003). Because of this multidimensionality, profound *incommensurability* obtains; and that again is why a value conflict in an individual or a group committed to a plurality of values, as we all are, may have no intersubjective solution. The values involved are not, as the philosophers Charles Larmore has said, "rankable with respect to a common denominator of value" (Larmore 1996, 159). As a result, we cannot do what another moral and legal philosopher, John Finnis, describes in the following way: "Aggregate the pluses, subtract the minuses, and pursue the option with the highest balance" (1998, 216). That is, in deliberative argumentation there may be no objective or intersubjective way to determine which side outweighs the other.

Perhaps the most articulate contemporary interpreter of the notion of incommensurability is Joseph Raz. He defines the condition of two reasons for action being "incommensurate" in the following way:

Two competing reasons (for specific actions on specific occasions) are incommensurate if and only if it is not true that one defeats the other, nor that they are of equal strength or stringency. They are incommensurate in strength, that is, reason does not determine which of them should be followed, not even that there is equal reason to follow either. When reasons are incommensurate, they are rendered optional, not because it is equally good (or right or reasonable) to choose the option supported by either reason, but because it is reasonable to choose either option (for both are supported by an undefeated reason) and it is not unreasonable or wrong to refrain from pursuing either option (for both are opposed by an undefeated reason). (2000, pp. 102-103)

Raz describes his own belief in the everyday occurrence of incommensurate reasons as a "classical" stance, as against a "rationalist" one. There are, according to Raz, three crucial differences between the two conceptions:

First, the rationalist conception regards reasons as requiring action, whereas the classical conception regards reasons as rendering options eligible. Second, the rationalist conception regards the agent's own desire as a reason, whereas the classical conception regards the will as an independent factor. Third, the classical conception presupposes the existence of widespread incommensurabilities of reasons for action, whereas the rationalist conception, if not committed to complete commensurability, is committed to the view that incommensurabilities are relatively rare anomalies. The three differences come down to a contrast between the rationalist view that generally rational choices and rational actions are determined by one's reasons or one's belief in reasons and are explained by them, as against the classical conception that regards typical choices and actions as determined by a will that is informed and constrained by reason but plays an autonomous role in action. (2000, pp. 47-48)

In other words, "rationalists" believe that reasons for one action are necessarily stronger than those for another, and hence that they "require" or "determine" that action. Classicists, such as Raz and the other moral philosophers I have cited, and everyone in the classical rhetorical tradition, including myself, believe that on moral and other practical issues there is option or choice, or if you will, legitimate enduring dissensus, not just in practice but also in theory.

The important insight from moral philosophy has now been fully spelled out for us argumentation theorists, and it is time for us to offer some insights to them in return. The point is that after philosophers realize there is no required or determinable solution to a practical issue, they tend to conclude that there is no more to be said, and people will just have to plump for one or the other solution. This probably leaves many philosophers feeling slightly uneasy. After all, philosophy trades in general solutions to problems. Not that they do not admit of heated discussions of alternative solutions, but usually the philosophical assumption is that *if* a solution to a problem holds, then it holds generally, that is, for all. Consequently, if an issue is indeed optional, philosophical argument about it stops.

What we can teach philosophers, if indeed we understand it ourselves, is that even if there is no determinable philosophical solution to an issue, that does not mean that we cannot or should not argue about it. Although practical issues are in principle optional, not determinable, argument about them certainly goes on, and it should. Although an individual is free to choose on practical issues, that individual may change his mind, and he may be worked upon.

The kind of argumentation through which we may work upon other individuals' free choice is rhetoric. The core of rhetoric is argumentation intended to work upon other individuals' choices regarding actions that they are free to undertake. This has been settled in the rhetorical tradition at least since Aristotle, who uses the verb *bouleuein/bouleuesthai* about the kind of reasoning that constitutes rhetoric. It is a word that we usually translate to "deliberate," and it is derived from *boulē*, a word with an original meaning of "will," related to the Latin *volo* and the English *will*. Aristotle repeatedly insists that what we may deliberate about is only actions we may choose to undertake. As he says in the *Nichomachean*

Ethics, III: "any particular set of men deliberates about the things attainable by their own actions" (1112a). So rhetoric is debate about choosing action, and by the same token it is aimed at individuals and does not pretend to find solutions that are binding for all. (For a fuller statement of this, see this volume, Ch. 2.)

If a philosopher now asks, "But how can we argue about individual options?" the obvious answer is that the points where we can work rhetorically on individual choices are the same points where dissensus may arise in the first place: the sources of reasonable disagreement identified by Rawls and systematized earlier on in this paper. First, we may discuss facts. Secondly, the categories we use to subsume facts. And thirdly, matters of degree based on circumstances. But then, in the practical domain, where the issue is not what is true but what to do, we have two further complications: there may be conflict between equally relevant reasons on both sides, and they are not objectively commensurable. Rawls says that these complications are "peculiar to reasoning about values" (1989, p. 236). An example might illustrate why.

As a model case of deliberation by a collective body on a practical issue we may take the case of a family considering the purchase of a large Chesterfield armchair. The parents, let us call them Dick and Jane, happen to agree that such a chair is comfortable, but also that it is somewhat inelegant, not to say ugly. So comfort and elegance are two value concepts shared by both Dick and Jane, but unfortunately they find that in this case these two value concepts conflict. Dick and Jane, too, are in conflict, because Dick values the chair's comfort so highly that he wants to buy it, while Jane finds its ugliness so prohibitive that she will have none of it. They have discussed the issue at length but find that there is no objective way for them to balance the comfort against the ugliness in a way they can both agree on. He finds that comfort trumps ugliness, she has it the other way around. We have a classic case of legitimate and enduring dissensus. This occurs because we are in the practical domain, and in that domain the issue is not about truth and facts, but on decisions based on values assigned to facts.

At this point, I cannot help citing one of my favorite examples of how people, when considering issues in the practical domain, may agree in principle that something has a positive value, yet their views may diverge widely as to just how great a positive value it has. In Jane Austen's *Pride and Prejudice* Mr Collins, the unctuous clergyman, says, in proposing marriage to Elizabeth Bennet: "My situation in life, my connections with the family of De Bourgh, and my relationship to your own, are circumstances highly in my favour" (II, xix). As we know, Elizabeth does not think these circumstances are as highly in his favour as all that.

These examples further show something that many argumentation scholars take to be rather scandalous, namely that at least as far as the "weight" or "strength" factor in practical reasoning is concerned, there is an ineradicable element of subjectivity in argument appraisal. To those who argue that the admission of such subjectivity compromises argumentation theory, branding it as relativism and the like, I reply that their own theories are deficient for not seeing what moral philosophers since antiquity have seen, namely the inherent audience-relativity of argumentation over issues where values are involved—as they are in deliberative debate. In argumentation theory, Perelman and Olbrechts-Tyteca (1969) were perhaps the first to fully understand this kind of subjectivity. The divergent "value hierarchies" of audiences is one of the concepts in which they find this subjectivity expressed. It is the same subjectivity that is brought in by Rawls's last two points, which, as you will recall, are "peculiar to reasoning about values."

Our examples also show that pro and con arguments in the practical domain typically have the status of advantages and drawbacks as perceived by the arguers. Dick and Jane happen to agree on all the advantages and drawbacks of the armchair. For both of them, those advantages and drawbacks are inherent in the chair. But Dick and Jane disagree on how much weight to assign to them. And no advantages or drawbacks are refuted, rebutted or defeated even if either Dick or Jane prevails. Even if the armchair scheme is abandoned, an armchair like this does not cease to be comfortable. If the family actually buys the chair, it remains inelegant.

In the epistemic domain, by contrast, pro and con arguments are only important by virtue of their probative or inferential force (or, with a word used by some theorists and derived from the same verb as "inferential": their *illative* force); that is, they are important for what they appear to signify or suggest, not for what they are. Once the issue has been decided one way or the other, the arguments supporting the discarded position lose their relevance.

The example of the armchair further shows that in the practical domain pro and con arguments may be real and relevant simultaneously. The advantages and drawbacks are real to the arguers and remain so. In epistemic argumentation, on the other hand, the pro and con arguments may in themselves be real circumstances, but the two opposite states of affairs signified by the pro and con arguments, respectively, may not both be real simultaneously.

Also, this means that in practical argumentation no party can be logically *proven* to be either right or wrong. In principle, arguments in the practical domain can never be "valid" in the sense of *entailing* their conclusion, nor can they be "sufficient" to entail a conclusion. No matter how many arguments you muster for your proposal, your opponent is never *compelled* by those arguments to accept it. This is why, as we have seen, the practical domain is one of choice.

Further, the strength or weight of arguments in practical argumentation is a matter of degrees. Advantages and drawbacks come in all sizes. Along with this comes the fact that practical argumentation typically persuades by degrees. An individual may gradually come to attribute more weight to a given argument, so he or she may gradually become more favorably disposed towards the proposal. This is one of the reasons why argument in matters of choice is meaningful.

Finally, let us repeat that practical reasoning crucially depends on individuals' subjective value assignment. That goes for each single reason given in the discussion of the issue, but also for the balancing of the multiple, incommensurable reasons relevant to the case.

The type of argumentation described here is really a branch of Carl Wellman's "conductive reasoning." Govier among others has adopted this term, but does not distinguish as I wish to between arguments in the epistemic and the practical domain. What I have just been describing is practical reasoning. All practical reasoning is conductive, but not all conductive reasoning is practical.

Now that we have established practical reasoning as a separate domain of argumentation with particular properties, we may ask: what norms may we appropriately apply to this kind of argumentation?

First, we may conclude that as criteria in argument evaluation, the notions of validity, inference, sufficiency all have to go; no arguments for or against actions have any of these properties. "Sufficiency" or "adequacy" are no change or improvement on the traditional "validity" requirement. If "sufficiency" is to have a clear meaning, it must mean, as in mathematics, that there is inference. And inference, in a nutshell, is the negation of choice.

Furthermore, since even reasonable people arguing reasonably cannot be expected to reach consensus, we may conclude that a set of norms that posits eventual consensus as the goal of reasonable discussion, such as the argumentation theories of Habermas or Pragma-dialectics, is not applicable to practical reasoning.

But if consensus is not the goal of discussion, and if it may even be legitimate for discussants to remain fully committed to their initial standpoints, a set of norms should perhaps be more concerned with what discussion can do for the audience.

The function of practical argumentation for its audience would more meaningfully be defined in terms of the enlightenment it might provide, i.e., the extent to which it equips the audience to make up their own minds on the issue. Since argumentation in the practical domain is never compelling, and since inference does not exist, and since the audience's needs are central, it seems reasonable that such argumentation should not be required to permit an inference to its conclusion, but rather to supply explicit and relevant informative reasons at any point of dispute.

Also, since there will usually be several relevant reasons and counter considerations, belonging to different dimensions, it becomes essential that debaters should, in the metaphorical sense, weigh those reasons and considerations up against each other. "Weighing" here does not mean "measuring," because there is no such thing, but it does mean "comparing." Each debater must use the resources of rhetoric somehow to hold the multidimensional pros and cons together, making a bid as to his or her own individual assessment of how they compare and balance, and giving audience members added input to make their own individual assessments.

From these principles we might derive rules such as the following:

For any point where dissensus exists, debaters must give reasons. This goes not only for the dominating standpoint for which each debater argues, but also for each argument given at a lower place in the argument hierarchy. More specifically, this implies that if a debater does not recognize the acceptability, relevance or weight of one of the opponent's arguments, he must give reasons for this non-recognition. Similarly, if a debater does not want an objection to one of his arguments to stand, he must give reasons why it does not stand.

We should note at this point that recognizing an argument given by the opponent does not mean that acceptance of his standpoint or proposal can be inferred. As we have seen, in the practical domain there is no such thing as inference. This is worth emphasizing, because political debaters often seem compulsively to deny each and every argument given by opponents, apparently for fear that if they did concede the relevance of any point made by the opposition, they would be compelled by inference to accept the opposing standpoint. This kind of behavior polarizes and distorts public debate, and it goes to show how mistaken it is to think of practical argumentation in terms of inference.

The explicitness principle, turned into a negative, further implies that on any point where dissensus exists, a debater should not implicitly assume his or her own view to be generally accepted. This sounds obvious, but this type of behavior accounts for many of the "spin" maneuvers and other misdemeanors we find in political debate. Discussions of issues such as abortion, taxation, or terrorism are full of linguistic maneuvers in which a view or assumption that part of the audience contests is taken for granted by means of framing language, presupposition, conversational implicature, and the like. On all such points argumentation scholars should insist that any assumption on which there is dissensus should be made explicit and supported by reasons. And the same principle also dictates that any reasons given by opponent should be answered—either rebutted or acknowledged, and if acknowledged, compared and "weighed," all on the assumption that in conductive reasoning there may be non-rebuttable reasons on both sides.

All in all, it can be said that in this revised set of norms for legitimate dissensus *answering* becomes essential. And because advantages and drawbacks are properties of the proposal they argue for, not just signifiers, and hence do not go away, there will often be relevant counter considerations. So, to recall the armchair example, an appropriate answer from Jane to Dick's argument that a Chesterfield chair is comfortable is not to deny this fact or its relevance to the issue, but to explain why, in Jane's view, this property counts for less than the chair's negative value on another dimension, that of elegance. Jane can never *prove* to Dick or to the audience, which in this case means Dick and Jane's teenage kids, Ethan and Chelsea, that this is so; consequently, Jane must try to make them *see* it. She will have to use rhetoric to win their support of the way she balances the incompatible and incommensurable values involved in the issue. She might not be able to win over Dick himself, but Ethan and/or Chelsea might eventually come down on her side, and that might settle the issue. What she should not do, neither for her own sake nor in the light of reasonable norms of legitimate dissensus, is to flatly deny or ignore the argument that the chair is comfortable. For an audience member who considers both comfort and elegance to be relevant, and who needs input to help them decide for themselves which is weightier, such a debater is no help at all.

The Australian political scientist John Dryzek is among those who deny that consensus is the reasonable theoretical endpoint of deliberative debates. Instead he has introduced the concept of *meta-consensus*. As we have done here, he sees deliberative debate as having three levels: that of normative values, that of epistemic beliefs ("facts"), and based on these two, that of preferences regarding action. Dryzek, writing with Simon Niemeyer, defines *normative meta-consensus* as "agreement on recognition of the legitimacy of a value, though not extending to agreement on which of two or more values ought to receive priority in a given decision" (Dryzek and Niemeyer 2006, p. 639; the term "normative meta-consensus" corresponds to "axiological consensus" in Rescher 1993). One norm of argumentation in the case of enduring dissensus is that a debater should recognize the legitimacy of a value to which his opponent appeals if he himself shares that value, even when he disagrees on its relative priority. Such a situation obtained between Dick and Jane on the armchair issue. Dryzek also notes that "adversarial processes (such as Anglo-American legal systems) may weaken normative meta-consensus if they frame issues in ways that induce advocates to denigrate the legitimacy of the values of the other side." He suggests that "one of the main tasks of deliberation could be to uncover existing normative meta-consensus obscured by the strategic actions of partisans who try to de-legitimate the values held by their opponents" (2006, p. 639).

The debate that has been going on for the last twenty years or so in my own country, Denmark, about issues relating to immigration and immigrants, provides many examples of argumentation flouting this norm. One controversial issue has been the legislation introduced by the current right-wing government regulating the residence in Denmark of couples where one spouse is a Danish national and the other is not. Among other things, both spouses must be at least 24; there are income, housing and employment requirements; and the combined "attachment" of the spouses to Denmark must be greater than their attachment to any other country. Supporters of these rules have argued that they help integration and prevent many forced marriages. Opponents have argued that these rules curtail personal freedom, including citizens' rights to live in their home country with spouses of their choice.

On the whole, opponents of this law have tended to focus single-mindedly on these values and have rarely addressed the law's alleged social benefits, including its presumed effects against forced marriages—a consideration that has made a certain number of immigrant women support the law. I would argue that while argumentation theory could not expect or require opponents on such an issue to reach consensus, they should not behave as if one principle might decide the issue as it were by inference; instead they should recognize the relevance of the alleged social benefits appealed to by the other side. We might add that arguably personal freedom is involved on both sides of the issue: on the one hand, the law curtails people's freedom of marriage and/or residence, but on the other hand the argument is that the law extends young people's freedom to avoid forced marriages. So what one might expect from the law's opponents is that they explain why, in their view, these alleged advantages do not outweigh the rather obvious drawback of curtailing certain personal freedoms. To supply such an explanation, opponents might spell out the effects of these curtailments based on specific examples, either authentic or devised; or they might seek to reduce the perceived benefits of the law by using statistics to show that forced marriages are a small or a dwindling problem; or they might make a pathos-based attempt to heighten the perceived weight of individual freedom as a principle; or they might analogize to other cases of freedom-curtailing legislation that most people would agree to condemn; or they might try to show that the legislation will create more social ills than benefits and in effect counteract integration. This amounts to saying that they might use any and all of the resources of rhetoric to help them *compare* the weights of the pros and cons. In fact, rhetorical resources are all we have to help us compare those weights and decide on the issue, since they cannot be weighed, measured or calculated in any objective way. But compare them we must.

We might add to this that such a meta-consensus might be called for not only where debaters disagree on the priorities of values in a given case, but also when they disagree on their very applicability to that case. The notorious affair of the Muhammad cartoons which a Danish daily published on September 30, 2005, and which, the following winter, caused a political crisis in Denmark and serious unrest with deaths and destruction in many Muslim countries, is a case in point. In Denmark, one side in the debate that ensued held that freedom of speech was at issue, while the other held that interpersonal respect was at issue. However, the issue separating the two opposed factions in the Danish debate was not, as they should both have recognized, their commitment to the value of freedom of expression, but their *interpretation* of the specific events of the affair. A similar view, highlighting the role of interpretation in apparently intractable conflicts, has been suggested by the philosopher Georgia Warnke in *Legitimate Differences* (1999). Since the dispute in Denmark was not really over principles and values, but over the interpretation of the cartoons in relation to those values, the debate ought to have been about that interpretation, not about whether certain people had betrayed the cause of freedom of expression. But the supporters of the cartoons on the whole did not enter into debate about their view that the publication of them was indeed a matter of defending freedom of expression; rather they argued in a way that took this contested interpretation for granted. This they did using linguistic mechanisms such as framing, presupposition, implicature, etc. What should have been the issue of explicit argumentation from both sides, namely the proper conceptual interpretation of the newspaper's act, was an issue on which the cartoon-supporters presented almost no explicit argumentation. Instead, they used their energy to say that those who had criticized the cartoons or failed to lend the newspaper their whole-hearted support, for example by refusing to reprint them, were to be roundly condemned for betraying freedom of expression. On February 26, 2006, Prime Minister Fogh Rasmussen said in an interview with a national daily: "Writers and others, who so much live by the freedom of expression, have, as you know, failed in this matter. ... As far as I am concerned, the sheep have been separated from the goats." Thus the pro-cartoon faction, led by the Prime Minister, illegitimately took their interpretation for granted instead of defending it; but the faction that was critical of the cartoons, in its insistence that the matter had nothing to do freedom of expression, but instead with lack of proper respect for religious minorities, perhaps did not sufficiently articulate their shared allegiance to freedom of expression and their concern that certain tendencies in Muslim populations were in fact a threat to that freedom. The reason for this was presumably their view that freedom of expression was not relevant to the case at all, since they had not questioned the newspaper's right to print the cartoons. Yet they might have helped bring about a meta-consensus by admitting that the situation seen in a broader perspective clearly did make freedom of expression an important concern. What happened subsequently in the Danish debate was a predictable orgy of name-calling. The pro-cartoon debaters in particular were uninhibited in taking their own contested interpretation as a given even though they must have known that their opponents did not acknowledge it—a maneuver that has been described as linguistic "bullying" (Harder and Kock 1976). Both factions in the heat of the squabble thrashed away at obvious straw men; for example, a past Minister of Foreign Affairs who had from the beginning been critical of the newspaper's publication of the cartoons was accused, by implicature, of advocating groveling surrender to the violent protesters in the Middle East. The whole debate showed all the symptoms of pernicious and pointless polarization. The diagnosis: no one made the attempt to find any kind of normative meta-consensus, on the basis of which there could have been a reasoned and explicit discussion of the interpretations and weightings over which debaters were actually, and legitimately, in dissensus.

For some appropriate concluding remarks to these reflections on norms of legitimate dissensus we might again turn to John Rawls. His listing of the sources of reasonable disagreement leads to what he calls "precepts of reasonable discussion." They are, in slightly abbreviated form:

> First, the political discussion aims to reach reasonable agreement, and hence so far as possible should be conducted to serve that aim. We should not readily accuse one another of self- or group-interest, prejudice or bias, and of such deeply entrenched errors as ideological blindness and delusion. …

> Second, when we are reasonable we are prepared to find substantive and even intractable disagreements on basic questions. …

> Third, when we are reasonable, we are ready to enter discussion crediting others with a certain good faith. We expect deep differences of opinion, and accept this diversity as the normal state of the public culture of a democratic society. (1989, pp. 238-239)

Another way of stating the same desiderata is to say, with Amy Gutmann and Denis Thompson in *Why Deliberative Democracy?*, that we need norms of dissensus "which permit greater moral disagreement about policy and greater moral agreement on how to disagree about policy" (2004, p. 65).

REFERENCES

Aristotle. 1995. *The Complete Works of Aristotle. The Revised Oxford Translation*. I-II. 6th printing with corrections. Princeton: Princeton University Press.

Austen, J. 1970 (1813). Pride and Prejudice. Oxford: Oxford University Press (The World's Classics).

Berlin, I. 1958. *Two Concepts of Liberty*. Oxford: Clarendon Press. Reprinted in *the Propers Study of Mankind: An Anthology of Essays*, H. Hardy and R. Hausheer (Eds.), London: Pimlico, 1998.

Cicero. *De officiis*.

Dryzek, J.S., and Niemeyer, S.J. 2006. Reconciling pluralism and consensus as political ideals. *American Journal of Political Science, 50*, 634-49.

van Eemeren, F.H., and R. Grootendorst. 2004. *A Systematic Theory of Argumentation: The Pragma-dialectical Approach.* New York: Cambridge University Press.

Finnis, J. 1998. Commensuration and public reason. In Ruth Chang (Ed.), *Incommensurability, Incomparability, and Practical Reason.* Cambridge, Mass.: Harvard University Press, 215-233.

Govier. T. 2004. *A Practical Study of Argument*, 6th ed. Belmont, CA.: Wadsworth.

Gutmann, A., and D. Thompson. 1990. Moral conflict and political consensus. *Ethics* 101, 64-88. Reprinted in R.B. Douglass, G.M. Mara, and H.S. Richardson (Eds.), *Liberalism and the Good*. New York: Routledge, 125-47.

Gutmann, A., and D. Thompson. 2004. *Why Deliberative Democracy?* Princeton: Princeton University Press.

Habermas, J. 1972. Wahrheitstheorien. In *Vorstudien und Ergänzungen zur Theorie des kommunikativen Handelns*. Frankfurt/M.: Suhrkamp, 127-183.

Habermas, J. 1997. *The Theory of Communicative Action. Vol. 1: Reason and the Rationalization of Society.* Thomas McCarthy (trans.). Cambridge: Polity Press.

Harder, P., and Kock, C. 1976. *The Theory of Presupposition Failure.* (Travaux du Cercle Linguistique de Copenhague, XVII.) Copenhagen: Akademisk Forlag.

Heath, M. 1995. *Hermogenes on Issues: Strategies of Argument in Later Greek Rhetoric*. Oxford: Clarendon Press.

Kock, C. 2003. Multidimensionality and non-deductiveness in deliberative argumentation. In F.H. van Eemeren, J.A. Blair, C.A. Willard and A.F. Snoeck Henkemans (Eds.), *Anyone Who has a View.* Dordrecht: Kluwer, 157-171. (See this volume, Ch. 6.)

Larmore, C. 1996. *The Morals of Modernity.* Cambridge: Cambridge:University Press.

Nagel, T. 1979. *Mortal Questions*. Cambridge: Cambridge University Press.

Perelman, C., and L. Olbrechts-Tyteca. 1969. *The New Rhetoric: A Treatise on Argumentation*. J. Wilkinson and P. Weaver (Trans.). Notre Dame: University of Notre Dame Press.

Plato. 1925. The Loeb Classical Library, Plato III: *Lysis, Symposium, Gorgias*. London: Heinemann.

Plato. 1975. The Loeb Classical Library, Plato IV: *Laches, Protagoras, Meno, Euthedemus*. London: Heinemann.

Rawls, J. 1989. The domain of the political and overlapping consensus. *New York University Law Review* 64, 233-255.

Rawls, John. 1993. *Political Liberalism*. New York: Columbia University Press.

Raz, J. 1998. Incommensurability and agency. In Chang, R. (Ed.), *InCommensurability, Incomparability, and Practical Reason*. Cambridge, MA: Harvard University Press, 110-128.

Raz, J. 2000. *Engaging Reason: On the Theory of Value and Action*. Oxford: Oxford University Press.

Rescher, N. 1993. *Pluralism: Against the Demand for Consensus*. Oxford: Clarendon Press.

Sinnott-Armstrong, W. 1988. *Moral Dilemmas*. Oxford: Basil Blackwell.

Stocker, M. 1990. *Plural and Conflicting Values*. Oxford: Oxford University Press.

Warnke, G. 1999. *Legitimate Differences: Interpretation in the Abortion Controversy and Other Public Debates*. Berkeley: University of California Press.

Wellman, C. 1971. *Challenge and Response: Justification in Ethics*. Carbonale, IL: Southern Illinois University Press.

10.

Dialectical Obligations
in Political Debate[*]

Political debate is a distinctive domain in argumentation, characterized by these features: it is about proposals for action, not about propositions that may have a truth value; there may be good arguments on both sides; neither the proposal nor its rejection follows by necessity or inference; the pros and the cons generally cannot, being multidimensional and hence incommensurable, be aggregated in an objective way; each audience member must subjectively compare and balance arguments on the two sides; eventual consensus between the debaters is not a reasonable requirement. From all this follows a view of the rhetor's special obligation in democratic, deliberative rhetoric on which it becomes crucial, in the interest of the audience, that political debaters acknowledge good arguments on the opposite side and explain why, on balance, they deem the arguments favoring their own side to be stronger.

The present paper has sprung from an intuitive sense that much is amiss in the way public political debate is generally conducted, even in societies with entrenched commitments to democracy and free speech. I believe any argumentation scholar who listens for some time to public debating by contemporary politicians, whether in legislative bodies or in the media, will agree that debaters routinely engage in dialectical moves that impede rather than promote the purposes of the debate, whatever they are. While subscribing to Johnson's seminal notion of a separate "dialectical tier" in argumentation (2000; 2002), I nevertheless believe that current theories of argumentation are not sufficiently sensitive to the distinctive properties of political and other deliberative argumentation to provide meaningful criteria for a normative critique of debate in that sphere. Therefore, the aim of this paper is, on the basis of a discussion of these distinctive properties, to indicate what I see as the central dialectical obligations of public

---

[*] Originally published in *Informal Logic* 27 (2007), 223-47. Reprinted with permission of the Editors.

political debaters, so that argumentation theorists will have firmer theoretical grounds for criticism of what they hear.

The nature of deliberative argumentation

Political debate, as a subcategory of deliberative argumentation, is ultimately about undertaking action, not about the truth or falsity of statements. Another way of saying this is that deliberative argumentation generally is not about propositions but about *proposals*. (An alternative term is *policies*; one advantage of it is that support of the *status quo*, i.e., the rejection of a proposal, can also be called a policy.)

To be sure, deliberative argumentation usually involves debate, often of a heated kind, over propositions that may be true or false, e.g., about whether a certain dictator has (or has had) weapons of mass destruction, or whether a certain tax reform will mainly benefit the rich; but the issues that deliberative argumentation is *ultimately* about are proposals for action, such as invading the dictator's country or adopting the tax reform. What is at issue in regard to such actions is whether to undertake them, not whether they are "true" or "false."

The proposition-proposal distinction in itself is not unfamiliar to philosophers. It is related to Aristotle's separation of the three domains of *theoria*, *poiēsis*, and *prāxis*, where proposals belong to the latter. It has correlates in contemporary thinking as well. Jürgen Habermas, for one, has emphatically pointed to the differences between various types of claims that people may argue for. In practical argumentation one does not, according to Habermas, argue about the truth of propositions, but about the rightness of actions (Habermas, 1997).

Not realized by many theorists, however, this distinction implies deep differences in the way argumentation works, depending on whether the issue is a proposition or a proposal.

One difference is that, in the standard case, there are often not just arguments on both sides, but *good* arguments on both sides. The non-technical word "good" reflects the fact that arguments about proposals are

---

[11] This is a simplification: by focusing on telic arguments, i.e., the "advantages" and "drawbacks" of proposals, we bypass arguments of a deontic nature, e.g., that a proposed war might be a contravention of international law. But acknowledgement of this and other types of arguments only lends increased strength to the points made in this section: that arguments for or against proposals refer to inherent properties of the proposals and do not cancel out each other.

typically different from arguments about propositions. Arguments about proposals primarily refer to alleged *advantages* or *drawbacks* of adopting the proposal or of rejecting it.[11] This is why there are "good" arguments both pro and con. If the proposal is for a war in a foreign country to depose its tyrannical dictator, then his elimination will be an advantage of that policy, but a drawback of it will be that in wars lives are lost. Notice that none of these facts can "cancel out" the other.

This example also demonstrates another distinctive property of arguments about proposals: although they may be perfectly real, relevant, and hence "good," they are never what logicians call "valid," in the sense that if the argument is true, then the truth of the conclusion follows by necessity (i.e., as an inference). Since proposals can be neither true nor false, validity is a misplaced concept in relation to argumentation about proposals. Not only could the "truth" of a proposal not follow from anything, but neither does the *adoption* of the proposal "follow" by any kind of necessity or inference from any number of "good" arguments. The proposed action may have *n* undeniable advantages speaking in its favor, which hence earn the status of "good" arguments, yet they are not valid in the traditional sense, nor are they even "sufficient," neither singly nor in conjunction. The tyrannical dictator's removal might, *per se* and all else equal, be seen as a great advantage of the war and hence as a very good argument in its favor, perhaps one of many, yet no number of convergent arguments would be sufficient to cause the war plan to follow as a *necessary* or "valid" inference; many people would still, legitimately, withhold support from it.

This is because the advantages (benefits) of any proposed action are always offset by its concomitant drawbacks (costs). War, for example, always has costs, measurable in lives, welfare, money, and other dimensions.

Generally speaking, since any proposal is likely to have both benefits and costs, and since they can both be true at the same time, it will be appropriate for those who are to decide on the proposal, not only to *consider* the pro and con arguments, but to *compare* them.

In argumentation about propositions, on the other hand, pro and con arguments are typically not about advantages and drawbacks. Instead, their relevance depends on their *probative* or *inferential* force (or, with a word used by some theorists and derived from the same verb as "inferential": their *illative* force). They are relevant *transitively*, i.e., by virtue of what they appear to point to, signify or suggest, not for what they are. This means that pro and con arguments cannot both signify truly at the same time. If several arguments speak for a proposition *p*, while several others speak for *non-p*, both sets may be well-considered, yet *p* and *non-p* cannot both be true at the same time. Once a dispute over a proposition has been decided one way or the other, the arguments signifying the truth of the rejected proposition have been determined to signify falsely or misleadingly and have been denied the illative force they were previously held to possess.

In contrast, an argument about a proposal, in referring to an advantage or drawback of it, refers to an inherent *property* of the proposed action. An action has many properties, instantiating many dimensions. Some of them will be seen as advantages/benefits, others as drawbacks/costs. Once the dispute over the proposal has been decided one way or the other (for example by democratic vote), the arguments referring to the advantages of the rejected policy have not thereby been judged wrong, nor have the arguments referring to the adopted policy's drawbacks. We opt for a policy because we place a higher value on its inherent advantages than we do on its inherent drawbacks, but in the standard case there will be advantages and drawbacks that remain in force simultaneously and do not cancel out each other.

The reason why properties on the pro and con side do not cancel each other out is that the warrants that valorize them are values which are mutually incompatible. We are faced here with what Isaiah Berlin called the "pluralism" of values, meaning that "not all good things are compatible, still less all the ideals of mankind." For example, "neither political equality nor efficient organization nor social justice is compatible with more than a modicum of individual liberty" (1958, repr. 1998, p. 238).

Value concepts, such as those cited here, constitute the warrants that deliberative argumentation relies on. For example, individual liberty, broadly defined, will serve as a warrant for many of those who support a war because it topples a tyrannical dictator. But Berlin insists that a value endorsed by one individual or party will often be incompatible with another value endorsed by another individual or party (this is value *diversity*); moreover, and more critically, the values held by any one individual (or one culture) may also be *incompatible*—in the sense that one of these values can only be fully realized at the cost of at least one of the others.

Several contemporary moral philosophers have argued that value pluralism, in this sense, is a condition of our everyday existence (cf., e.g., Sinnott-Armstrong 1988, Stocker 1990, Lukes 1991, Larmore 1996, Finnis 1998, Raz 1998). This is why arguments that we recognize as real and relevant about a policy may still be contradictory: argument A *for* the policy is warranted by a certain value to which we are committed, but argument B *against* the policy is warranted by another value to which we are *also* committed.

Even so, value pluralism might not be a major difficulty in deliberation (and in argumentation theory), and a form of value monism might yet be derived, if these values were not also *incommensurable*—meaning that no "common denominator" can be found, providing "a common basis for determining, in given situations, the respective weights of the conflicting commitments" (Larmore 1996, p. 157).

Incompatibility and incommensurability are often confused, and both concepts are sometimes confused with value diversity. Drawing on Lukes (1991, pp. 10-11), we may distinguish between them as follows. *Diversity* means that different people are committed to different values (which may be incompatible). *Incompatibility* means the potentiality of conflict between two values; if they are held by the same individual or group, we have value pluralism, meaning that the values to which that individual or group is committed are not one, but many. Value pluralism may be superficial if the conflicting values may both be converted into a common denominator; but it is profound if *incommensurability* also obtains, that is, if the arguments relying on the conflicting values are not "rankable with respect to a common denominator of value" (Larmore 1996, p. 159). As a result, we cannot do what John Finnis describes in the following way: "Aggregate the pluses, subtract the minuses, and pursue the option with the highest balance" (1998, p. 216). That is, in deliberative argumentation there may be no objective or intersubjective way to determine which side outweighs the other.

The underlying reason for this is that arguments for and against a proposal often belong to different "dimensions": they refer to properties of irreducibly different kinds. That is, we are not talking about situations like a business investment that has involved a cost of a certain size and brought a return of a certain size; return and cost have the same dimension (money), and when one is deducted from the other we get the net result: the profit. Also, we are not just talking about the sort of incommensurability first identified by the ancient mathematicians who found that, e.g., the side of a square and its diagonal are incommensurable. Although the ratio between the two can never be expressed by rational numbers, they still instantiate the same dimension: length. Hence they are objectively comparable, and it is easy to demonstrate that the diagonal is longer than the side (cf. Stocker 1990, p. 176).

In contrast, the benefit gained by freeing a foreign country of its tyrannical dictator versus the loss of many lives (one's own troops as well as the foreign country's citizens) are two arguments (among many) which, while relating to the same policy, represent qualitatively different dimensions. There is no intersubjective, algorithmic way of measuring them on the same scale. They do not have comparable "lengths" or "weights." The cost on one dimension is not restored on the other dimension; to outweigh the cost, a qualitatively different benefit is sought (cf. Stocker 1990, pp. 272-277). We may refer to this property as the irreducible *multidimensionality* of deliberative argumentation (Kock 2003).

But although relevant arguments in deliberative argumentation may be incompatible, as well as incommensurable, they are not, as everyday experience will remind us, *incomparable*. When facing a choice where relevant arguments are contradictory, individuals do compare them and choose. So incommensurability precludes neither comparability nor choice; this observation is made emphatically by, e.g., Larmore (1996), and Raz (1986, 1998).

What is less strongly emphasized in moral philosophy is that since there is no intersubjectively compelling reasoning determining such choices (and if there were, they would not be choices), they are in fact subjective. In deliberative debate over a proposal to go to war each legislator and, ideally, each citizen, must choose individually ("subjectively") which policy to support. This is so not because "truth" is subjective (e.g., on whether the dictator has weapons of mass destruction) but because the values that function as warrants in deliberation are subjective as well as incommensurable.

Add to this the facts that all individuals may not *interpret* the values they share in the same way when applying them to specific phenomena (this is the central issue in Warnke 1999); and that although they may be committed to shared values, their commitments may be differently *ranked* (this is the meaning of Perelman and Olbrechts-Tyteca's "value hierarchies"); and that they may not be committed to *all* the same values. All this means that when deliberating individuals compare pro and con arguments—and they do, defying incommensurability—the choices ensuing from these acts of comparing will differ from one individual to the next; in other words, the choices will, in all these respects, be subjective—and *legitimately* so.

A last, important characteristic of deliberative argumentation is that, for all the reasons just laid out, it cannot be expected, not even as a theoretical ideal, that it will lead towards consensus. For example, even individuals sharing the same values will, facing a proposal of war in a distant country, opt for different policies, if for no other reason because their value hierarchies (or "priorities") are different. Some will decide that large-scale war, with heavy foreseeable losses, is a sad but acceptable cost to pay to win democracy for that country; others will accept some casualties, but not on the scale anticipated by the first group; and some will not endorse any war for such a gain. Very likely only a minority in each of these groups will change their stand, even after prolonged debate (although some might); and their different stands may be grounded in *legitimately* different ways of comparing pros and cons. Hence any theory of argumentation which sees it as a theoretical norm that they should reach agreement seriously misunderstands the nature of deliberative argumentation.

But if not consensus, what could then be the purpose of proponents of different policies engaging in deliberative debate? Briefly stated, the main reason why such debates are potentially meaningful is that *other* individuals facing such a choice (legislators and citizens) may hear, consider and compare the arguments relating to the choice. How debates may best fulfill their function vis-à-vis these third parties will be the subject of the last part of this paper.

The inadequacy of alternative models of deliberation

The above overview of the properties of argumentation about proposals, and by extension, of all deliberative argumentation (indeed all practical reasoning), has focused on a handful of distinctive features which may be summarized as follows:

> *There will always be several good but contradictory arguments. Contradictory arguments do not cancel out each other.*
>
> *A good argument never entails a policy by necessity or inference.*
>
> *Contradictory arguments often rely on plural values which are not objectively commensurable.*

Contradictory arguments must nevertheless be compared for choices to be made. Choices rely on individuals' value commitments and are subjective.

Debates between exponents of opposite policies cannot be expected to lead towards agreement, but may help other individuals consider and compare the pro and con arguments relating to a policy.

The view that these statements reflect will recall the notion of "conductive argument," coined by Wellman (1971) and adopted for textbook use by Govier (2005). The acceptance of several good arguments on both sides and the abandonment of the notions of validity and sufficiency are the same (although Govier retains notions like "cogency" and "enough reasons"). The nuances that my view of deliberative argumentation adds to their "conductive argument" are primarily these: First, I insist on the distinctive, non-alethic nature of the issues in deliberative argumentation and on the consequent "non-probative" and "non-cancelable" nature of arguments in that domain; Wellman and Govier offer no clear demarcation of the domain of conductive argument, although they note that, for reasons they do not analyze, it tends mainly to occur in practical and moral reasoning. Further, because of the evaluative nature of warrants in deliberative argumentation, I insist on the pervasiveness in those warrants of subjectivity, and, because of their multidimensionality, of their incompatibility and incommensurability. Finally, the legitimacy and the frequent inevitability of dissensus follow from all this.

A look at these views of deliberative argumentation will soon reveal that they are at odds with several dominant assumptions in contemporary argumentation theory. I will briefly consider some current theories of argumentation and try to show that they need revision as far as deliberative argumentation is concerned. If that is so, then it is to be expected that their views of dialectical obligations in that domain would be off the mark as well, despite the fact that reflection on the dialectical nature of argumentation as such is a common and central concern of contemporary argumentation theory.

For example, the pragma-dialectical school sets up "critical discussion" as the model for all argumentation. As is well known, in critical discussions the shared aim of both discussants is the *resolution* of their difference of opinion. Also crucial in Pragma-dialectics is the concept of *reasonableness* in argumentation; being reasonable means avoiding fallacies, which again are defined as argumentative speech acts that obstruct the goal of critical discussion: resolving the difference of opinion.

So the notion of "reasonableness" and the normativity that are both intrinsic to the pragma-dialectical approach are similarly bound up with the ideal of resolution of the difference of opinion (in another word, consensus). In what we might call the "classic" stance of Pragma-dialectics (as in, e.g., van Eemeren and Grootendorst 1992, and most recently van Eemeren and Grootendorst 2004), it remains an alien and suspect idea that both discussants' driving motive might be to "win" the discussion rather than to reach consensus. However, several publications by van Eemeren and Houtlosser (e.g., 1999, 2000, 2001, 2002) represent a newer phase characterized by a wish to integrate rhetoric in the theory, where "rhetoric" is identified with a wish to "win" that results in "strategic maneuvering." Such maneuvering is now seen as legitimate so long it is not "derailed." My contention is that although this new version of Pragma-dialectics shows great understanding for rhetorical devices and has contributed insightful analyses of strategic maneuvering, it has no way of explaining how both discussants may at the same time be legitimately strategic, i.e., legitimately committed to "winning," and yet also committed to consensus, as Pragma-dialectics continues to insist that they are. What Pragma-dialectical theory does not take into account, I suggest, is precisely the fact that rhetoric is rooted in deliberative argumentation, a domain where consensus is not to be expected, eve as a theoretical ideal, owing to the domain's distinctive properties, as laid out above.

It is a curious fact that outside of argumentation theory proper, there is another school of thought which has central notions in common with Pragma-dialectics, and which has had an even wider resonance, yet the two schools seem to have almost no cognizance of each other. The political philosophy of Jürgen Habermas and many who are inspired by him is centered around the ideal of a public discourse where participants obey "den zwanglosen Zwang des besseren Arguments" ("the unforced force of the better argument") (1972, p. 161), reaching (or approximating) consensus along this road.

As we have seen, Habermas, unlike the pragma-dialecticians, recognizes differences between various types of claims that people may argue for. Arguing about actions is different from arguing about the truth of propositions in that the warrants we appeal to will not be other propositions we hold to be true, but *norms of action* we hold to be "right." This rightness is a very different kind of validity claim (*Gültigkeitsbedingung*) from the truth that validates constative speech acts; and both are different from the sincerity that validates expressive self-representations and from the adequacy of value standards that validates evaluative expressions.

Argumentation theorists might pay more attention to the distinctions that Habermas lays down here. However, his main thrust is to say that even though a proposal for action makes a distinctive kind of validity claim, it is still just one form of a communicative practice "which, against the background of a lifeworld, is oriented to achieving, sustaining, and renewing consensus—and indeed a consensus that rests on the intersubjective recognition of criticizable validity claims" (1997, p. 17).

Several contemporary thinkers in political philosophy—especially those concerned with "deliberative democracy"—have either followed this consensus-oriented line of thought in Habermas, or have thought along parallel lines; these include Joshua Cohen (e.g., 1989a, 1989b, 1998), Joseph Bessette (1994), and Seyla Benhabib (e.g., 1994, 1996), or a rhetorician like Thomas Goodnight (e.g., 1993). Then again, other recent thinkers, united mainly by their background in moral philosophy and their acknowledgment of real moral conflict, have pointed to the intrinsic incompatibility, incommensurability and subjectivity in practical reasoning based on plural values. I have drawn on some of these thinkers in the discussion above.

In argumentation theory proper, another widely held notion is "presumptive reasoning" as discussed in particular by Walton (1996). As one of the few philosophical argumentation theorists today, Walton sees practical reasoning as a separate domain (Walton, 1990) and has (recently) recognized the simple fact that in practical reasoning people argue about a proposal, not about a proposition or assertion (2006). But Walton's attempt to see practical argumentation in terms of presumptive reasoning leads to rather counterintuitive results. As in argumentation theory generally, a "good" argument in his model of practical argumentation is one that licenses an inference; however, the inference is *presumptive* or *defeasible*, and what is inferred is not a proposition but an action. Thus if we have a goal G, and if an action A may serve to bring about G, then it is an inference that we should do A—a presumptive inference, that is. This, one might object, implies that any action which may serve to bring about any agreed goal may be presumptively inferred from that fact. But the presumption is canceled again for arguments that can be rebutted, and that happens when any one of a list of critical questions about the argument has an affirmative answer. One such question is whether the agent planning the action has *other* goals that should be taken into account (since the action might interfere with them). That, however, is, as we have seen, the standard case: the benefits conferred by *any* action always have concomitant costs and hence interfere with other goals. So presumptive inference as a model of deliberative argumentation implies that, in the first round, *any* action may be (presumptively) "inferred" if it brings *any* benefit, i.e., serves *any* goal; but then, in the second round, for each of these actions the benefits/goals cited on their behalf are rebutted and canceled because of the other goals interfered with. Presumptively, then, *any* action that might bring *any* benefit should be undertaken; eventually, however, *no* arguments for any action are any good, so *no* action should be undertaken at all.

Such a model of deliberative argumentation is of little help in describing how we actually use and evaluate deliberative arguments. Argumentation theory paints itself into this kind of corner because it has not taken seriously these intuitive insights: (1) that in deliberative argumentation it is the standard case that there are good arguments on both sides; (2) that a good argument for an action does not license an inference to that action; and (3) that good arguments on opposite sides do not cancel out each other. (For a fuller statement of my criticism of Walton's "presumptive" view of practical reasoning, see this volume, Chapter 5.)

Debaters' dialectical obligations

In this final section of the paper I will discuss what the view of deliberative argumentation presented above implies in regard to debaters' dialectical obligations, and I will point out some of the ways in which the current assumptions just discussed need, in my view, to be amended.

Because good, non-cancelable arguments are likely to exist on both sides in deliberative argumentation, it follows that in order to come to a reasoned decision one will need to juxtapose, compare and balance them; and this goes for the audience as well as for the debaters themselves. It is not enough that each argument relating to the issue is appraised singly, or even that all the arguments on one side are appraised conjunctively to see if there are "enough" or "sufficient" grounds for the proposed action to be inferred.

Walton's model based on presumptive inference suggests, misleadingly, that if an argument for the opponent's policy is recognized as good, then, by virtue of this very fact, it already triggers an inference to that policy (albeit presumptively). Such a view would urge a debater to seek to "rebut" every counterargument at any cost (possibly by turning it into a "straw man" that is easy to rebut), or alternatively to ignore it. In fact this kind of behavior is what we often see in public political debaters, to the frustration of their deliberating audiences. Another misleading implication of the "presumptive" model is that an argument which has been "rebutted" is henceforth counted as null and void, having no strength at all, as if a toggle switch had been clicked. Rather, the standard case is that some arguments on both sides have *some* strength; they do not trigger an inference, but they are not null and void either. So the audience very much needs to hear what a debater has to say in regard to such arguments presented against him from the other side; nothing short of this will be trustworthy help for the audience in assessing whether arguments in the debate are in fact relevant, and if so, how they compare and balance. What audience members do not need is to hear each debater either systematically deny the acceptability or relevance of all the opponent's arguments, or distort them (in order to avoid recognizing them): this will compromise the individual audience member's chance to *compare* the pros and cons. If each debater instead offers his own comparison of pros and cons, trying sincerely to advise the audience as to why he sees the arguments on his own side as outbalancing those on the other side, then audience members will be substantially helped in making their own comparison of pros and cons. They will have two contrasting bids for an appropriate comparison to consider; and they will have the opportunity to see how well each debater can make his case stand up against counterarguments. Only by fulfilling these duties can the debater be trustworthy and hence helpful to the deliberating audience member.

The fact that the comparison of pros and cons will often involve an essentially subjective weighing of them is just another reason why the audience will need the debaters' help and advice in this process: the debaters presumably are individuals who have themselves found or devised ways to compare the pros and cons on the issue, in spite of their incommensurability, and reached assessments they are confident with (however mutually contradictory). The debaters can be helpful advisers in offering their individual assessments and the considerations that led to them, while recognizing that alternative assessments are legitimate. Audiences will not need an attitude on the part of the debaters which suggests that the comparison can only have one correct result, and that consensus on that result ought ideally to ensue; any such view, which effectually delegitimizes continued dissensus, suspends the anchoring that individuals' deliberative decision-making cannot do without: their value hierarchies, such as they are.

In sum, precisely because there usually are, in the nature of the case, legitimate, non-cancelable arguments on both sides (or all) in political debate, and in view of all that follows from this, it becomes central to a political debater's dialectical obligation that he should pay proper and explicit attention to arguments supporting the opposite side. I suggest that the main consequent specifications of this general requirement are the following:

The debater's main dialectical obligation is to make motivated comparisons between contradictory arguments. As we have seen, it is a standard situation that contradictory arguments do not (because of their incommensurability) cancel each other out and cannot be objectively aggregated and weighed against each other; on the other hand, individuals who would choose between rival policies must, and usually somehow manage to, compare the arguments supporting them in ways that assist their choice. Public debaters, who cannot be required or expected to find a consensus, might instead see it as their primary function to help individuals who are third parties to their debate in this choice. This the debaters could do by explaining how contradictory arguments compare in *their* subjective view, and why.

Often it is not appropriate to try to rebut, refute or deny arguments that contradict one's own policy. As we have seen, good arguments contradicting a debater's policy are often grounded in values shared by the debater himself; it is just that the con arguments do not register in the debater's subjective comparison of pros and cons with the same strength as the pro arguments, or the values grounding the con arguments are lower in his value hierarchy than the values grounding the pro arguments. Whichever is the case, the appropriate thing for that debater to do is probably just to explain why it is so. "Appropriate" in this context means: likely to serve the purpose of the debate, insofar as the purpose of the debate is not to achieve consensus between the debaters, but rather to help the third parties in their process of choice.

Some of the things the debater might do in this attempt at explaining might be to offer *specifics* about the benefits and/or costs involved in adopting either his own or the opposite policy, thereby enhancing the *presence* of these benefits/costs, and thus perhaps causing others to share the assessment on which the pros subjectively outweigh the cons. He might also try to invoke *parallels*, either of a similar or opposite nature, adducing analogies, precedents, similarities, contrasts, or differences; or he might employ *metaphors* and other verbal devices to enhance the pros or attenuate the cons relating to his policy. In many cases it will probably be to his own advantage and to the audience's enlightenment if he chooses the same devices in addressing the audience as have perhaps caused himself to assess the present case as he does, thereby possibly causing individuals in the audience to adopt a similar assessment. It might also happen that, on a somewhat deeper level, the listener is caused to revise the hierarchical ordering of those values in terms of which he sees the issue, because the specifics and parallels that have been adduced make him, e.g., find the costs in terms of one value unacceptable compared with the benefit in terms of another value that he has so far favored.

The attentive reader will not have failed to notice that the devices I have mentioned here, which are just a sample of the moves a rhetor might employ, are all central resources in the traditional discipline of rhetoric. The justification of all these devices, and of rhetoric as such, is that they are all we have in situations where no objective algorithm can determine our choice, i.e., in deliberation.

No quantity of good arguments on one side is in itself sufficient to decide the matter. Just as attempts at blank rebuttal of counterarguments are often not appropriate, because the counterarguments are in fact perfectly good, so also does a debater not sufficiently honor his dialectical obligation merely by marshaling all the good arguments speaking for his own policy. A *comparison* of the arguments on the two sides is still called for, and if this is not offered, the third parties have still not been helped in making their own comparisons. Failing an objective, algorithmic procedure for the commensuration of incommensurable pros and cons, a special act of incommensurability-transcending comparison remains necessary, employing, e.g., strategies based on specifics or parallels, as described above.

Looking back, one might skeptically ask what purpose is actually served by political debate, even when dialectical obligations like those discussed above are respected. Since debaters cannot be expected to reach consensus, and since audience members cannot expect sufficient grounds to be offered for any one policy but will still have to choose subjectively, might public political debate not be dispensed with altogether? My answer is of course negative. While public political debate as brought to us by the media is often at its worst, a kind of debate that would respect the dialectical obligations as sketched in this paper might indeed help deliberative democracy become just that: a democracy that not just votes but deliberates, i.e., considers contradictory arguments and tries to weigh them against each other, as in a *libra*, a pair of scales. Although the decision that the individual makes about deliberative issues will be subjective, it can still be a reasoned decision; just because no objective balancing of contradictory arguments is possible, we should not conclude that individuals facing political decisions are left with mere gut feeling to help them decide, or rather, simply plump for one or the other policy. Public reasoning by debaters in front of decision-makers about the decisions they face is still possible and can be helpful. True, individuals' decisions will be subjective, but the subjectivity comes in because the warrants relied on in deliberative reasoning are *values*, and because individuals' sets of values, their interpretations of them, and their hierarchical rankings of them are not identical. Nevertheless, it is a need for every individual facing a decision to gain understanding of what is implied by competing proposals and policies in terms of that individual's values—such as they are, or such as they may dynamically evolve as a result of the reasoning offered. Public debate in respect of obligations like those discussed above would promote that kind of understanding.

REFERENCES

Benhabib, S. 1994. Deliberative rationality and models of democratic legitimacy. *Constellations* 1, 26-52.

Benhabib, S. 1996. Toward a deliberative model of democratic legitimacy, in *Democracy and Difference: Contesting the Boundaries of the Political*. Princeton: Princeton University Press, 67-94.

Berlin, I. 2002. Two concepts of liberty. In *Liberty, Incorporating Four Essays on Liberty*. Oxford: Oxford University Press, 166-217.

Bessette, J.M. 1994. *The Mild Voice of Reason: Deliberative Democracy and American National Government*. Chicago: University of Chicago Press.

Cohen, J. 1989a. Deliberative democracy and democratic legitimacy. In A. Hamlin and P. Pettit (Eds.), *The Good Polity*, Oxford: Blackwell, 17-34.

_____. 1989b. Moral pluralism and political consensus. *New York University Law Review* 64, 233-55.

_____. 1998. Democracy and liberty. In J. Elster and A. Przeworski (Eds.), *Deliberative Democracy*. Cambridge: Cambridge University Press, 185–231.

Eemeren, F.H. van and R. Grootendorst. 1992. *Argumentation, Communication and Fallacies: A Pragma-dialectical Perspective*. Hillsdale, NJ: Lawrence Erlbaum Associates.

_____. 2004. *A Systematic Theory of Argumentation: The Pragma-dialectical Approach*. Cambridge: Cambridge University Press.

Eemeren, F.H. van and P. Houtlosser. 1999. Strategic manoeuvring in argumentative discourse. *Discourse Studies* 1, 479-497.

_____. 2000. Rhetorical analysis within a pragma-dialectical framework. *Argumentation* 14, 293-305.

_____. 2001. Managing disagreement: Rhetorical analysis within a dialectical framework. *Argumentation and Advocacy* 37, 150-157.

_____. 2002. Strategic maneuvering: maintaining a delicate balance. In F.H. van Eemeren and P. Houtlosser (Eds.), *Dialectic and Rhetoric: The Warp and the Woof of Argumentation Analysis*, Dorcrecht: Kluwer Academic Publishers, 131-159.

Finnis, J. 1998. Commensuration and public reason. In Ruth Chang (Ed.), *Incommensurability, Incomparability, and Practical Reason*. Cambridge, MA: Harvard University Press, 215-233.

Goodnight, T. 1993. A "new rhetoric" for a "new dialectic": Prolegomena to a responsible public argument. *Argumentation* 7, 329-342.

Govier, T. 2005. *A Practical Study of Argument*, 6th ed. Belmont, CA: Wadsworth Publishing Company.

Habermas, J. 1972. Wahrheitstheorien. In *Vorstudien und Ergänzungen zur Theorie des Kommunikativen Handelns* Frankfurt/M.: Suhrkamp, 127-183.

_____. 1997. *The Theory of Communicative Action, Vol. 1: Reason and the Rationalization of Society*. Thomas McCarthy (trams.). Cambridge: Polity Press.

Johnson, R. 2000. *Manifest Rationality: A Pragmatic Theory of Argument*. Mahwah, NJ: Lawrence Erlbaum.

_____. 2002. Manifest rationality reconsidered: Reply to my fellow symposiasts. *Argumentation* 16, 311-331.

Kock, C. 2003. Multidimensionality and non-deductiveness in deliberative argumentation. In *Anyone Who Has a View: Theoretical Contributions to the Study of Argumentation*, F.H. van Eemeren, J.A. Blair, C.A. Willard and A.F. Snoeck Henkemans (Eds.). Dordrecht/Boston/London: Kluwer Academic Publishers, 157-171. (This volume, Chapter 6.)

_____. 2006. Multiple warrants in practical reasoning. In D. Hitchcock, and B. Verheij (Eds.), *Arguing on the Toulmin Model: New Essays on Argument Analysis and Evaluation*. Dordrecht: Springer, 269-280. (This volume, Chapter 4.)

_____. 2007. Is practical reasoning presumptive? *Informal Logic* 27, 91-108. (This volume, Chapter 5.)

Larmore, C. 1996. *The Morals of Modernity*. Cambridge: Cambridge University Press.

Lukes, S. 1991. *Moral Conflict and Politics*. Oxford: Clarendon.

Perelman, C., and L. Olbrechts-Tyteca. 1958. *La Nouvelle Rhétorique: Traité de l'Argumentation*. Paris: Presses Universitaires de France. American edition, *The New Rhetoric: A Treatise on Argumentation*, J. Wilkinson and P. Weaver (trans.). Notre Dame: University of Notre Dame Press, 1969.

Rawls, J. 1993. *Political Liberalism*. New York: Columbia University Press.

Raz, J. 1986. *The Morality of Freedom*. Oxford: Clarendon Press.

_____. 1998. Incommensurability and agency. In Chang, R. (Ed.), *Incommensurability, incomparability, and practical reason*, pp. 110-128. Cambridge, MA: Harvard University Press.

_____. 2000. *Engaging Reason: On the Theory of Value and Action*. Oxford: Oxford University Press.

Sinnott-Armstrong, W. 1988. *Moral Dilemmas*. Oxford: Basil Blackwell.

Stocker, M. 1990. *Plural and Conflicting Values*. Oxford: Oxford University Press.

Toulmin, S.E. 1958. *The Uses of Argument*. Cambridge: Cambridge University Press.

Walton, D.N. 1990. *Practical Reasoning: Goal-driven, Knowledge-based, Action-guiding Argumentation*. Savage, Maryland: Rowman and Littlefield.

_____. 1996. *Argumentation Schemes for Presumptive Reasoning*. Mahwah, N.J.: Lawrence Erlbaum Associates.

_____. 2006. How to make and defend a proposal in a deliberation dialogue. *Artificial Intelligence and Law*. DOI 10.1007/s10506-006-9025-x.

Warnke, G. 1999. *Legitimate Differences: Interpretation in the Abortion Controversy and Other Public Debates*. Berkeley: University of California Press.

Wellman, C. 1971. *Challenge and Response: Justification in Ethics*. Carbonale, IL: Southern Illinois University Press.

11.

Virtue Reversed: Principal Argumentative Vices in Political Debate[*]

Contributing to an understanding of the true virtues of argumentation, this paper sketches and exemplifies a theoretically reasoned but simple typology of argumentative vices or "malpractices" that are rampant in political debate in modern democracies. The typology reflects, in negative, a set of argumentative norms, thus making a bid for something that civic instruction might profitably teach students at all levels about deliberative democracy.

Introduction

In order to highlight the true virtues of public argumentation, I will sketch and exemplify a theoretically reasoned but simple typology of argumentative vices that are rampant in political debate in modern democracies.

The typology is based on reflections on what functions political debate might have and ought to have in a modern mediated democracy. This functional understanding underlies a view of what "virtuous" political argumentation might be like, which again implies the proposed typology of vices. It integrates, revises and extends concepts from, primarily, informal logic, such as the triad of *acceptability, relevance*, and *sufficiency*, and the notion of *dialectical obligations*. I further draw on insights from several practical philosophers and political theorists.

My typology, I suggest, could be a useful tool not only for academic observers of political debate but also for political reporters and commentators and journalists acting as interviewers or moderators in debates; with it, they might better identify and respond to the argumentative vices they meet. Moreover, I propose the theory, the set of norms, and the typology as a bid for something that civic instruction might

---

[*] Originally published in *Virtues of Argumentation*. (Proceedings of the 10th Conference of the Ontario Society for the Study of Argumentation). University of Windsor, Windsor, ON, Canada. 2013. http://scholar.uwindsor.ca/ossaarchive/OSSA10/. Reprinted with permission of the Society.

profitably try to teach students at all levels about deliberative democracy—or, with a term I prefer, "rhetorical citizenship" (Kock and Villadsen, 2012).

What Citizens Need

I believe we should assess the virtues of political argumentation from the point of view of *citizens*. In contrast, political commentators and pundits tend to primarily estimate or second-guess how politicians' pronouncements and debate behavior will benefit politicians themselves. They speculate on their underlying strategy and on which voter segments or political factions will respond favorably. This strategic framing (Cappella and Jamieson, 1997) represents a prevailing, while often implicit, view that politicians are motivated, mainly or exclusively, by a desire to strengthen or consolidate their positions of power. According to the strategic framing politicians try to do this by pleasing other politicians and mainly by pleasing the voters, or certain segments of voters. To counterbalance this trend I suggest that we argumentation scholars should come forward in the public sphere and assess to what extent politicians' contributions to the debate are of any use to us citizens.

We need norms on the basis of which this can be done. So what must political debates and debaters deliver in order to meet citizens' needs? My starting point is that political debate should function as citizens' *basis for making choices*. It should help each of us estimate what problems we face, what ought to be done about them, and who has the best approach to them. Debates should help each one of us take a stand on what should be done—*before* it is done. In short, public debate should be deliberative to help us citizens deliberate.

The political theorist Robert Goodin has referred to this stand-taking by citizens as "deliberation within" (2000). Simone Chambers, another political theorist, similarly believes that deliberation is central to democracy, but we should realize that "the mass public can never be deliberative" in the active sense of the word, i.e., we shall never see all the members of the mass public engage in deliberative debate with each other. However, the public rhetoric we hear, mainly through the media, does have a potential for providing deliberation to serve deliberating citizens' needs—but only a potential. Most public rhetoric is what Chambers calls "plebiscitary," based on pandering and manipulation. So scholars should critically assess public rhetoric, and the media that provides it, in hopes of "making the mass public more rather than less deliberative." She says: "If rhetoric in general is the study of how speech affects an audience then deliberative rhetoric must be about the way speech induces deliberation in the sense of inducing *considered* reflection about a future action" (2009, p. 335).

I agree with Goodin and Chambers that we need public political debate that is deliberative, not plebiscitary, mainly in order that we citizens may be optimally prepared for "deliberation within." This is the basic normative consideration on which I build a categorization of argumentative virtues and vices. The proposal aims to be simple and useful, for example in teaching citizenship and for journalists who want to contribute to the quality of deliberation in the media.

The cardinal virtues, in brief, are these: First, debaters who seek our adherence should do so by explicitly offering arguments, rather than trying to gain it with strategies that bypass arguments. Second, the arguments offered should themselves have merit, judged by criteria to which I will return. Third, debaters should provide answers to counterarguments and criticisms from opponents or questioners.

The typology of argumentative vices I propose is a mirror image of this triad. The first major category of vices comprises strategies by which our adherence to policies is sought without any arguments being given. In the second category, reasons are offered, but they are deficient or useless from a citizen's point of view. The third category comprises ways in which responses to criticism or counterarguments may be lacking or deficient.

Vices, Type I: No Arguments

First, a look at some strategies by which politicians try to win voters' adherence to policies without providing argumentation. In my critical work with political debate, most explicitly in my book in Danish for a general audience *De svarer ikke* ("They Are Not Answering," 2013) I discuss four related ways of presenting debatable ideas for the hearer's acceptance without making it explicit that this is what one is doing, i.e., without asserting these ideas or arguing for them. Because the ideas have not been asserted, chances are that hearers will accept them unreflectingly and without asking for arguments.

The range of linguistic features that can work like this includes such phenomena as Orwellian "Newspeak," i.e., words and expressions "intended to impose a desirable mental attitude upon the person using them," as Orwell explains (1949); also, second, "framing" language as discussed by, among others, George Lakoff (1996, 2004), for example the term *death tax* for *estate tax*; third, illicit use of presuppositions (Harder and Kock, 1976). This refers to assumptions tied to words and expressions which are taken for granted even if the sentence in which they occur is negated or turned into a question. In the standard case, such assumptions should be shared by the speaker and the hearer; the illicit use of them occurs when a speaker introduces presuppositions not shared by the hearers in order to get the hearer's unreflecting acceptance of them.

I will discuss a fourth phenomenon: implicatures—ideas that hearers understand and derive from an utterance, often involuntarily, although they are not asserted in it. Linguists, following Grice (1975), tend to distinguish between two types: *conventional* implicatures, which attach to a statement whenever it is uttered, regardless of context; and *conversational* implicatures; which hearers derive from a statement as a function of its specific context. Perelman and others have reminded us that what we call style is an integral part of argumentation. One of the merits of Jeanne Fahnestock's *Rhetorical Style* (2011) is to have shown this in detail. For example, in her chapter about "interclausal relations" she demonstrates how rhetors can call on readers' or hearers' *discourse knowledge*, a knowledge of the kinds of meaning relations that *can* exist between clauses (p. 356). This triggers a process in which listeners' minds are basically made to act involuntarily, constructing possible links between the parts of an utterance.

Consider this passage from George W. Bush's "State of the Union" speech on January 28, 2003.

Before September the 11th, many in the world believed that Saddam Hussein could be contained. But chemical agents, lethal viruses and shadowy terrorist networks are not easily contained.

In the first sentence, why is it relevant to say, in the past tense, that many believed Saddam could be contained? The most obvious reason would be that now people no more believe this. That may also provide relevance to the phrase *Before September the 11th*. Ostensibly, that day people gave up their former belief—for if they had kept it even after September 11, it would be irrelevant to specify the date. But if precisely that date refuted the belief that we can contain Saddam, then the most obvious reason for that would be that Saddam was partly or fully responsible for what happened that day. (There might be other reasons, and

Bush did have another, much more convoluted reason in mind, but this is certainly the most obvious one.)

Next consider both sentences together. Now more implicatures may arise, most obviously that Saddam *had* chemical agents, lethal viruses and shadowy terrorist networks, and that these were involved in 9/11. Otherwise the second sentence would be irrelevant to the first.

Many similar examples from the Bush administration's rhetoric on Iraq could be cited. The point is that the use of implicatures is one of a range of devices by which politicians may transfer debatable beliefs to citizens without explicitly giving arguments.

Vices, Type II: Deficient Arguments

Now for the second main category of argumentative vices. If arguments are in fact given, what criteria may we apply to them? Taking the reverse view, what can be wrong with them?

I start with the observation that there are usually "good" arguments both for and against a particular policy.

From this it follows that a good argument is not the same thing that logicians call a "valid argument"; we need to say this because many textbooks still cling to "validity." In standard logic "valid" means that the truth of the conclusion necessarily follows from the truth of the arguments (premises). When this is so, we speak of "deductive reasoning," "entailment," or "demonstration." But to Chaïm Perelman (Perelman and Olbrechts-Tyteca, 1958), argumentation is reasoning where demonstration is precisely *not* attainable; and argumentation thus defined is "the realm of rhetoric." Similarly, it is arguably the defining feature of informal logic that it looks at how argumentation can be reasonable *without* being deductively valid.

Is the validity criterion any use to us, then? Yes, it is of some use, because we often hear debaters pretend, explicitly or implicitly, that their arguments for a proposal *entails* an adoption of that proposal. And such false pretenses should be exposed. In politics the logical yardstick of deductive validity has this, rather limited, purpose. Where policies and decisions are concerned, we are dealing with what many philosophers, inspired by Aristotle, call practical reasoning; here I claim that there are never, in principle, any deductive entailment from the arguments for a proposal to the adoption of it. Although there are good arguments for it, there are, as a rule, also good arguments against it. As the philosopher

Anthony Kenny has it, "if a project or proposal or decision is good, that does not exclude its being also, from another point of view, bad" (1979, p. 146). Hence we cannot blame debaters for not presenting arguments which *entail* their proposal; we can, however, blame them if they will make us *believe* that they do.

Add to this that for any problem one would like to do something about, there are often several alternative policies. Even if one of them is good, another might be better.

All in all, assessing argument merit is much more complicated in politics, and in practical reasoning generally, than in logic. This is so not just in practice, but also in theory. So how *can* we go about it?

Building on the work of informal logicians such as Johnson and Blair (2006), Blair (2012), Johnson (2000), and Govier (1987, 2009), I would posit the following three dimensions of argument appraisal in practical reasoning. Arguments should be:

1. Accurate
2. Relevant
3. Weighty

Accurate means that one can answer "Yes" to the question, "Is that so?" I prefer the term "accurate" to the informal logicians' preferred term "acceptable" because "accurate" refers more to the relation between statements and reality, whereas "acceptable" refers more to the relation between statements and hearers. This is the ground covered by fact-checking organizations like the websites Factcheck.org or Politifact.com. Political debate is replete with alleged facts and statistics that should not go unchecked.

It is important that outright falsity is not the only vice here. Accountants and lawyers use the expression "true and fair." This means that alleged facts and numbers provide *a good and trustworthy account* of how things really are—not just that the numbers, taken in isolation, are "true," but that we get a *full* picture.

Further, terms used in such information must, as Jamieson and Waldman (2002) have discussed, have a clear definition—and one that tallies with how the same terms are used by other debaters and understood by the public. But loose and idiosyncratic use of terms is one major vice in political debate; I suggest calling it the vice of "fuzzy facts."

Another major vice, one degree worse, is what we may call "fudging facts": "factual" information which is not downright false but which invites us to believe falsehoods. We have just seen how deftly worded communication can invite people to believe things that aren't so.

The rampant use of fuzzy and fudging facts makes public debate near useless for citizens. That is why Daniel Patrick Moynihan famously said: "Everyone is entitled to their own views, but not to their own facts."

Relevant. Relevance concerns the relation between arguments and their warrants, whether these be explicit or implicit, as they often are. Problems arise in two kinds of situations: when an argument is not in fact covered or subsumed by the warrant it depends on, and when the warrant it depends on is one that the hearers cannot endorse. The warrants appealed to in practical argumentation will often be value concepts and ideological positions endorsed by the debater, but not by his opponents or hearers. Warrants are often differentially recognized by different individuals. It is a fact that the Falkland Islanders have voted overwhelmingly for staying British, but Argentina does not recognize popular majority as a warrant and instead bases her claim for the islands on a territorial warrant—which in turn is not recognized by Britain. This example makes it clear that relevance appraisal in argumentation, more than the assessment of factual accuracy, allows for a certain amount of disagreement, even deep disagreement, and if you prefer, subjectivity.

The insight that underlying values are sometimes not shared should also tell us that if we want to influence our opponents' views, we should search for values on even deeper levels that we do share with them. The principle that there has to be this sort of common ground is central to Perelman's concept of argumentation. In principle, we should expect debaters on public issues to base their case on warrants that are shared by *every* member of the public. And a corresponding vice is to base one's case on values and other warrants that are only shared by a narrowly targeted faction. We should expect public argumentation that does not simply pander to the pre-existing policy preferences of selected segments, but which tries to *change* some people's policy preferences by appealing to underlying shared warrants.

Also, whether an argument is covered by a warrant is often a matter of interpretation. Everyone agrees that killing innocent human beings is wrong, but does this notion cover abortion? We need debates in which debaters recognize that their disagreement with opponents is not necessarily a disagreement over deeply held values, but a difference in the *interpretation* of these values (Warnke, 1999).

Coming back to what we actually get, a rampant relevance-related vice that is objectively and unconditionally vicious is argumentation directed at "straw men," i.e., distorted versions of opponents' standpoints or of their arguments (these are two different things). A straw man version of an opponent's standpoint tends to radicalize and transmogrify it into a caricature that is easy to reject; we may call it a "detestable straw man." While a "straw" version of one's opponent's standpoint may well be detestable, however, there is no warrant for concluding from this that one's opponent's real standpoint is detestable too. As for straw versions of an opponent's *arguments,* these are routinely weakened and emasculated into something we might call "pitiable straw men."

Another subtype of relevance-related vice which is perhaps not quite so objectively and unconditionally wrong is the ascription of sinister ulterior motives to opponents. The possible presence of such motives has at most marginal relevance, or none at all. There are accuracy problems as well—how can we know whether an opponent really has the hidden motives ascribed to him if they are hidden? Even if it shown that some of those who advance a proposal do have hidden motives, should the proposal not be judged on what it actually does, rather than what someone intended it to do?

Even if an argument is clearly relevant, and factually accurate too, our argument appraisal is not done. Since the warrants for arguments in political debate are typically value concepts, we come to a further fundamental complication. As we have seen, a policy might be good according to one relevant value, for example that one should keep one's promises; but it might be bad according to another relevant warrant, for example economic prudence. A government may have made pre-election promises to implement certain policies—but doing so turns out to be disastrously expensive. Many citizens in such a case would probably feel that both these warrants have some relevance, so the task for citizens engaged in "deliberation within" would be to *prioritize.* That would be each citizen's *personal* responsibility, since there is no pre-ordained or intersubjective way to determine whether the ethics of promises or economic prudence has more weight in a particular case.

This shows that relevant warrants in practical argumentation are typically multiple (Kock, 2006), and that they can easily be in conflict

(Stocker, 1990), and that they are not commensurable (Raz, 1998) in any agreed and pre-ordained way.

As you may have noticed, the *weight* criterion just popped up here. In choosing the term "weight" I deviate from the term most frequently used by informal logicians such as Anthony Blair: "sufficiency." The problem is that sufficiency is dichotomous. A quantity is either sufficient for some purpose, or it isn't; it cannot be "rather sufficient." Do I have sufficient time to catch my plane? I cannot catch my plane to some extent. Also, sufficiency is known in mathematics in phrases like "the necessary and sufficient condition." A condition is sufficient for something to be the case if that something *necessarily* follows; that is, deductive inference obtains. Informal logicians rightly want to abandon deductive inference as a necessary criterion of good argumentation; but if they include "sufficiency" in their criteria, that either means that deductive inference is still required—or it has some other meaning which is fuzzy and idiosyncratic.

Furthermore, the weight of an argument is of a peculiar, metaphorical kind because one cannot assess it for one argument taken by itself; one has to look at it in relation to the other good arguments on the same issue—and there are usually several on both sides. So *weight* means *relative weight*. All the arguments on both sides are in play when we want to "weigh" an argument.

This metaphorical weighing of arguments against each other will be additionally complicated by the presence of the elements of individuality or subjectivity. As I have shown, these complications arise in regard to the recognition and the interpretation of warrants, and they arise even more when arguments are to be prioritized or "weighed."

This is because, for one thing, arguments belong to different dimensions. Should the economic argument that cutbacks are (perhaps) prudent trump the moral argument that promises to the contrary were made? There is no objective or "philosophical" answer, so citizens must try to decide for themselves. But before they do, they need all the help they can get, and this kind of help they should expect from public debaters—as well as from journalists, pundits and academics in the public sphere. They need to hear the good arguments on both sides, and to be able to weigh them against each other they especially need debaters on each side to *hear* and *answer* arguments from the other side.

Vices, Type III: No Answers

This brings us to our last category of vices. Flouting the "dialectical obligation" (Johnson, 1996, 2000, 2002; Kock, 2007) to sincerely hear and answer counterarguments or critical questions is perhaps the chief vice that makes public debate near useless for citizens. There is reason to believe that a great deal of what communication consultants do for the politicians they serve is teach them how to respond in ways that superficially *appear* to answer counterarguments and critical questions, but which in reality bypass them. Not every response is an answer. The obligation to answer can in principle only be satisfied in two ways:

Either one tries to show why the counterargument is deficient— i.e., that it is either inaccurate or irrelevant, or both.

Or if the counterargument happens to fulfil the accuracy and relevance conditions, as it often does, then one explains why one still sees the arguments for one's own position as weightier than the arguments against it.

These two kinds of behavior are rarely found in public debate. Instead we get responses in which counterarguments are either bypassed in silence, distorted into pitiable straw men, or blankly dismissed, i.e., without any reasons being offered for the dismissal. These vices are often camouflaged with repetitions of stale talking points, or talk about other subjects, including straw man versions of opponents' views and condemnation of their alleged hidden motives.

It is the discussion of arguments pro and con, as in 1) and 2), that constitutes true deliberation. That is the kind of input that will most help citizens and voters engage in "deliberation within." It will help them muster the available arguments on both sides, what the issue involves, what arguments pertain to it, which arguments are accurate and relevant, and what the other party has to say in answer to them.

That kind of deliberation will not result in universal consensus; there are reasons why we have such a thing as "reasonable disagreement" (Rawls, 1989, 1993). Perhaps there will not even be many people who will change their views. Even if none of these things happen, it will probably still be the case that a citizen who engages in "deliberation within" will realize that other citizens who disagree with him in regard to their preferred policies often have reasons to do so which may make him wiser. He may understand that their reasons may say something about reality that he has not yet thought about, but which may be accurate and relevant, and which may even have some weight. Such an insight does not entail that our citizen should necessarily endorse his opponents' preferred *policies*. As we saw at first, that kind of entailment has no place in practical reasoning. This implies that we should not be afraid to admit that our opponents may have some points that we have not yet given enough thought. In other words, even though we may never agree on divisive issues, it might do us good to sit down and talk. It might even do our politicians good.

REFERENCES

Benoit, W.L. 1989. Attorney argumentation and Supreme Court opinions. *Argumentation and Advocacy,* 26, 22-38.

Blair, J.A. 2012. Relevance, acceptability and sufficiency today. In Blair, *Groundwork in the Theory of Argumentation.* Dordrecht: Springer, 87-100.

Cappella, J., and K.H. Jamieson. 1997. *Spiral of Cynicism: The Press and the Public Good.* New York: Oxford University Press.

Chambers, S. 2009. Rhetoric and the public sphere: Has deliberative democracy abandoned mass democracy? *Political Theory* 37, 323-350.

Goodin, R.E. 2000. Democratic deliberation within. *Philosophy & Public Affairs* 29, 81-109.

Govier, T. 2009. *A Practical Study of Argument,* 7th ed. Belmont: Wadsworth Publishing Company.

Grice, H.P. 1975. Logic and conversation. In P. Cole and J.L. Morgan (Eds.), *Syntax and Sermantics: Speech Acts,* vol. 3. New York: Academic Press, 41-48.

Harder, P., and C. Kock. 1976. *The Theory of Presupposition Failure.* (Travaux du Cercle Linguistique de Copenhague, XVII.) Copenhagen (Akademisk Forlag).

Jamieson, K.H., and P.Waldman. 2002. *The Press Effect: Politicians, Journalists, and the Stories that Shape the Political World.* New York: Oxford University Press.

Johnson, R.H. 1996. The need for a dialectical tier in arguments. In D.M. Gabay and H.J. Ohlbach (Eds.), *Practical Reasoning: International Conference on Formal and Applied Practical Reasoning.* Berlin: Springer, 349-360.

Johnson, R.H. 2002. Manifest rationality reconsidered: Reply to my fellow symposiasts. *Argumentation*, 16, 311-331.

Kenny, A. 1979. *Aristotle's Theory of the Will*. London: Duckworth.

Kock, C. 2003. Multidimensionality and non-deductiveness in deliberative argumentation. In F.H. van Eemeren, J.A. Blair, C.A. Willard, and A.F. Snoeck Henkemans (Eds.), *Anyone Who Has a View: Theoretical Contributions to the Study of Argumentation*. Dordrecht: Kluwer Academic Publishers, 157-171. (This volume, chapter 6.)

_____. 2006. Multiple warrants in practical reasoning. In D. Hitchcock and B. Verheij (Eds.), *Arguing on the Toulmin Model: New Essays on Argument Analysis and Evaluation.* Dordrecht: Springer, 269-280. (This volume, Chapter 4.)

_____. 2007. Dialectical obligations in political debate. *Informal Logic* 27, 233-247. (This volume, Chapter 10.)

_____. 2013. *De svarer ikke: Fordummende uskikke i den politiske debat*, 2nd ed. Copenhagen: Gyldendal.

_____, and L. Villadsen. 2012. Introduction: Citizenship as a rhetorical practice. In C. Kock and L. Villadsen (Eds.), *Rhetorical Citizenship and Public Deliberation*. University Park: Penn State Press, 1-10.

Lakoff, G. 1996. *Moral Politics: What Conservatives Know that Liberals Don't*. Chicago: University of Chicago Press.

Lakoff, G. 2004. *Don't Think of an Elephant: Know Your Values and Frame the Debate*. White River Junction, VT: Chelsea Green Publishing.

Orwell, G. 1949. *Nineteen Eighty-Four*. London: Secker and Warburg.

Raz, J. 1998. Incommensurability and agency. In Chang, R. (Ed.), *Incommensurability, Incomparability, and Practical Reason.* Cambridge, MA.: Harvard University Press, 110-128.

Stocker, M. 1990. *Plural and Conflicting Values*. Oxford: Oxford University Press.

Warnke, G. 1999. *Legitimate Differences: Interpretation in the Abortion Controversy and Other Public Debates*. Berkeley: University of California Press.

12.

Rhetoric That Shifts Votes:
An Exploratory Study of Persuasion
in Issue-oriented Public Debates[*]

This article summarizes a study of 37 televised debates on political issues in Denmark, conducted live before representative audiences, with polls on the issue before and after each debate. These debates are of interest to research because they were authentic, and for the data they supply indicating persuasive effects. Various rhetorical features were observed and related to debaters' success in attracting votes. In a qualitative interpretation of the observations, we suggest that debates such as these are likely to be won by debaters whose argumentation is fair and thoughtful. Audiences may respond differently depending on whether they are voters or merely viewers. The debate format may enhance such a response, for the benefit of the democratic process.

Two important efforts in the study of persuasion are analyses of authentic political communication and experimental effect studies. The first kind, as exemplified in the work of Kathleen Hall Jamieson (e.g., 1992; Jamieson and Birdsell, 1988), has brought important insights but generally lacks data to link specific features and effects. On the other hand, experimental studies developing the tradition of the Yale group (as in Hovland *et al.*, 1953) focus specifically on effects, isolating one variable at a time and controlling for disturbing influences; however, this very methodology makes it problematic to transfer results to the world of authentic political communication, in which countless variables are constantly at play. The empirical study of persuasion might benefit from observations of persuasion taking place in authentic settings, but with built-in controls that make it possible to link causes and effects.

---

[*] This article was co-authored with Charlotte Jørgensen and Lone Rørbech. It was originally published in *Political Communication* 15 (1998), 283-299. Reprinted with permission of the Publisher.

Our study is based on videotaped events that meet this dual requirement.[12] Over the years 1975-1985, the Danish Broadcasting Corporation televised 37 one-hour debates, titled *Town Parliament (Bytinget)*. In each, two debaters took opposing sides on such issues as "Should the electoral age be lowered to 18?" and "Should legal abortion be restricted?" Debaters were often prominent figures, noted for their interest in the issue. Each debater brought three "witnesses," interrogating each for four minutes; the opponent would then cross-examine for three minutes. The studio audience, a panel of a hundred "jurors" who served for three or four debates, were a randomized sample of the citizens of Silkeborg, where the debates were held—then Denmark's political "Middletown," mirroring the national party distribution in elections. Unlike most studio audiences, these were reasonably representative of the electorate.

Two secret push-button polls were taken in each debate; the first after both debaters had briefly presented their views and the other at the end, after two-minute concluding speeches by the debaters. Jurors had three options: yes, no, and undecided.

Of the 37 debates, we had at our disposal 30 on videotape and one on audio-tape.[13] For all debates, we knew the issues, the participants, and the net polling results. For 20 of the available debates, we also knew the internal movements between yes, no, and undecided.

In sum, the issues debated were real and important; debaters argued views that they truly held because they wanted to persuade; the jurors were a representative sample; what jurors voted on was not who "did best" but by whom they were persuaded; and finally, if votes were shifted between the two polls, this must have been caused by the debaters' and witnesses' persuasive efforts because the audience was under no other influence.

---

[12] The study reported here was supported by the Danish Research Council for the Humanities and published in our Danish monograph *Retorik der flytter stemmer: Hvordan man overbeviser i offentlig debat* ("Rhetoric That Shifts Votes: How to Persuade in Public Debate"; Jørgensen, Kock, and Rørbech, 1994). There, we present extensive analyses of data and examples of all features studied, as well as thorough discussions of our methodology and statistical procedures. Many methodological questions that might be raised are discussed in the book; they have necessarily been compressed here to give an international audience an outline of our study within article length. Our consultant on statistics was Knut Conradsen, Professor of Mathematical Statistics and Operations Research at the Technological University of Denmark.

[13] The earliest of these debates were held before videotape recorders became common. The debates missing in this study do not exist in the archives of the Danish Broadcasting Corporation nor in any other collection of which we have inquired.

Hence, we believe the debates are important data for a study in persuasive effects.[14]

Method

Exploratory Nature of the Study. Given the exceptional value of these debates as data, it was clear to us that our study would have to be exploratory and hence different from traditional experimental studies. We did not approach the material with any one hypothesis to test. Naturally, we had ideas concerning what to look for. But to exploit the material optimally, we tried not to be guided by preformed hypotheses that might blindfold us to unexpected observations.

For all features studied, we tested for correlations with the voting results. We emphasize that our tests and p values cannot be given a strict probabilistic interpretation but instead are used in a descriptive way to indicate how well the data correspond to the persuasive effects for which we were looking. We used one-tailed tests only when a unidirectional hypothesis was obvious. If we had no *a priori* reason to hypothesize that a possible effect would be either negative or positive, we did two-tailed tests; these cases are explicitly indicated.

"Featurizing" authentic persuasion was a complicated task. For example, in a forensic format with testimony and cross-examination, a debater's witnesses act as co-debaters. Still, the debater is the team leader. Certain features are ascribable to debaters, others concern witnesses, and others again concern the performance of the whole team. However, the audience does not vote for the witnesses or the teams but for the debaters' claims; hence, for statistical tests we attributed all features to the debaters.

Debaters and witnesses, facing a real audience, employ a wide range of constantly intermingling appeals. We wanted to study the full range of appeals, from *actio* over *inventio* to overall strategy. Yet there are undoubtedly many patterns we have overlooked. On the other hand, many features that we considered including in the study were left out, either because they turned out to be practically absent or because they could not be coded with any degree of precision. Such difficulties are inherent to authentic communication. What we explore is not the effect of single features in contexts where all others are held constant but features

---

[14] A study such as ours only offers insight into short-term persuasive effects and yields no data on what long-term effects would be. Also, because all the debates took place between 1975 and 1985, it is possible that the effects we hypothesize may not be valid now.

recurring across many debates in interaction with countless others; this creates complexities but also a realism hard to achieve in experimental studies.

Coding. Conveniently, our criterion variable—the persuasiveness of the debaters—had been quantitatively coded by the 100 jurors. For the coding of the independent variables, we relied on our own judgment.[15] When in doubt, we reached consensus on the coding after extensive discussion among the three of us.

We used dichotomous coding, not gradation, for two reasons: First, there would have been additional reliability problems in applying graded coding of, for example, "intense gaze"; second, quantification of a feature (as in content analysis) would assume that the effect of a feature is proportional to the degree of its presence. However, even one use of a highly aggressive gesture by a debater may have an immense effect on the audience, rendering strict quantification pointless. For some features, however, we did use relative quantification, estimating which of two debaters had more of the feature in question.

Cases in which dichotomous coding remained problematic were coded as undecidable. We did not use subjective features such as high versus low credibility.

Statistical Tests. For each feature, we identified all debaters who had it and tested their success in terms of winning votes. A debater might be in the minority in both polls yet be more successful than his opponent by gaining more votes. We looked at net gain, not proportional gain (i.e., the debater's net gain in proportion to his initial number of votes); a minority debater gaining 10 votes is hardly more successful than a majority debater who does the same. In parliamentary elections, the winner is considered to be the party, large or small, making the largest net gain. Our data confirm this interpretation: debaters who are in the minority in the first poll gain

---

[15] Charlotte Jørgensen worked on audience response, hostility, nonsupportive testimony, and types of grounds. Christian Kock worked on demographic features, ideology, rhetorical strategy, and claim demarcation. Lone Rørbech worked on nonverbal features, stylistic features, and the last word strategy.

An obvious question is how we dealt with possible "success" biases. Because we knew the outcome of the votes in advance, we might have been inclined to find justification for this outcome in the coding. Extended discussion of doubtful cases among the three of us cannot completely eliminate this problem, but the temptation to bias would have been stronger if we had had any specific hypotheses to prove. As we did not, we had no *a priori* wish to code any given debater in any particular way for any feature.

more votes in exactly as many cases as do majority debaters. Thus, to win was to gain more votes than the opponent; a tie was when the opposing debaters made equal gains.

Tied debates, and debates in which both debaters, or none, have a particular feature (F), cannot in themselves show anything about the effect of F. When these are discounted, we have a set of debaters with F confronting debaters without F. The winner-loser distribution among F-debaters allows us to do a binomial test. For brevity, we shall say, for instance, "F-debaters won 10 times and lost once;" this should be understood to refer to the 11 debates that were not tied and in which F-debaters confronted non-F-debaters.

The binomial test, using nominal data only and excluding many debates, does not fully exploit the data; it would be desirable to include all debates in which a feature appears and to define degrees of success. But we cannot simply compare all debaters' net gains because some debaters, presumably, have stronger opponents than others; however, this problem is reduced for groups of debaters. Also, it may be harder to gain votes on some issues than on others. In fact, it turned out that debaters' average gains were roughly proportional to the number of undecided voters in the first poll, both in debates with many undecided votes, in debates with an average number (about 10), and in debates with few undecided votes. Hence, we postulated that the jurors' volatility in a given debate is proportional to the number of undecided votes in the first poll. (The number of undecided votes does not, we believe, reflect any other factor, such as jurors' view of the salience of an issue—a factor that usually affects the turnout in referendums and the like. In these debates, the jurors already had turned out.) Thus, if there are n_1 undecided voters in the first poll, and if a debater's net gain is G_N, then the formula $G_N:n_1$ yields comparable "success factors" for all debaters. Notice that in this definition, two opponents' success factors are not mere reciprocal figures.

The success factors were not normally distributed (there were several extreme values). Therefore, we chose a nonparametric statistic: we converted success factors into a rank order and applied the Mann-Whitney U test.

One problem remained: we could not lump together all debaters. That would have placed the winner and the loser of a given debate in the same rank order, resulting in Type I errors. Instead, we used one rank order for "A" debaters (those who spoke first in each debate) and one for "B" debaters (those who spoke last). The risk now is Type II error: to obtain significant results in both these half-sized groups is a stiff requirement. Thus, the rank order test and the binomial test have complementary advantages. Also, because they are quite different, we assumed that whenever they confirmed each other, our results would be bolstered.

Because data on some features (e.g., debaters' age) were available outside the debates, the rank order for these features includes all 37 debates. Most features (e.g., types of evidence) could be studied only in the debates; hence, the rank order for these features is based on 31 debates. Other features (e.g., gestures) could only be studied on video-tapes; here, only 30 debates were included.

Some features make a third statistic meaningful. When there were two extremes on a scale, with an undecidable in the middle (e.g., the feature *voice,* which may be modulated, monotonous, or undecidable), we used "winner versus loser" as the independent variable and the three-point scale as a rank-ordered criterion variable. This, unlike a Chi-square test, allowed us to capture a skew toward, for example, more modulated voice in winners.

Results

Demographic Features. Does persuasive effect correlate with *professional status?* This feature was elusive because debaters tended to have multiple or borderline professional identities, such as politician/lawyer/businessman. The only profession category that we found operational was "member of Parliament" (MP; past or present). It is perhaps surprising that MPs (41 out of 74 debaters) did not excel in persuasion: their average rank was 18.8 against a total average of 19.

What about *educational background?* In Denmark, the word *academic* means a person with a full university degree (Master's or above). Academic debaters won 10 times and lost twice ($p = .0193$). The rank order test yielded $p = .13$ for the A group and $p < .01$ for the B group. The reason academic debaters won, we assume, is that they had special skills in supporting a case. "Initial ethos" (McCroskey, 1997, pp. 91-95) cannot explain their success: in most cases no information on debaters' educational background was given and there generally seemed to be no way for the audience to make inferences about it; we ourselves had to research extensively to find out.

As for non-university backgrounds, one might expect journalists and schoolteachers to show persuasive skills. However, both groups were too small for statistical testing, they both ranked well below average (journalists, 12.4 against 19; schoolteachers, 13.3).

The hypothesis that academics have special persuasive skills corresponds with observations on *witness roles.* Debaters bringing professional researchers as witnesses (academics in the American sense) won nine times and lost twice ($p = .0327$). In the rank order test, the result for the A group was nonsignificant; for the B group, $p = .06$.

Another witness role is the professional expert, for example, a general testifying on a military issue. We also found witnesses without professional expertise on the issue but with special personal experience that was used by the debater to exemplify the issue (we return to these below under the heading *Types of Grounds*).

The residual group of witnesses was typically used to express the views of ordinary people. Debaters using such witnesses won three times but lost eight times ($p = .2266$, two-tailed); the rank order test went in the same direction but was of course nonsignificant.

As for *gender,* women ranked slightly below men. In male-female confrontations, the men won eight times, the women twice ($p = .1094$, two-tailed). Results in the rank order test were nonsignificant.

We also looked at cases in which all-male debate teams confronted mixed teams; this is relevant because there was only one all-female team, whereas 34 teams—nearly half of all teams—were all-male. All-male teams won 12 times and lost five times *($p = .1434$, two-tailed).* The rank order test had a *p* of .05 for the A group, whereas *p* for the B group was nonsignificant.

Probably, however, these results are best explained in terms of education. Only *seven* (44%) of the female debaters held university degrees but those did well above average (21.1). There was a positive correlation between men and academics ($\chi^2 = 1.89$, $p = .17$, two-tailed). That mixed teams lost to all-male teams may stem from the fact that female witnesses always (with one exception) appeared as "ordinary people."

Age. Age as such had little correlation with rank (Pearson's $r = .18$ for the A group, .13 for the B group). We also grouped debaters in age intervals of *five* years, with about the same number of debaters in each. Here, for example, the middle-aged (46-50) lost 12 times and won twice (p = .0130, two-tailed), whereas the old (those *over* 55) won nine times and lost three times *($p = .1460$, two-tailed).* Again, these results probably have to do with education as only 26.7 percent of the middle-aged were academics, against 85.7 percent of the old.

Overall, the only demographic feature correlating plausibly with persuasiveness was a university degree. This suggestive fact foreshadows the general picture that emerges from our analysis.

Nonverbal Features. Several significant winning or losing features related to nonverbal aspects. We identified four categories: *voice, facial expressions, posture, gestures.*

Voice. One would expect debaters speaking in a monotonous voice to do less well than debaters with a modulated voice, that is, a voice with a broad range of variation in pitch, speed, or volume. (An intermediate group was coded as undecidable.) Indeed, modulated debaters won 9 times and lost 3 times ($p = .0730$); monotonous debaters lost 10 times and won once ($p = .0059$). In the A group, modulated debaters ranked only slightly above average, but monotonous ones ranked significantly lower ($p < .01$); in the B group, modulated debaters ranked higher ($p = .11$), and monotonous ones ranked lower to a similar degree. In a rank order test on degree of modulation, winners were significantly more modulated than losers ($p < .01$).

Articulation is another classic feature of effective delivery. On a three-point scale (energetic, undecidable, and sloppy articulation), energetic debaters won 12 times and lost five times ($p = .0717$); sloppy debaters lost eight times and won twice ($p = .0547$). The rank order test yielded no significant results, but a test on degrees of articulation showed that winners ranked significantly higher than losers ($p = .03$).

Facial Expressions. The feature friendliness versus unfriendliness yielded nonsignificant results, though with some skew toward friendliness. We noticed another feature, though: a noticeably intense gaze fixed on the witnesses or the audience at appropriate moments. Debaters with an intense gaze won 11 times and lost no debates ($p = .0005$). The rank order test yielded qualified support to this finding (A group, $p = .11$; B group, $p < .01$).

Posture. We identified three recurrent features. The open posture is one in which the speaker generally holds his or her arms in an open position, away from the body, and the chest open and upright; in the closed posture, speakers tend to crouch and cover their chest with their arms. (There also was an intermediate undecidable class.) Debaters with an open posture did marginally better than average, and debaters with a closed posture did slightly worse, but a rank order test showed that winners were significantly more open than losers ($p = .03$).

A combination of closed posture and unfriendly facial expression struck us as a recurrent syndrome; we call it the *dismissive attitude*. Six debaters had it: Five lost, one won ($p = .1094$). All were in the B group; a rank order test suggested that the dismissive attitude is, indeed, for debaters opposing a proposition, a losing feature ($p = .04$).

Like energy in articulation, we hypothesized that an energetic posture might also be a winning feature. We noted a tendency in some debaters to sit alertly on the edge of their chairs with sustained muscle tension, as if ready to pounce. Eleven debaters with this posture won, and one lost ($p = .0032$). Rank order test results were as follows: for A debaters, $p = .09$; for B debaters, $p = .02$.

Gesticulation. Again, we found three recurrent patterns. Some debaters gesticulated eagerly, others hardly at all, with an undecidable group in between. Eager debaters won 12 times and lost twice ($p = .0193$); on the rank order test, they were average in the A group but significantly better in the B group ($p = .05$). However, debaters who hardly gesticulated were not losers: they won nine times and lost 11 times; on the rank order test, they were slightly above average in the A group but were significantly below average in the B group ($p = .04$).

Another pattern was open, embracing gestures. Debaters with this feature won eight times and lost twice ($p = .0547$). On the rank order test, the p for the A group was nonsignificant; for the B group, $p = .05$.

Firm, directive gestures were typically fist, edge-of-hand, or index finger movements, performed energetically and selectively to underscore key points. Debaters with this feature won 13 times and lost twice ($p = .0037$). On the rank order test, the p for the A group was .05; for the B group, $p < .01$.

A look at the whole range of nonverbal features suggests that while energy and liveliness are certainly important, the most persuasive nonverbal features are those that are used in a selective, precise, and directive way to emphasize specific, crucial features of content. We do not believe that any standardized nonverbal feature will guarantee success. Persuasiveness cannot be assured by adding a few effects extraneous to the nature of one's arguments, strategy, or general ethos. For instance, firm, directive gestures comprise an indefinite number of different movements; the indiscriminate use of any one gesture would appear robotic. More generally, we believe that when nonverbal features are persuasive, it is because they are integrated with spoken words to highlight and structure ideas also presented verbally.

Stylistic Features. Testing the persuasive effects of linguistic and stylistic features would be a time-consuming project, which we gave low priority because probes suggested that such features *per se* have little persuasive effect. Debaters using rhetorical figures in their concluding speeches did only averagely. Results might have been different if we had been able to test for apt use. Perelman and Olbrechts-Tyteca (1969) distinguish between figures used argumentatively and as embellishment, but we lacked an operational way to apply this distinction.

A few debaters used what we might call "nutshells" (Flower, 1985). These are repeated and pointed one-word or one-line formulations that sum up the main reason for their stand. An example is "Babies will become merchandise," used in support of a ban on surrogate motherhood. Debaters with this feature were all large winners.

A related observation concerns debaters whose concluding speeches used what we call *rhythmical pith.* These debaters ranked high and won seven times, while losing three times. This feature resembles another aspect of verbal pith: A small group of debaters had an unusually low average T-unit length (10-12.5 words per T-unit) in their concluding speeches (a T-unit is an independent clause and all subordinate elements attached to it, whether clausal or phrasal, cf. Hunt, 1965). These debaters seemed to us to project energy and precision and were in fact large winners.

Apart from this, both general T-unit length and percentage of long words, as used in readability tests, were persuasively neutral. We believe that energy and purposeful variation—features that we did not attempt to operationalize—are more relevant, especially in oral communication, than average values.

Audience Response. Inspired by Atkinson (1984), we examined the occurrence of audience response.[16] In this civilized format there was little of it; no instances of directly hostile response occurred. Of the four teams that evoked clapping from the audience, one won and three lost. As for

---

[16] Atkinson (1984) assumed, reasonably, that applause is indicative of attention and approval. However, no theoretical reason predicts that applause indicates persuasive effect: one should remember that the audience in Atkinson's material is generally a partisan group, typically a national party convention.

laughter, although it was nearly always given in a spirit of sympathy, laughter-evoking teams ranked below average. When we asked which of two sides got laughter more often, the negative effect became pronounced: six of those teams won and 14 lost ($p = .1154$; two-tailed). This does seem to suggest that the audience is not persuaded just by being amused nor by any assumed ethos appeal of a person with humor. Possibly, the appeal to laughter in issue-oriented debates is a boomerang: in the final count it may leave the impression that a debater lacks sincerity.

Hostility. There is a widespread notion of debate as inherently eristic; Walton (1989/1992) places debate on a level below the "critical discussion" as a semi-quarrel—a description we find misleading (Jørgensen, 1998). We define hostile debate behavior, or eristic behavior, as any impoliteness toward the opponent unnecessary to elucidate the difference of opinion. Hostile debaters attack the person (Infante *et al.*, 1992); they seek divergence, making the gap as broad as possible; they show disrespect for their opponents and their views. Not only does this behavior pose an unavoidable threat to the opponent's face (Goffman, 1955), it also deliberately attacks it. Within this broad definition, we established three categories of features that identify the eristic: (1) *hostile interrogation*—untimely interruption, demanding an unwilling yes or no answer, or distorted summary; (2) *direct personal* attacks—slurs on the opponent's external characteristics, such as looks, age, or sex; attacks on the opponent's character such as truthfulness or motives; verbal aggressiveness, such as derogatory expressions, insults, and name calling; (3) *non-verbal expression of* hostility—through voice, facial expressions, body postures, or gestures.

There are, of course, degrees of hostility. We identified hostile debaters by asking whether their team had a number of the hostile features or used one of them repeatedly or emphatically, in such a way that the impression of hostility attached to the whole. By this criterion, 10 out of 62 debate teams were clearly eristic. Eight were more hostile than their opponents: four of these were winners, four losers.

The picture is thus inconclusive. However, one eristic feature that we found meaningful to test in isolation did seem to have a negative effect. This is a subtype of conspiracy arguments that we call the *coup argument:* The debater accuses the opponent of having a hidden agenda behind his or her claim. Teams with this feature won twice but lost seven times ($p = .1796$, two-tailed). Their average rank was 10.8 (against a total average of 16). Eight of nine debaters using coup arguments were in the B group;

these defenders of the status quo ranked significantly lower than the rest ($p = .05$, two-tailed).

Nonsupportive Testimony. A few debaters used witnesses who explicitly did not support their claims. We found two types: (1) neutral witnesses, who took no stand on the claim, and (2) disagreeing witnesses, who supported the opponent's claim.

These strategies recall the distinction between biased, unbiased, and reluctant testimony (Arnold and McCroskey, 1967). They reflect the debater's confidence that "bare facts" will persuade the jurors. Apparently, they do not. Only one debater using non-supportive testimony won; four lost. Their average rank was 9.3 (against 16). The reason might be that if the testimony offered by the witness does not warrant the claim in the eyes of the witness him- or herself, why should it impress the jurors? There may also be an ethos effect: a debater who says, "We just lay down the facts, we don't tell you what to think," may seem not to care about the audience's opinion, thus wasting its time and, in fact, declaring his or her own evidence irrelevant.

Types of Grounds. The types of grounds offered by debaters formed a major part of our study. (We adopt the layout and terminology introduced by Toulmin, 1958, revised in Toulmin *et al.*, 1984.) Four types recurred constantly and cover most of the argumentation in the material: (1) examples used as precedents, which again were of three kinds—precedents from the past, contemporary precedents from other countries, and precedents based on analogy; (2) grounds involving statistical evidence; (3) specific instances; and (4) ideological grounds. A fifth main type, appeal to authority, was disregarded because the use of witnesses created a hybrid of expert testimony and external appeal to authority, making the distinction between them inoperative.

Contemporary precedents from other countries were used by one or both debaters in 23 of 31 debates. They appear to be a productive modern *topos,* an element in any debater's heuristics. By contrast, the past was rarely referred to and then mainly for negative precedents. A few positive models from the past were used to show the proposed action as one step in a long progression. Ideals were located in the future, not in the past as in the *topoi* of Founding Fathers and the Golden Age in the classical tradition (Finley, 1975; Zarefsky, 1990).

We saw no persuasive effect of precedents as such. The important distinction, one might assume, is between using them well and badly. The lack of an operational criterion of good precedents prevented us from testing this assumption.

A similar dim picture emerged concerning the effect of statistical evidence. Debaters who used expert witnesses to present a high concentration of numerical information won four times and lost four times. Four teams that used decidedly more statistical evidence than their opponents won, and seven lost.

An interesting type of ground was the single, specific instance of the issue at hand. In our definition, a specific instance should narrate a specific episode, real or hypothetical, or introduce a representative specimen, such as a witness who testifies on the impact of a proposed action for the company where she works, without narrating one evolving event. Such specific instances, however, appeared in most debates. We did not test how users compared with nonusers because there were issues for which specific instances would have been less appropriate. However, the few debaters who, in our view, might have relied much more on them than they did ranked far below average.

Sharpening our criterion, we identified debaters who devoted an entire testimony (out of three) to a first-hand account by the witness of a specific instance. These 22 debaters ranked above average, but not significantly. Second, we ventured to apply qualitative criteria. We defined a good specific instance as one that was relevant and weighty. A similar requirement relating to arguments generally was suggested by Hitchcock (1992). Five debaters had obvious problems with the relevance or weight of the instances they presented. We applied the criterion with caution, eliminating only instances whose off-the-point or trivial characters was, in our view, blatant. Of those who remained, nine won and two lost ($p = .0327$); the rank order test yielded $p < .06$ for the A group and $p < .05$ for the B group. This strongly suggests that first-hand testimony relating a relevant and weighty specific instance is persuasive.

We hypothesized, more generally, that any good use of specific instantiation is persuasive. To test this, we considered the amount of specific instantiation presented by each debater, firsthand or secondhand. A debater was considered to have more specific instantiation than his or her opponent if the difference was at least of the order of one elaborated instance or two instances that were somewhat extended. Again, we disregarded specific instances that we considered obviously irrelevant or trivial. Of the 17 debaters who had more relevant, weighty specific instantiation than their opponents, 12 won and five lost ($p = .0717$). We take this as confirmation that in issue-oriented debates, what we may call extended use of good specific instances is a persuasive feature.

A very different strategy is what we call ideological grounds. We are not using the term in the Marxist sense of "false consciousness." Rather, in a non-evaluative way, "ideological" for us refers to argumentation in which a debater supports his or her claim by identifying the issue as an instance of a more abstract evaluative concept.[17]

Ideological grounds abounded in a debate on abortion; one side argued that "No one should have the right to *exterminate others,*" and the other said that "Every woman should have the right to *control her own life*" (our italics). "Exterminate others" and "control one's own life" are evaluative terms far higher on a ladder of abstraction than the issue at hand: abortion. Twelve debaters clearly offered ideological notions (as defined here) as important, independent grounds for their claim. Their average rank was 11.0 (against 16). In the eight debates in which ideological debaters confronted non-ideological opponents, they lost every time ($p = .0078$, two-tailed). As the groups were small, a two-tailed rank order test gave less impressive results ($p < .20$ in both groups). All 10 debaters using ideological grounds more than their opponents lost ($p = .0020$, two-tailed).

As with many other features, we realize that the apparent preference in the audience for non-ideological grounds, even if internally valid, may not transfer to other situations; however, in a forensic debate format like *Town Parliament,* the use of ideological grounds seems to be a losing strategy.

Why? One reason might be that ideological grounds offer no new information. Placing abortion under the category "extermination of life" does not extend or deepen the audience's store of facts about abortion.

In this sense, ideological argument and specific instantiation represent opposite extremes on the same dimension. Specific instantiation is about the concrete, everyday consequences of a proposition; moving down on a ladder of abstraction, the debater finds instances of the issue, giving information that is perhaps new to the audience and in any case "enhancing

---

[17] Recently, there have been several attempts to redefine ideology, separating the concept from the false consciousness notion of critical and Marxist theory and bringing it in line with the more intuitive way it is used in everyday political commentary (Flood, 1996; Hinich and Munger, 1994). An ideology, in these attempts, is a system of generalized, evaluative concepts that subsumes many specific phenomena. An individual holding an ideology is able to take a stand on an issue as soon as the issue is subsumed under an ideological concept, without requiring additional or specific information about it. Argumentation that seeks to persuade by subsuming phenomena in this way is, in our terminology, ideological.

presence" (Perelman and Olbrechts-Tyteca, 1969). Ideological grounds represent an upward move on the same ladder, classifying the issue as one instance of an evaluative abstraction. The two opposite strategies are independently distributed, permitting us to add up the two results; in conjunction, they indicate strongly that persuasiveness in an issue-oriented debate increases with the amount of relevant and weighty instantiation.

Rhetorical Strategy. Gradually, we became aware of two opposite tendencies in overall argumentative strategy. Some debaters tended to base their claims on multiple grounds: parallel, mutually independent grounds in direct support of their claim. Others used a single ground: one central or overarching reason, which may be supported by subordinate grounds or supplemented by rebuttals of the opponent's grounds. To make this distinction manageable, we coded debaters' strategy on the basis of their concluding speeches.

Single-ground debaters won 11 times and lost three times ($p = .0574$). The rank order test for A debaters yielded $p = .14$; for B debaters, $p = .08$. Multiple-ground debaters lost 12 times and won twice ($p = .0130$). The rank order test for A debaters yielded $p = .10$; for B debaters, $p = .28$ (two-tailed). A rank order test on degrees of singularity showed that winners ranked significantly higher on this feature than losers ($p < .01$, two-tailed).

This result might be taken to suggest that jurors prefer simplistic views, but it might also be attributable to the presence of a focus in the debater's performance. Much work in writing pedagogy and rhetoric emphasizes the importance of structuring utterances around one organizing viewpoint: a well-formed text should "say one thing" (Meyer, 1975; Murray, 1984). Such a strategy creates a hierarchy, rather than a battery, of arguments. The dominance of one ground means that more evidence and instantiation may be offered in its support, and this may account for the persuasiveness of the single-ground strategy. This fits with the observation that several debaters whose concluding speeches were not of the single-ground type but who all along dwelled much longer on one ground than on others also did very well.

A related criterion is whether debaters' concluding speeches were largely repetitions of their opening remarks or largely presented material not found there. Debaters of the former type won six times and lost three times; debaters of the latter type won three times and lost eight times. A rank order test on degree of repetition showed that winners tended to rank higher on this feature than losers ($p = .07$).

This feature seems related to another strategy: having the last word. Some debaters managed to make an interrogation end in a way that emphasized an important point of their own—either by leading the witness to give the exact answer needed to emphasize the point or by stating it in a remark of their own. Debaters who failed to have the last word let interrogations end at points that seemed arbitrary, often because they could think of no further questions, or they tried to have the last word but were beaten to it by the witness. Last-word debaters, remarkably, won 19 times and lost twice ($p < .0001$). The rank order test yielded $p < .01$ for both groups. We do not interpret this as showing that jurors prefer slogan-laden or repetitive argumentation. Instead, we suggest that they reward the last word debater's manifest energy and will to present a unified argument.

Finally, what we call *claim demarcation* helps complete the picture of winning strategy. In the debate on abortion, the anti-abortionist demarcated his claim, stating that the issue was "not whether abortions may occur at all, but whether abortions may be performed for *any reason whatever, however trivial or frivolous.*" The function of this maneuver is to indicate that one's claim is narrower than some people might think. Logically, this is unnecessary, but rhetorically it is meaningful to signal to the jurors that they should only change their views in a specified respect, not adopt an entirely new outlook. Debaters whose concluding speech demarcated their claim won 12 times and lost three times ($p = .0352$, two-tailed). The rank order tests yielded $p = 0.01$ for the A group, $p = 0.05$ for the B group.

We believe this feature tallies with other observations we have made on argumentative strategy. What the typical winning debater did was to press one point (a single ground) with comprehensive support (specific instantiation) in an insistent manner (last word) to gain adherence to an explicitly limited claim (claim demarcation).

Discussion

Overall Pattern and Underlying Persuasive Qualities. The features we have identified above are situated on different levels of abstraction: some are specific and local, others represent more abstract properties.[18] To

---

[18] In addition to the statistics described, we used two types of multivariate analysis: logistic regression and CART (classification and regression trees). In their way, these may reveal whether any features have special power to predict winners. (Only the winner/loser parameter was used, not rank orders.)

Logistic regression, performed on all debaters for whom data on all features were

extract a pattern and explain how it portrays the persuasive debater, we now shift to a more speculative, qualitative mode, looking for underlying qualities that may be too abstract to be testable.

We suggest that the following four factors may be seen as the fundamental persuasive qualities in the debate format we studied: precision, firmness, energy, and commitment. Clearly, these are interrelated and partly overlapping constructs.

They are all instantiated in the winning nonverbal features discussed above: modulated voice, energetic articulation, intense gaze, energetic posture, eager gesticulation, and firm, directive gestures. All of these instantiate energy and commitment. Intense gaze and firm, directive gestures signal firmness. Firm, directive gestures are highly specific and selectively used; that is, they demand and signal precision. Similarly, modulated voice and energetic articulation are used to reinforce selected aspects of content, thus reflecting the speaker's energy and commitment to what he or she says. Energy in articulation similarly signals insistence and hence firmness. Conversely, the significant losing features—monotonous voice and sloppy articulation—suggest the absence of all four underlying qualities.

The other results may, in retrospect, be reduced to the same denominators: If the evocation of applause and laughter is not persuasive, this may be because the debater seems to lack commitment and precision, expending energy on peripherals. Lack of precision might also explain the ineffectiveness of hostility and the negative effect of *coup* arguments: by

---

available, yielded the following features: (1) having the last word, (2) dismissive attitude (negative loading), (3) modulated voice, (4) the single ground (positive loading) versus multiple grounds (negative loading), (5) age over 55, (6) ordinary people used as witnesses (negative loading), and (7) full firsthand testimony giving a relevant and weighty specific instance.

When the A and B groups were analyzed separately, three additional features emerged: for the A group, claim demarcation and all-male debate team and for the B group, ideological grounds (negative loading).

CART yielded an inverted tree in which each node bifurcated into a winner branch and a loser branch. The winner's route in the CART analysis (based on the 30 debaters for whom all data were available) contained the following three features: (1) having the last word, (2) multiple grounds (negative loading), and (3) monotonous voice (negative loading). In other words, any debater in our material who had the last word, did not use multiple grounds, and did not speak in a monotonous voice was a winner.

CART analysis also yielded an alternative ordered list of highly predictive features, which included, in addition to features already mentioned, the winning nonverbal features discussed above and conspiracy arguments (negative loading).

stooping to personal attack rather than concentrating on the issue, the debater expends energy diffusely. Nonsupportive testimony obviously reflects noncommitment. Ideological grounds are weak in issue-oriented debates-possibly because the concepts they appeal to are by nature vague. Specific instantiation embodies precision by supplying in-depth, detailed information; the insistence of debaters who stay on one specific instance throughout a whole testimony signals energy and firmness. The power of the single-ground strategy, and the weakness of parallel grounds, bespeaks jurors' preference for argumentation that concentrates its energy rather than being wasted across a wide range. Similarly, in claim demarcation the claim is circumscribed with careful precision. Finally, debaters who want to have the last word must stick firmly to their line of argument and energetically drive home their precise point at the strategic moment.

It is natural here to raise a question that has hovered in our minds throughout this project: does our profile of the winning debater bring alarm or reassurance for those who are concerned about norms of discourse in public debate? In incisive analyses, Kathleen Hall Jamieson (1992) called for "fair, accurate, contextual, comparative, engaged campaign discourse" (p. 11). She also demonstrated that whereas campaigning politicians failed to honor this ideal, in congressional debates they

> delivered thoughtful speeches that engaged the ideas of others, examined evidence, and moved with care to warranted conclusions. ... The members of Congress spoke a language of good will, presuming the integrity of those in disagreement. Rarely were the motives or integrity of those in disagreement impugned. (Jamieson, 1992, pp. 203-204)

Does our typical debate winner resemble the dirty campaigner or the thoughtful lawmaker?

Our answer is that the representative audiences in our debates cast their vote for evidence and thoughtful reasoning. Our winning debaters, we suggest, would on the whole be applauded by those who, like Jamieson, call for reasoned argument in public debate.

Vote-Gathering Versus Vote-Shifting Rhetoric. The two faces of the modern politician portrayed by Jamieson (1992) resemble two modes of political rhetoric exemplified in *Town Parliament.* As explained, we have, for 20 of the 37 debates, data on how many jurors moved between the yes, no, and undecided groups. We did not use these incomplete data statistically, but they suggest an interesting pattern.

In bipartisan debates there are two ways to win votes. Vote-gathering is to win undecided votes; vote-shifting is to win votes from the opposition. Winning debaters generally do both, but some debaters are much better in one of these respects than in the other. Typical vote-gatherers seem to prefer ideological arguments; they lean toward categorical, polarized formulations; and they tend to use attention-getting devices reminiscent of popular journalism. They are "telegenic." Typical vote-shifters, by contrast, tend to use the single ground strategy; they use much specific instantiation; they often demarcate their claims; and they are generally moderate and polite verbally as well as nonverbally. They are less sprightly than vote-gatherers, but more earnest and insistent.

An interesting point is that whereas vote-gatherers are undoubtedly favored by television and other popular media, the winner in debates of the type we studied was more likely to be a typical vote-shifter.[19]

The reason is simple. On two-way issues, votes won from the opposition count twice: down for them, up for us. And although partisan voters are no doubt less volatile than the undecided, they were also, in our material, more numerous: on the average, there were 10 undecided voters in the first poll (of which about eight took sides in the second poll) against 90 partisan voters (of which about nine changed sides and about two joined the undecided). Hence, when a pure vote-gatherer confronts a pure vote-shifter, the latter is likely to win. In other words, a strategy in issue-oriented debates that concentrates on those of the opponent's followers that can be shifted, rather than on the undecided, leads to higher standards of argument, and it pays.

Such a result flouts much contemporary campaign strategy, perhaps especially in the United States. A likely explanation is that in American presidential elections, the turnout is usually about 50 percent, which means that an obvious strategy is to gather (mobilize) some of the passive 50 percent. Even John Kennedy was a typical vote-gatherer: an interview survey (Lang and Lang, 1962) showed that in the Kennedy-Nixon television debates, he won 18 new votes (out of 95). However, only three of these 18 were shifted from Nixon's side, whereas 15 had been undecided (who all declared that they were basically Democrats). By contrast, with only 10 percent undecided in our study (paralleling the fact

---

[19] It is suggestive that of five politicians who were singled out in a newspaper article by two noted media experts as exceptionally able to "communicate on TV" *(Politiken,* March 14, 1989), four had appeared as debaters in *Town* Parliament—and lost.

that the turnout in Danish elections usually is between 80 percent and 90 percent), typical vote gatherers had fewer latent followers to mobilize.

How far are the hypotheses in this study generalizable to other types of debate, particularly the "vote-for-me" debates so typical of political campaigns? We cannot be sure, but we assume that, all else equal, those by whom we are persuaded in deliberative debate, that is, those we trust to advise us best, are also those we trust to lead us best. The qualities we have posited in our interpretation of the data—precision, firmness, energy, and commitment—all seem as relevant in leadership as in deliberation. Of course all else is *not* equal. There is more to leadership than these qualities, but why should there be a contradiction? If vote winning in presidential campaign advertising, for example, seems to follow different rules from what we see in our study, then the reason may have to do with the medium and the format rather than with any intrinsic difference between issue-oriented and candidate-oriented debates. Determining how far the similarity goes between winning behavior in deliberative and personalized debate is a task for further studies.

On an even more general level, we may also ask whether the effects we have suggested will transfer from a Danish context. Cultures differ, and political cultures differ even more, so we might well have to do with purely local patterns. For example, our results on the effects of hostility or the inducement of laughter and applause might merely reflect the fact that this is an audience of Scandinavians, whom cultural cliché portrays as cool, inhibited, and conflict shunning.

Even so, there is a marked difference between the winner's profile in our *quasi* forensic debate format and the features that are considered winning in typical television-mediated communication. Our main hypothesis, then, is that debate format makes a difference and that this difference is hardly culture specific. Even if vote-gatherers have better chances in a typical American context, we hypothesize that a live debate in a format such as ours would still be more congenial to fair, evidence-oriented rhetoric, as represented by our winner's profile, than typical television-mediated formats. Future research and experience might put this hypothesis to the test. If it finds support, political communication scholars would have reason to take a heightened interest in alternative political debate formats. David Weaver (1994), among others, has discussed how nontraditional media, such as electronic and televised town hall meetings, contribute to political agenda setting, enhancing voter involvement. Our study suggests, apart from this effect, that a town hall meeting format, if administered by the producers in proper respect of its deliberative functions, may also enhance the quality of political debate by rewarding engaged, thoughtful, accurate discourse.

Indeed, we might speculate whether political debates, even when candidate or party oriented, might not, in the public interest, be turned more toward sustained deliberation on issues. Leaders could be figures with visions of what to do and engagement to persuade a majority that they are right, rather than figures who promise to do what a majority wants. What the media could do would be to let candidates holding opposite views on key issues engage in sustained forensic-type debates with, for instance, one issue per debate; the journalists might then act more as mere keepers of order.

Perspective: A Future for Deliberative Rhetoric

In recent years, the role of television as a medium for political debate has caused increasing concern. Appearing on Danish television on August 15, 1993, the Nestor of television journalism, Walter Cronkite, expressed disillusionment over the state of democratic debate mediated by television:

> Our use of television for political campaigns has been absolutely disastrous to the democracy. Here is this magnificent medium to carry meaningful debate on the serious subjects under consideration by the government to the people, and it is not used in that fashion at all. Our debates are a laugh. They are not debates at all, they are shows.

Our main point is that debates in a format like the *Town Parliament* are generally not a laughing matter. Voters here tend to reward debaters who act out principles of serious deliberative argument, highlighting an ironic contradiction between what television as a medium appears to demand and the criteria for deliberative debate. Jurors laughed at the entertaining debater's wisecracks—and voted for the opponent. This calls to mind Bennett's (1992, p. 402) paradox: "people tune in, but ultimately turn against, the politicians and journalists who make the news." As voters, ballot in hand, we seem to judge the persuasiveness of a debater's case by criteria other than those by which we, as viewers, remote control in hand, respond to television programs.

Currently, political communication seems dominated by viewers' needs, not voters'. Political debate is equated with quarrel and telegenic spectacle. But if television continues to disregard our needs as voters, we may become a body of cheering or jeering spectators, with no real participation in the political process.

However, scholars in communication and rhetoric should not turn cynical. We believe our study suggests that there is indeed a place, even today, for deliberative public debate. Television has, irreversibly, become the town hall where most public communication is transacted; our interpretation of the *Town Parliament* supports a call for debate formats on television that rely on deliberative argument. Whatever fare television viewers prefer, we suggest that as voters, watching such debates, they demand and reward thoughtful, engaged persuasion, delivered in the language of good will.

REFERENCES

Arnold, W.E., and J.C. McCroskey. 1967. The credibility of reluctant testimony. *Central States Speech Journal* 18, 97-103.

Atkinson, M. 1984. *Our Masters' Voices: The Language and Body-language of Politics.* London: Methuen.

Bennett, W.L. 1992. White noise: The perils of mass mediated democracy. *Communication Monographs* 59, 401-406.

Finley, M.I. 1975. *The Use and Abuse of History.* London: Chatto and Windus.

Flood, C. 1996. *Political Myth: A Theoretical Introduction.* New York: Garland Press.

Flower, L. 1985. *Problem-solving Strategies for Writing.* New York: Harcourt Brace Jovanovich.

Goffman, E. 1955. On face-work: An analysis of ritual elements in social interaction. *Psychiatry* 18, 213-231.

Hinich, M. J., and M.C. Munger. 1994. *Ideology and the Theory* of *Political Choice.* Ann Arbor: University of Michigan Press.

Hitchcock, D. 1992. Relevance. *Argumentation* 6, 251-270.

Hovland, C.I., I.L. Janis, and H.H. Kelley. 1953. *Communication and Persuasion: Psychological Studies of Opinion Change.* New Haven: Yale University Press.

Hunt, K.. 1965. *Grammatical Structures Written at Three Grade Levels.* Champaign, IL: National Council of Teachers of English.

Infante, D.A., K.C. Hartley, M.M. Martin, M.A. Higgins, S.D. Bruning, and G. Hur. 1992. Initiating and reciprocating verbal aggression: Effects on credibility and credited valid arguments. *Communication Studies* 43, 182- 190.

Jamieson, K.H. 1992. *Dirty Politics: Deception, Distraction, and Democracy.* New York: Oxford University Press.

Jamieson, K.H., and D.S. Birdsell. 1988. *Presidential Debates: The Challenge of Creating an Informed Electorate.* New York: Oxford University Press.

Jørgensen, C. 1998. Public debate—an act of hostility? *Argumentation* 12, 431-443.

Jørgensen, C., C. Kock, and L. Rørbech. 1994. *Retorik der flytter stemmer: Hvordan man overbeviser i offentlig debat.* Copenhagen: Gyldendal.

Lang, K., and G.E. Lang. 1962. Reactions of viewers. In S. Kraus (Ed.), *The Great Debates: Kennedy vs. Nixon, 1960.* Bloomington: Indiana University Press, 313-330.

McCroskey, J.C. 1997. *An Introduction to Rhetorical Communication,* 7th ed. Boston: Allyn and Bacon.

Meyer, B.J.F. 1975. *The Organization of Prose and its Effects on Memory.* Amsterdam: North-Holland.

Murray, D.M. 1984. *A Writer Teaches Writing.* Boston: Houghton Mifflin.

Perelman, C., and L. Olbrechts-Tyteca. 1969. *The New Rhetoric: A Treatise on Argumentation.* Notre Dame, IN: Notre Dame University Press.

Toulmin, S.E. 1958. *The Uses of Argument.* Cambridge, England: Cambridge University Press.

Toulmin, S.E., R. Rieke, and A. Janik. 1984. *An Introduction to Reasoning.* New York: Macmillan.

Walton, D.N. 1989. *Informal Logic: A Handbook for Critical Argumentation.* Cambridge, England: Cambridge University Press.

Walton, D.N. 1992. *Plausible Argument in Everyday Conversation.* Albany: State University of New York Press.

Weaver, D. 1994. Media agenda setting and elections: Voter involvement or alienation. *Political Communication* 11, 347-356.

Zarefsky, D. 1990. *Lincoln, Douglas, and Slavery: In the Crucible of Public Debate.* Chicago, IL: University of Chicago Press.

13.

The Rhetorical Audience in Public Debate and the Strategies of Vote-Gathering and Vote-Shifting*

We argue in this paper that public political debates should not be seen as "dialogic," but instead as "trialogic," i.e., staged for the benefit of the audience, whose members may use a debate as help to take a stand, or as reason to change a stand they already hold. We criticize the view reflected in opinion polls and much political journalism that the voters, except for the undecided, have already taken permanent stands. Recalling and exemplifying our own distinction between vote-gathering and vote-shifting rhetoric, we argue that many voters can indeed be shifted. We propose a simple taxonomy of voters, based on the two parameters "involvement" and "assurance," which yields four types: spectators, partisans, abstainers, and deliberating citizens. The latter, high on involvement but often less high on assurance, are the ones most likely to be shifted, and rhetoric aimed at them would, we suggest, give us more democratically useful debates.

In the pragma-dialectical approach to argumentation, as represented by van Eemeren and Grootendorst (e.g., 1992) or Walton (1989, 1992, 1995*),* *critical discussion* provides the normative model for rational argument. But do the norms for critical discussion also apply to political *debate?* As rhetoricians, we insist that critical discussion and political debate are different genres with different norms. Critical discussion is *dialogical,* debate is *trialogical* (Dieckmann 1981, Klein 1991). The arguers in the discussion address each other with the cooperative goal of *resolving the dispute;* debaters do not argue in order to persuade each other, but to win the adherence of a third party: the audience (Jørgensen 1998).

Because of its trialogical nature, a debate must answer the needs of the

* This article was co-authored with Charlotte Jørgensen. It was originally published in *Proceedings of the Fourth International Conference of the International Society for the Study of Argumentation*, F.H. van Eemeren, R. Grootendorst, J.A. Blair, and C.A. Willard (Eds.): Amsterdam: SIC SAT 1999, 420-423. Reprinted with permission of the Publisher.

audience. This means that a debate should be evaluated in relation to the functions it fulfils. This does not mean that our approach is oriented toward uses and gratifications in the traditional sense. We are interested not only in the functions of debate, but also in the specific features of debates that serve these functions: and our approach is normative.

We shall concentrate on *issue-oriented debates,* such as the Irish debate over the Ulster peace plan, or the Danish debate over the Amsterdam treaty. What we have to say about the rhetorical audience and the quality of public debate has particular reference to how debate is conducted on TV.

Opinion polls will tell us that the audience of such debates consists of three groups: those in favor, those against, and the undecided. Commentators typically refer to the undecided as those who have not made up their minds yet, implying that all the others have indeed made up their minds. Accordingly, it is assumed that the outcome depends on the remaining undecided voters.

But this is misleading. Both among those in favor and among those against, there are many who have not made their minds up, and who may well change sides—under the influence of events or arguments. To document this, we may cite a poll in the French daily *Libération* shortly before the referendum in France on the Maastricht treaty in 1992. Here—interestingly—voters were asked whether they might change sides on the issue. No less than 37 % of those who intended to vote yes admitted they might also vote no, and conversely for 34 % of those who said they intended to vote no. It is probably true that especially in matters concerning the European Union many voters are of two minds; they feel that there are arguments on both sides of the issue, and they are constantly weighing them against each other.

What this means is that on any issue, the audience represents a spectrum of opinion, with unmovable partisans at both ends, and with a fair number of voters near the middle of the road who lean to one side but who may be shifted. But debaters and TV programmers tend to make the undecided their primary target because they falsely believe that the static and simplistic Yes-Undecided-No model says all one needs to know about the debate audience. They forget the lesson of the Danish referendum which rejected Maastricht because many voters changed sides at a late stage, even at the polling station.

To understand how some voters can thus be of two minds, we shall propose a model of the debate audience (inspired by Tonsgaard 1992).

This, in turn, will allow us to distinguish between the different functions of debate for the public audience.

In Figure 1 (next page), the undecided are represented by the area beneath the curve. The area above it represents the decided voters, i.e., those who say that they are going to vote yes or no, respectively. Those near the curve are the hesitant voters. The point is that there are two variables which may explain why voters hesitate. These are represented by the two axes.

The *x-axis* represents *involvement in the issue,* that is, how important the voter perceives the issue to be. The *y-axis* represents the voter's feeling of *assurance* on the issue. Those high in both assurance and involvement belong in the area marked "P" (for partisans). What they will want from debates is mainly reinforcement of their existing views. Those low in both assurance and involvement will belong in the area marked "A" (for abstainers, because these people will probably end up not voting at all). But it is also possible to have a quite fixed and assured view of the issue, either for it or against it, and yet feel that it is all quite distant and uninteresting. These voters—high in assurance but low in involvement—will be in the "S" area (for Spectators). They will probably feel little need for guidance because they know what they think—but more of a need for entertainment, and some need for reinforcement. Finally, many voters—certainly in Denmark—see the European issue as highly important, but also as complex and baffling; and that is why they are hesitant. These voters—who are high in involvement but low in assurance—belong in the "D" area (for deliberating citizens). Although they lean to one side, they feel they need to know and understand more, because they are still of two minds; hence they want the ongoing debate to give them guidance for the decision they confront.

This segmentation of the debate audience reflects the analysis of three of the audience roles defined by Gurevitch and Blumler (1977). Their account also includes roles for "media personnel" and "party spokesmen," as seen in table 1 (next page).

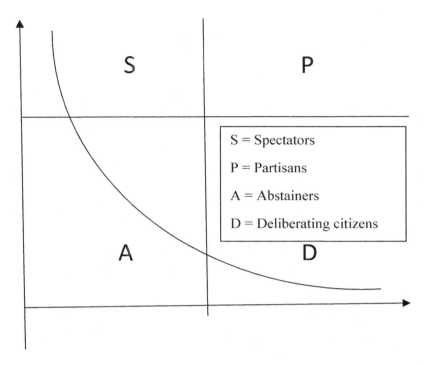

Figure 1: The Rhetorical Debate Audience

Audience	Media Personnel	Party Spokesmen
Partisan	Editorial guide	Gladiator
Liberal citizen	Moderator	Rational persuader
Monitor	Watchdog	Information provider
Spectator	Entertainer	Actor/Performer

Table 1: The Complementarity of Roles in
a Political Communication System

In our context, we may disregard the "monitor" role, since we regard it as less relevant for members of a debate audience, and more applicable to, for example, political scientists and commentators. What the voter seeks when he appears in the partisan role is precisely "reinforcement of his existing beliefs"; as a spectator, he seeks "excitement and other affective satisfactions"; as a deliberating citizen— or, as Gurevitch and Blumler have it, "liberal citizen"—the voter seeks "guidance in deciding how to vote" (1977, p. 276).

Our model of the debate audience explains the notion of audience roles and their underlying parameters. The model also implies that there are two basically different ways that a debater can try to increase adherence to his view, depending on to which segment of the model he is mainly appealing.

1) The debater can prefer to appeal mainly to those who are rather high in assurance, but low in involvement. These people will basically tend to choose the spectator role. Since they are rather assured about their views, the debater must concentrate on those voters in this group who lean to his side already. Those who plan to vote for the side anyway will merely have their enthusiasm boosted. Those who might not have voted may be stimulated to come out and do so. Thus the way this strategy may gain votes is by mobilizing some of the undecided vote. We call this strategy *vote-gathering.*

2) The other general strategy is to appeal to those voters who lean to the other side but who may be won over. These people are high in involvement, that is, they think the issue is important; but they are low in assurance. Typically, they arc deliberating citizens who acknowledge that there are two sides to the issue and that their decision should be based on the weight of the arguments. As we have pointed out, there are often a substantial number of such voters on both sides. We call this strategy *vote-shifting.*

The distinction between vote-gathering and vote-shifting was one of the perspectives we became aware of in a study of televised public policy debates in Denmark (Jørgensen, Kock, and Rørbech 1994; 1998; this volume, Chapter 12). In these debates we found voting patterns suggesting that some debaters are particularly good at vote-gathering, others at vote-shifting. For example, in one debate, in front of a hundred representative jurors, one debater gathered no less than 14 votes from the undecided group, but she shifted only one from the opposite side; the opponent gathered just 5, but shifted 9. This is shown in Figure 2, where the blue columns show votes gathered and the red ones show votes shifted.

The typical vote-gatherer will tend to claim fundamental, black-and-white differences and introduce a series of further points of contention that will broaden the front between the two sides. He will claim a fundamental ideological opposition between the two sides: he will impute a series of further claims and positions to the opponent that have not been mentioned by the opponent himself; he will see the opponent's proposal as "the thin end of the wedge," as part of a large campaign, or even of a conspiracy; he may attack his opponent's motives, he may bring in matters that cast doubt on the opponent's intelligence, ethics, or good will; he will typically attack the weakest arguments made by the opponent, trying to make them out as ridiculous, or as self-contradictory. Front-broadening arguers generally spend much energy on refutations of arguments made by the opponent, and on counter-refutations of refutations, and so on *ad infinitum.*

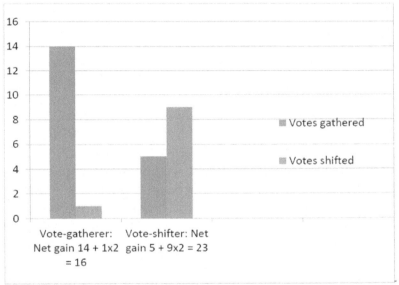

Figure 2: A vote-gatherer vs. a vote-shifter

Figure 2: A vote-gatherer vs. a vote-shifter

In all this, the issue at hand will often disappear in a confusing verbal duel. As audience, we may find ourselves turning our heads back from right to left and back again, as if watching a tennis match. Refutation and counter-refutation are what we would call *secondary* argumentation, as distinct from *primary* arguments. These are the grounds offered by the debaters in direct support of their standpoints—i.e., the main merits of their own proposal, or the drawbacks of the opponent's. Throughout, the front-broadening debater introduces topics of disagreement that are not necessary to elucidate the disagreement at hand.

The vote-shifter, on the other hand, will argue so as to narrow the front, concentrating on the specific issue that separates the opponents. He will, for example, concede that the opponent has certain weighty arguments, but he will then try to show that his own arguments are weightier. He will typically narrow or demarcate his claim, stating, for example, that he does not advocate a federal super-state in Europe, but that he does strongly advocate a union of nation states for certain reasons. He will concentrate on his own *primary* grounds for his claim; for example, he will concentrate on the main reasons why he thinks the Amsterdam treaty is a good idea (or, if he is against it, a bad idea), and he will spend less energy refuting the opponent's grounds, or counter-refuting the opponent's refutations. We might add that this emphasis on primary grounds, rather than on refutation, is one point where our normative criteria, based on audience needs, differ from the norms for critical discussion.

Furthermore, the front-narrowing debater will treat his opponent with politeness and respect and avoid face-threatening attacks on his person, ethics, and competence. In all these maneuvers, the debater seeks to find and preserve whatever common ground there is between the opposite sides, narrowing the front to what is absolutely necessary.

In terms of the traditional rhetorical appeals, the vote-gatherer will rely heavily on *pathos* and will, for instance, use Atkinson's "claptraps" in abundance (Atkinson 1984). As is well known, Atkinson described two principal types of claptrap: *the contrast*, which is clearly a front-broadening feature, and the *list of three*, a schematic figure of great dynamism, known from ritual and folk literature. Both are clearly front-broadening devices to enhance the feeling of "us" against "them." The use of these devices will help the vote-gatherer boost the partisan's spirit and give the spectators a good show. The vote-shifter, in contrast, relies mainly on *logos* appeals and avoids devices that may appear cheap or facile. As for *ethos,* the vote-gatherer will tend to impress by being either sparkling or passionate, while the vote-shifter tends to be a more academic type, perhaps slightly stiff and dry, but serious and knowledgeable.

All in all, it is clear that of these two types of argumentation, the vote-gathering, front-broadening type is by far the more "telegenic," as media people say. This brings us to the role of TV in public debate.

Now, our point in contrasting the two types is of course not that debaters should become pure vote-shifters and never try to be vote-gatherers. Surely good debaters are those who manage to combine elements from both strategies. Nor do we claim that vote-gathering is bad rhetoric at all times. Many situations call especially for vote-gathering; but issue-oriented debate does not. The problem is that many forces in modern TV-mediated democracy unite in suppressing the kind of political argument that aspires, and inspires, to vote-shifting debate. TV debates, when best, are both entertaining and informative. But at times there is a conflict. What works well as TV is often front-broadening features that leave little opportunity for vote-shifting rhetoric to unfold; what boosts and entertains partisans and spectators often alienates the deliberating citizen looking for guidance. In consequence, the media furthers the transformation of citizens to a body of, in Jamieson's words, viewers "observing the 'sport' of politics" (Jamieson 1992, p. 191).

Front-broadening, vote-gathering TV debates thus appear to be the modem version of sophistic rhetoric. Sophistic debate is basically a type of combat, with debaters in the role of gladiators, in Gurevitch and Blumler's term. Such a debate may serve a mobilizing purpose for us if we are partisans of the gladiators, but that role easily slips into the purely *spectatorial* role where debaters are as much actors, at whose performance we either applaud or hiss. This audience role echoes Aristotle's description of the auditor as "spectator'"" in epideictic speech, vs. the role as "judge" in political and forensic speech. According to Aristotle, the spectator is concerned with the ability of the speaker (*Rhetoric* III, 1358b). The spectator, as George Kennedy explains, "is not called upon to take a specific action, in the way that an assemblyman or juryman is called upon to vote"; the whole event becomes "an oratorical contest" (Aristotle 1991, p. 48, note 77)—which is also how commentators see it when they discuss which politician "did best" in a TV debate. Thus the deliberative function of debate is suppressed by the simplistic question, so dear to the media, of "who loses and who wins." While spectators see such debates as sporting events, their effect on partisans may be described in the words of Perelman and Olbrechts-Tyteca commenting on the epideictic genre: "the argumentation in epidictic discourse sets out to increase the intensity of adherence to certain values" (1969, p. 51).

What is problematic with the spectator and partisan roles according to the deliberative ideal is that they tend to turn the audience into mere bystanders rather than participants in the political process. Only as deliberating citizens do we become a genuine rhetorical audience in Bitzer's sense of the word—an audience of decision-makers "capable of being influenced by discourse and of being mediators of change" (Bitzer 1968; 1992, p. 7).

We may compare our view here with Walton's pragmatic approach: Walton is critical of debaters who have *fixed* positions, so that there is no "genuine chance of either side persuading the other" (1992, p. 157). However, Walton ignores the trialogical nature of debate, which makes it quite acceptable for debaters to be unwilling to be persuaded by each other. What threatens the legitimacy of debate is when it is conducted in such a way that there is no chance of anyone in the *audience* shifting to the other side.

To sum up, what we advocate in issue-oriented debate is that vote-shifting argumentation be allowed to unfold—i.e., argumentation strongly characterized by the features we have called front-narrowing. The purpose, of course, is not the shifting of voters as such. We call for more vote-shifting argumentation for normative reasons. We propose that if debaters argue with the shiftable voters on the opposite side as their primary addressees, this would stimulate them to produce *convincing argumentation*, i.e., arguments that those on both sides of the boundary who recognize the force of argument would consider weighty—whether they are persuaded by them or not. Thus, the deliberative goal would not be lost, namely that of providing citizens with the best arguments on both sides, to be weighed against each other, in order to reach a decision. The net result at the polling station would perhaps be pretty much the same. But decisions would be made on a firmer basis, and debates would better serve the purpose of informed political argument. They would not degenerate into mere sports events for spectators or pep talk for partisans, and citizens might remain active participants in the political process.

REFERENCES

Aristotle. 1991. *On Rhetoric: A Theory of Civic Discourse.* G. Kennedy, (Ed.). New York: Oxford University Press.

Atkinson, M. 1984. *Our Masters' Voices: The Language and Body Language of Politics.* London: Methuen.

Bitzer, L.F. 1968. The rhetorical situation. *Philosophy and Rhetoric* 1, 1-14. (Reprinted in Supplementary Issue 1992.)

Eemeren, F.H. van & R. Grootendorst. 1992. *Argumentation, Communication, and Fallacies. A Pragma-Dialectical Perspective.* Hillsdale, NJ: Lawrence Erlbaum Associate.

Gurevitch, M., and J.G. Blumler. 1977. Linkages between the mass media and politics: A model for the analysis of political communication systems. In J. Curran, M. Gurevitch, and J. Woollacott (Eds.) *Mass Communication and Society.* London: Edward Arnold, 270- 290.

Jamieson, K.H. 1992. *Dirty Politics: Deception, Distraction, and Democracy.* New York: Oxford University Press.

Jørgensen, C. 1998. Public Debate—an Act of Hostility? *Argumentation* 12, 431-443.

Jørgensen, C., C. Kock, and L. Rørbech. 1994. *Retorik der flytter stemmer: Hvordan man overbeviser i offentlig debat.* Copenhagen: Gyldendal.

_____. 1998. Rhetoric that shifts votes: An exploratory study of persuasion in issue-oriented public debates. *Political Communication* 15, 283-299. (This volume, Chapter 12.)

Klein, J. 1981. Zur Rhetorik politischer Femsehdiskussionen. In Dieckmann, Walther. *Politische Sprache, Politische Kommunikation: Vortriige, Aufsiitze, Entwiirfe.* Heidelberg: Carl Winter Universitatsverlag.

Perelman, C., and L. Olbrechts-Tyteca. 1969. *The New Rhetoric: A Treatise on Argumentation.* J. Wilkinson and P. Weaver, trans. Notre Dame, IN: Notre Dame University Press.

Tonsgaard, O. 1992. A theoretical model of referendum behaviour. In P. Gundelach and Karen Siune (Eds.), *From Voters to Participants. Essays in Honour of Ole Borre.* Aarhus: Politica.

Ueding, G. (Ed.). 1991. Rhetorik zwischen den Wissenschaften. In *Geschichte, System, Praxis als Probleme des Historischen Wörterbuchs der Rhetorik.* Tübingen: Max Niemeyer. 353-362.

Walton, D.N. 1989. *Informal Logic: A Handbook for Critical Argumentation.* Cambridge: Cambridge University Press.

Walton, D.N. 1992. *Plausible Argument in Everyday Conversation.* Albany: State University of New York Press.

Walton, D.N. 1995. *A Pragmatic Theory of Fallacy.* Tuscaloosa: The University of Alabama Press.

14.

Evaluation of Public Spokespersons[*]

Based on empirical studies employing factor analysis, this paper proposes to see the two constructs "credibility" and "charisma" as two separate factors, both of which comprise properties desirable for a public spokesperson. This result contrasts with earlier studies of the credibility construct, which take it to merely be a covering umbrella term for all the properties that a public spokesperson might wish to have. We find credibility to comprise properties like intelligence and competence, but also—which is perhaps more noteworthy—ability to see a matter from different angles, balance, respect for others' opinions, and ability to admit a mistake. Charisma, in contrast, is comprised of properties including extroversion, passion, dynamism, and self-confidence.

"...but when I was speaking in America, they told me that there were 105 million TV sets in America ... It is a strange feeling to speak to millions of people. I think one feels it. There is something strange about television, very odd, also in another way. They told me over there that television is dangerous, it gives you away, you can't hide your true nature, appearing on television. They said that McCarthy, then a very popular person, was ruined in one or two days, after appearing on television. People did not believe him, or they did not trust him any more ... . In general, people who appeared on television over there were kind of "waterproof."

(Quotation from radio interview with Karen Blixen, 1955)

Background

In our generation, audio-visual media have become a dominant force in the public arena, for political debate, transmission of news, business, and for many other purposes. In this context, the *credibility* of public persons has become an important item in the public sphere. For example, in Denmark the current Prime Minister, Mr Poul Nyrup Rasmussen, is said by

---

[*] Co-authored with Flemming Hansen. Originally published in *Nordicom Review* 24 (2003), 25-30. Reprinted with permission of the Publisher.

many commentators to have a severe "credibility problem." This liability is said to have brought him defeat in the referendum he had called on the common European currency in September, 2000, which was won by the anti-Euro coalition, and it is also cited as grounds for his likely upset in the upcoming general election. Such claims are current in spite of the fact that Mr. Nyrup Rasmussen's administration is admitted to have performed well by objective standards, at least as far as the economy is concerned.

It is not a new fact that credibility is considered important. For the last 50 years or so, communication scholars have studied it intensively. Hovland et al. (1953) initiated this effort, Andersen & Clevenger (1963) summarized work so far, followed by, among many others, J. McCroskey (e.g., McCroskey 1966; Whitehead 1968; Tuppen 1974).

After the heyday of empirical credibility studies, a new facet to the issue came into focus as television became the main source of political and other public communication. The ability to communicate well on TV was highlighted in the 1980's in press commentaries as well as scholarly studies centering on President Ronald Reagan as a "master communicator." Reagan's masterful handling of the specific demands of this all-important medium were scrutinized. Since then, it has been a standard assumption that the ability to perform well on TV and in other mass-mediated contexts is crucial to success in politics as well as in business and public opinion generally, and there is a strong tendency to equate the notion of a source's credibility with that source's ability to handle TV and other media well and to "come across" in a way that will ingratiate viewers.

That raises the question as to what connection there might be between these two constructs: 1) credibility, as analyzed in the many empirical studies since the 50's, and 2) the status as mass-mediated "master communicator," as instantiated by Ronald Reagan, or in later decades, Bill Clinton or British PM Tony Blair. Are these two constructs basically the same? Or are they different but correlated? Or are they perhaps clearly separate?

To return to the case of Prime Minister Nyrup Rasmussen, it is generally said not only that his credibility is low, but also that his performance on TV is often toe-cringing. One way to see such a case is to conclude that credibility and the qualities that make a master communicator are closely connected, and that this is why a public figure would rank low in both respects.

On the other hand, there are observations that might suggest a different hypothesis. A point of departure for this study has been the regular appearance of credibility ratings for public persons, media, and organizations. One source of such ratings in Denmark has been the business weekly *Børsens Nyhedsmagasin*, which publishes an annual "credibility barometer." More than once, we have been struck by the fact that the people and organizations usually considered "master communicators"—for example those politicians most praised by the media and by communication experts as being "telegenic," capable of "coming across" on TV, of communicating in "headlines," etc.—are often quite low on the list. Conversely, figures or organizations at the top of the list are generally such as usually appear to lack or to shun these qualities; more typically, they appear reflective, balanced, measured, and even reticent in their media appearances.

From these observations we have built the hypothesis that in this age of mass-mediated communication there might well be more than one dimension on which the public communication of, e.g., politicians and organizations are evaluated by the general public. Further, we hypothesize that these dimensions may well be separate and perhaps even negatively correlated. Specifically, we hypothesize that the "master communicator" dimension might be separate from the "credibility" construct.

In studies done over the last decades, scholars have tended to find that credibility has as one of its dimensions a factor revolving around "dynamism" or "charisma." The work of Berlo *et al.* (1969) has been influential in this respect. What Berlo and his associates did was to compile a set of semantic differentials (statements) by asking a number of people to name qualities that would be found in people of whom they might say (rather vaguely perhaps), "If it's good enough for him, it's good enough for me." They then had a number of individuals rate a set of "message sources" along these differentials and subjected the data to factor analysis. Other researchers, working largely along similar lines, included a growing number of differentials in their studies.

The problem with this tendency was that it became increasingly unclear whether all these differentials were actually relevant to the concept of credibility, or whether the construct whose factors were being studied was a larger, less coherent one. Berlo *et al.* chose, in the title of their paper, to use the term "Acceptability of Message Sources," a term which leaves some obscurity as to whether this is the same as "credibility" or perhaps a vaguer, more inclusive concept.

An impressive number of studies on credibility and ethos continued to appear in the Seventies, designed largely along the same lines: more and more semantic descriptors were selected and subjected to increasingly sophisticated factor-analytic procedures. At the same time, however, one of the originators, and perhaps the key figure, of this whole line of research, J.C. McCroskey, was beginning to doubt the soundness of the direction it was taking (McCroskey and Young, 1981). He felt that credibility scholars, including himself, had distorted the credibility construct by including an ever wider battery of descriptors, while still assuming that they were dealing with the same concept: credibility (or as McCroskey preferred to call it: *ethos*). By doing this they confounded credibility with other source characteristics unrelated to it. Source credibility, McCroskey now found, was merely a subset of a much larger construct of "person perception," and scholars would have done well to limit their factor analysis of it to the original Aristotelian *ethos* construct, with its main factors of competence (*phronesis*), moral character (*arete*), and good will towards the audience (*eunoia*)—a formula which had proved its robustness in one empirical study after the other, including McCroskey's own.

The present study is based on a hypothesis that heeds McCroskey's warning: credibility, we hypothesize, is a quite narrow concept that is separate from other important and desirable source characteristics. Among these other desirable characteristics are, for example, "telegenic" qualities enabling a person to come across well on TV, as well as such personable qualities which might easily allow audiences to relate to and identify with that person.

In order to test this hypothesis, we have assembled a set of scales that might be involved in creating either of the overall impressions of a source that we wish to analyze. Among these are a number of statements that are typically used to refer to a public person's media performance. This is one respect in which our study differs from the long line of pre-1980 studies, in which media performance was not a specific issue in relation to credibility. A further difference is that in a methodically simple but perhaps debatable move, we have included our main dependent variable, credibility, in the list of scales. We did this in order to see how the other scales would correlate with it, and whether a factor would actually emerge that might meaningfully be called "credibility."

Just as we believe that there is a tendency to confound unrelated aspects of source evaluation under the term "credibility," we also hypothesize that differentiation is called for in another respect: credibility, for different categories of public persons, may depend on different characteristics. This should really be a rather obvious point, yet is one that was not explicitly made in credibility research until Cronkhite and Liska (1976).

It is likely that credibility and overall source evaluation for different public persons depend upon quite different characteristics of the source. The present study presents an attempt to develop an instrument which can give a more precise and more detailed picture of the way in which public spokespersons are perceived. At the same time it is an initial attempt to establish data that can show how such evaluations look in an European (Danish) context.

Hypotheses

To sum up: In the present study, we want to test the following hypotheses.

H1. Evaluation of public persons is made along several dimensions, among which credibility is one and just one.

H2. The dimension of credibility is separate from the dimension that might characterise telegenic "master communicators."

H3. Different public persons are evaluated differently, along evaluative dimensions.

H4. In particular, credibility depends, for different public persons, on different aspects of the overall impression made by that person.

In testing these hypotheses, ideally, a large number of different public persons should be evaluated along a large number of scales. To do so would require a questionnaire so extensive that it was feared that it would influence the response-rate and the quality of the responses.

For this reason, it was chosen to limit the study to five different public persons, with expectedly very different profiles.

Methodology

For the study, a battery of statements were developed, covering items that might be used meaningfully in describing public spokespersons.

Inspiration came from past studies of source effects (McCroskey et al. 1972), from corporate image studies (Worcester 1972), and from other evaluative measurement instruments, such as Osgood's Attitude scales (Osgood, Suci and Tannenbaum 1963). After some sorting and testing, a battery of 45 items was decided upon. The battery includes statements of the type: "is informative", "is eloquent," etc.

In the study, five high-profile public figures were included. These were two well-known political leaders with very different political orientations: Mr. Svend Auken (57), a leading Social Democrat, currently Minister of the Environment, and Ms. Pia Kjærsgaard (53), leader of the right-wing, anti-immigration Danish People's Party; Denmark's most notable businessman, Mr. Maersk McKinney Møller (87), owner of the huge and successful A.P. Møller group; Ms. Bodil Nyboe Andersen (60), Governor of the National Bank; and a celebrated sports personality who has moved into politics: Mr. Ulrik Wilbek (42), former manager of the Danish ladies' handball team, which he led to a series of international triumphs in the 90's. Each of these persons was rated on a five-point Likert scale for each of the 45 statements. Respondents were 78 students in a graduate class of Marketing and Communication.

Data analysis

Self-rating of the respondents' awareness of the five spokespersons was also included in the questionnaire. Since the respondents were graduate students in business economics, we find it surprising that Mr. Møller and Ms. Nyboe Andersen were judged by several to be "not very well-known."

	Svend Auken	Pia Kjærsgaard	Maersk Mckinney Møller	Bodil Nyboe Andersen	Ulrik Wilbek
Others	1	1	1	5	1
1			11	28	3
2	4	1	10	19	9
3	15	9	18	12	16
4	20	23	17	9	15
5	25	31	16	4	23
6	13	13	5	1	11

Table 1: Awareness. 1-6 reflect degrees of awareness,
6 being the highest, and 1 = do not know.

In the following analysis, respondents' ratings of persons they do not know, or do not know very well, are excluded. Awareness and average scores on self-rated credibility for the five public figures are shown in Table 1. It is obvious that considerable variation in the data exists. The two most credible figures, by far, are the non-political Governor of the National

Bank and the leading business personality, but they are also the least known.

Factor analysis was conducted for each of the five persons. For a description of this technique, applied in the manner done here, see, e.g., Green and Tull (1978).

It appears that the solutions emerging here has significant similarity across individuals. This we take as an indication that the dimensions along which the different public persons are evaluated are similar, even though the precise evaluation of the persons may differ markedly. For this reason, we decided to define the dimensions based upon a combined analysis for all five public spokespersons. In this manner, the number of observations on which the analyses are based is increased from 78 to 391. The stability of the solution thereby improves significantly.

With three factors, 47 percent of the total variance in the data is accounted for. Adding more variables only slightly increases the amount of explained variance. As in other analyses of this kind, "noise" in the raw data (the ratings), combined with effects of skewness of the distribution of answers for many of the items, may account for this. It is a common observation that one can rarely explain more than 50-60 percent with factors which each accounts for at least as much variance as one single question. In the present case, to reach this level, the inclusion of nine factors would be required (64 percent explained variance). However, each of the last six factors explains only a little more variance than any single question. For this reason—and since the three-dimensional solution lends itself easily to a meaningful interpretation—we chose to focus on this. The solution is shown in table 2.

The first factor, accounting for more than half of the explained variance, centers on credibility, which comes out with the highest loading of all statements. This lends support to the notion that "credibility" is indeed a separate factor, and that its name is an apt one. Moreover, the loadings of the other statements on this factor suggest some of the aspects that enter into the perception of credibility. On average for the five public figures, to be "irritating" (not surprisingly) detracts from credibility, whereas the perceptions that a person is intelligent, objective, and competent add to it. These are clearly representative of the Aristotelian "phronesis" dimension (cf. Aristotle's *Rhetoric*). Further, it is noteworthy that being able to see matters from different angles and being balanced and respectful of others' opinions are properties with high loadings. These represent a dimension that bear some resemblance to the Aristotelian *arete* and *eunoia* dimensions, but which may more properly be described as standing for judge-like qualities—independence, objectivity, incorruptibility, etc.

The second separate dimension in the evaluation of the five persons can be labelled "charisma." Public spokespersons having this characteristics are extrovert, entertaining, telegenic, passionate, and able to explain things in a down-to-earth manner. Such people are the darlings of talk-show hosts and debate moderators on TV because they come across so well on the screen.

It is no surprise that this is a dimension in source evaluation. The interesting thing is that this dimension is separate from credibility proper. This finding may explain the observation which originally instigated this study: that political and public figures high in telegenic qualities and the ability to "sell tickets" on the screen (to translate a favourite Danish term) often ranked low in credibility ratings, while precisely people like Ms. Nyboe Andersen—high in expertise, independence, and balance, but soft-spoken and low in media magnetism—were invariably rated most credible.

Credible	0.88
Irritating	-0.85
Professional	0.80
Intelligent	0.79
Competent	0.78
Unappealing	-0.77
Person I often agree with	0.76
Realistic	0.76
Appealing	0.75
Can see matters from different angles	0.72
Pleasant	0.71
Calm	0.70
Balanced	0.69
Stupid	-0.69
Seen to often	-0.66
Sincere	0.65
Dishonest	-0.64
Respects other people's opinions	0.60

Artificial	-0.56		
Eloquent	0.55	0.48	
Informative	0.54		
Exciting personality	0.52		
Not able to lie	0.46		
Extrovert		0.68	
Entertaining		0.67	
Straightforward		0.59	
TV appeal		0.58	
Passionate		0.55	
Brings matters down to earth		0.54	
Has charisma	0.41	0.51	
Imaginative		0.51	
Good popularizer	0.45	0.50	
Lacks TV appeal		-0.50	
Good at making debate		0.49	
Dynamic		0.48	
Self-confident		0.47	
Dull personality		-0.45	
Knowledge		0.44	
Sensitive			0.62
Warm			0.60
Unassuming		0.41	0.53
Capable of admitting mistakes	0.48		0.49
Incapable of admitting mistakes	-0.39		-0.47
Doesn't respect other people's opinions	-0.40		-0.43

Table 2: Three-dimensional solution

The third dimension has a more emotional side to it. Important traits of persons scoring high on this factor are: sensitive, warm, folksy, plain, and able to admit mistakes. The common denominator for these perceptions might be a homey, "one-of-us" quality.

Three-dimensional evaluation of spokespersons

Having determined three dimensions along which people evaluate public persons, we may try to profile the five public spokespersons individually on the three dimensions. This we could do by averaging each person's scores on the more important items belonging to each of the three factors. A more sensitive and elaborate procedure, however, is to compute factor scores for each respondent's evaluation of each public person on each of the three dimensions. The average factor score for each dimension then represents the degree to which each of the three public persons is associated with that dimension. These scores are shown in table 3:

	Factor I	Factor II	Factor III
Svend Auken	-0,24	-0,24	0,29
Pia Kjærsgaard	-0,91	0,43	-0,51
Mærsk McKinney Møller	0,70	-0,19	-0,54
Bodil Nyboe Andersen	0,52	-0,50	0,00
Ulrik Wilbek	-0,07	0,51	0,77

Table 3: Average factor scores on each dimension for each person

It is evident that the way in which the five spokespersons are regarded is very different. Mærsk McKinney Møller is most credible, but he scores less well on the other factors. Least credible is Pia Kjærsgaard. However, along with sports celebrity Ulrik Wilbek, the right-wing party leader scores highest on charisma. This dimension is one that the low-key National Bank Governor, Bodil Nyboe Andersen, completely lacks. On the other hand, she is the only one to come anywhere near Møller on credibility. On the emotional "one-of-us" dimension, Auken and especially Wilbek stand out.

The nature of credibility

The way the five spokespersons achieve such credibility as they have varies significantly. At one end of the scale, we find Nyboe Andersen, at the other end Kjærsgaard (Table 3). But as we shall see, what explains the degree of credibility that each of the five persons has varies much between them.

The *overall* nature of credibility can be inferred from the statements that load high on the credibility dimension in the analysis shown in Table

2. It is, however, possible to analyse credibility in a slightly different way as well. By using the credibility score as a dependent variable in a correlation analysis, and using answers to the 45 statements as independent variables, it is possible to single out exactly what constitutes credibility for each spokesperson. To achieve this, a regression analysis for each of the five persons was carried out. Here the amount of explained variance in the credibility score varies from 85 to 99 percent.

From this analysis, it is obvious that credibility for the different spokespersons has to do with different perceived qualities in them. Findings are shown in table 4. Only few statements correlate significantly with credibility for more than one of the five spokespersons

Clearly, each of these public figures has a different "credibility profile"; credibility has a somewhat different meaning depending on whose credibility we are talking about. The perceived credibility of Svend Auken, the Minister of Energy and the Environment, seems to have to do with his being realistic, respectful of the opinions of others, and informative, but not with any willingness to admit mistakes nor—surprisingly perhaps— with his being eloquent or extrovert. Many people would probably agree that Auken has these qualities; it seems, then, that there might be a tendency for his eloquence and extroversion to strike people as "too much," detracting from his credibility. For Pia Kjærsgaard, the right-wing, anti-immigrant party leader, the most significant findings are that those who find her credible also perceive her as disrepectful of the opinions of others, and that they do not see her as warm; they do not agree that she is unable to admit mistakes (but, somewhat contradictorily, will not go so far as to agree that she is able to admit them). For Mr Mærsk Møller, the business tycoon, those who find him credible tend to find him intelligent, pleasant, and objective, while they reject the notion that he is dishonest. National Bank Governor Bodil Nyboe Andersen is seen as credible by people who see her as calm, competent, pleasant, and, perhaps surprisingly, entertaining; they feel that she is not dishonest, nor is she warm or someone they often agree with. For Ulrik Wilbek, the celebrated sports personality, credibility seems to depend on his being seen as straightforward, calm, and unable to lie; those who see him as credible do not feel that he is telegenic or charismatic, nor that he is stupid.

Regression Analysis	Unstandardized Coefficients		Standardized Coefficients	t	Sig.
	B	Std. Error	Beta		
Svend Auken					
(Constant)	2,25	1,32		1,71	0,10
Capable of atmitting mistakes	-0,35	0,13	-0,31	-2,60	0,01
Eloquent	-0,26	0,12	-0,27	-2,16	0,04
Informative	0,36	0,10	0,37	3,60	0,00
Respects others opinions	0,25	0,12	0,24	2,17	0,04
Dull personality	-0,23	0,11	-0,27	-2,02	0,05
Realistic	0,41	0,10	0,40	4,10	0,00
Extrovert	-0,21	0,10	-0,20	-2,16	0,04
Knowledge	0,18	0,09	0,15	1,91	0,06
Pia Kjærsgaard					
(Constant)	1,84	1,52		1,21	0,24
Doesn't respect others opinions	0,19	0,09	0,27	2,07	0,05
Warm	-0,24	0,13	-0,22	-1,77	0,09
Not capable of atmitting mistakes	-0,17	0,09	-0,23	-1,94	0,06
(Constant)	1,38	1,75		0,79	0,44
Professional	0,23	0,15	0,26	1,50	0,15
Pleasant	0,26	0,17	0,29	1,51	0,15
Dishonest	-0,29	0,16	-0,25	-1,89	0,07
Intelligent	0,33	0,19	0,29	1,69	0,10
Bodil Nyboe Andersen					
(Constant)	0,51	1,44		0,36	0,73
"I often agree with"	-0,48	0,12	-0,48	-3,87	0,00
Competent	0,54	0,15	0,58	3,61	0,00
Entertaining	0,50	0,12	0,45	4,30	0,00
Warm	-0,45	0,15	-0,31	-3,06	0,01
Apealing	0,32	0,11	0,37	2,88	0,01
Dishonest	-0,36	0,10	-0,32	-3,50	0,00
Ulrik Wilbek					
(Constant)	0,86	1,33		0,64	0,53
Positive TV appearance	-0,15	0,11	-0,21	-1,34	0,19
Entertaining	0,18	0,11	0,28	1,58	0,13
Is straightforward	0,16	0,11	0,24	1,52	0,14
"Not able to lie"	0,19	0,10	0,26	1,89	0,07
Charisma	-0,25	0,13	-0,32	-1,88	0,07
Calm	0,22	0,13	0,25	1,69	0,10
Stupid	-0,19	0,12	-0,22	-1,58	0,13

Table 4: Regression analysis–significant items in relation to credibility

Discussion

The analysis clearly suggests that our evaluation of public persons takes place along several separate dimensions. Here, it has been proposed to work with a three-dimensional analysis: credibility, charisma, and "one-of-us" emotional appeal. This analysis supports our hypotheses 1 and 2: credibility is just one factor in the evaluation of a public communicator; and more specifically, credibility is separate from other qualities that public communicators may also wish to possess, such as a) charisma and b) "one-of-us" emotional appeal. To be even more specific: the much vaunted charismatic, "master communicator" quality that politicians and other public figures are often said to need in order to "come across" on TV is not the same thing as credibility.

To say this is not tantamount to saying that credible "master communicators" do not exist, or that the "mastery" they possess is not a valuable and important one. That claim would fly in the face of facts, e.g., the case of Ms. Kjærsgaard, who is undoubtedly, in some way, a master communicator with charismatic traits. Such a figure is clearly effective and persuasive in terms of building popular support. That raises the intriguing question of what the different *kinds* of persuasiveness or effectiveness are that we find in communicators who are strong on each of our three dimensions: credibility, charisma, and "one-of-us" appeal, respectively. The present study gives us no basis for theorizing on that. However, the question calls to mind a perspective raised by an empirical study of persuasion in which one of the authors was involved (Jørgensen, Kock and Rørbech 1994; 1998; this volume, Chapter 12). In that study, it became clear that we may distinguish between two different kinds of persuasive effectiveness, each corresponding to a separate persuasive strategy. These are *vote-shifting* and *vote-gathering*, respectively. Vote-shifting is the ability to win over votes from the opposite side. Vote-gathering is the ability to mobilize latent followers from the "undecided" group and to galvanize the enthusiasm of followers already mobilized. The typical vote-shifter, it turns out, is very reminiscent of the typical "credible" person of the present study; the typical vote-gatherer has most of the qualities that constitute our "charisma" factor. In fact, a public debate featuring Ms. Kjærsgaard was a key case in the earlier study, and it turned out then that in persuasive strategy as well as in measurable persuasive effect she was perhaps the most typical vote-gatherer of all debaters studied (out of 74).

We began with a reference to the case of Denmark's Prime Minister, Poul Nyrup Rasmussen. Looking back, we may now state that although in many people's estimate he has neither credibility nor charisma, this should not lead anyone to think that the two dimensions are the same. They are identifiable and separate dimensions in the evaluation of public communicators.

However, when that is said, it also seems likely that these dimensions involve somewhat different qualities for different communicators. For example, our everyday judgement of the credibility of different communicators relies upon different traits. This lends support to our hypotheses 3 and 4. When we look for reasons why this should be so, it is natural to point to the fact that these five figures belong to very different spheres. First, we may assume that respondents have not rated their credibility *in abstracto*, but on the assumption that they should be seen as communicating within the particular sphere in which they are active. When Mr. Møller communicates to the public at all (a rare event), he talks about business and how various policies will affect it, not about sports. So the credibility ratings he achieves refer to what he says within that sphere. Secondly, it is natural to assume that the qualities which make Mr. Møller credible on business matters are different from those which make Mr. Wilbek credible on (certain) sports. Our readers may explore our tables for themselves to look for qualities that may be constitutive of credibility in politics, business, sports, etc., respectively. Suffice it here to conclude that differences in what makes for credibility in people from different life spheres are to be expected and have indeed emerged, yet the more interesting fact is perhaps that in spite of these differences there is a relation and an overlap between the credibility profiles of these very different figures—enough to allow us to conclude that credibility is an identifiable and separate construct, as are the other two factors in our analysis.

Based upon the present study, it would be possible to devise a meaningful instrument of manageable size for the profiling of spokespersons along the three dimensions suggested here. To estimate someone's credibility, one would concentrate on those items in the analysis that contribute strongly to the credibility of at least one of the spokespersons. With regard to the second and third dimension, it would be advisable to work with at least three statements for each, providing a total battery of 16-20 statements, to be used for each person to be evaluated.

REFERENCES

Andersen, K., and T. Clevenger, Jr. 1963. A summary of experimental research in ethos. *Speech Monographs* 30, 59-78.

Applebaum, R.L., and K.W.E. Anatol. 1973. Dimensions of source credibility: A test for reproducibility. *Speech Monographs* 40, 231-37.

Aristotle. 1995. *Aristotle's Rhetoric.* E. Garver (Ed.). Chicago: University of Chicago Press.

Berlo, D. K., J.B. Lemert, and R.J. Mertz. 1969. Dimensions of evaluating the acceptability of message sources. *Public Opinion Quarterly* 33, 563-76.

Cronkhite, G., and J. Liska. 1976. A critique of factor analytic approaches to the study of credibility. *Communication Monographs* 43, 91-107.

Green, P.E., and Donald S. Tull. 1978. *Research for Marketing Decisions.* 4th ed. Englewood Cliffs: Prentice-Hall.

Hovland, C.L., I.L. Janis, and H.H. Kelley. 1953. *Communication and Persuasion.* New Haven: Yale University Press.

Jørgensen, C., C. Kock and L. Rørbech. 1994. *Retorik der flytter stemmer. Hvordan man overbeviser i offentlig debat.* København: Gyldendal.

_____. 1998. Rhetoric that shifts votes: An exploratory study of persuasion in issue-oriented public debates." *Political Communication* 15, 283-299. (This volume, Chapter 12.)

McCroskey, J.C. 1966. Scales for the measurement of *ethos. Speech Monographs* 33, 65-72.

McCroskey, J.C., and T.J. Young. 1979. The use and abuse of factor analysis in measurement of *ethos*: Another attempt. *Speech Monographs* 39, 269-301.

_____. 1981. *Ethos* and credibility: The construct and its measurement after three decades". *The Central States Speech Journal* 32, 24-34.

Osgood, C.E., G.J. Suci, and P.H. Tannenbaum. 1957. *The Measurement of Meaning.* Urbana, Illinois: University of Illinois Press.

Tuppen, C.J.S. 1974. Dimensions of communicator credibility: An oblique solution. *Speech Monographs* 41, 253-60.

Whitehead, J.L., Jr. 1968. Factors of source credibility. *Quarterly Journal of Speech* 54, 59-63.

Worcester, Robert M. 1972. *Consumer Markets Research Handbook.* London:Elsevier Publishing Company.

15.

Argumentation Democracy 101: Deliberative Norms Made Easy

This chapter—an adaptation of the first chapter of my book in Danish De svarer ikke *("They are not answering," 2011)—sets forth in everyday terms a theory of democratic debate: what its constitutive conditions are, and what ideal requirements it ought to fulfill in order to serve its democratic function best. Along the way, some current theories of democracy and the roles of rhetoric and argumentation in it are invoked as either supports or targets.*

In Western democracies, political debate is—fortunately—intense. Especially when an election is drawing near, hopeful candidates as well as incumbents find themselves busy with pronouncements, signals and branding. Attack and counter-attack fly back and forth. Moreover, there is vigorous debate between opinion leaders who aren't politicians themselves. Unlike politicians, they are not running for office, but like politicians they seek acceptance of their positions from citizens and voters.

Particularly in regard to what politicians say and do the media delivers commentary and evaluations. This often takes the form of judgments of what strategic intentions may have motivated a given pronouncement, and whether its actual effects are likely to be desirable from the strategic point of view of the politician who made it, or his or her party or block. In other words, these assessments concern how well this politician is doing from his or her own perspective. Will a given move win votes? Which voter segments or factions will like it? Is it clever?

Below, a different perspective will be taken. It, too, serves to render a qualitative assessment of public debate—but from the point of view of *citizens.*

While the media's political commentators tend to pontificate—often as self-appointed authorities, without supporting reasons—on whether and how the politicians' contributions to the debate benefit the politicians themselves, the question in this essay will be whether the politicians' contributions to the debate are of any use to citizens; that is to say, whether they deliver what *citizens* need.

According to a widespread view, politicians themselves are exclusively or primarily driven by a need to strengthen or consolidate their power positions by pleasing other persons of power and, most of all, by pleasing the voters. But citizens–voters—what do *they* need? What should political debates deliver in order to meet their needs? And do they get it?

Even if we assume that all politicians aim merely to strengthen their power positions as much as possible, as political pundits tend to assume (but this is a very questionable theory), then that is not likely to give citizens what *they* need. In fact it is impossible for the simple reason that all the competing politicians cannot strengthen their positions at the same time.

What Norms Should Count?

If one aims to make qualitative evaluations of political debates from citizens' point of view, then one must have a set of norms on the basis of which this can be done. That is, norms that deal with what citizens, not politicians, actually need.

Think about the public debate that takes place in a Parliament or in Congress. It probably has to be there according to the Constitution or tradition. But why do citizens need it? What good does it do? What good *could* it do? What is its purpose?

One would think that a Constitution, for example, would say something about these questions; or perhaps other rules or statutes or treatises of constitutional law. But, on the whole, this is not the case.

That one can, from the citizens' side, formulate requirements and norms for political debates—norms that reflect citizens' needs and not just the strategic interests of politicians—is nevertheless a perspective that is slowly gaining validity, even in the media. One can see this in the way several websites, TV/radio stations and newspapers have begun fact-checking claims that politicians put forward, especially during election campaigns.

We must go further down this road. Indeed, politicians' arguments should not distort or misrepresent facts—but that is just one of the norms in political debate that reflect what citizens need (and do not need). There are other needs we should also wish to see fulfilled if a debate is to be useful.

The main thesis here is simply that we citizens should be able to use public political debate as *a basis for making decisions*. It is, for example, for this reason that we should demand that we are neither lied to nor given misleading representations of facts that leave out important information and thereby lead us to believe things that aren't so. As citizens we need debates that help us acquire a view of reality that is, as they say in the auditing profession, "true and fair." More generally, debates fulfilling this and other quality standards are needed in order for us to judge who we think has the best approach to the political problems and what should be done about them. Based on such a judgment we can each take a position on who deserves to be elected. And between elections we can influence our politicians by communicating with them or letting our voices be heard in the political debate in other ways.

If this is citizens' primary purpose in hearing (and reading) political debate, then our first and most elementary requirement as citizens, all things considered, is that we deserve debates containing *arguments*—that is, *reasons* why given policies under consideration are right or wrong.

This is not the only purpose we citizens can have in attending to debate. Debate can also be entertaining, suspenseful, exciting. We may sometimes withdraw to a position as mere observers and wonder "who loses and who wins, who's in, who's out," as Shakespeare's King Lear said to his good and virtuous daughter, Cordelia. Who is the frontrunner? Who makes outrageous claims? Who makes gaffes? Who is in a tight spot? There can be a particular satisfaction in following a debate where the side one roots for does well while the others embarrass themselves.

Another important purpose in having debates, such as those held in a Congress or Parliament, is that by learning elected politicians' public reasons for their decisions, we can afterwards hold them accountable for those decisions. We can say, for example, "You supported this because you thought it would bring such and such a benefit—but now look what has happened."

But the primary purpose must still be a forward-looking one: we need debates so that we can each take a position on what should be done— *before* it is done. What are the exigencies, problems and challenges we face? What can be done? What proposals are there? What will be best? There are issues enough: economic crises, taxes, unemployment, health care, schools, the environment, immigration, the climate, terrorism, military involvements ... Taking positions on such issues may help us take positions on whom to vote for. And our votes are not our only means of influence. Politicians can be influenced by opinion polls, by debate pieces in newspapers and on blogs, and by direct contact via, for example, e-mail or the social media.

We need debates to provide us with input we can use to take stands on all the issues facing our society, and to decide, on that basis, whom to vote for. Perhaps we even want to interfere in ongoing debates and raise our voices ourselves. This input that we need for all this consists of several things. There should be alternative *proposals* or policies for our consideration. These policies should be supported with *arguments*[20], and those arguments should be good ones, which means, among other things, that they should not be untruthful, deceptive or misleading. In addition, debates should offer *counterarguments* and criticisms of proposed policies and their supporting arguments, and all these too must meet certain critical standards. And finally, debates should provide good *answers* to counterarguments and criticisms, for it is only by hearing opposing arguments *and* the respective answers to them that we are really in a position to evaluate them.

But all this, which we as citizens need and require from political debates, is something we aren't getting in any satisfactory measure. We get personality contests, performance, spin, slogans, talking points, one-liners, and we get mutual accusations and mudslinging. All these things are what political analysts, commentators and "pundits" like to analyze and applaud or disparage in their commentaries, where they pontificate on "who loses and who wins, who's in, who's out"; and sometimes, when these analysts are hired as communication consultants, as they often are, this is also what they teach politicians to be good at. As a result, we often know little more about a candidate we have voted for than a slogan, a few one-liners, a party affiliation and how he or she looks on a lot of identical posters. Communication consultants know that superficial and casual impressions and expressions are often the only input that many voters manage to

---

[20] The expression "an argument" will be used as synonomous with "a reason," i.e., a statement that is seen as given in support of some conclusion (a proposition or proposal). Thus, "an argument" is *not* used in the sense often heard of "an exchange between disagreeing people." Nor is it used in the sense often found in scholarship of "a constellation of reasons and the conclusion they support." When something like that is meant, the term "argumentation" will typically be used.

receive before an election. True enough, more and more media compete for our limited time. The result is that "so much political rhetoric today looks more like advertising than like deliberative argument," as political theorist Bryan Garsten has noted (2011, p. 160).

There is nothing wrong in itself with one-liners, slogans, TV commercials and snappy advertisements on buses. It is in order, after all, that there are short, to-the-point messages; and color on a campaign poster is better than if all is black, white and grey. But things have gone wrong if we get all this *instead* of proper debates with arguments that can help us find our positions.

And such arguments we are hard pressed to find. The fact that commercials, one-liners, etc., play a big role is not the main focus here. Rather, the concern is with much of what is put forward as being proper debate with usable argumentation in it—because usually it isn't.

To be sure, there is a great deal of debate. But, first, much of the debate is marked by the fact that it contains no real arguments; instead a range of techniques are used to get us to buy policies and assumptions that are *not* backed by arguments (many of these techniques are the ones known from advertising). Second, many of the arguments (and counterarguments) that we do get are *bad* ones. And third, the *answers* that should be given to the counterarguments and criticisms are often of miserable quality, or they aren't there at all.

This is why we need to evaluate the quality of public debate from the point of view of the *citizen*'s needs. Citizens should think of themselves as *critical consumers* of debate. We should hold public and political debaters responsible for giving us input that serves *our* needs as citizens. The important question about political communication is not how well it serves *politicians'* purposes. We are consumers of debate because we *need* debate; but we should also be critical monitors of what we get. We should learn to detect and identify the typical shortcomings and tricks in political communication by which we citizens get shortchanged.

A covering term for these tricks and shortcomings that tend to make much political communication useless or even stultifying could be *vices*. Below I try to sketch the principal criteria that we, as critical consumers, might apply to the political communication we get; that will enable us to define the principal types of vices that occur when these criteria are disobeyed. These vices can be placed under the three main categories I have indicated: *no* arguments—*poor* arguments—poor *answers* to arguments.

What we have a shortage of in our public sphere is not talk about problems, it is not debate, nor is it proposals for solutions; what has been lacking is rather real elucidation of the problems and of the proposed solutions in the form of good argumentation.

We need to specify what that is. One cannot begin to criticize someone or something without making clear on what basis one is doing it—that is to say, without identifying and motivating the criteria for evaluation that one claims are not being met.

But Can Voters Be *Bothered* with Argumentation?

A critical question might be raised in response to what I have said so far: are citizens and voters really *interested* in argumentation? Don't they already know what they want, and don't they just expect politicians to give it to them? And in that case, what would they need argumentation for?

That the individual voter merely wants particular policies, period, and is therefore not much interested in argumentation is a widespread assumption that is firmly held by many political scientists, but also by politicians themselves and political journalists. Arguably, a majority of political reporting and analysis in the media is based on the understanding that the electorate is composed of certain "segments," all of which have given interests at heart, and to have those interests satisfied is what they care about; so all a politician can do to win voters' support is simply to make them think that he or she gives them what they want—not to try to *change* their views on issues or policies by means of argumentation.

An important political initiative in the United States springing from this notion was the so-called "Contract with America," a document written by Conservative politicians before the mid-term Congressional election in 1994, in which they set out very specifically a long series of promises that the Republican party were to enact if they were to gain a majority in the election. It was signed by all but two of the party's members of the House of Representatives and all its non-incumbent candidates. In the election the Republicans gained 54 seats in the House and 9 seats in the Senate and won a majority in both houses. This set a trend in the US, and in other countries as well, that has sometimes been referred to as "contract politics." It is a way of political thinking according to which voters know what they want, so that the role of politicians is to say, "We promise to give you what you want, and in return you vote for us."

It is also a way of thinking where argumentation plays a very small role. There is, on this view, no need for it, precisely because voters are already supposed to *know* what they want, and what could change that? Politicians' hands, on this view, are tied by the promises that get them elected: if they make good on those, they may be reelected, and if they don't, they can be thrown out in the next election.

It is clear that when such a view of politics dominates, politicians see no reason to present much in the way of argumentation for what they intend to do, or to answer counterarguments. More nearly the opposite is true: counterarguments and critical considerations should simply be passed over and ignored, because even mentioning them, let alone answering them, would just give them attention and media coverage that one doesn't want them to get. And certainly if one considers one's policies to be fixed by a "contract" with the voters, and if voters are not likely to be swayed by arguments, one need not argue for those policies. Instead, one is simply bound to do what the contract says. To even enter a debate or argument about one of them can be interpreted as if there is doubt about it. For that reason "contract" politicians tend to discourage such debates.

So, even though it is an advantage of "contract politics" that politicians are obligated to say in advance what they intend to do, and also to some extent to stand by what they have said, a problematic side of contract politics is that it tends to suspend or sideline open debate and argumentation. That is precisely because it is based on the presumption that each individual voter wants something quite definite that is not debatable—and that debate therefore cannot affect or change what voters want. In other words, here again we have the underlying notion that voters have fixed, given positions ("preferences" is the term often used by political scientists)—so they will not let themselves be moved by arguments.

This way of looking at things not only lies beneath contract politics, it also, as pointed out a moment ago, lies beneath a great deal of political debate and journalism. And it is reinforced by some of the prevalent tendencies in political science—a discipline in which increasing numbers of politicians, journalists, commentators and administrators are schooled.

Democracy as Cutting up the Cake

A connected and deeply entrenched view in political science is that politics is purely and simply the fight over the distribution of society's goods. Democracy, on this view, means that goods and influence in a society are distributed among social segments in proportion to their relative strength. On this view, the citizens of a society only care about their own wishes in the distribution process; to them politics is to promote their own and their segment's interests. Everyone, by this interpretation, is a "utility maximizer"—to borrow a phrase from classic economic theory, which assumes that individuals are (primarily) driven by one motive: getting the maximum value ("utility") out of all the choices they make. Democracy is likewise seen as a system in which everyone's concern is to maximally satisfy his or her preferences—and in principle the preferences of all individuals are then channeled ("aggregated") into an authoritative decision procedure; that procedure is how democracy works.

A problem in this connection that is of concern to many political scientists aligned with what they call "Social Choice Theory" is that in principle no system seems to exist that can accurately and unambiguously transform the aggregate preferences of all citizens into policies; depending on which voting procedure is used, various contradictory policies may result from the same set of voter preferences, and politicians have ample opportunities for manipulating what happens in this process. In other words, even in systems where citizens have the right to vote as they wish, "democracy" in the sense that the state is ruled by the will of the people does not really exist, because the notion "the will of the people" has no clear and unambiguous meaning. The work of the political scientist William Riker has been very influential in stating this view (see, e.g., Riker 1982).

But perhaps the dominant mode of thinking in political science is that "democracy" is a notion that does have a clear meaning: it means that citizens get their preferences satisfied and are allotted their proportionate share of society's goods according to their strength. Democracy is cutting up the cake of society between competing groups that all want the biggest possible slice. The Canadian political scientist David Easton (1917-2014) proposed a general theory of political "systems" that has been widely adopted to the degree of being considered the basic doctrine for a whole generation of political scientists. It includes, among other things, a famous definition of politics as the "authoritative allocation of values for a society" (1965, p. 50). In this lies also the idea that we citizens are basically seen as consumers who are always trying to get the political system to apportion us values—and the system tries to give us what we want because then we will support it and thereby secure its continuation. Easton's "systems" model has for decades been a staple in what we might call "Political Science 101."

Another leading political scientist, Anthony Downs, whose theories have long been part of academic curricula, says it as follows: "Because the citizens of our model democracy are rational, each of them views elections strictly as a means of selecting the government most beneficial to him" (1957, p. 138—an article that political scientists have cited thousands of times).

But if people think only of maximally fulfilling their self-interest, then their political attitudes will depend only on what they think will benefit them most, as viewed from their position in the social structure, and—according to this line of thinking—they tend to know this already and be firmly convinced of it; in which case they will not set much store by any arguments they hear, or feel much need for arguments in the first place. For example, pensioners will want their public pensions to at least stay the same, or, better, to be increased; they will want more money for home-care, and probably less for education. In short, people from a particular segment of society want to have precisely this and that. And a lot of debating won't change what they want. This is how a dominant way of thinking goes.

A Less Simplistic Picture

But it is, in the first place, a simplistic and false idea that people seek only their own "maximum utility." One might get the impression that scholars in the emergent field of Political Science seized on theories by thinkers like Easton and Downs because they offered views of the political world as beautifully clear and rule-governed as the view of the universe offered by Newton's laws. It is a fact that theories that inject this kind of beautiful mathematical simplicity in a murky and complicated field exert a tremendous attraction to some scholars. Interestingly, Adam Smith, the father of another beautifully simple theory, classical economics, was also a rhetorician, and he was very aware of this effect (we might call it the "Newton effect"). He defined the Newtonian method as follows: "we may lay down certain principles, primary, or proved, in the beginning, from whence we account for the several phenomena, connecting all together by the same chain" (1971, p.140)—and he added: "It gives us pleasure to see the phenomena which we reckoned the most unaccountable, all deduced from some principle." So, if this is right, we may assume that theories like Easton's or Downs's reduction of politics to one grand, materialist principle have gained acceptance partly because their quasi-mathematical simplicity provides *pleasure* to people with a certain mindset.

But the fact that these theories are wrong in their seductive simplicity doesn't mean that they are *all* wrong. Most people probably do think about their self-interest and their wallets a lot of the time, such as when they consider whom to vote for. But most voters *also* think about a wider range of issues than their personal economy. Other values than economic ones do influence the positions they take on concrete issues. It is not for nothing that in the last few years there has been considerable talk about "value politics," for it reflects precisely the view that politics is about much more than economy: citizens believe in certain values that they want legislation and other public action to reflect, so, for one thing, citizens' "preferences" are not exclusively determined by what benefits them most economically. Also, research shows that voters do not choose a standpoint on policy solely with a view to what they think will best serve their special interests and preferences, but also to a significant degree with a view to what they think is best for the community.

In the second place, the assumption that people's standpoints on all sorts of concrete issues are fixed it also a simplistic and mistaken idea. Many people in many social segments (to use the accepted terminology) actually change or modify their standpoints after they have heard arguments. Granted, it is no doubt true that most of us have rather fixed attitudes on several issues; but no one has fixed views on *every* issue. For one thing, for most people there are many issues on which they have no views at all. They may not even know that an issue exists until a pollster asks them to state their opinion on it. Or they will have views on it that are very superficially informed, undecided and volatile. Many people will tell the pollster that they support one or the other of the views he presents to them, but only because they feel they have to choose something and may not want to appear stupid. The pollster will then put them down as having taken a stand, and only those who didn't choose any of the suggested options will be put down as "undecided." If, for example, a referendum is upcoming (as in Britain on EU membership in the summer of 2016), those who have told the pollster what option they support will be put down as having taken a stand, and only the rest will be referred to in the media as those who have not yet decided. But the truth in such situations is that a large proportion of those who have declared a stand in a poll are *also* undecided; they may well change sides before the voting day, perhaps several times. Unfortunately the way the media, and pollsters themselves, tend to refer to opinion polls does not reflect this. But the fact remains that even on issues where an individual might have a rather firm view it is still possible—and often seen in practice—that this individual changes that view after having some experience, or hearing some argument. All this goes to show that citizens *can* be affected by argumentation—and, by the same token, that they *need* argumentation.

What Is Good Argumentation?

If it is assumed that citizens do need to hear arguments on political issues, then the question arises as to what sort of arguments. As already said, often those arguments that are in fact used in political debates, if any are used at all, are, unfortunately, bad ones. But what does that mean? When are arguments bad, when are they good?

A starting point in regard to this is the observation that *there are often good arguments both for and against a particular decision or policy.*

From this it follows, among other things, that "good" arguments are not the same as what philosophical logic calls "valid" arguments; it is necessary to say this because a good number of textbooks in argumentation and logic still build on this concept.

In logic the meaning of a "valid" argument is an argument that *entails* the conclusion it supports. This amounts to saying that if the argument is true, then it follows *necessarily and automatically* that the conclusion is also true. One authoritative formulation of this understanding of "valid" is this: "For a valid argument, it is not possible for the premises to be true with the conclusion false. That is, necessarily if the premises are true, then the conclusion is true." (This is from the article "Argument" in *The Internet Encyclopedia of Philosophy.)* This kind of argumentation is best known from geometry and other branches of mathematics. For example, if a is longer than b, and b is longer than c, then it follows necessarily that a is longer than c; or if is true that a given triangle is right-angled, then it follows necessarily that the square on its long side equals the sum of the squares on the two shorter sides. This insight is called the Pythagoras theorem; proofs that demonstrate its truth were known centuries before Christ.

Logic textbooks tend to equate a *good* argument with a *valid* argument, and they like to show examples of bad arguments like this one: "All birds lay eggs; this animal lays eggs; so this is a bird." This is of course an *in*valid argument, and every schoolchild probably knows that. It is clearly important that when someone in a political debate claims that the policy or claim he advances follows necessarily from argumentation like this—and that does happen—then that kind of argumentation should be exposed as false. Invalid arguments should not be allowed to pass as valid.

But using "validity" as a yardstick in political argumentation is a problem if it is our *only* yardstick. The problem is that in politics a lot of the relevant arguments that we would all agree are "good" in some sense are not valid—the conclusion they argue for does *not* follow necessarily.

Take for example this argument that has been used a great deal in the debate about Britain's membership of the EU: "If Britain leaves the EU, then it has more freedom to pass its own laws." This is surely true, and one cannot deny that it is a relevant argument. Surely for a country to have more freedom to pass its own laws is, taken in itself, a good thing—no one would call it a bad thing or an irrelevant thing. So as an argument for leaving the EU it surely is relevant and has some weight. However, the conclusion it argues for—that Britain should leave the EU—does *not* follow necessarily from it. And why not? Because there are many other considerations that are relevant in regard to the issue. For example, what will happen to Britain's foreign trade if it leaves the EU—and to its economy generally?

Practical vs. Epistemic Argumentation

The issue of whether Britain should be a member of the EU or not is an example of what is sometimes called a *practical* issue: it is about *what to do*. The issue of whether a given animal is a bird is different; it is an example of what is sometimes called an *epistemic* issue: it is about what is true. To put a crucial difference between practical and epistemic issues in a simple way we can say that an epistemic issue is *one-dimensional*: it concerns one dimension only, namely this: what is the truth. Here the validity yardstick helps us a long part of the way. That is also the reason why in logic textbooks the examples used to illustrate good and bad argumentation are nearly all drawn from the epistemic realm—they are mainly or exclusively issues about what is true, not about what to do. Practical issues, on the other hand, are *multi-dimensional*: for example, in the case of Britain's membership of the EU there is a dimension that has to do with national independence, but there is also the economic dimension; and there are many more. This, essentially, is the reason why, on political issues (and other practical issues), we cannot expect that arguments should be "valid" in the sense that their conclusion follows necessarily from them. They can be good without being valid; in fact it is arguable that arguments on practical issues can never be valid in the strict logical sense. However, they can still be good—and they can certainly also be bad.

To sum up: in regard to political argumentation (and practical argumentation generally) we cannot use the logicians' "validity" yardstick as our only normative evaluation tool. It is not for that reason superfluous, though. In politics we can, among other things, use the logical measuring stick to expose and criticize people if they try to fool us into thinking that their political views follow as necessary conclusions from their arguments. Conclusions do this extremely rarely where politics are concerned. Even though there may be good arguments for something—for example, in Britain's case, for either leaving the EU or staying in it—then there are, as a rule, also good arguments for the opposite view. Therefore, on the whole, that something or other is to be done is arguably never a "logical" (that is to say, necessary) consequence of there being good arguments for it. And for that reason we cannot criticize debaters for not bringing forward arguments which logically *entail* that we must agree with their policies; we can, on the other hand, criticize them if they try to make us *believe* that they have such arguments.

This brings us back to the initial point made a while ago: in politics there are typically both good arguments *for* a course of action—and good arguments *against* it. One cannot conclude that we *must* undertake a certain action—nor that we *must* refrain from doing it. This kind of situation is an everyday experience both in our daily lives and in politics, but validity-based logic cannot really account for it; according to it, there cannot be "valid" arguments on both sides, since two opposite courses of action cannot both follow by necessity from the arguments brought forward.

Added to this is the fact that in relation to every problem one would like to *do* something about, there are not only several arguments both for and against any proposed action, but also there are often several alternative possible actions. And even if one of them can be said to be good, this does not exclude the possibility that another alternative action is even better.

What Citizens Need from Debates

For this reason the matter of judging what is a good argument in politics (and in practical argumentation generally) is much more complicated than in the logical world. Among other things, what we need as citizens (and voters) in relation to political debates is two things:

The first thing: we need to *hear* the arguments on both sides of a given issue—pro and con.

(In fact we need to know the good arguments for *all* the different, alternative actions. But it is simpler to say that we need to hear the arguments both for and against every policy or action.)

The second thing: we need to *weigh* the arguments on the two sides. (Remember that the term "weight" popped up a while ago in relation to the argument for Britain's leaving the EU that this will give Britons more freedom to pass their own laws. By contrast, no one would say that one of the steps in the proof of the Pythagoras theorem has a certain "weight.")

As a general rule, no argument or set of arguments arguing for a certain action may entail the *necessity* to undertake that action. So we must "weigh." And our most important help in weighing is that those who defend a particular policy must *answer* the arguments on the other side.

Now back to the initial question, whose complications we have just tried to disentangle: if we cannot use "validity" as our sole yardstick, how do we judge whether an argument in a political debate, for example, is a good one?

The answer to be given here relies mainly on work within the philosophical school that calls itself "Informal Logic," in particular work by the philosopher Trudy Govier. Not everything in this chapter aligns completely with Govier and the other Informal Logicians, in particular not the rather essential distinction advanced above between epistemic and practical argumentation, but an important point of agreement is that it is useful to consider the following three dimensions of what a good argument is. Here they will be designated as follows:

1. Accurate

2. Relevant

3. Weighty

Accurate—it means, in simple terms, that one can answer *Yes* to the question, "Is that so?"

Why not just say that any arguments used should be *true*? The answer is that the word "true" says at the same time too much and too little. It is "too much" in the sense that the concept of truth in itself is one whose meaning philosophers have never stopped arguing about. It is better to avoid getting entangled in a philosophical quarrel about what it means that something is "true." An eminent contemporary philosopher, Donald Davidson (1996), has written an article titled "The Folly of Trying to Define Truth." Most people, on the other hand, have a commonsense notion of what it means to say something that isn't so. Aristotle said: "To say of that which is that it is and of that which is not that it is not is true" (*Metaphysics* 1011b). What someone says about reality must not mislead others about reality so that they do stupid things, such as walking off a cliff that they have been told wasn't there. We need statements about the world that we may reliably act upon; if that is the case, then they do not have to include every last detail, and there may even be a few minor errors in them. In that sense a strict notion of truth may be too much to ask.

In another sense it is too little. Auditors and lawyers use the expression "true and fair." A company's annual accounts must be true *and* fair. What this means is among other things that the numbers and other information given must provide *a good and trustworthy picture* of how things really are—one that may be acted upon. It does not just mean that the information and the numbers given, taken in themselves, are "right" or "true"—but also that the accounts present a *full* picture, meaning that no important information and numbers are left out so that we're misled about how things really stand.

So one thing that is suggested by the word *accuracy* is that statements used as arguments should not just "say of that which is not that it is," but also they should not tend to make us *believe* that it is. This is worth emphasizing because there are ways of saying things that are true in themselves, but in a "fudging" way that will make some people believe something untrue.

Regrettably, numbers are precisely one form of argument where a lot of fudging is going on, both in the selection and the presentation of them, as well as with the terms used, etc. So what we get in political debate is often a very foggy or even misleading picture of how things are. It is a sad fact that it has come to this, because if we do not have reliable numbers and other factual statements about reality we cannot have a reliable political debate. A concern about accuracy in argumentation implies, among other things, that one must look out for fog-mongering, obfuscation and fudging with numbers.

Next, what does *relevant* mean? One can also say "pertinent to the issue." It is no doubt pertinent to the issue of whether Britain should remain in the EU that this will give the country greater freedom to pass its own laws. On the other hand it is also relevant to the issue if it seems likely that leaving the EU will negatively affect much of Britain's foreign trade.

A crucial problem with an issue like this is that there is no way one can objectively weigh and balance these two arguments against each other. It is not just that the notions involved in these arguments are all rather vague and uncertain. Just how much freedom would Britain actually have, in practice, to pass its own laws outside the EU? On the other hand, just how certain is it that its foreign trade would be affected, and how much? None of these questions can be answered with any precision.

Over and above these problems, however, there is the overriding problem that there is no "official" way to determine how much the "freedom" consideration weighs against the "trade" consideration. And there are any number of additional considerations besides these—all relevant to the issue.

Besides the relevant considerations on issues like this there are, of course, a great many others being advanced that are clearly *ir*relevant, or whose relevance is much less clear. An example from a different debate is the view that if an American President wants to restrict people's ability to buy automatic firearms, then many opponents of such a step will argue that the President's motive is really to completely take away *all* the American citizen's constitutional rights to have guns, and in a sinister next step, to suspend all individual freedoms. This is, in all probability, not true, so this argument fails the "accuracy" criterion; but moreover, even if we were to assume for a moment that it were true, it is arguably still irrelevant: such a President would not have a chance to have his way with a plan like that, and it could be stopped a hundred times before ever being implemented— so the argument that the President has this hidden motive really has little or no relevance in regard to his actual proposal to limit the accessibility of automatic firearms somewhat.

A related type of bad argument is the *straw man* argument. If the President proposes to put certain restrictions on the sale of automatic guns, then to claim that he has proposed to ban *all* guns altogether is a straw man. To make a straw man is to attribute a claim or a proposal to someone who hasn't made it. One can also make straw man versions of other people's arguments. This is what happens when someone attributes an argument to someone who hasn't advanced it. An example would be to say that the President in our example argues for his proposal by saying that it will completely eliminate homicides in the US. Probably no one, no matter how strongly in favor of gun control, would advance such an extravagant argument, and if a spokesman for gun ownership claims that his opponents argue like this, then the debate is quickly turning absurd. Nevertheless arguments of the irrelevant types just exemplified are heard much too frequently—usually from both sides (or all sides) on any given issue.

Weighty: this concept, which has been mentioned a few times already, becomes crucially important in practical argumentation precisely because there are more than one dimension to them, and probably several considerations belonging to each dimension. How much weight an argument has becomes worth considering if it is deemed accurate and relevant. (If it is not accurate or relevant, it can, of course, not have any weight either.)

It is a peculiar complication in considering the weight of an argument that one cannot do it for that argument taken by itself; one has to do it in relation to other relevant arguments on the same issue—and of those there are, as we saw, usually several on both sides. *Weight* therefore really means *relative weight*. All the arguments on both sides are in play when we are out to "weigh" an argument.

The weighing of all the arguments against each other will be additionally complicated by the presence of interpersonal variance—or, in a word, "subjectivity." For example, on the topic of Britain's EU membership, some will hold that freedom for Britain to pass its own laws without any interference from "Brussels" carries a tremendous weight and outweighs all other considerations. Others, however, will feel that this aspect of national freedom is in practice pretty restricted anyway, and that on the whole it doesn't matter all that much; economy is more important.

Here we see in a nutshell the difficulty in weighing arguments in politics: there are no objective truths about relative weight.

We can *criticize* and *evaluate* arguments, and debaters and experts can help us understand what, for example, certain facts and numbers mean, and how certain they are. On these points there is much that is objective, and subjective views will not all be equally plausible; some factual claims simply *are* inaccurate, not to say false or untrue. It is not the case that "everyone has a right to his own statistics," as an American politician is reputed to have said. And some arguments really *are* irrelevant in a way that should be exposed.

However, the *weighing* of arguments is another matter; everyone must somehow weigh or balance the arguments for him- or herself, and in that there is considerable room for different subjective perspectives.

This is because, for one thing, arguments are of different *kinds* (or dimensions, as we said above). Should the economic argument trump the "freedom" argument? We have no physical pair of scales on which we can literally "weigh" the arguments on an issue against each other; the weighing is not a literal, physical and hence objective one, but is basically characterized by subjectivity. The philosopher Carl Wellman (1971) was aware of this; he not only coined the term "conductive reasoning" for the situation where we try to balance the pro and con arguments on an issue (that is, we bring those arguments together, so we "con-duct" them)—he also used the old term "hefting" for what we do when we "weigh" arguments against each that cannot be weighed in an objective sense.

But despite all these complications and despite the ineradicable presence of subjectivity on the scene—or precisely because of it—it is still the case that an individual trying to take a stand on a disputed issue needs all the help he or she can get in the form of good arguments on both sides. And in order to be able to weigh them against each other one especially needs the debaters on each side to *hear* and *answer* the arguments from the other side.

A Public Debate Based on Common Values

Let us imagine to ourselves an argument about Britain's EU membership in which someone says: "We bankers have really made a bundle with Britain in the EU, so let's remain so we can continue to rake it in." Is this a good argument?

Many will say: No—it may be true, but it is not good, because it is not a relevant argument for staying in the EU—for the rest of us who are not bankers, that is. Or take this argument: "We Conservatives believe Britain should leave the EU because if we don't say that a lot of our voters will go over to UKIP" (a party whose main platform is that Britain should leave the EU). That kind of argument would also jar the ears, and in fact one rarely hears politicians say such things—in public, that is.

The reason is that both these arguments are built on *special interest*. The first argument builds on the fact that a certain group of voters (bankers) have a selfish interest in preserving a state of affairs that they profit from. The second is built on the idea that a given political party would rather gain than lose votes—and we can well understand that, but it is nevertheless something that the rest of us voters need not care about. Both arguments are probably accurate enough because they both invoke something that is probably a fact; but neither of these facts appears to be really relevant to the voter who is about to choose a standpoint.

The point is that arguments that are put forward in public debate should be related to *the common good*. To put it simply, arguments in *public* debate should refer to concerns that matter to the *public*. They should refer to values or effects that everyone, or a lot of people, recognize as important. This is just a special case of the principle that if you want to persuade someone you should refer to some belief that this person or group already shares. Most citizens don't believe it is very desirable in itself that bankers make a bundle—in fact a lot of citizens probably think that if they do, then some change is called for, because it isn't really *just* that one profession should rake it in while many others in our society are in dire straits.

The principle we are dealing with here is essentially the same that has been stated in Chaïm Perelman and Lucie Olbrechts-Tyteca's *The New Rhetoric* (1969) as the necessity of there being some "common ground" that serves as a "starting point" for anyone's attempt to convince someone of something. In democracy theory, Amy Gutmann and Denis Thompson have formulated the principle of "reciprocity," which means, essentially, that "a citizen offers reason that can be accepted by others who are similarly motivated to find reasons that can be accepted by others" (2009, p. 53). Note how it is implied here that a debater is *motivated* to find such reasons—because they constitute his chance of having his conclusion or policy accepted by others. But the fact that debaters find—and *need* to find—reasons (arguments) that can be accepted by others does *not* imply that others will necessarily accept their conclusions—for example, the policies they argue for; as Gutmann and Thompson also emphasize, reciprocity does not always produce agreement.

To argue on the basis of the common good can also be defined as arguing with reference to values that are commonly shared. They have to be values that others share, *including* those who do not agree with the policy one argues for; if they don't somehow share a value invoked in the argument we make, then our chance of persuading them is nil. That a particular group or a particular party wants to protect its self-interest has nothing to do with common values. And for that reason such an argument has no place in *public* political debate. It is something that may be said in closed groups, behind closed doors. The argument that bankers will continue to do well if Britain stays in the EU will have traction among bankers, but not much outside that segment. Similarly, a Muslim fundamentalist (or a fundamentalist Christian) probably (and hopefully) would not get far in a public debate with an argument to the effect that we should ban homosexuality because the Koran (or the Bible) condemns it. These books are not expressions of common values, at least not if they are interpreted literally and in a fundamentalist way.

Here we have one of the advantages of public debate (there are disadvantages too): in public it is a bad idea to argue with reference to self-interest; one must do it with reference to values that are held in common— if not by all, then by most. Purely group-related arguments have little or no *public* traction. To promise financial payments to members of a particular group if they cooperate in getting one elected is not argumentation at all, but more like a business transaction. "If you give me this, then I will give you that. You scratch my back, and I'll scratch yours." Said in a private context something like this is sometimes called "log-rolling." Said in a public context to a broad group it is sometimes called "pork barrel politics." One could also call it political marketing.

It is a fact that in political campaigns nowadays we do see a great deal of political marketing. Political campaigners and their consultants are becoming increasingly adept at using current technology to home in on carefully selected segments of the electorate and appeal to their particular self-interest in communication that only they receive. This kind of selective communication will become ever easier, in part because of the new digital media and advanced databases in which citizens are divided into segments this way and that. For example, a politician running for a seat in a constituency with many well-off homeowners may distribute flyers or send out emails to this group of people saying: "Here in our district there are many homeowners for whom the freeze on property taxes proposed by Party X will save thousands every year. If you want that, then vote for me, the candidate for party X." If a candidate were to argue to the population at large for a freeze on home-owner tax on the ground that it would particularly benefit owners of big houses, it might cost him votes rather than win them. He would instead have to defend this policy with reference to "common" values—for example, financial security for *all* homeowners, or the social desirability of a general tax freeze.

In these times of precisely targeted political marketing appealing it becomes increasingly important that there should be public argumentation appealing to common values. There are many divisive forces at work that will pull us apart from each other for the sake of placing us in separate segments or interest groups. To go down this road is to approach a society of mutually isolated "parallel societies."

Answering as Crucial in Argumentation Democracy

In public debate in a democracy it is important, not only that those who argue for a candidate or a policy try to live up to the three criteria: accurate, relevant, weighty—it is equally important that those who debate with others, or who are asked to defend their policies in the media, attend to arguments and criticisms coming from others and *answer* them. It is arguably the real acid test of useful democratic debate that debaters in principle *answer* arguments from others.

But what does it mean to answer? Not every reply is an answer. What is required?

The obligation to answer can in principle be satisfied in two ways—and in two ways only:

– *Either* one explains why the opponent's or questioner's argument is bad. It can be bad in two ways—by having a problem with accuracy or with relevance (possibly with both).

– *Or* one acknowledges that the opponent's argument is good enough (i.e., it fulfills the accuracy and relevance criteria); but then one explains why one doesn't think it is especially weighty, that is to say, why the arguments *for* one's own position still outweigh the opponent's arguments *against* it.

It is this final comparison of pro and con arguments that constitutes weighing. It is what every single voter must do for him- or herself. The weighing has to be a kind of "comparison," since it cannot be an actual physical weighing in terms of pounds or kilograms or some other objective unit. (For that reason let us put "weighing" in quotes from now on.) And because of this we need to do the "weighing" ourselves and assume the responsibility for it ourselves. We cannot call in experts to do it for us. There *are* no experts that can do it for us.

This does not alter the fact that in advance of this personal "weighing" of arguments there is a great deal we do need—both from the politicians who want us to adopt a particular standpoint and from people with experience on the issue as well as experts of all kinds. By listening to all of them we may hope to acquire a basis for our own "weighing" of the arguments. This will help us get an overall view of what the issue involves, what arguments pertain to it, which arguments from each side are accurate and relevant, what the other party has to say in answer to them—and how much "weight" we then feel we can assign to them, in relation to the other relevant arguments.

Perhaps the fundamental principles of public debate that have just been sketched sound obvious, almost banal. But they imply a number of not-so-banal consequences:

– Democracy is not just the principles that people can vote, and the majority rules. There also has to be public debate in which the parties give relevant arguments for their standpoints and answer opposing arguments.

– Consensus, i.e., complete agreement on an issue, cannot be expected to arise, and no one can expect to win over all the others to his or her side.

– There will be *some* individuals on both sides who will change their standpoints, but only some.

– Some of those who did not have a standpoint initially will choose a standpoint.

– All who participate in the debate, or listen to it, will, however, become better informed about the issue. Even though most of those who have a standpoint will probably continue to hold it, many of them will be likely to find additional support for it, extend it, modify it or attach some qualifications to it.

– Arguments should appeal to shared values; arguments based on the arguer's personal value system or on his or her pure self-interest have no weight for those who do not share that value system or that self-interest.

– Answers to an opposing argument must include either a reasonable criticism of it or an acknowledgment of it, plus a "weighing" of the arguments for and against.

A democracy that has public debates like these can be called an *argumentation democracy*. A current term used by an increasing number of thinkers and scholars is *deliberative democracy*. Its key notion is *deliberation*, which is simply a Latin word that means "weighing." One could say that what has just been described is one notion of what a "deliberative" democracy implies.

A related concept is that of a "conversation democracy" (or "dialogue democracy"). This term was used in a book written in 1945 by a forerunner of the deliberative democracy strand of thinking—the Danish theologian and educator Hal Koch. For him the central features of democracy were not just that general elections are held and that the majority decides, but also that there is ongoing debate. The rules and principles for such a debate are similar to those outlined above.

Importantly, "conversation democracy" does not mean that the discussants must necessarily come to agreement but only that through conversation one "seeks to get the matter looked at from all sides and that the parties to the conversation strive to ... reach a more correct and reasonable understanding of the problem behind the conflict" (1945, p. 16).

Koch's thinking has been criticized because it was thought that he was beating the drum for a kind of *consensus* democracy—a democracy in which it is expected that all will come to agreement if only they continue to talk reasonably with each other. Such an ideal is attributed—rightly or wrongly—to the German social philosopher Jürgen Habermas. But that was not what Koch meant, and a conversation-based or argumentation-based democracy does not build on this idea at all. There are many good reasons why a group of people will not necessarily come to an agreement, no matter how much and how well they argue. To believe that deliberation or argumentation or conversation is essential to democracy does not entail the view that argumentation must lead to agreement among the debaters. It *can* do that, or at least bring it closer—but much of the time the debaters continue to hold exactly the same positions after the debate that they did before it. However, even so, debate is essential to democracy; it is, after all, not for the sake of the debaters that debates are held but for their audiences (citizens, voters).

Debates should be held and evaluated with a view to what citizens need. What they need is open discussion of what is best for the society—discussion that brings bring accurate and relevant arguments onto the stage, and makes sure that citizens are helped in their attempts to "weigh" them—which requires that they are properly answered.

That ideal has become increasingly distant in debates in contemporary Western democracies in the last ten to twenty years. This essay tries to set up a yardstick that can help us assess what we get—and be conscious of what we lack.

REFERENCES

Davidson, D., 1996. The folly of trying to define truth. *The Journal of Philosophy,* 93.6: 263-278.

Downs, A., 1957. An economic theory of political action in a democracy. *The Journal of Political Economy*, 135-150.

Easton, D., 1965. *A Framework for Political Analysis*. Vol. 25. Englewood Cliffs, NJ: Prentice-Hall.

Garsten, B., 2011. The rhetoric revival in political theory. *Annual Review of Political Science* 14: 159-180.

Govier, T., 1987. *Problems in Argument Analysis and Evaluation*. Dordrecht: Foris.

Gutmann, A., and D. Thompson, 2009. *Democracy and Disagreement*. Cambridge, MA: Harvard University Press.

Koch, H., 1945. *Hvad er Demokrati?* Copenhagen: Folkevirke-Serien.

Perelman, C., and L. Olbrechts-Tyteca. 1969. *The New Rhetoric: Treatise on Argumentation*. Notre Dame: University of Notre Dame Press.

Riker, W. H. 1982. *Liberalism Against Populism: A Confrontation between the Theory of Democracy and the Theory of Social Choice*. San Francisco: Freeman, 1982.

Smith, A. 1971. *Lectures on Rhetoric and Belles Lettres*. J. M. Lothian (Ed.). Carbondale: Southern Illinois Press.

Wellman, C. 1971. *Challenge and Response: Justification in Ethics*. Carbondale: Southern Illinois University Press.

Part 4: Rhetoric and Practice

16.

Non-Truth-Conditional Quantification*

It is argued here that vague quantification, one of the most common constructions in natural language communication, cannot and should not be accounted for in terms of truth conditions—a dominant notion among linguists and philosophers of language who wish to account for all semantic meaning in terms of referential meaning. Instead, a huge class of common quantifying expressions should be seen as essentially "argumentative" or "persuasive." Their only clear meaning lies in their aptness to support a conclusion of a certain kind.

This article—or rather, this collection of rambling remarks—allows itself an amount of irreverence which calls for some apology. The motivation behind it is certain simple observations I believe to have made and wish to communicate. They have been made by others, but those treatments of them which I have seen have, I feel, tried to explain away these observations rather than to take them seriously. The observations I mean all involve what has been called *vagueness* in quantification, either of amounts or degrees, in natural language. I believe there are countless cases of vagueness in quantification in natural language where the vagueness is crucial and unresolvable. Now if my linguistic intuition tells me about all these cases of unresolvable vagueness, I look for a theory to explain *why* the vagueness is there, not for one that tries to say that it isn't. I make the assumption that a truth-conditionally based semantics cannot put up with unresolvable vagueness in quantification. If this is not the case, my remarks become inoperative as far as truth-conditionalism is concerned. However, the claim that unresolvable vagueness is common in natural language remains, and my wish is to make it implausible to say that it isn't. I confess that I am either unfamiliar or unimpressed with existing attempts to resolve vagueness in quantification—mostly because they

*This his article was originally published in *Possibilities and Limitations of Pragmatics: Proceedings of the Conference on Pragmatics, Urbino, July 1979.* Amsterdam: John Benjamins. 1981, 359-366. Reprinted with permission of the Publisher.

employ an amount of logical formalism that make them opaque to me. For example, there is Altham and Tennant (1975), whose "sortal quantification," as far as I understand it, has recourse to the classes-and-norms idea discussed below; and there is Kamp (1975), which, for the student who can comprehend that sort of thing, might contain something that refutes my claims. Be that as it may, I still think somebody has to make new observations about natural language. Logicians may then try to explain the mechanisms in what they have seen, not to explain it away. It cannot be satisfactory to let logicians set up a theory of natural language based on "The King of France is bald" and other bits and scraps made up to illustrate what they are looking for in the first place.

Currently, logically oriented semantic theories are much attracted by the project of accounting for meaning in terms of truth conditions. This seminal idea is the sort of notion that is capable of grabbing hold of the minds of a large body of students within a subject, while others in the same subject, who are in the hold of some other seminal idea, tend to be impatient with it, and conversely. It will be no secret in the following that the present writer, not exactly a linguist and much less a logician, belongs to the class of impatients as far as truth conditions are concerned. In a general way, I think that linguists and other researchers in academic fields to a large extent have their views dictated to them by the *charm* that various seminal ideas exercise over their senses. And the charm that certain ideas have to certain people is again derived from certain ruling instincts in their conscious and unconscious minds. This is no less true, I believe, of logicians than anybody else. Furthermore, the whole point of the following remarks is coherent with the idea that the primitive function of natural languages is to help satisfy the conscious or subconscious needs of individuals, as dictated by certain basic instincts.

As a believer in this, I am likely to say things like "The contribution made by truth conditions to the meaning of utterances in natural languages is small, while the contribution made by other mechanisms is large," whereas believers in logical semantics would put it the other way round. For instance, Ruth Kempson (1977, p. 41), after conceding that areas of meaning like non-indicative sentences may not be describable in terms of truth conditions, adds a footnote saying: "A small and inhomogeneous group of lexical items also seems to resist analysis in terms of truth conditions. These include *even, but, deplore,* and some uses of *if*' (!). What I want to suggest is that a *large* group of lexical items seems to resist analysis in such terms. And in anticipation of what I have to say, let me direct your attention to the first sentence in the quote, and to the first sentence of my own following it.

The final, and boldest, claim I am going to make below is precisely that the meaning of such uses of *small* and *large* as we find here cannot in any respectable way be accounted for truth-conditionally, but only if natural language is seen as purposive action for the furtherance of speakers' interests and needs.

Thus, a great many adjectival and adverbial quantifiers appear to be much more easily accounted for in terms of speaker's purpose than in truth-conditional terms. Take a sentence like

(1) *The dictator had several clergymen arrested*

This would typically occur in a newspaper report, e .g., about social riots in some Latin American country. It would be evidently suitable to support the reporter's statement as to what sort of a country it is, or what sort of man the dictator is. But it does not give the reader much idea of just *how* many clergymen were arrested. However, if it was substituted with a sentence that does, such as

(2) *The dictator had 117 clergymen arrested*

it would probably be of much less use in conveying the reporter's idea, and the reader might be inclined to ask: "So what? What do you *make* of that?" On the other hand, the item *several* would not be of much use to the dictator himself in the situation where he wants his National Guard, or whatever, to go out and arrest a certain number of clergymen taking part in a demonstration or something. The order:

(3) *Arrest several of those clergymen!*

would be rather inappropriate here and probably put the National Guard in a state of disorientation.

The point is that the purpose of *several* is not so much truth-conditional as it is *argumentative,* in the sense suggested by Ducrot (1973), Anscombre and Ducrot (1976, 1978). Leaning on their formulation of argumentative properties of items like *almost (presque),* we might say that the most important lexical feature of *several* is the following: it may be used in a sentence S_1 to support any sentence S_2 which is such that S_2 receives stronger support the *more* members of a class are referred to in S_1. It is not important, in a sentence containing *several,* to know just *how* many members of a class it refers to. The important thing is that the kind of statement it is meant to support is the kind just defined, e.g., the statement *The dictator has taken a harsh course on political dissent within the church.* Now in a situation where, say, 1,000 clergymen have been demonstrating and 117 arrested, one reporter might write *The dictator had several clergymen arrested,* whereas another might write *The dictator only had a few of the clergymen arrested.* The meaning of *several* and *only a few* is non-truth-conditional in the sense that there is no saying whether the actual state of affairs described by the two statements fulfils the truth conditions of one or the other. But so much is certain to any reader familiar with the lexical properties of the two items in question: only the writer of the first statement may, with coherence, go on to say *the dictator has taken a harsh course on political dissent within the church.*

An interesting adverbial quantifier is *a bit.* Suppose I say

(4) *Scotland is a bit rocky*

Again it is quite unclear just what degree of rockiness I wish to predicate of Scotland. I am not saying anything that you could go to Scotland and test to see if Scotland satisfies the truth conditions of it. Truth-conditionally, I am probably only saying that there *are* rocks in Scotland. But I *am* saying more than this. I am saying that *whatever* degree of rockiness can be truthfully predicated of Scotland, it is *too much for my taste.* A typical situation for (4) to occur in would be a discussion with my wife over where we ought to go on holiday. A likely reaction to (4) would be to say, *What do you mean? Rocks are LOVELY!* Such a reaction would be a purposive act—trying to get me to see the nice side of rocks—against the purposive act represented by (4), which is an attempt to *avoid* going to Scotland on holiday.

Consider now a statement like (5), which is quite likely to be heard in the current debate over nuclear energy:

(5) *Nuclear plants often have uncontrolled radioactive blowouts*

As before, my claim is going to be that the quantifier contained in this sentence, *often,* carries a kind of meaning that cannot be described in terms of truth conditions. It should begin to be clear by now that if this claim can be validated the carpet is drawn away under the truth-conditional account of an enormous amount of quantifying expressions.

As far as I can see, the only notion truth-conditionalism can rely on to keep the carpet under its feet against attacks of this sort is the notion of implicit *norms.* The idea is that apparent vagueness in adjectives or adverbials is resolved in each individual case by looking at what class, or sort, of thing, or event, the vague expression applies to. The argument is usually advanced in connection with what Lyons (1968, p. 465) calls "implicitly graded antonyms," i.e., pairs like *small* vs. *big,* where the apparent vagueness of *This elephant is big* is resolved by implying that the elephant is bigger *than the norm* for that sort of thing, i.e., elephants. I wish to return to items like *big* and *small* below, but I would like to take a first skirmish with the "norm" theory now. In the case of (5), what norm could one adduce in order to resolve the vagueness of *often?* The example is chosen expressly with a view to exclude such a resolution, yet I claim that (5) is a perfectly natural and meaningful sort of thing to say, as in fact we all do all the time. You can't explicate *often* by saying that radioactive blowouts happen often in nuclear plants compared to the "norm" for, e.g., power plants in general, for in other power plants radioactive blowouts do not occur at all. Hence there is no such norm. It is interesting that (5) is a statement that one would very likely hear from an opponent of nuclear power, whereas it would probably never come from one of its advocates. The case is quite analogous to that of *several.* Two opposed participants in a hearing or panel discussion on nuclear power might be quite agreed as to just *how* many radioactive blowouts have occurred in nuclear plants within a given period, e.g., 117; yet one will probably maintain that they happen *often,* while the other will maintain that they do not—or perhaps that they do happen often, *but* represent no danger. The meaning of *often* is thus argumentative, not truth-conditional; in the sense that the basic bit of lexical information about *often* is that it may be used to describe a certain state of affairs if you have a certain kind of conclusion you want to support in doing so; if you reject this kind of conclusion, you may only use it if you follow it up with a sentence containing *but* or a synonym of *but.*

I would ask the reader, without further comment, to consider the functioning of items like *repeatedly, again and again* and *all the time* in terms similar to those just suggested.

Now consider (6):

(6) *Uncontrolled radioactive blowouts from nuclear plants are frequent*

It would take a great deal of hair-splitting to claim that (5) and (6) are not synonymous. That is to say, if my argument about *often* in (5) holds good, it also applies to *frequent* in (6). And in that case it will turn out that an enormous amount of utterances in daily communication involve non-truth-conditional predication, *viz.* all those where adjectives of the type *frequent/rare, small/big* are operative in the predicate. These are Lyons's "implicitly graded antonyms," or, in the terminology suggested by P.T. Geach (1956): "logically attributive adjectives." These he distinguishes from "logically predicative adjectives" like *red* or *round,* which apply to any individual in the same way regardless how it is specified. In contrast, it is characteristic of a logically attributive adjective that the individual it applies to must be specified as a member of some class for which some norm may be indicated (regarding size, or whatever it is). Fink (1973, p. 26) also calls such adjectives "logically comparative" because the positive form of such an adjective is "logically dependent on its comparative and not vice versa. A big mouse is not bigger than other mice because the property *bigness* is realized in it in an especially high degree; it is a big mouse simply because it is bigger than most other mice." This, as far as I can see, amounts to saying that there is a norm for bigness in mice which can be defined as a degree of bigness such that half the mice in the world are bigger and the other half smaller. Lyons makes essentially the same point when he remarks that "such words as *big* and *small,* or *good* and *bad,* do not refer to independent, 'opposite' qualities, but are merely lexical devices for grading as 'more than' or 'less than' with respect to some implicit norm" (1968, pp. 465-66).

But whereas this idea is nicely applicable to paradigmatic cases like *This mouse is big,* it is hard to see how it can apply to (6). The application of an implicit norm regarding the quality attributed to the subject is, as we have seen, dependent on the reference of the subject to some class. While it is easy enough to refer an individual like *this mouse* to the class of all existing mice, what is one to do if the subject is not an individual, but a whole class in itself? The only way seems to be to regard it as a subclass of some super-class—but what is that to be? As we have already seen, we cannot in (6), any more than in (5), have recourse to a super-class of "uncontrolled radioactive blowouts in *all* kinds of plants," for this super-class would have no more members than the sub-class. If pressed, we might try to establish as super-class either "*all* kinds of blowouts in nuclear plants" or "*all* accidents in *all* kinds of plants" or an unlimited number of other super-classes, none of which are in any way suggested by (6) itself.

It is possibly the case that in *most* sentences with a logically attributive in the predicate the subject *may* be referred to some class with some implicit norm. But the point is that this operation is not possible in *all* such sentences. Hence I claim that the cases where a class and a norm may be appropriately adduced are special cases of a more general phenomenon. The more general phenomenon is that predicates with logically attributive adjectives in them are basically argumentative, not truth-conditional; however, they may be so directly, or *via* some norm. In order to salvage the "norm" account as a general ploy to resolve vagueness, one might, in a last desperate move, suggest that each occurrence of a logically attributive adjective in the predicate either refers to some pre-existent implicit norm, *or*, if this is not possible, sets up an idiosyncratic, *ad-hoc* norm. In order to test this suggestion, let us consider one more example of the kind that resists the simpler analysis. Let us imagine a man and a wife who have to part from each other for a certain period, say, three weeks. In parting they tell one another to cheer up and not be too sad about it, and one of them says,

(7) *Three weeks is not long*

Now in many such cases it would be implausible to suggest that the couple already have, in their shared background knowledge or whatever we want to call it, an implicit norm regarding the length of periods of separation according to which three weeks is not "long." At any rate, one cannot in such a situation, along the lines suggested by Fink, interpret *not long* to mean "shorter than most periods of separation"; it may be the couple's first and even their only period away from each other. Now the "last desperate move" consists in saying that the utterance of (7) *establishes* a norm where none existed before; that is, we now have to do with a "norm" that is *not* implicit. But all we know about this very ephemeral, *ad-hoc* norm is that according to it, three weeks is *not long*. Now if we wish, as a logical semanticist would, to resolve the vagueness and find the truth-conditional meaning of (7), this is all we have to work with, and hence all we can do is to substitute, for the phrase *not long*, the phrase *three weeks* in which case we end up with *Three weeks is three weeks*. On a pragmatic account this might indeed have some meaning, but certainly not the same as the original utterance. On any account, *Three weeks is three weeks* is, on the face of it, tautological, and on a truth-conditional account it would then have no meaning at all.

As we see, the truth-conditional account in cases such as this only manages to eliminate any meaning the utterance might have had. An alternative account, which I am not in a position to develop fully here, ought instead to interpret the meaning of the utterance in terms of what sentences it may *cohere* with. *Three weeks is not long* in the given situation may cohere with any sentence that serves to encourage mental fortitude in the hearer and/or to discourage sorrow. Thus the speaker, in saying *Three weeks is not long*, is not making an assertion as to how long three weeks are in relation to any norm, but he/she is acting to encourage fortitude, etc., in relation to the length of the period of separation, *such as it is*. This interpretation is of course situation-dependent (in that it assumes, among other things, that the speaker and hearer are unhappy about being separated). But it may be made independent of such contextual factors if we say the following: The meaning of the utterance is that it may cohere, in a supporting function, with any sentence which is such that it receives stronger support the *shorter* the period of absence is. Conversely, there will be no coherence with any sentence which does not fulfill this condition. Thus, in terms of coherence, the meaning of *Three weeks is not long* may be understood and described without vagueness even though there is no actual sentence for it to cohere with, and without making it circular by imputing to it a reliance on any volatile, *ad-hoc* "norm." The meaning of the utterance, if truth-conditional, is void.

Such a radically non-truth-conditional use of logically attributive adjectives is not limited to situations of the emotional nature suggested in the above example. On the contrary, it is found all the time in such allegedly non-emotional, matter-of-fact types of communication as newspaper reporting and political debate or statement. To illustrate this, let me choose just one example, quite randomly, from a newspaper I picked up on my way to the pragmatics conference at Urbino, *The International Herald Tribune* from Thursday, July 5, 1979. One of the cover stories of this issue is headed "EEC Aides See OPEC Drive to Set Oil Ceiling" and reports on talks held in London between high-ranking EEC and OPEC representatives. The reporter, Joseph Fitchett, writes:

> In the London talks, the European team, which apparently did most of the talking while OPEC listened, concentrated on conveying 'confidence-building measures' aimed at demonstrating the intentions of industrial countries to cooperate over energy matters. The French industry minister, for instance, reportedly spent much of his time trying to convince the OPEC team that the U. S. commitment at the Tokyo summit to a ceiling on oil imports until 1985 was a sincere, important step by the Carter administration to promote energy-saving.

Consider the adjective *much* in the second sentence. The function of this sentence, which gives it coherence with the first, is to establish support for the assertion made in the first—the sort of conjunctive relation that Halliday and Hasan (1976, p. 248) would call "exemplificatory apposition" and place under the heading of "internal additive relations." My point is that *much* cannot be referred to any norm that gives us any clue as to just *how* much of his time the French minister spent trying to convince the OPEC team. The contribution made to meaning by *much* is not truth-conditional. Its purpose is simply to get the reader to accept the assertion contained in the first period, not to supply information on the actual amount of time spent by the minister doing this or that.

Further down in the article, the reporter quotes Mr. Guido Brunner, the EEC commissioner for energy, on the outcome of the talks: "Despite the inauspicious start in London, Mr. Brunner said that 'we stand a fair chance to continue' some form of dialogue, perhaps in another framework." Consider the word *fair* in the quote from Mr. Brunner. Just how big a chance could he have meant there was for a continuation of the talks? 25 %? 50 %? More than 50 %? There is no way for the hearer or the reader of Mr. Brunner's statement to assess this. Most likely Mr. Brunner himself did not have any figure in mind at all. The function of his statement is simply what we might call *persuasive*; its meaning emerges when one considers the various continuations it might think ably cohere with in a supporting function. All we know about these is that they must be such that they will receive *stronger* support, the *fairer* the chance is.

We may now revert to the quarrel as to whether the group of lexical items unaccountable for in truth-conditional terms is "small" or "large." The difference between logical semanticists and more instinctive ones like myself is that I would say it was large, and they would say it was small. I have tried above to show that it is certainly larger than they think. But even if they concede that some of my points are correctly taken, they will probably still say it is small, and I will still say it is large. Both statements are vague when interpreted truth-conditionally; in fact there is no deciding whether the actual state of affairs, if it could be agreed upon, comes closer to satisfying the truth conditions of my statement or those of theirs. My whole point is that this is quite as it should be, if you believe in the sort of theory of language that I think ought to be developed; but not if you believe in theirs. People who believe that all sentences, or even all *declarative* sentences, have a statable truth-conditional meaning, ought to be biting their tongues a lot of the times they use predicates involving words like *big* or *small*; the rest of us may go on using them unabashedly, as we always have. The use of unresolvably vague, non-truth-conditional quantification in natural language is, I believe, as omnipresent as people's attempts, in whatever they do or say, to further their interests, dictated by instincts.

REFERENCES

Altham, J.E.J., and Neil W. Tennant. 1975. Sortal quantification. In E. Keenan (Ed.), *Formal Semantics of Natural Language*. Cambridge: Cambridge University Press, 46-58.

Anscombre, J.-C, and O. Ducrot. 1978. Échelles argumentatives, échelles implicatives, et lois de discours. *Semantikos* 2.2-3, 43-66.

Anscombre, J.-C., and O. Ducrot. 1976. L'argumentation dans la langue. *Langages* 42: 5-27.

Ducrot, O. 1973. *La preuve et le dire*. Paris: Mame.

Fink, H. 1973. *The Analysis of Goodness*. Oxford: University of Oxford.

Geach, P. T. 1956. Good and evil. *Analysis* 17, 33-42.

Halliday, M.A.K., and R. Hasan. 1976. *Cohesion in English*. London: Longman.

Kamp, H. 1975. Two theories about adjectives. In E. Keenan (Ed.), *Formal Semantics of Natural Language*. Cambridge: Cambridge University Press, 123-155.

Kempson, R.M. 1977. *Semantic Theory*. Cambridge: Cambridge University Press.

Lyons, J. 1968. *Introduction to Theoretical Linguistics*. Cambridge: Cambridge University Press.

Wittgenstein, L. 1966. *Lectures and Conversations on Aesthetics, Psychology and Religious Belief*. Oxford: Blackwell.

17.

Inception: How the Unsaid May Become Public Knowledge[*]

This paper is a case study of how language may be used by a politician in ways apt to make people believe propositions that have not been made, and which may be highly controversial or debatable. The corpus from which the examples are drawn is President George W. Bush's public speeches during the months before the invasion of Iraq in March 2003, and the controversial but implicit proposition that they may have helped putting over to many Americans is that Iraq's Saddam Hussein had some complicity in the terrorist attacks of 9/11. To analyze the linguistic mechanisms that may have allowed this to happen, the paper invokes H.P. Grice's notion of "conversational implicature," but also two other mechanisms that may work in similar ways, and which are, it seems, less explored in linguistics pragmatics and rhetoric.

Introduction

Arguably, the discipline of rhetoric can be defined as the study of communication as it impacts on the minds of audiences. This paper will look at examples of one category of such impact: it will study how utterances by a speaker may—more or less strongly—invite audiences to interpret them as conveying semantic content that is not explicitly expressed. In other words, some people in the audience take that content as part of what the speaker meant to say, yet it is not manifestly there in the speaker's utterances.

It is of course a trivial insight that speakers' utterances imply more than they explicitly state. There have been insightful studies of how politicians implicitly convey views they want their audiences to accept, as for

[*] Originally published in *Rhetoric, Discourse and Knowledge*, M. Załeska and U. Okulska, (Eds.). Frankfurt am Main: Peter Lang, 2016, 276-286. Reprinted with permission of the Publisher.

example the rhetorician Anders Sigrell's study of persuasion "between the lines" in modern political argumentation (1995), or the discourse analyst Teun van Dijk's study of "political implicatures" in Spanish Prime Minister Aznar's rhetoric on his country's participation in the Iraq war (2005). The views conveyed in these ways generally are ones that the speakers in question *also* state explicitly, and indeed in any way they can; however, what is common to the phenomena I will look at below is that they may, in the understanding of some hearers, convey content that the speaker a) is *not* willing to state explicitly, and b) would deny if asked point-blank whether he intended to convey it. In fact, in the case studied, the speaker did deny it.

The case concerns public speeches given by President George W. Bush during the half year that preceded the invasion of Iraq in March 2003, and the particular notion that I believe some hearers believed he meant to convey, but which he did not assert, was that Iraq's dictator Saddam Hussein had somehow been involved in the terrorist acts of September 11, 2001.

Without discussing whether Bush and his speechwriters deliberately intended their words to convey this notion, I wish to emphasize that there may be the following advantages for a public speaker in conveying certain notions in this manner. First, the speaker cannot be held responsible for them since he did not state them or otherwise convey them in a manner that is manifest and unquestionable (e.g., by direct assertion or by presupposition). Second, these notions are likely to "fly under the radar" of many in the speaker's audience, since non-explicit semantic content is ubiquitous in human communication. In the standard case, it helps securing speedy and unimpeded communication between people, and hence it is normally processed rather automatically by hearers and out of their mental focus; for these reasons at least some hearers are likely to accept such content unreflectingly as being part of the speaker's meaning, and maybe even as being true. Third, for the same reasons, the speaker is not so likely to be expected to offer argumentation in their support. Because of these potential advantages a public speaker may have a strong motive for using language inviting hearers to imply views that the speaker does not wish to state or to argue for—views that he does not want to be consciously processed, questioned or scrutinized. To the extent the speaker is successful in this, such views may become part of what many in the audience consider public, shared knowledge.

An important pioneer in the study of implicit semantic meaning is the philosopher H. Paul Grice. The first of three phenomena that I will exemplify belongs to the category he, in a celebrated paper, called *conversational implicature* (1975; 1989). I will then discuss examples of two related concepts inspired by his approach; I call them *fuzzy reference* and *suggestive sentence collocation*. I will discuss these three mechanisms in descending order of what we may call "suggestive force." Conversational implicature is the type I think most likely to suggest unasserted ideas in hearers' minds; hence these are the ones that make it most relevant to blame the speaker for manipulation. The other two types may also act suggestively and automatically in varying degrees, but here a smaller part of the blame may be laid to the speaker and a correspondingly larger part to the carelessness of hearers.

In my rhetorical analysis, I will specifically suggest that several pronouncements by President George W. Bush shortly before the invasion of Iraq had the capacity to prompt, invite or sustain in the minds of hearers the idea that Iraq's Saddam Hussein was somehow complicit in the terrorist acts of September 11. This idea, which Bush never explicitly asserted, became widespread in the US population in the months preceding the invasion of Iraq, concurrent with the rhetorical campaign by the Bush administration from which I draw my examples.

More generally, I will suggest that an explicit and nuanced awareness of such phenomena can help rhetoricians and other students of public and political communication expose and illuminate phenomena that deserve such exposure. Because they work the way they do, many hearers may accept ideas conveyed in this way without reasons for them being asked, or given. Moreover, I believe much of the mental work in the minds of hearers who accept these ideas is automatic and subliminal; and that is another reason why it is useful to be distinctly aware of what goes on. Hence it is particularly useful to know these devices and to be able to distinguish between them. That way we citizens, and also the media, may better recognize them and engage in analysis and deliberation when we hear them; and we may consider to what degree politicians who use such devices are to blame for it, and to what degree we should blame ourselves for letting them work on our minds without giving them proper attention.

In this analysis concepts and approaches drawn from linguistic pragmatics are adduced to provide a more explicit conceptual understanding of the mechanisms involved; on the other hand, the understanding and assessment of precisely how these mechanism function and are used (or exploited) in actual political rhetoric in a specific historical context is a task for rhetorical criticism. The two disciplines may thus mutually aid and supplement each other.

Conversational implicature

First, the mechanism that H.P. Grice has called *conversational implicature*. An implicature of an utterance is the hearers' understanding of something that is not said, but which the hearers believe the speaker *means* them to understand. Grice thinks implicatures arise because of what he calls the "Cooperative Principle" underlying all normal conversations. It states: "Make your conversational contribution such as is required, at the stage at which it occurs, by the accepted purpose or direction of the talk exchange in which you are engaged" (Grice 1989, p. 26). Speakers (and writers) are normally expected to adhere to this principle, and hearers' (and readers') implicit awareness of this may cause them to assume, often inadvertently, that certain ideas are implicated as part of the speaker's intended meaning—because if they were not, the speaker would be perceived as violating the Cooperative Principle.

From this principle Grice infers a set of "conversational maxims" (Grice 1989, pp. 26–27). At issue in the present context is, primarily, the second "maxim of Quantity," which says: "Do not make your contribution more informative than is required." Because our default expectation is that speakers will obey this rule, we tend, in the default case, to automatically believe that all the information they put into their utterance and all the choices it reflects have meanings that they intend us to grasp.

There is also the "maxim of Relation," which says, simply: "Be relevant." This makes us automatically expect that speakers *intend* everything in their utterances to be relevant; for example, conjoined sentences should be relevant to each other somehow, that is, have some semantic coherence. This will be in evidence in some of the examples discussed below.

The first example comes from Bush's "State of the Union" speech shortly before the invasion of Iraq.[21]

(1) Before September the 11th, many in the world believed that Saddam Hussein could be contained.

---

[21] Held in Congress on January 28, 2003. All quotations from the documents discussed have been taken from the site http://georgewbush-whitehouse.archives.gov/infocus/iraq/archive.html.

Example (1) has the implicature that those who believed, before 9/11, that Saddam could be contained, stopped believing it that day—otherwise it would be pointless to say that they believed it *before* 9/11, and (1) would be "more informative than required." But *why* did they stop believing it after that day? Bush does not state the reason explicitly. But surely the minds of many hearers would automatically have set to work on it. If 9/11 changed people's view of Saddam, then the most obvious reason would be that Saddam was involved in 9/11. There may be other reasons, as we shall see, but none as obvious.

Now consider the next sentence in the speech:

(2) But chemical agents, lethal viruses and shadowy terrorist networks are not easily contained.

Here, new implicatures may arise. The preferred one will probably be that Saddam *has* these agents and viruses and *supports* these networks; otherwise (2) also would be "more informative than required."

If, then, (1) invites an implicature that Saddam was indeed involved in 9/11, then (2) coheres with that idea since the phrase *shadowy terrorist networks* could now be heard as referring to the same terrorist network(s) that perpetrated the 9/11 attacks. However, the chemical agents and viruses cannot connect with this idea, since nothing of those kinds was involved in the attacks. The two sentences together, including their implicatures, may then be heard as implicating that Saddam was involved in 9/11 through his connection with terrorist networks, and that he *also* has chemical and biological weapons that he may lend to a new attack.

However, Bush's official reason why 9/11 should make Americans change their view of Saddam only contained the second idea: that Saddam might equip a new terrorist attack, not that he was involved in the first one. Consider this passage from a press release:

(3) We felt secure here in the country. There's no way we could have possibly envisioned that the battlefield would change. And it has. And that's why we've got to deal with all the threats. That's why Americans must understand that when a tyrant like Saddam Hussein possesses weapons of mass destruction (...).[22]

In other words, we now know that terrorists can attack the mainland, and all villanous dictators like Saddam who could equip them with WMD's should therefore be seen as threats that we must deal with.

---

[22] "Bush, Prime Minister Blair Discuss Keeping the Peace," September 7, 2002.

But surely this reason for connecting Saddam and 9/11 is less plausible than the simple idea that he was *involved* in 9/11. First, the need to deal with *all* threats from villainous dictators who might act like this does not explain why Saddam in particular is such an urgent concern, or why Saddam is singled out for mention in (1) there rather than *all* villanous dictators. Secondly, as for terrorists bringing WMD's to America, nothing really seems to have changed. For them to bring nuclear weapons is probably out of the question, and always has been; as for chemical and biological WMD's, these can be so small that it has always been possible to bring them into the US, so here too there is nothing new. Moreover, terrorists can probably get these things elsewhere if Saddam is deposed. So Bush's reasoning as to why 9/11 suddenly reveals the necessity of deposing Saddam is much more complex than the idea that Saddam was involved in 9/11, and also rather implausible. Thus the most natural implicature in (1) and (2) is still that Saddam was involved in 9/11.

On January 31, 2003, Bush received British Prime Minister Blair, and in a joint press conference a journalist asked them: "Do you believe that there is a link between Saddam Hussein, a direct link, and the men who attacked on September the 11th?" Bush replied:

(4) I can't make that claim.

And he never did.[23] Yet when the invasion of Iraq was begun in March 2003, and for some time after, most Americans had come to believe that there was such a link. I am arguing that several public utterances by Bush and his staff in the months before the invasion were apt to suggest or sustain the idea in hearers' minds that Bush believed in this link. Is this denial such an utterance?

At any rate Bush's denial of the claim about the direct link between Saddam and 9/11 is worded in a peculiar way. The default wording of a denial when asked whether one believes something that one in fact does not believe would be something like *No, I don't.* The linguist and social anthropologist Stephen Levinson proposes a heuristic for what he calls "marked" formulations, based on Grice's maxim of Quantity (i.e., that one should not be more informative than required): "What's said in an abnormal way, isn't normal; or Marked message indicates marked situation" (2000, p. 33). Hearers' minds, using this heuristic, may

---

[23] As late as 2009, former Vice President Dick Cheney also denied the Saddam-9/11 link, see "Cheney: No link between Saddam Hussein, 9/11," http://edition.cnn.com/2009/POLITICS/06/01/cheney.speech/.

automatically proceed to interpret Bush's "abnormally" worded denial as implicating that even though he *cannot* make the claim, he would still *like* to, perhaps because he believes it to be true but just does not (yet) have the evidence that would allow him to do make it (thus obeying Grice's second "maxim of Quality": "Do not say that for which you lack evidence.") The rhetorician Jeanne Fahnestock, in a paper on Perelman and Olbrechts-Tyteca's view of style as argument, makes a similar observation about "the marked term being the less expected choice that can draw attention to itself and initiate a Gricean implicature to detect intentions behind its use" ("No neutral choices," 2011, p. 36). On that principle, some hearers might reason that Bush intended them to understand that he holds the claim to be true.

Concluding on the examples considered so far, Bush bears a responsibility for speaking in ways that are apt to mislead hearers as to his intended meaning—and understanding a speaker's intended meaning is, according to another seminal insight by Grice (1957, 1969), the criterion for understanding what someone's utterance means. Bush probably made a number of Americans take him to mean something that he neither asserted nor gave reasons for. And the people that were thus duped are only partly to be blamed for it.

Fuzzy reference

Our second suggestive mechanism is "fuzzy reference." Certain phrases in Bush's speeches may be heard as having *either* a relatively vague reference, *or* a more specific one that suggests a connection between Saddam and 9/11; both interpretations are possible and natural. On the vague interpretation, Bush's sentences do not violate any maxims of conversation and do not become pointless. Hearers in whose minds the more specific interpretation pops up thus have themselves to blame in a higher degree than in the examples we have seen so far.

In a long speech on "the Iraqi threat" we get this passage:

(5) We've experienced the horror of September the 11th. We have seen that those who hate America are willing to crash airplanes into buildings full of innocent people. Our enemies would be no less willing, in fact, they would be eager, to use biological or chemical, or a nuclear weapon.[24]

---

[24] "President Bush Outlines Iraqi Threat," October 7, 2002.

Whom do the phrases *those who hate America* and *our enemies* refer to? Here contextual information must help the hearer work that out. Surely Saddam must belong to at least one of these sets, or be connected with it, since the passage is part of a speech in which "President Bush Outlines Iraqi Threat." Are the referents of these two phrases the same sets of people? If we expect a "rich" coherence between sentences we might take Bush to mean just that. Saddam is clearly cast as America's central enemy in this speech, and it is also natural to accept that he is among *those who hate America* (although in the eighties, during the Iran-Iraq war, Saddam was a friend of the US and was visited by US officials like later Defense Secretary Rumsfeld); but if he is among *those who hate America*, then he is also among those we know are *willing to crash airplanes*. We *have seen* them do so, so the nominal phrase must include the perpetrators of the 9/11 terrorist acts. In other words, Saddam must somehow be connected with this lot. That is a line of automatic reasoning that may easily be triggered by this passage.

Later in the speech we have this:

(6) The attacks of September the 11th showed our country that vast oceans no longer protect us from danger. Before that tragic date, we had only hints of al Qaeda's plans and designs. Today in Iraq, we see a threat whose outlines are far more clearly defined, and whose consequences could be far more deadly. Saddam Hussein's actions have put us on notice, and there is no refuge from our responsibilities.

Again, an impulse to hear a "rich" connection between sentences might make hearers assume that what connects the terrorists referred to in the first two sentences of (6) and the agents named in the last two sentences (Iraq and Saddam) is not only that they threaten Americans, but also that there is a *personal* overlap between them. This understanding may be strengthened by the phrase *Saddam Hussein's actions*, since it is plausible, in the context, to hear this phrase as referring to Saddam's supposed part in 9/11.

The last two examples demonstrate that *definite nominal phrases* are potent devices for suggestion. In the following passage too a definite nominal phrase may put a hearer's mind to work to identify a specific referent:

(7) ... the best way to secure the homeland is to chase the killers down, one at a time, and bring them to justice. (Applause.) And that's what we're going to do.[25]

The date is December 2002; Bush and his staff are campaigning for an invasion of Iraq. That makes it natural for hearers to assume that the proposed invasion is the same as the plan to *chase the killers down*, since that is *what we're going to do*. But then Saddam and Iraq become in some sense co-referential with the definite noun phrase *the killers*. The definite article, as used here, normally requires that the killers are already *known* to hearers as killers. Where would hearers have that knowledge from? An obvious answer is: from 9/11.

Later we get this:

(8) (…) out of the evil done to this country, is going to come incredible good (…)

The *evil done to this country* surely refers to 9/11; the *good* probably refers to the imagined results of a war against Saddam. The causal claim that *this* good comes out of *that* evil makes much more sense to hearers if they assume that the phrase about evil also refers to something Saddam was involved in—in this case, 9/11.

On February 13, Bush said this:

(9) The terrorists brought this war to us—and now we're taking it back to them. (Applause.)[26]

Here, *the terrorists* and *them* are surely coreferential; *them* is anaphoric, as Halliday and Hasan (1976) would say. Since *them*, uttered at this point in time, clearly means Saddam and his regime, whom the US is preparing to attack, it also seems natural to hear the phrase about the terrorists as referring to, or including, Saddam—unless both *the terrorists* and *them* are taken to refer very broadly to, say, all terrorists in the world.

In all these examples of fuzzy reference, and many similar ones, we find ambiguous nominal phrases which may or may not be taken to identify Saddam as involved in 9/11; another term for the same phenomenon might be "semantical underdeterminacy" (Atlas 2000). Even when these phrases are interpreted in the vague sense they do not flout any conversational maxims; so hearers who hear a more specific reference to Saddam should realize that they are letting themselves be duped.

Suggestive sentence collocation

---

[25] "Remarks by the President in Terrell for Senate and Louisiana Republican Party Luncheon," December 3, 2002.

[26] "President Salutes Sailors at Naval Station Mayport in Jacksonville," February 13, 2003.

Jeanne Fahnestock devotes the fourth section of her monograph on *Rhetorical Style* to "passage construction." This term comprises concepts such as coherence and cohesion (Halliday and Hasan 1976), "given/new," and "topic/comment." As a motto for the section she quotes the 18th Century rhetorician George Campbell's classic work *The Philosophy of Rhetoric* (1776) as saying that "as there should always be a natural connexion in the sentiments of a discourse, there should generally be corresponding to this, an artificial connexion in the signs. Without such a connexion the whole will appear a sort of patchwork and not a uniform piece" (from the chapter on "Connectives Employed in Combining the Sentences in a Discourse"; Fahnestock 2011, p. 345).

This is a clear anticipation of Grice's thinking about implicatures—the point being that if hearers (or readers) do not perceive an "artificial connexion," i.e., explicit "connectives" (coherence-signaling devices) in a text, then it will be natural for them to try to construct a "natural connexion in the sentiments" (i.e., in the semantic meaning) of the discourse because if such connection is absent, the text will appear a "patchwork and not a uniform piece."

This is in fact an apt description of the third type I will discuss of suggestive mechanisms in Bush's rhetoric on Iraq. Here, where we have to do with "passage construction," i.e., with collocations of sentences, the hearer bears even more responsibility for hearing what is not said than in the first two types. It is a default expectation, as both Campbell, Grice and Fahnestock are aware, that collocated sentences in well-written texts cohere semantically; but just *how* much coherence across sentences and what *specific* semantic ties the speaker has intended is partly guesswork on the hearer's part.

Consider these sentences:

(10) The entire world has witnessed Iraq's eleven-year history of defiance, deception and bad faith.

We also must never forget the most vivid events of recent history. On September the 11th, 2001, America felt its vulnerability—even to threats that gather on the other side of the earth.[27]

It is a clear possibility to hear all three sentences as describing the actions of the same agent, namely Saddam's Iraq; on the other hand, the

---

[27] "President Bush Outlines Iraqi Threat."

passage does not violate any conversational maxims when not heard like this. In the same speech, we get this:

(11) We've learned that Iraq has trained al Qaeda members in bomb-making and poisons and deadly gases. And we know that after September the 11th, Saddam Hussein's regime gleefully celebrated the terrorist attacks on America.

Here two sentences are not just collocated but conjoined with *and*. That conjunction is rich in potential meanings. One might say, for example, that Grice's Maxim of Relevance prompts us to hear conjoined sentences as maximally relevant to each other, and/or jointly relevant to some encompassing purpose or direction. But a hearer's mind is likely to wonder: relevant in what way, for what purpose, in what direction?

Levinson states that "when events are conjoined, they tend to be read as temporally successive and, if at all plausible, as causally connected" (2000, p. 122). In fact, a temporal reading of *and* is clearly possible; moreover, one may read both sentences as relevant support for an unsaid conclusion to the effect, for example, that Saddam is a villain. But a causal reading is also inviting: Iraq has been training terrorists; the 9/11 terrorists were among them, and *that* caused Saddam's regime to celebrate their act—this is how such an interpretation might go. On the other hand the passage is still meaningful when not heard like this.

George W. Bush's speeches before the Iraq invasion contain many passages where similar phenomena are in evidence. Sentences referring to 9/11 repeatedly rub shoulders with sentences referring to Saddam. Those who heard these statements as implicating that Saddam was involved in 9/11 bamboozled themselves; but Bush and his speechwriters gave them ample opportunities to do so.

Conclusion

In 2007, a group of communication scholars (John *et al.*, 2007) issued a call that has not yet, I believe, been adequately answered:

Research that examines with analytical precision the specific mechanisms of Implication of September 11, al Qaeda, and Saddam used by Bush in his public communications, as well as how these implications were buttressed by public claims of other administration members, is an important task for future scholarship. (p. 207)

More specifically, John *et al.* said: "Using threat rhetoric, Bush over time adroitly associated terrorists such as al Qaeda, which evoked the horrors of September 11, with Saddam and Iraq, without necessarily connecting the two directly" (2007, p. 207). Also they pointed out:

> In 2006, two national polls showed that more than 40 Percent of American adults still believed Saddam was involved in September 11. The president and his administration denied ever making any such claim, and nowhere in these texts did Bush *directly* say Saddam supported either the September 11 attacks or al Qaeda. However, our findings confirm the view expressed by growing numbers of critics that the impression was conveyed, even implied, by the rhetoric of Bush and his administration. The result was a political advantage for the administration and Republicans, but the cost was a misinformed public and a political discourse that pushed—largely unchecked by those in the mainstream—toward war with Iraq. (John *et al.* 2007, p. 212)

What is said here clearly motivates studies like the present one. Many have felt that the Bush administration's public communications *somehow* conveyed the assumption that Saddam was involved in 9/11, although he never made that direct claim (declaring that he couldn't); but the exact mechanisms by which they did it have remained less illuminated.

Steuter & Wills (2008) report that Frank Luntz, a communication consultant for the Bush administration, wrote a memo in June 2004, advising Bush to justify the war in Iraq indirectly, rather than directly, avoiding arguments about preemption and relying instead on references to 9/11. The memo was titled *Communicating the Principles of Prevention & Protection in the War on Terror* and offered advice on what language to use in referring to the war in Iraq:

> His advice was to connect the war on terror to the war in Iraq by ensuring that "no speech about homeland security or Iraq should begin without a reference to 9/11." Luntz's recommended phrases such as "It is better to fight the War on Terror on the streets of Baghdad than on the streets of New York or Washington" and "9/11 changed everything," became staples of Republican rhetoric. (Steuter and Wills 2008, p. 14)

The examples in this paper provide good reasons why citizens in a democracy should learn about the automatic (or if you prefer, "subliminal") impact of political discourse on audiences' minds. There are several rhetorical devices that depend on automatic cognitive mechanisms in audiences. Practicing rhetors (such as Presidents and speechwriters) use them routinely and skillfully; rhetorical critics may notice them and point them out, and they should. Concepts and insights inspired by work in other disciplines such as linguistic pragmatics may help them do so more explicitly and with more nuance and a better basis for pronouncing critique and caution. The devices studied above are apt to create phony public "knowledge" in our minds, or as rhetoricians might say, dubious *doxai*—without our conscious knowledge.

REFERENCES

Atlas, J. D. 2000. *Logic, Meaning, and Conversation: Semantical Underdeterminacy, Implicature, and the Semantics/Pragmatics Interface.* New York: Oxford University Press.

van Dijk, T.A. 2005. War rhetoric of a little ally: Political implicatures and Aznar's legitimatization of the war in Iraq. *Journal of Language and Politics* 4, 65-91.

Fahnestock, J. 2011. *Rhetorical Style: The Uses of Language in Persuasion.* New York: Oxford University Press.

Fahnestock, J. 2011. 'No neutral choices': The art of style in *The New Rhetoric.* In J.T. Gage, (Ed.), *The Promise of Reason: Studies in The New Rhetoric.* Carbondale: Southern Illinois University Press, 29-47.

Grice, H. P. 1957. Meaning. *The Philosophical Review* 66, 377-388.

Grice, H. P. 1969. Utterer's meaning and intention. *The Philosophical Review* 78, 147-177.

Grice, H. P. 1975. Logic and conversation. In P. Cole, and J.L. Morgan (Eds.), *Syntax and Semantics.* New York: Academic Press, 41-58. Reprinted in Grice, *Studies in the Way of Words.* Cambridge, MA: Harvard University Press 1989, 22-40.

Halliday, M.A.K., and R. Hasan. 1976. *Cohesion in English.* London: Longman.

John, S. L., D. Domke, K. Coe, and E.S. Graham. 2007. Going public, crisis after crisis: The Bush administration and the press from September 11 to Saddam. *Rhetoric & Public Address* 10, 195-219.

Levinson, S.C. 2000. *Presumptive Meanings: The Theory of Generalized Conversational Implicature.* Cambridge, MA: MIT Press.

Sigrell, A. 1995. *Att övertyga mellan raderna.* Åstorp: Retorik-förlaget.

Steuter, E., and D. Wills. 2008. *At War with Metaphor: Media, Propaganda, and Racism in the War on Terror*. Lanham, MD: Lexington Books.

18.

A Good Paper Makes a Case: Teaching Academic Writing the Macro-Toulmin Way[*]

In this paper, we contend that students' problems with genre and task definition in the writing of academic papers may be helped if we adapt Toulmin's argument model to explain what the genre requirements of the academic paper are, as opposed to everyday argumentation. The student should be encouraged to apply the model as an assessment criterion and, at the same time, as a heuristic tool during her work on the paper. This involves a "macroscopic" or "top-down" approach to the evolving draft, not a "microscopic" analysis of individual passages. The paper suggests a number of class activities that will help students apply a "Macro-Toulmin" view to their own work.

Faculty across all departments, perhaps especially in the liberal arts subjects, have trouble teaching students what an academic paper is, and how to write it. Central to the problem is students' difficulty with "task definition" (Flower *et al.* 1990), i.e., in making the appropriate "task interpretation" (Nelson, 1990). Another way of saying this is that what many students lack is not the motivation or even the ability to write good academic discourse, but an understanding of the *genre* of the academic paper. They fail to understand one or more of the following: the overall *purpose* of the academic paper, its *components*, and how the components *contribute* to the overall purpose. This is frustrating for teachers, but it is even more frustrating for students. Often they find themselves lavishing high hopes and hard work, only to receive the dampening response that they are trying to do the wrong thing.

We suggest that Toulmin's argument model (1958), in a particular interpretation, is a significant help against this frustration, for teachers and students alike. To argumentation scholars, there is nothing new in using the

[*]Co-authored with Signe Hegelund, this article was originally published in *Teaching Academic Writing in European Higher Education*, L. Björk, G. Bräuer, L. Rienecker, and P. S. Jörgensen (Eds.). Kluwer Academic Publishers 2003, 75-85. Reprinted with permission of Springer Publishers.

Toulmin model for pedagogical purposes; however, its use in general argumentation courses is, in many people's experience, very debatable—a view also taken in Fulkerson's comprehensive discussion (1996), with which we tend to agree. But what we shall suggest in this paper is that the model, while not particularly successful in general argumentation pedagogy, is highly useful precisely when it comes to teaching *academic* writing.

In our view, the main problem with the Toulmin model in relation to general argumentation from everyday life is that it sends students searching for warrants in texts where the warrant, ever so often, is simply not there. Instead, such texts often contain multiple grounds or data for the claim they support. Armed with Toulmin's model, students tend arbitrarily to label some of these "warrants" and others "data," but they often realize that there is no real difference in status between the elements thus labelled—and confusion ensues.

A better approach, but still a problematic one, is to point out that everyday argumentation is often based on tacit "assumptions" of a general kind. Toulmin's model may then be invoked, with "warrant" serving as a synonym for such assumptions. This is the approach taken in one of the better argumentation textbooks, John Gage's *The Shape of Reason* (1991). However, the explicit formulation of other people's tacit assumptions—what many argumentation theorists call "reconstructing" the argument—is, we believe, a questionable practice, especially when it amounts to formulating those unstated premises that will make the argument deductively "valid" (cf. van Eemeren *et al.* 1993).

But the typical absence of stated warrants in everyday argumentation is precisely one of the major features that separate it from argumentation as it is supposed to be in academic papers. Thus, what amounts to a weakness in the Toulmin model when applied to the analysis of ordinary argument is a strength when we use it as a tool in teaching the academic paper. We contend that students' problems with genre and task definition in the writing of academic papers may be significantly helped if we adapt the model to explain what the genre requirements of the academic paper are.

The adaptation implies that we use the model in a *macroscopic* way—hence our neologism, "Macro-Toulmin." We suggest that we should use the model to attack the difficulties of the academic paper top-down, saying to students, "The overall purpose, components, and inner functioning of an academic paper *as a whole* can be better understood by means of this model."

What this means in practice is that the student is encouraged to apply the model as an assessment criterion and, at the same time, as a heuristic tool during her work on the paper. The idea is not to use it microscopically, looking at individual sentences in her text and checking for data or warrants for claims that occur (or do not occur) in them. This is the way the model is often used in attempts to adapt it to the analysis of everyday argumentative texts. Instead, we suggest that the student should learn to apply the model to her evolving draft in a top-down manner, asking herself, "Does my draft contain material that will fit into each of the six categories represented by the model?" As a general rule we suggest that a "default" good academic paper contains material representing each of the six categories. The accompanying graph (see next page) will illustrate how.

As the figure suggests, the *Claim* in a typical academic paper is something that will often be located in the conclusion. This feature, incidentally, is one that often annoys non-academic readers, who (understandably) expect to be told or at least warned from the outset what the drift of the paper is going to be. Wise instructors, especially in academic sub-genres that come close to non-academic writing, such as literary criticism, comply with this expectation by asking students to offer the reader some pre-understanding of their line of argument in the Introduction. But in many academic papers, perhaps most, the claim cannot be located in one or two single passages. Even so, a good paper does make a claim. It should not merely be the kind of paper that many students write, and which some are even required to write, titled "An Analysis of ... ." Such a paper is not a valid instantiation of what academic research is about; rather, it can be seen as an exercise that sharpens a skill necessary for doing "real" papers, i.e., real research work. A good paper is not merely an "analysis" of something; it may use analysis as a tool, but its end is to make a point or claim.

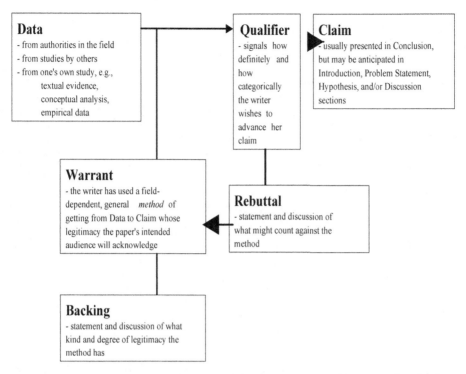

There are many criteria that the claim in an academic paper should live up to, more than can be discussed here; but the first criterion is simply that the claim should be there. The student should have something to say—she should make a statement that is hers, not just reiterate or summarize statements made by the scholars she has studied.

The second category is, of course, *Data.* It usually constitutes the body of the paper. Basic criteria for the data include: 1) Data should support the claim. 2) Data that are irrelevant to the claim should be omitted. 3) Data that the student can be expected to know, and which might serve to undermine or qualify the claim, should be discussed.

Data may be of at least three kinds; what a specific paper, including the present one, has to present by way of data is often a combination of all three types:

1) Theoretical data, i.e., theories, concepts, definitions drawn from authorities, either esteemed individuals (for example, "Habermas says ... .") or current paradigms (for example, "it is generally assumed in Generative Grammar ... "). Such general assumptions belonging to a

current paradigm that the writer subscribes to are often presupposed rather than stated.

2) Specific data, drawn from studies by others.

3) Specific data, drawn from one's own study.

Specific data may include, according to field: textual evidence, conceptual analysis, examples, qualitative or quantitative empirical data, and many more.

The *Warrant* category: One of the defining features, perhaps the constitutive feature, of academic writing is that the writer should carefully discuss the warrant for the data she presents. Debaters in practical argument are generally not required to do so, and rarely do it—which is part of the reason why we find it so hard to teach the proper understanding of warrant in practical, extended argument. What happens when students try to apply the Toulmin model to instances of practical argument is often that they arbitrarily label some of the statements in the text "data" and others "warrant," while other students analysing the same text may have applied these labels the other way around.

In academic writing, as opposed to practical argument, the notion of warrant has much more meaning. This will be clear when we specify that what we propose to call warrant in academic writing is what academics often refer to as *method*. The method in a piece of research can be defined as its manner of collecting, selecting, and interpreting data. A given academic field allows and makes possible the use of certain types of data, and it prescribes ways these data may or may not be interpreted.

In some fields the methods are few, strictly defined and rigorously adhered to. In other fields, it is common that new studies give methodology a slightly new twist, e.g., by suggesting new types of data (as, for example, a new type of qualitative interview). In such cases it is essential that the paper clearly explain how these data are collected, selected, and interpreted. It may be that the method is drawn or at least inspired by studies in a neighbouring field; the method may also be a combination of traditional features, borrowed or adapted features, and new features. By codifying how to interpret data, methods constitute the bridge between data and claim; and this is why warrant is really another word for method.

Like warrants, methods are field-dependent. In fact, warrants or methods are not only field-dependent; they are actually constitutive of fields. The mastery of the codes we call method or warrant is at the heart of what constitutes professional competence in any academic field. Bazerman

(1981) presents an instructive study of how professional competence in three highly separate academic fields is largely constituted by differing norms as to what counts as warrants in the respective fields.

Backing, according to Toulmin, is what we come up with if we are asked "why *in general* this warrant should be accepted as having authority" (1958, p. 103). That is, the "backing" category should be represented by statements about how and why we are justified in adducing and interpreting the data we offer in support of our claim. And that implies discussing and defending not only this way of interpreting, but also the way we collect and select our data. Here again we have various options. We may refer to authority, either "authority figures" (here again, Habermas may be our example) or a current paradigm that sanctions such an interpretation; or we may point to parallel studies where a similar or related method has borne fruitful and reliable results. The synonym generally used for what the model labels backing is *theory*.

Rebuttal indicates "circumstances in which the general authority of the warrant would have to be set aside" (Toulmin 1958, p. 101). The criterion that there has to be something in the rebuttal category means that the paper must show awareness of what counts against allowing the step from data to claim. Hence the rebuttal category is connected to the warrant category; notice that rebuttal in this sense does not include data that seems to count against the claim; such data should be discussed in the paper as well, but belong in the data category, as mentioned above.

Rebuttal may take many forms, according to field. On a very general level, a specific study might lead to the kind of fundamental problems of theory or paradigm known to many fields, for example as to whether the study of human phenomena is better or worse off by limiting itself to the observation of behaviour, or whether introspection is allowable or preferable, and the like. In other situations, there might be specific questions, of either a theoretical, a practical or even an ethical nature, which might be raised to question the warrant of the data used.

What we see generally is that awareness of what might count in rebuttal of one's method of interpreting is central not only to the merit of an individual paper, but also to the professional competence and identity of the writer.

Taken together, the three elements Warrant, Backing and Rebuttal constitute what we might call a full-blown statement and discussion of Method. Depending on how known and accepted that method is by the intended audience, the categories Backing and Rebuttal may be represented by more or less material. The liminal case is research papers written so squarely within a paradigm accepted by the intended audience that the warrant may be taken for granted. This may be so, for example, in certain schools of literary criticism where the use of biographical data in the interpretation of texts by a given writer is seen as a matter of course (whereas other schools, as is well known, do not take that view at all). Here we may in fact see papers consisting exclusively of data and claim—and perhaps some instantiation of the last of the six elements in the model: the qualifier.

The *Qualifier,* in Toulmin's own words, indicates "the strength conferred by the warrant" on the step from data to claim. For the academic paper, this means that the student should discuss or at least signal how definitely and how categorically she wishes to advance her claim. There need not be any separate passage that can be labelled "qualifier"; more often a certain amount of qualification is indicated along the way by means of phrases like "this rather strongly suggests" or "a plausible interpretation would be."

We believe that the Toulmin model, thus interpreted, may not only help students understand the definition of the task of that problematic genre, the academic paper; it may also be a procedural help to them in producing such papers: While work on the paper is in progress, the student may use the model as a criterion for assessing material already in the draft, as well as a heuristic for inventing material still missing—by asking, "What have I got in this draft to fit into each of the categories represented in the model?" Thus, the model may help giving an awareness of the overall function of the genre, as well as of its component parts. Also, just as it may help in assessing one's own writing-in-progress, it may also help students read and assess academic writing by others.

In our experience, the main pedagogical advantage of using the Toulmin model as a macroscopic layout of the academic paper is that it increases the student's sense of the paper as one focused or functional unity. Students get a better understanding of what intimidating words like "data," "method," and "theory" refer to if they understand more clearly what these elements *do*. This in turn helps them tie the components of their paper together. This is also true on the verbal level, where we may see an increased and more discriminating use of meta-discourse—signposts telling the reader how the parts of the text work together.

On the level of substance, students may, for instance, suddenly realize how theories may supply the Backing that legitimizes or even prescribes a certain methodological choice; this again may help them collect, select, and interpret the material that constitutes their data. They may realize the various functions that theory may have in academic discourse, which may in turn help them generate theoretical ideas of their own and give them a critical understanding of what goes on in professional debates within a field. A functional awareness of Backing and Rebuttal may help them make a Claim that is no greater than their data will plausibly permit, and with the appropriate degree of qualification. Students realize how important it is for the plausibility of their claim that Method is made explicit (Warrant), legitimized (Backing) and scrutinized (Rebuttal). Essentially, students may learn to *assess* critically the merit of their own work—a skill high in the Bloom hierarchy of educational goals. This in turn may help them assess strengths and weakness in the work of others, either their peers or established authorities in their field.

Many students have difficulty applying theories in a critical and constructive way. This, we believe, is especially so in those fields in the humanities where methodological considerations are usually implicit rather than explicit, e.g., literary criticism. Student papers in these fields often leave the impression that theories are adduced, not in order to strengthen the writer's argument, but in order to please the instructor. Students whose papers seem to use theories in this way may benefit from seeing how theories function in an overall argumentative plan; they may realize that theories matter to method, both as legitimization and as criticism. And they may see that theories themselves may be subject to analysis in terms of argument structure.

Finally, approaching the academic paper as one argument may benefit students by heightening their awareness of the uses of metadiscourse to signal the overall plan of a paper. As noted by, among others, Prosser and Webb (1994), the presence of meaningful metadiscourse significantly makes for higher grades; Hyland (1998) has shown how meta-discourse in academic writing functions not only as a help for the reader to understand the intended structural relations within the paper, but also text-externally, (i.e., relations to discourse outside the text itself), by alluding to presupposed disciplinary assumptions and by helping the reader construct appropriate contexts.

Admittedly, the approach to the paper as one and just one argument is a pedagogical simplification. Many academic papers can better be described as making several claims, either parallel or hierarchically arranged (or a combination of both). Still, the model has the pedagogical advantage of facilitating novices' overall understanding of the genre, as well as of the specific paper they are working on. In our experience, the model does not inhibit creativity; instead, the overview of the paper's constituent parts that the model affords often allows students to improve further on its design.

We have used the model in teaching academic writing in a variety of formats. In the most basic version, it is possible, in a one-hour period, to introduce the model and offer a few examples of its elements with reference to excerpts or projects contributed by students in the class. A more spacious format is a seminar of two separate three-hour sessions. This allows for more elaborate presentation of the model, more extensive exemplification from students' papers in progress with class discussion, and some exercise activities, of which we will describe a few.

Activity: Early Claim Formulation

This is the instruction given to the class for this activity:

1. Write freely for 8-10 minutes on "the essence of my papers is ... "
2. Boil down the essence of your paper to one sentence—either a statement or a question.
3. Based on this sentence, state the claim of your paper. To help you do this, ask yourself the following question: "If I were to hand in this paper to-morrow, what would my conclusion be?"
4. Read aloud—let us all hear what claims in research papers may sound like.
5. (Optional question to the class:) Which of these claims would you choose to base a paper on?

Activity: Analysis of Model Examples

We generally use fairly short excerpts from selected student papers (max. 3 pages, preferably with line numbers). These papers are not by participants, but it is still important to use student papers so as to encourage the response "Whatever they can do, I can do." After silent in-class reading, everyone is instructed to locate claims, data, warrant, rebuttal, backing, and qualifiers. The aim is to teach students to identify the various elements, which are not always separate or neatly marked off, and assess the balance in the argument as a whole—e.g., will this set of data support a claim as large as this, is there enough backing, shouldn't the qualifiers be stronger? This activity is a useful exercise before analysing the participants' own papers-in-progress.

Activity: The Devil's Advocate—Critical Assessment of Argumentation in Others

The class looks closely at the argumentation in a paper and discusses whether each element is sound in itself, and whether the elements are in harmony. As an aid in this discussion, a checklist with these questions is handed out:

- What is the main claim? Given the argumentation presented in the paper, is it reasonable to make this claim?
- From where is data drawn to support the claim? Is the data credible and sufficient?
- What is the warrant, i.e., what method is used? Has the method been used in a sound way?
- What problems are there in connection with this method? What possible rebuttals are there?
- Why is the method applicable? What backing is there that may eliminate or minimize the effect of the rebuttals?
- How certain may we be of the soundness of the claim when we consider rebuttals and backing? In other words, what kind of qualification is called for?

Activity: Apply the Model to Your Own Paper-in-Progress

This activity plays a large role in our seminars. We have developed the following rubric, which we ask students to fill in with answers relating to their own papers-in-progress. If they are able to fill in all the slots and find that the elements are in reasonable balance, then the paper is probably on the right course. We find that this rubric has a capacity to get many students going. Some realize that they have a great deal more material in the right places then they thought, while others are confronted with holes that should be filled, or with a claim that needs modification, etc.

Questions on the overall argument in my paper. (Model examples, drawn from an archaeology paper, are given in *italics*.)

Claim: "What is my claim at this point in the writing process?"

Model example: The ancient city of X has directly influenced the architecture of city Y. Hence, there must have been a migration from X to Y.

My paper: …

Data: "What will I use as data for this claim?"

Model example: The bricks used in X and Y are identical to the millimetre.

My paper: …

Warrant: "What is my warrant (what method will I employ)?"

Model example: Description of how I will proceed as to selection of samples, measurement, number of bricks selected, etc.

My paper: …

Rebuttal: "What may be said in rebuttal of this method (what makes it problematic)?"

Model example: Only one parameter is used. The identity, rather than suggesting an influence, could be a coincidence.

My paper: …

Backing: "What supports the warrant (the use of this method), in spite of rebuttal(s)?"

Model example: It is extremely unlikely that such a similarity could be a coincidence, hence an influence must have taken place: the bricks must come from he same mould.

My paper: …

Qualifier: "Given the rebuttal and backing cited above, I expect to make my claim with the following qualifier."

Model example: It is highly probable that a migration has taken place from X to Y, but…

My paper: …

In our experience, students benefit particularly from analysis and assessment of argumentation in model excerpts drawn from papers in the top third of the scale. In one and the same process, students are trained in applying the model, recognizing well-made academic argumentation, and making critical but constructive assessment of each other's work. Thus, this activity may be used in the early part of a course, and it may be a help even for novice writers of academic papers.

Special non-credit courses, featuring activities such as those described above, are not the only way to heighten students' awareness of the academic paper as a genre. In "content" courses, especially on the more advanced levels, there will be frequent opportunities to apply the model to heighten students' awareness of the demands of the genre.

For example, it is customary in such courses to include excerpts from scholarly books, papers from journals, etc., as required reading in coursepacks or the like. As a rule, such readings are discussed only for the content, i.e., the results, theories, or ideas that they present. However, the instructor may also make a point of discussing such readings with regard to how they relate to the argument model.

For example, in history courses where actual historical studies in the form of journal articles or book chapters are studied, it will be relevant to dwell on passages where the writers discuss the validity of their sources. Such passages, in which some of the key skills that constitute "historical method" are called for, usually represent the "warrant" category. The sources used are, of course, the data. The claim is the historical interpretation derived from the sources.

In papers reporting empirical studies, it will generally be easy to locate passages where the elements of the model are in evidence. Often there is a separate "Method" section, which will usually contain most of the "Warrant" material in the paper. The theory underpinning the study, i.e., the Backing, may often be found in the introductory section, and/or under the discussion of Method. The Claim may be found near the beginning in the form of a hypothesis, and in the "Discussion" section in the form of an actual claim. Often, the Discussion will also contain elements of Rebuttal, as well as material that may be identified as Qualifier. As an example, chosen at random, we may cite this passage from a journal article on advertising (McQuarrie and Mick 1999, p. 52). In the subsection "Limitations and Future Research" (under "General Discussion") we read:

> We did not demonstrate that replacing, say, the visual pun in the almond ad with a verbal pun conveying the same brand attitude would, in turn, produce the same impact on consumer response. This limits our ability to assert that, for instance, a pun is a pun, whether visual or verbal, with the same characteristic impact.

A propos a discussion of the points the writers are trying to make about visual effects in advertising, the teacher may also point out to students that such a passage constitutes a Qualifier, and that its presence (together with several others) increase the credibility of the article as a whole. If it is part of the course requirement to write a research paper, we think the teacher should go out of his way to point out that the use of appropriate qualifiers, like this one, is one of the criteria by which these papers will be graded.

More generally, in any content course there will numerous opportunities for the teacher to make statements or initiate discussions on the functions and merits of specific passages in the course materials. This practice is a modern version of what ancient rhetoricians called *imitatio*: we read important writers not just in order to learn what they have to say, but also in order to learn from them how to say what *we* have to say.

An important part of this kind of reading is to be as critical as we are when reading papers or drafts by our peers. Here, too, the teacher will probably have to show the way. Statements by the teacher like: "This is an interesting study, but I think part of the data is irrelevant, and the writer ought to have discussed the following obvious objection to his method ..." may be eye-opening to students. They will realize that published research by esteemed scholars is not necessarily beyond reproach; that the merits of such research is not a black-or-white matter, but one in which there may be pros and cons; and that the criteria the teacher will apply in assessing the students' own papers include these, by which he finds others to fall short.

Even when only textbooks are being used (as opposed to actual research papers), it is still possible for the teacher to make observations like this: "What the textbook does here is something you should never try to do in a research paper. These are two different genres. It carefully introduces and explains Habermas's theory of the public sphere, but does not supply backing for its application to talk shows on TV; in your paper it should be the other way around."

To sum up, we suggest that there is indeed a use for the Toulmin model, despite much frustration with it in the teaching of general argument analysis among faculty and students alike. Coming as it does from a philosopher and ex-scientist, it is perhaps not surprising that more than anything it models the ideal case of *academic* argument. Moreover, we suggest that its real usefulness is only brought out when we give up applying Toulmin's labels microscopically to individual sentences and phrases in existing texts—and turn it upside down, as a tool for searching a text top down for material representing each of the categories. Finally, what we propose is using the model as an aid in production rather than in analysis, i.e., as a set of criteria to guide the tentative unfolding of a paper-in-progress. What it does in that capacity, judging by the responses of the hundreds of students who have attended our non-credit seminars, is to furnish them with an understanding of the academic paper as one kind of purpose-driven speech act.

REFERENCES

Bazerman, C. 1981. What written knowledge does: Three examples of academic discourse. *Philosophy of the Social Sciences* 11, 361-387.

Van Eemeren, F.H., R. Grootendorst, S. Jackson, and S. Jacobs. 1993. *Reconstructing Argumentative Discourse.* London/Tuscaloosa: The University of Alabama Press.

Flower, L., V. Stein, J. Ackerman, M.J. Kantz, K. McCormick, and W.C. Peck. 1990. *Reading-to-Write: Exploring a Cognitive and Social Process.* New York: Oxford University Press.

Fulkerson, R. 1996. The Toulmin model of argument and the teaching of composition. In B. Emmel, P. Resch, and D. Tenney (Eds.), *Argument Revisited; Argument Redefined.* Thousand Oaks: Sage Publications, 45-72.

Gage, J.T. 1991. *The Shape of Reason: Argumentative Writing in College*, 2nd ed. New York: Macmillan.

Hegelund, S. 1997. Argumentationen i universitetsopgaver. In L. Rienecker (Ed.), *Den gode opgave.* København: Gyldenda, 162-207.

_____. 2000a. *Akademisk Argumentation.* Frederiksberg: Samfundslitteratur.

_____. 2000b. Opgaven som ét argument og argumentation i opgaven. In L. Rienecker, and P.S. Jørgensen, (Eds.), *Den gode opgave* (revised edition). København: Samfundslitteratur, 227-276.

Hegelund, S., L. Rienecker and P.S. Jørgensen. 1999. Opgaven som et argument. Hvordan lærer vi de studerende at argumentere videnskabeligt? In L. Rienecker and P.S. Jørgensen (Eds.), *Opgaveskrivning på de videregående uddannelser: en læreRbog.* Frederiksberg: Samfundslitteratur, 162-199.

Hegelund, S., and C. Kock. 1999. Macro-Toulmin: The argument model as structural guideline in academic writing. In H.V. Hansen, C.W. Tindale, (Eds.), *Argumentation at the Century's Turn*. St. Catherines, ON: OSSA.

Nelson, J. 1990. This was an easy assignment: Examining how students interpret academic writing tasks. *Research in the Teaching of English* 24, 362-396.

Prosser, M., and C. Webb. 1994. Relating the process of undergraduate essay writing to the finished product. *Studies in Higher Education* 19, 125-138.

Toulmin, S.E. 1958. *The Uses of Argument*. Cambridge: Cambridge University Press.

19.

Generalizing Stasis Theory
for Everyday Use[*]

This paper attempts to revitalize an important source of rhetorical thinking from antiquity: the stasis (or status) system. It is argued that a "generalized" version of the system would be useful today as a resource for the production and assessment of argumentation about matters of shared concern in a society—not just as an aid for defendants in criminal cases. One generalizing move suggested is to integrate the sub-system known in antiquity as the "status legales," treating it as a subcategorization of the second of the "status rationales": that of "definition." A second generalizing move is to see the resulting conceptual system as a taxonomy of disagreements and controversies of all kinds that may occur in a society: ethical, political, etc.—not just criminal accusations. The paper suggests that those who learn to think about disagreements with this taxonomy in mind will be better able to understand what ongoing controversies are essentially about; however, it may also be a resource for debaters, helping them focus their argumentation on those points where they stand the best chance of persuading opponents.

Introduction: Public debate as trench warfare

When debaters disagree, it is important to understand the exact nature and scope of their disagreement. Each debater has an interest in knowing the precise reasons that make his opponents disagree with him, because if he wants some of his opponents to change their minds, those are the reasons he should try to refute. The onlooker, too, has an interest in knowing them, because they are probably the reasons that will best help him decide for himself.

However, public debaters often misrepresent and widen their disagreements. They distort each other's standpoints and reasons,

---

[*]Originally published in *Bending Opinion: Essays on Persuasion in the Public Domain*, T. van Haaften, H. Jansen, J. de Jong, and W. Koetsenruijter (Eds.). Leiden University Press, Leiden, 2011, 81-94. Reprinted with permission of the Publisher.

representing them as either bizarre or toothless (two subtypes of the 'straw man' fallacy). Or they ignore the opponents' real reasons and attribute imaginary reasons to them. They speculate on their opponents' base, hidden motives. Often they see an opponent as part of a large, monolithic block, so that he is either a member of a conspiracy or at least a "useful idiot". Attacks on the opponent's ethics, intellect, and personality often follow. Partisanship and polarization flourish. Debaters see their own standpoint as representing righteousness, while any divergent standpoint is seen as opposite, usually in a dichotomous sense: there are no third positions, no neutral ground. This way, political and social debate may resemble trench warfare as in the First World War. In both, we can see a typical widening of the front zone where the two parties clash.

For onlookers who look to debates for enlightenment to choose a standpoint there is little help. They would be better served if the debate would focus on those smaller sectors of the front where debaters crucially disagree, and where a true breakthrough might most likely occur. Litigation lawyers know the need to focus their argument on potentially decisive points and present a coordinative argumentation rather than a multiple set of unconnected reasons—to use the terminology of Franciska Snoeck Henkemans (2000). Interestingly, an empirical study of televised political debates where representative audiences voted on issues before and after each debate showed that here too the coordinative strategy is superior: what we called "single ground" debaters performed significantly better in terms of votes than "multiple ground" debaters (Jørgensen, Kock and Rørbech 1994; 1998, this volume, Chapter 12). Readers of a famous essay by Orwell (1946) will know that to shoot a mad elephant (as young Orwell once had to) one should place one bullet in the exact right spot with great force. A similar piece of advice seems to be sound regarding deliberative argument.

Status theory as a focusing tool

Ancient stasis (status) theory was a tool to help forensic debaters focus their case. The central part of the theory was the *status rationales*: the conjectural, the definitional, and the qualitative, equivalent to the questions: What are the facts? How are the facts to be categorized? What particular circumstances characterize them?

These *status rationales* question the facts at issue, but another main part of *status* theory was the *status legales*, which question the laws by which the facts were to be judged.

Usually, four types of disagreement are mentioned. In all of them the debater argues that there is no clear one-to-one match between a law and a fact. *Ratiocinatio* is when there is no norm that meaningfully covers the fact, so we must reason by analogy from existing norms about something else. *Ambiguum* is where there is one relevant norm that may cover the fact, but it is ambiguous or abstract. In *scriptum et voluntas* there is also one relevant norm, but this time it is too specific; it may literally cover the fact, but the argument is that we should read the spirit of the law, not the letter. Finally, *contrariae leges* is where two or more norms which may cover the fact, but they point to different conclusions.

Notice that here we pass logically from cases with no applicable norms, to cases where one norm may apply, which is either too abstract or too specific, to cases with more than one applicable norm.

Ancient *status* theories also included lists of so-called "practical issues," such as legality, justice, advantage, feasibility, honor, consequence. All these are examples of relevant norms (or norm systems) that may legitimately be invoked in social and political argument, but they are mutually heterogeneous, i.e., the set of relevant norms is "multidimensional," and hence the norms will necessarily tend to clash. For example, a debater might support a policy as advantageous; another might oppose it as dishonourable. This is the practical parallel to the issue of *contrariae leges*. But the main components of the *status* system—the *status rationales* and the *status legales*—were intended for legal argument; they presupposed the existence of explicit, formal rules (*leges*), which were meant to cover the facts of the case, i.e., to correlate *ius* and *factum*.

I suggest a way to generalize and integrate all these strategies into one scheme which can help identify and narrow down the decisive reasons not just in legal argument, but in deliberative argument as well, that is, in any social disagreement over action. Such a scheme might help clarify, for debaters and onlookers alike, what current disagreements are essentially about, and in particular what they are not about.

We should note that the differences between legal and political argument are not absolute. Legal argument often relies on informal norms used in practical reasoning; political argument often invokes legal considerations. Both kinds are about action—legal argument is about legal action in response to past acts, political argument is mainly about future action but also about evaluating and modifying past acts. In both cases acts are being supported or opposed with reference to norms of right action, which function as "warrants," to use Toulmin's term (1958). The difference is mainly that legal norms are typically written statutes which are recognized as valid and operative by all; norms underlying political argument are usually informal, unwritten and not always recognized as valid by all, or to the same degree. Also, they are most often implicit rather than explicitly stated, and they are more heterogeneous or "multidimensional" than legal norms: some may be purely prudential and are perhaps only concerned with economic consequences; others may be virtue-ethical norms about moral conduct, fairness or justice; others again are in fact formal and legal, for example considerations as to whether a policy is constitutional.

Applying status theory to social and political argument

Status theory is a typology of the problems we may meet in correlating norms and facts, and since these problems are analogous in the two fields, I propose we use *status* theory to consider not just legal argument, but social and political argument as well.

For this purpose, I further propose to integrate the *status legales* in the *status rationales*. In the *status of definition*, we discuss how a fact can be subsumed under a norm. The *status legales* are about the same kind of discussion, but they start from the other end: the norms. The reason they are useful is that they specify the problems raised by the correlation of norms and facts. Finally, I also propose to include the "practical issues" of political argument among the many norms that are invoked, implicitly or explicitly, in political argument.

So this is how we may integrate and generalize the various components of ancient *status* thinking into a comprehensive typology of disagreement in social debates. 1) We generalize the formal legal concept of "laws" into a broader, more varied concept of norms. 2) We see the *status legales* as specifications of the ways in which the correlation between facts and norms may be contentious. 3) We use the "practical issues" to specify some of the varied norms that may clash in social debates.

The complete, integrated *status* system for practical debates is given in the following table (see table on pp. 338-339). I have named the cells with letters and number, filled in some terms drawn from ancient status theories and supplied examples for the different types of disagreement. We will look at some of these. (Notice that the table also contains examples and comments not cited in the text of this paper.)

But you may ask, Why do all this? Is this meant to be a better interpretation of what ancient rhetoricians meant? No, I propose it as a useful tool for handling current social and political disagreements. If public debaters and audiences would think about disagreements in terms like these, they might better avoid the characteristic widening of disagreements where debaters impute imaginary standpoints, policies, reasons, intentions and personality features to each other. With greater awareness of the specific type of disagreement in a particular case, debaters may be more conscious of the norms that their own argument relies on, and of those on the other side.

Let us look at some of the types of disagreement that our generalized and integrated version of the *status* system specifies. Those that primarily call for comment are those representing the four *status legales*, seen as specifications of the *status finitionis* (C5-F5 in the table). This is where the traditional system of *status rationales* is most notably enriched; the *status conjecturae* and the *status qualitatis*, on the other hand, are defined and subdivided by the present scheme in the same way as we find in ancient theory (more specifically that of Hermogenes).

If for example the disagreement is one where no pre-existing norm clearly and indisputably applies (cell C5 in the table), then that understanding might be a starting point for a discussion where both parties collaborate to find a relevant norm. Issues where such a search for relevant norms is indicated concern such "new" phenomena as are currently emerging in fields like bioethics and information technology: Cloning of higher organisms and stem cell research are activities where there is indeterminacy as to what categories may relevantly apply to the entities in question—and hence there are also quandaries as to what exisiting norms, if any, may relevantly apply to them. Various forms of digital file sharing are technological phenomena which, at least according to some, fundamentally question existing norms relating to property and intellectual rights, thus necessitating the formulation of new norms.

1	Classical terms	1. *Status conjec-turae*	2. *Status finitionis* (the *status legales* are inserted here: C4-F4)			
2	What are we de-bating?	What are the facts?	What norms apply to the facts? (Legal norms [statutes], ethical norms, ideological norms, value concepts, "doxai", "common sense", formal and informal topoi …)			
3	Argumentation theory	Truth/ Accepta-bility	Relevance			
4	Classical subtypes		Assimilation *Ratiocinatio*	Ambiguity *Ambiguum*	"Letter and Intent" *Scriptum et voluntas*	Conflict of law *Contrariae leges*
5	Disagree-ment type and appro-priate rhetor-ical strategies	Disagree-ment about facts Give evidence Increase prob-ability	No norms clearly apply Argue from either conse-quences or analogy	One disputable (vague) norm applies Interpret norm to either include or exclude facts	One disputable (strict) norm applies Dissociate between literal and intended meaning	Two or more contra-dictory norms apply: Argue to show that norms on own side have more relevance and/or weight than those on other side
6	Com-ments		Mostly novel pheno-mena	Many debates in politics and ethics belong here (cf. Warnke)	Often a last resort in argument	Many debates in politics and practical ethics Cf. "conductive reasoning" "Value pluralism" "Incommensurability" "Normative meta-consensus" Norms invoked include: legality, justice, advantage, feasibility, honour, consequence
7	Examples:		Cloning, Stem cell research, File-sharing,	Abortion	Anti-abolitionists: "Black slaves not intended by 'all men created equal'"	Invasion of Iraq: Spread democracy, Depose tyrant, Self-defence *vs.* Legality, Human and material costs Resulting chaos Muhammad cartoons: Defend free speech internationally *vs.* Gratuitous offense to minority locally
	A	B	C	D	E	F

338

3. *Status qualitatis*					
What specific features and circumstances of the facts should be considered?					
Weight, Strength, "Sufficiency", "Good Grounds" (= gradual and quantitative considerations)					
Counterplea *Antilepsis*	Counter-statement *Antistasis*	Counter-accusation *Antenklema*	Trans-ference *Metastasis*	Mitigation *Syngnome*	Mortification
Norm recognized, but breach justified by extraordinary circumstances "It is just"	Norm recognized, but set aside "It is necessary"	Norm recognized, breach blamed on object of breach "They asked for it"	Norm recognized, breach blamed on external party "They made us do it"	Norm recognized, breach attenuated "Mitigating circumstances"	Norm recognized, breach deplored, forgiveness asked "I apologize"
All these resemble, or are even identical with, those issues where contradictory norms apply (F5); the difference, if any, is that in the *status qualitatis* (as we are here), one argues for an exception to the strict application of a certain general norm, the relevance of which is not contested					
Liquidation of informers under German Occupation; Whistleblowing	Torture, "extra-ordinary rendition" ; "illegal combat-tants"	Retaliation in war	"We were under orders"	Victim gets back at tormentor	"I misled people, including even my wife. I deeply regret that."
G	H	I	J	K	L

Disagreeing debaters might also find that they both agree on a certain norm, but that their disagreement is about interpretation, that is, about whether the fact they discuss can indeed be meaningfully subsumed under this norm that they both happen to support (cell D5). The philosopher Georgia Warnke (1999) has written about this sort of "interpretive" disagreement. The abortion issue in the United States is a prime example; the problem is that the participants in that debate do not realize it. Both sides are surely "pro life" as well as "pro choice," but the disagreement is on whether the removal of a new foetus, or fertilized egg, constitutes the taking of a human life, and whether a woman's choice to have a new foetus removed from her body can be seen as her own choice.

Disagreements belonging in cell E5 are those where a strict and literal understanding of a norm (either written or unwritten) is opposed by one that will read a different underlying spirit into that norm. For example, anti-abolitionists in the debate on slavery in the US in the Nineteenth Century were apt to believe that the words in the Declaration of Independence about "all men" being "created equal," when read in the right spirit, did not really apply to black slaves, although they admittedly saw them, in a certain sense, as men.

Again, two disagreeing debaters in the abortion controversy might find that they mutually endorse the other side's interpretation of the norms that are invoked. Then we have a dispute belonging in cell F5: there is agreement on two relevant norms which in the specific case point to opposite conclusions, and the crucial point is now whether the argument relying on one of these norms can be made to appear weightier than the argument relying on the other.

Column F in the table is the deliberative counterpart of *contrariae leges*—cases like those where two or more normative concepts are used as warrants on opposite sides. We face such issues all the time. The invasion of Iraq was supported by some with reference to defence against terrorism, dissemination of democracy and the need to overturn tyrants, but it was opposed by others with reference to its non-compliance with international law, the loss in human and material terms, and the dangerous chaos that would be its likely consequence.

All of these considerations were in some sense potentially relevant to the issue, so we had a case of what Carl Wellman (1971) and Trudy Govier (1987, 2004) have called "conductive reasoning," i.e., we must somehow weigh the pros against the cons. Such situations exemplify the "value pluralism" propounded by Isaiah Berlin (1998, 2002), that is, the understanding that several norms may be relevant to a given issue, but argue for opposite decisions—and this not only between two disagreeing debaters, but also inside the mind of an individual. Other philosophers have recently emphasized the "incommensurability" that obtains between such norms, which implies that it cannot be objectively determined whether one or the other norm should have priority because the relevant norms belong to different dimensions (see, e.g., Raz 1998, and Kock 2003; this volume, Chapter 6). In legal argument the status of *contrariae leges* describes such situations, and if we apply status thinking to social disagreements we are reminded that similar contradictions are common there as well, probably more so.

Besides value pluralism and incommensurability, another concept that may be illuminative in polarized debates about controversial issues is that of normative metaconsensus. The political theorist John Dryzek defines it as "agreement on recognition of the legitimacy of a value, though not extending to agreement on which of two or more values ought to receive priority in a given decision" (see, e.g., Dryzek & Niemeyer 2006, p. 639). In the Iraq debate, both supporters and opponents of the invasion might probably agree on values such as spreading democracy as well as respecting international law. The dispute would then be narrowed down to one about the priority, in the specific case, of one norm over the other; that is, there would be normative metaconsensus. Normative metaconsensus might also be said to exist between the two sides in the abortion debate. Life and choice are two values that both sides recognize, and their dispute is either one of interpretation because both these notions are vague, or one of priorities.

In proposing to apply status thinking to deliberative disputes I do not suggest that we can expect consensus on issues like the ones I have mentioned. The belief that rational argumentative discourse will necessarily lead to consensus (or towards consensus) has been championed by Habermas in philosophy and by political theorists such as Elster (1986). In argumentation theory, the pragma-dialectical school builds on the hypothetical assumption that the purpose of all argumentation is for the discussants to resolve their dispute. But as John Rawls and others have maintained, there are reasons why people may not ever agree on issues where values are involved; hence his term "reasonable disagreement" (1989, 1993). One of these reasons is precisely the fact that people may, even within the bounds of reasonableness, interpret values differently; this is the main idea in Georgia Warnke (1999). Another reason that people may prioritize values differently; or, in the terminology of Perelman and Olbrechts-Tyteca (1969), their value hierarchies differ.

Nevertheless, although consensus cannot, for these reasons, be expected to emerge, in some cases it actually might, and of course that would be welcome. But in the absence of consensus, to realize that there is normative metaconsensus is also an achievement. It would reveal that a dispute is not always an all-out clash between monolithic blocks that reject each other's values. Thus it would help narrow down the scope of the disagreement and focus everyone's attention on where it actually is rather than on where it is not. The polarization and the trench warfare we often see in public debates would lose some of their fuel. Moreover, debaters on both sides might find more persuasive arguments for their views. The status system in antiquity had this kind of purpose. The reason it might work like that is that it helps us focus on the decisive points of disagreement. If one could change opponents' minds about those, then one might change their minds about the whole issue. Similarly for undecided onlookers. They too would more likely take our side if we were to focus on the decisive point of disagreement and make them accept our case on that precise point.

To complete the picture, let us briefly consider the types of disagreement represented by the cells G5-L5. In G5, we have issues where a norms is recognized, but where the presence of "exceptional" circumstances is invoked to justify the suspension of that norm. For example, during the Nazi occupation of various European countries, including my own country, Denmark, many individuals known or assumed to be informers against members of the resistance movements were summarily liquidated by resistance men. No law or social norm was invoked to justify these killings or the fact that no legal steps were taken against them after the war, only the completely exceptional nature of the situation was invoked.

Cell H5 represents issues of a partly similar nature, including the use of "extraordinary rendition" and physical pressure bordering on torture against so-called "illegal combatants" captured in Iraq, Afghanistan, etc. Whereas in G5 cases the basic norm outlawing the liquidation of one individual by another is simply suspended by exceptional circumstances, in H5 cases there is more of a weighing of contradictory norms against each other, with one being regretfully "bent" because trumped by another, based on self-defence.

Cases represented by cells I5-L5 show gradually increasing degrees of recognition of the norm that is being broken: In I5 cases, the victim of the norm breach is cited as giving cause for it and deserving retaliation ("they asked for it"). In J5 cases, no degree of mitigation of the norm breach itself is sought, yet the perpetrator seeks acquittal or at least mitigation for himself by seeking to shift the blame to a third party, supposedly so powerful that no alternative was available for the perpetrator ("we were under orders"). In K5 cases the perpetrator admits his transgression and his responsibility for it, yet he seeks mitigation in the fact that, e.g., the victim had long tormented or provoked him—a circumstance that may indeed explain and even mitigate the transgression but never justify it. Finally, in L5 the perpetrator fully recognizes the transgression and his own responsibility, seeking mitigation only as an act of mercy, following his avowal of guilt and contrition. This strategy may be exemplified by former President Clinton's words, "I misled people, including even my wife. I deeply regret that" (words which came after a series of attempts at some of the strategies discussed above).

Let me reiterate that what I see as the most useful feature of this proposal to generalize status theory to everyday disagreements is the integration of the four *status legales* as a series of specifications of how we may disagree about the definition or nature of the act we debate. As an example, consider the debate on the Muhammad cartoons published by a Danish newspaper in 2005. In October of 2008, the debate was revived in another newspaper between its editor, Tøger Seidenfaden, a leading critic of the cartoons, and Frederik Stjernfelt, a well-known academic (Mogensen 2008). Seidenfaden argued that the cartoons were an act of gratuitous offence denying due empathy to a domestic minority not deserving such treatment, namely all those Muslims in Denmark who are peaceful and want integration, and thus the cartoons were likely to set back integration. Stjernfelt, a self-declared enlightenment thinker, argued that the cartoons were part of a global struggle for freedom of speech, against special rights for cultural groups, and he rebuked Seidenfaden for wearing "blinkers" and seeing only "the tiny Danish corner" of the issue, ignoring the global aspects.

As an onlooker, I cannot help wondering why these two debaters, both highly articulate and intelligent men, did not see more clearly the simultaneous relevance of two contradictory norms, both of which they probably both support. In other words, there was normative metaconsensus between them, but they did not realize it. Stjernfelt persisted in assuming that opposing the cartoons constituted a betrayal of the principle of free speech, and rejected the relevance of the "gratuitous offence" argument as "tiny"; Seidenfaden, on the other hand, appeared similarly insensitive to the global context, where some Muslims in fact acted violently to curtail freedom of speech, and he was unwilling to concede that the cartoons might relevantly be seen in that context—in which the domestically-based criticism of them (and of the Danish government's no-comment attitude to them) might appear as a failure to stand up for free speech. As an onlooker, I find it obvious that the quarrel between the two sides in this debate was not about any one of them betraying one or the other of the norms invoked (empathy with deserving minorities and free speech, respectively), but about how to interpret these norms, how they were relevant to the case, and in particular what relative weight or priority should be assigned to them. In other words, the disagreement was primarily an instance of the deliberative counterpart of *contrariae leges* (cell F5), with elements of interpretive disagreement (cell D5)—and the debaters should have realized that, or have been made aware of it. As a general principle, I would argue that onlookers looking for guidance on a controversial issue are let down by a debate where each debater only insists on the exclusive relevance of his "own" favoured norm. What might have helped onlookers more would be mutual recognition by the opposite sides that contradictory norms are relevant, plus a motivated bid from each side as to why its favoured norm should be given priority in the case at hand.

Even more generally, I suggest that democracies like ours need a greater awareness among debaters, audiences, journalists and educators that social disputes should not be seen as all-out clashes along enormous front lines, but may usually often be narrowed down to focused disagreements on more specific, but also more potentially persuasive points. I suggest that the insights contained in status theory as presented here can help promote such an awareness. Let us not be like the two lovers in Matthew Arnold's famous poem "Dover Beach," who feel that "we are here as on a darkling plain/ Swept with confused alarms of struggle and flight, / Where ignorant armies clash by night."

REFERENCES

Berlin, I. 1998. The pursuit of the ideal. In *The Proper Study of Mankind: An Anthology of Essays* (by Berlin), H. Hardy and R. Hausheer (Eds.). New York: Farrar, Straus, and Giroux, 1-16.

Berlin, I. 2002 [1958]. Two concepts of liberty. In *Liberty, Incorporating Four Essays on Liberty*. Oxford: Oxford University Press, 166-217.

Dryzek, J.S., and S.J. Niemeyer, and J. Simon. 2006. Reconciling pluralism and consensus as political ideals. *American Journal of Political Science* 50, 634–649.

Elster, J. 1986. The market and the forum. In *Foundations of Social Choice Theory*, J. Elster and A. Hylland (Eds.). Cambridge: Cambridge University Press, 103–122.

Govier, T. 1987. *Problems in Argument Analysis and Evaluation* Dordrecht: Foris.

_____. 2004. *A Practical Study of Argument* (6th ed.). Florence, KY: Wadsworth.

Jørgensen, C., L. Rørbech and C. Kock. 1994. *Retorik der flytter stemmer*. København: Gyldendal.

_____. 1998. Rhetoric that shifts votes: A large-scale exploratory study of persuasion in issue-oriented public debates. *Political Communication* 15: 283-299. (This volume, Chapter 12.)

Kock, C. 2003. Multidimensionality and non-deductiveness in deliberative argumentation. In *Anyone Who has a View: Theoretical Contributions to the Study of Argumentation*, F. van Eemeren, J.A. Blair, C.A. Willard, A.F. Snoeck Henkemans (Eds.). Dordrecht: Kluwer Academic, 157-171. (This volume, Chapter 6.)

Mogensen, L.T. 2008. Interview: Frihed for Frederik såvel som for Tøger. *Politiken*, October 4, section "Debat".

Orwell, G. 1946. *Shooting an Elephant and Other Essays*. London: Secker & Warburg.

Rawls, J. 1989. The domain of the political and overlapping consensus. *New York University Law Review* 64, 233-255.

_____. 1993. *Political Liberalism*. New York: Columbia University Press.

Raz, J. 1998. Incommensurability and agency. In *Incommensurability, Incomparability, and Practical Reason*, Ruth Chang (Ed.). Cambridge, MA: Harvard University Press, 110-128.

Snoeck Henkemans, A.F. 2000. State-of-the-art: The structure of argumentation. *Argumentation* 14, 447-473.

Toulmin, S. 1958. *The Uses of Argument*. Cambridge: Cambridge University Press.

Warnke, G. 1999. *Legitimate Differences*. Berkeley: University of California Press.

Wellman, C. 1971. *Challenge and Response: Justification in Ethics.* Carbondale: Southern Illinois University Press.

20.

Rhetoric in Media Studies:
The Voice of Constructive Criticism[*]

Rhetoric takes a view of media and of public communication generally that we may call functionalist. Rhetoricians tend to think that we use public discourse to do certain things for us with words. Rhetoric is a practical subject, which also implies that it is normative: it will teach us, not only to do certain things with words, but also to do these things well with words. Because rhetoric is about doing things well with words, it is also central to it that we should always be very aware of what we are trying to do, for we can do many different things with words, and they need to be done with different words; in general rhetoric teaches us that the function a message is meant to serve very largely determines all the properties that the message should have, which again implies that messages meant to serve different functions will have very different properties.

Rhetoric is not just a subject about how each individual can do his or her own thing with words, sometimes at the expense of others. It also holds that we have language and communication to perform certain vital functions in society. Rhetoric has always been seen by some of its practitioners as the ongoing public discourse that has helped establish human societies and hold them together; society would not have existed without the constant workings of rhetoric. In fact, the way rhetoricians figure that is that they believe that if everyone is enabled and allowed to do their own things with words, then that is the way in which the interest of society is best served.

Today, the media are the forum where public discourse is conducted. It follows that we should criticize the media when they fail to perform this function, and we should try to suggest how they could do it better.

By taking this stance toward the media, rhetoric distances itself from a couple of other positions that are strongly represented in today's academic

[*] From *Nordicom Review* 25 (2004: 1-2) (Special issue), 103-110. See no. 15.

world. In Critical Discourse Analysis and similar orientations there is, as in Rhetoric, an emphasis on the utterance and its specific properties, and on how discourse is always an attempt to further the encoder's interests; but there is also, inspired by Foucault, a constant assumption that public discourse serves to maintain a hegemony, that is, to preserve and extend power structures.

The strong suit of Critical Discourse Analysis, as practiced by Fairclough and others, is its meticulous observation of verbal messages revealing how even the smallest linguistic features of public messages may work to impress a view on us—a view which fits the agenda of the ruling powers. Critical Discourse Analysis, as Fairclough and others define it, is an astute attempt to incorporate linguistic analysis into social science so as to understand the transformations of modern capitalism. So basically, Critical Discourse Analysis is a purely descriptive pursuit. There is no theory of how public communication ought to be in order for it to fulfil a constructive role in society. There seems to be no theory of public communication as a necessary factor in a modern coherent society, no notion of a constructive function for public discourse at all.

Rhetoric, in contrast, is based on the premise that public discourse is beneficial and indeed necessary in human societies—but not any kind of discourse. Rhetoric shares with Critical Discourse Analysis the wish to look very closely at utterances in the public sphere and to analyse what they do and how they do it, but Rhetoric believes that there is good discourse and bad discourse, i.e., some properties of public discourse will hinder and some will serve the functions for which public discourse in needed. Hence Rhetoric is informed by the wish to identify these properties and to suggest or demand specific changes in current social discourse practices.

There are other voices in the study of public communication which also represent a purely descriptive stance, but with an orientation that is a far cry from the systematic suspicion of the critical discourse analysts. Polemically, one might refer to these other scholars as *un*critical analysts in that they seem to have taken it upon themselves to defend the media *en bloc* against any criticism. The outstanding British-American scholar Pippa Norris, it might be argued, is a representative of this trend. In her recent book, *A Virtuous Circle: Political Communications in Postindustrial Societies* (2000), she broadly dismisses what she refers to as "media malaise" and demonstrates with a wide battery of empirical data that there is a consistently positive correlation between attention to the news media and political knowledge, trust and participation. Hence, runs the argument, we should not "blame the messenger" but should look elsewhere to understand and confront the more deep-rooted flaws in current representative democracy.

But it is hardly surprising that there is a positive correlation between media use and political engagement; how could it be otherwise? Still this obvious fact does not acquit the media from any criticism of how, and how well, they perform their social functions. As a rhetorician one must find it disappointing that a media scholar like Norris never descends from the bird's-eye-view to look at specific types or even instances of political journalism. Also it is striking that Norris and other leading media scholars refrain from entering into any normative judgments; she has nothing to say as to which types of political journalism might be better than others in some way, nor as to types of political debate or engagement. Such media studies can be of very little help both to society and to the media themselves.

In contrast to these two broad orientations, which we may polemically call the paranoid and the obsequious, a rhetorician looks at public communication and the media with a functionalist eye. It recognizes that we need public communication for society to exist at all, and it asks not only: "How well does public communication perform the social functions it is meant to perform?" but also: "How could it perform them better?"

A trend in media studies that rhetoric has much in common with is uses-and-gratifications theory. Rhetoric shares with it the notion that utterances are used for different, specific purposes. However, uses-and-gratifications theory assumes, optimistically and individualistically, that each user selects and uses media content for his or her individual purposes. Rhetoric takes the social angle: how can we have communication that will perform these social functions for us? As a result, rhetoricians look closely at specific properties of media content, often with a view to how it could be different, whereas uses-and-gratifications theory, in a much broader approach, describes what each medium, considered as such, is used for.

Rhetoric acknowledges that the function of verbal communication is mainly to impress our views and our will on others. However, its view of interpersonal communication has more to it than this. If citizens have the means and the opportunity to make a case for their views in open debate, then that is the best way to build a human society that will endure.

What we are talking about here is often called the deliberative function of public communication. Deliberation actually means to weigh something, as on a pair of scales, and what we weigh when we deliberate is decisions. Where decisions are concerned you cannot prove anything, i.e., make a logically "valid" case one way or the other; instead, you have to see if you can increase your audience's adherence to your proposal. It follows that the best we can do in public debate is to make sure that the best reasons on both sides of a case are *heard, understood* and *given attention*.

The criteria for public debate just given have several implications. Public communication on politics should give much attention to the reasons that may be offered for or against a proposed policy. Hence, rhetoricians would, for example, look critically at the ways in which the media present reasons for a decision to go to war. Do the media, in particular, manage to make the available arguments on both sides of the issue accessible and understandable to the public? Also, rhetoric would look carefully at how spokespersons on each side of an issue make their case, and what treatment they in turn are given by the media. For example, it would expect would-be deliberative debaters to acknowledge legitimate arguments on the opposite side. Good reasons should be stated, heard and attended to, also by those who disagree. One important complaint against the way politicians and other decision makers argue is precisely that they tend to suppress, ignore or distort the reasons that the opposite side has to offer—especially the good ones. The media should try to make politicians attend to good reasons offered by the other side, and media critics should watch that the media do so. This is because the necessary function of deliberative debate is to identify, in Aristotle's phrase, "the available means of persuasion" (cf. *Rhetoric* 1355b) on *both* sides, thereby helping audiences form their own reasoned standpoints.

As an example of how scholars with a rhetorical approach would look at the media and their performance, we might consider the studies that Kathleen Hall Jamieson and Joseph Cappella presented, in their book *Spiral of Cynicism* (1997), of how the media reported the political activities around a possible health care reform in the US during the early years of the Clinton presidency. What Jamieson and Cappella found was essentially that the media, instead of focusing on "issues," i.e., the problems facing the American health care system, their possible solutions and what cases could be made for them, focused overwhelmingly on "strategy," i.e., the moves of the warring parties and political figures in the legislative process. The view of politics underlying this kind of coverage is that, as a general assumption, politicians are driven by a wish to preserve and extend their personal power, not by ideas about what policies are best for society. Further, Jamieson and Cappella argued that this strategic focus was instrumental in bringing the legislative process to a deadlock so that no reform came about. The book presents a series of studies suggesting that strategic coverage of specific issues tends to infect media users with a general cynicism regarding the *entire* political process; also, that media users do not want or demand strategic coverage of politics to nearly the extent that media people think they do, and that as cynicism grows, so does also public distrust of the media themselves—hence the term "spiral of cynicism."

Regina Lawrence (2000) did a further study of the dysfunctional workings of political coverage in the media, showing how media, in the phase where a piece of legislation was still in the making, would concentrate on the strategic aspects of the political process; only *after* it was made effective would they begin to describe how it would affect citizens.

There are several other empirical data which suggest that the media and their users do not see eye to eye as to what aspects of politics political journalism ought to focus on. In a 1999 study of the presidential election in 1996, two University of Connecticut researchers found that the way the media covered that election was grossly out of touch with how voters wanted it covered (Dautrich and Hartley 1999). Consistently throughout the campaign, voters found that the media focused too much on candidates' personalities, on "horse race" and on strategy and tactics, but too little on their standpoints on issues, on the effect if either of them were elected, and on the views of third parties.

For two years I directed a project financed by the Danish Newspapers Association to investigate current and alternative ways of doing political journalism in print media. The project is reported in the book *Forstå verden: Politisk journalistik for fremtiden* (Frederiksberg: Samfundslitteratur, 2002). In one study, I did a content analysis of all articles in the Danish daily newspapers about the budget negotiations for the year 2000. The articles, it turned out, were mainly about strategic maneuvering by the various parties involved in, or excluded from, negotiations about the upcoming budget. In addition, there was a good number of articles about minor, controversial items or proposals, many of which never materialised. But there was virtually no coverage of the overall structure of the budget, for example the fact that out of the 400 billion kroner in the Danish state budget, the vast majority is bound by other laws and hence untouchable, whereas less than 10 billion may in fact be shifted about in budget negotiations. But what, then, are the purposes for which we set aside nearly all of our national household money? How big are these programs in relation to each other and in relation to corresponding accounts in other countries? Which have grown most, and why? Why does a rich nation not have enough for health, education, and care for the elderly? How much *do* we spend on these accounts, by the way? In short, what are we spending our household money on? These are the questions that traditional budget negotiation coverage in newspapers leaves unanswered. Imagine a family living in similar ignorance of what their available income is spent on.

Moreover, there is no empirical evidence to suggest that newspaper readers or even TV audiences actually want the coverage of national budget affairs to be the way it traditionally is.

Media researchers ought to intervene here and point out that this is the way the media treat a subject like this; they might try to work out what users actually feel about it, and what the objective effects of it is; and they might suggest alternatives and do research to find out what users might think of them.

A group of journalism students who had heard of the critical stance our project was taking towards traditional political journalism did a study to see whether a sample of ordinary readers were in agreement with the media's own criteria as to which types of news stories they found most interesting (reported in the book). They constructed a list of 10 made-up news headlines, five reflecting "traditional" criteria of newsworthiness, and five which reflected a focus on broader structural issues. They asked political editors at five national newspapers and 76 ordinary readers to select the five stories that they would be most eager to print, respectively to read. This brought out a strong discrepancy between editors' and readers' preferences. The most attractive story to the editors was one that stated that the Minister of Culture would withdraw from politics in connection with the upcoming birth of her third child. This story was the one that readers were least likely to read. Instead, they gave top priority to a story whose headline asked the question: "Euthanasia—murder or charity. We have the right to live. Should we also be given the right to die?"

An interesting wider implication of this study was that some of the stories ranked highest by readers were in fact not about news. Their number 3 favourite was one whose headline said, "A multicultural democracy—Europe is the cradle of democracy, but are we willing to give immigrant citizens full democratic rights?" To this one editor objected that such a headline was "dreadfully abstract," and editors ranked this story eighth.

The interesting general issue here is that the media apparently do *not* necessarily give the audience what they want. There have been many claims that the media nowadays are run by money people, not by news people, and that this is the reason behind much of the current media malaise. But what we see in the case of political journalism is that what the media offer us is to a large extent not what the market forces would dictate. The forces that give us cynical, horse-race-oriented, unenlightening political journalism are not the market forces of public demand, but perhaps rather the forces of journalistic myth and orthodoxy.

One article of orthodox journalistic faith is precisely the cynical view of politics—the view of politicians as self-serving individuals whose every action or statement is dictated by a will to preserve or extend their power. This attitude, on the one hand, supplies an explanatory framework that is characteristic of the journalistic profession; it makes the journalist who adopts this attitude look like a seasoned expert, someone with savvy and no illusions, who is not easily taken in; however, with this framework to explain anything that goes on in politics, the journalist is not obliged to have any substantive knowledge of any actual policy areas. For example, in commenting on politicians' moves on health care legislation, the journalist needs no medical expertise or knowledge of health care economics, but may fall back on the same type of catch-all theory as for any other area of political debate: the power struggle framework. Adopting this framework is thus not only gratifying for the journalist, because it gives him a distinctive journalistic angle on politics; it is also cheap: with this one simplistic framework applied to everything any cub reporter can be a professional, because he needs no real knowledge of anything. For this stance I would like to suggest the term "Instant professionalism."

The cynical view that gives political journalists Instant professionalism is only one of several myths that haunt the media. It is a myth in the sense that contrary to what many journalists believe, it is not good for society, and since readers do not particularly want it, it is not good for business either. Another myth that specifically plagues newspaper journalism has to do not with the ideological but with the formal or structural dimension of messages. It is the myth of the "inverted news pyramid." This term refers to the traditional structure of news copy where everything is arranged in a linear sequence, beginning with whatever has most news value and then presenting additional chunks of information in order of descending importance. This often means: irrespective of chronology, logic and clarity.

The inverted pyramid is similar to the set menu at some restaurants, where the chef alone decides what we are having and in what order. Except that when we read it is easier to rebel and either drop out, which is what most readers do most of the time, or skip around, in which case one often has to skip pretty much at random, because it is usually not possible to see in advance what the individual parts of the article contain.

As stated before, it is a key point in a rhetorician's approach to the media that a given medium has several widely differing functions. Consequently, it makes little sense to speak of the function of that medium as such, or to assume that the medium as such imposes specific conditions on whatever content it is used to mediate. The function of a medium is to mediate the functions of the content that it carries. And each medium may carry many types of content, each with its own distinctive function.

It is clear that each medium will be better suited for certain functions than for others. Still, it is a mistake to believe that a given medium, e.g., television, imposes certain specific requirements on all of its content regardless of function. For example, there has been a strong desire in TV programming to inject narrative qualities into material that is not by nature narrative. This often involves an entire dramaturgy with heroes, villains, build-up, point of no return, etc. However, it is not necessarily the case that such a dramaturgy is functional in dealing with political issues, and while many viewers who watch a TV documentary based on these principles may feel that they are offered a strong narrative experience, they may also feel that somehow they are not given a fair and useful understanding of the issue involved.

Media scholars might perhaps expect a rhetorician to say to them, "Go ahead, learn all the tricks of the rhetorical trade, and use them. Use metaphors, symbols, tropes and figures, narrative suspense, identification and all the other tools that rhetoricians have identified." But no, what this rhetorician would say above all is, "Learn all these tricks of the trade but also learn to use them for what they are good for, for the functions that they will serve well and not for other functions where they tend to have a confounding effect."

An example of how rhetorical devices tend to confound some functions while pretending to serve others is a study by Michael Milburn and Anne

McGrail on "The Dramatic Presentation of News and its Effects on Cognitive Complexity" (1992). What they did was to show authentic, dramatic news stories to two groups, for example an item about election unrest in Chile, where one group saw the original while the other saw a version with the most dramatic scenes cut out. What they found was that "exposure to the dramatic news stories significantly decreased subjects' recall of the information in the stories and reduced the complexity with which individuals thought about the events reported."

More generally, as a rhetorician one would welcome more studies of the use of visuals in news programs on TV, such as what types of visuals are used for particular types of content, what effects they have, for example in terms of recall, learning, etc., and what other types might be used, if indeed visuals are necessary regardless of the type of story that is being presented.

Similar types of studies might be conducted on the use of visuals in newspapers. One aspect of this that deserves closer study is the use or non-use of graphics such as diagrams, maps, tables, etc. What are such devices good for, what are they not good for, where may graphs do a better job than pictures or verbal copy, what types are better than other types, what is current practice, and what suggestions for reform and experimentation might we make?

The use of graphics is one of the important but neglected issues for any medium that wishes to present quantitative information about national or international issues, and even more if one wants to help readers understand correlation, causation etc. Any important political issue involves quantitative dimensions and question of what causes what, for example global warming, the Israeli-Palestinian conflict, and budget balancing. This is one question that cannot be left to the media themselves. For one thing, the use of graphs requires specialized knowledge of statistics and mapping techniques that are generally not part of journalism programs and certainly not of traditional journalistic skills. Also, the proper use of any such communicative device requires empirical studies, qualitative as well as quantitative, for which news organizations have neither the skills nor the means. As part of our political journalism project we did a study of the actual use of graphs in a leading newspaper, and the results clearly suggest that practical journalists grapple in the dark as to what types of graphic presentation of data exist, and what they can do.

Graphics are just one example of a type of rhetorical-communicative devices that is available to the media but is not used at all to serve the functions that it might. There seems to be a prejudice in the profession to the effect that graphics are trite and superficial, and another to the effect that they are nerdy and hence boring. So what some media have done, e.g., the American daily *USA Today*, is to use banal graphics that are pepped up with much colour and cartoon-like artwork. What few people in the profession have realized is that graphics of the type used by *USA Today* are perhaps boring *because* they are banal; no amount of four-colour hysterical artwork will conceal the fact they generally communicate nothing.

Graphics, then, represent one aspect of media rhetoric that media studies might give more attention to. By nature, they are two-dimensional and they may be packed with information and even insight at a ratio that is hard to match with other means. All this suggests that they are particularly suited for print media. And that brings us to the general question: which rhetorical devices are particularly suited for which media?

In addition to this, we already have another equally general question: which rhetorical functions are particularly suited for which media? That is the kind of question that our project asked itself in relation the daily newspaper, especially regarding its coverage of politics. Our answer was one that involved not only the physical makeup of the newspaper, including what we call its enormous, easily navigable user interface, but also the fact that it appears once a day and once only, as well as the fact that most newspapers have a long-established credibility or *ethos* to draw upon. Moreover, the newspaper is under increasing pressure as to the time readers will have or want to spend on it, given competition from other media and activities. All these particular conditions and constraints go together to suggest that what the newspaper of tomorrow should increasingly focus on as far as political coverage is concerned is well-researched material that tries to illuminate structures and issues that are currently debated or which will be in the time to come; and they should do this with an increased emphasis on two-dimensional devices, i.e., an array of elements, verbal or visual, that illuminate separate aspects of an issue, and which are easily identifiable as to what they offer. For example, it should be possible to "read" a graphic separately, or an item specifying historical background, or a narrative item representing the human side of the issue, or an analytic piece predicting likely outcomes, or setting out reasons on both sides of the issue. All this means less emphasis on breaking news, less use of the so-called inverted pyramid in reportage, which, as a linear and purely verbal structure, makes little advantage of the newspaper's two-dimensionality and fails to take account of readers' time constraints and reading behaviours. Also it means less opinionated preaching of party lines and correct opinions and more respect for readers who want help to form a considered view for themselves.

An obvious objection to all these claims would be that political journalism which follows these guidelines would not be read because it would be boring.

There are two answers to this. The first is that of course it is a good thing not to be boring, and the media should try to make sure that material about society and its problems is interesting. It might be argued that a piece which actually managed to explain something like the makeup of the national budget would be scary rather than anything else, and what's scary is at least not boring.

The second answer is that interest in this kind of material should come from its capacity to illuminate, that is, to bring insight, not necessarily from its entertainment quality. We all want entertainment, but many of us also want enlightenment, and the two functions, as any rhetorician remembers, are different. Some genres are good at one of these functions; others are good at the other.

These have been a few examples of how media experts might look rhetorically at the media. The main emphasis has been on that old-fashioned medium that media studies perhaps tend to neglect: the newspaper. But as we know there are several other media to look at, and several other functions that we would like these media to perform in society, so there are countless opportunities to ask questions of the type, "What functions should this particular medium be used to serve, which ones is it particularly good at, for which does it have constraints that call for special solutions, which rhetorical devices could this medium use to perform this function? What is current practice, and how could it be changed or reformed? What will users think of such a change, and what will its effect on them be?" These are what I, as a rhetorician speaking to media scholars, would call true rhetorical questions.

REFERENCES

Cappella, J.N., and K.H. Jamieson. 1997. *Spiral of Cynicism: The Press and the Public Good.* Oxford: Oxford University Press.

Dautrich, K., and T.H. Hartley. 1999. *How the News Media Fail American Voters: Causes, Consequences, and Remedies.* New York: Columbia University Press.

Kock, C. 2002 (Ed.). *Forstå verden: Politisk journalistik for fremtiden.* Frederiksberg: Samfundslitteratur.

Lawrence, R.G. 2000. Game-framing the issues: Tracking the strategy frame in public policy news. *Political Communication* 17, 93-114.

Milburn, M.A., and A.B. McGrail. 1992. The dramatic presentation of news and its effects on cognitive complexity. *Political Psychology* 13, 613-632.

Norris, P. 2000. *A Virtuous Circle: Political Communications in Postindustrial Societies.* Cambridge: Cambridge University Press.

Index

251, 269, 276-277, 289-291, 316, 340-341, 349, 352

demonstration 32, 42, 69, 76, 109, 117, 211

deontic principles 59, 61, 191

derailment 29

Descartes, R. 66

dialectical obligations 12, 29, 190-207, 208, 217

dialectical tier 27-28, 190

dichotomous, dichotomy 1-2, 4-5, 38, 108, 148, 153-154, 161, 214, 222, 238

direction of fit 31

directive 31, 95

disagreement 4-5, 11, 15, 141, 143-144, 160, 169, 173-174, 179, 187, 214-215, 237, 249, 333, 335-337, 340-344

dissensus 10-11, 62, 126, 142-144, 169-189, 197, 201

domain 2-3, 6, 8, 10, 26-42, 44-46, 50, 53, 73, 83, 85-87, 94, 98, 123,124, 137-141, 160, 168-171, 177-180, 188-189, 195-197, 337

Downs, A. 63, 277-278

Dryzek, J. 60, 140, 181-182, 345, 140, 159, 212-213, 279, 282

Ducrot, O. 14

Ehninger, D. 53, 68, 74

Einstein, A. 34

emotion 56

entail, entailment 2-4, 116-118, 124

epideictic 31, 33, 35-36, 109, 251

epistemic reasoning 1-2, 8, 10-11, 50, 57

Erasmus of Rotterdam 7

ergasia 107

ethics 6, 8-9, 11, 23, 37, 45, 52-56, 59-61, 63-64, 69-70, 74, 76, 79, 82, 89, 108, 118, 120, 129, 155, 159, 161

ethos 28, 32, 46, 61, 64, 70, 225, 228, 230-231, 250, 257, 356

eudaimonia 108

Eudemian Ethics (Aristotle) 23, 37, 44, 54-55, 155, 173

Euro debate 94-97, 100

Fahnestock, J. 35, 81, 97, 150-151, 211, 310, 313

flattery 8, 19, 52-53, 111

forensic 15, 31, 35-36, 38, 61, 63, 109, 120, 233, 239-240, 251, 334

formal logic 2

Fortenbaugh, W.W. 54

Fortunatianus 40

fox-hunting 29, 73, 116-117, 121

Freese, J.H. 33

Fuhrmann, M. 74

Fumaroli, M. 41

fuzzy logic 92-93

Garver, E. 35, 46

Geach, P. 301

genre 6, 14, 35-36, 38, 106, 109-110, 119, 244, 251. 318-320, 324, 326, 329-330, 357

George of Trebizond 41

Godden, D. 83

Gorgias (Plato) 6, 8, 21, 171

Gorgias 7-8, 18-24

Govier, T 96-97. 157-159, 175-176, 181, 197, 213, 282, 340

gradation 57, 59, 156, 163, 298

Grice, H.P. 14, 211, 304, 306-307, 309-310, 313-314

Griffin, J. 73, 137

Gross, A. 35, 37

Habermas, J. 10, 28, 62, 126, 130-131, 141, 171-173, 191, 198-199, 291, 330, 341

Hansen, F. 13

Harder, P. 187, 211

Hauser, G. 36, 43

Heath, M. 40, 174

Hegelund, S. 14, 128

Hermagoras of Temnos 38

Hermogenes 40, 110-111, 337

Hesiod 32

Honorius of Autin 41

Houtlosser, P. 8, 27-30, 35, 45, 116, 198

illative 27, 139, 180, 197

imperative 88, 90, 93, 107, 132, 154-155

incommensurability 5, 9, 11, 37, 44, 60, 68, 71-75, 78, 80-82, 110-111, 120, 137-138, 155, 162, 169, 176-177, 183, 190, 194-197, 199, 201-203, 341

inference 10-11, 44, 80, 85-87, 90-96, 98-100, 112-113, 118-119, 131-132, 137, 140, 151-154, 156-157, 169, 173, 181-183, 185, 190, 192, 196, 199-201, 216, 225

informal logic 12, 27-28, 82, 91, 120, 136, 157, 167, 188, 206, 211-212, 214

Institutio oratoria (Quintilian) 39, 107

Institutiones oratoriae (Vico) 42

Isidore of Seville 41

Isocrates 24, 40, 143

Janik, A. 74

Johnson, R. 8, 26-31, 94, 190, 213, 217

Johnstone, C.L. 60-61

Jonsen, A. 76, 79, 120, 128-129

Jørgensen, C. 12, 114, 220, 223, 230, 244, 248, 266, 334

Kant, I. 19, 42-43

Kempson, R. 295

Kennedy, G. 33-34, 37-38, 40, 42, 53, 251

Kenny, A. 11, 54, 57-58, 148, 151-152, 154, 156, 213

Kock, C. 47, 54, 62, 71, 74, 88, 114, 128, 132-133, 138, 176, 187, 195, 209, 211, 215, 217, 221, 223, 248, 266, 334, 341

probability 3-5, 45, 52, 54-56, 59, 64, 76, 129, 149

Prodicus 18

proof 2, 4, 6, 121, 171, 279, 282

proposal 9-11, 13, 44-46, 58, 68, 70, 77, 85, 88-94, 107-108, 112-114, 120-121, 124, 130, 132, 138, 140-142, 148-150, 152, 164

proposition 6, 9-11, 14, 33, 35, 41, 44-46, 55,57-58, 64, 68, 70, 76, 86, 88-90, 106-108, 112, 114, 130-132, 138, 142, 148-149, 152, 154-155, 164, 172, 190-193, 198

Protagoras (Plato) 8, 20

Protagoras 18, 21, 32

prudence, prudent, prudential 60, 64, 86, 88-90, 107-108, 132, 136, 175, 215-216, 336

Pythagoras, Pythagorean 2, 112, 279, 282

quantification 13, 162, 223, 294-302

Quattrocento 42

Quintilian 7, 38, 40, 43, 55, 110-111

Rabanus Maurus 41

Rackham, H. 37, 77

rational choice theory 63

rationalism, rationalist 9, 28, 68, 70, 72, 75, 78, 81, 130, 177-178

Rawls, J. 5, 47, 142, 173-176, 179-180, 187, 217, 341

Raz, J. 72-74, 78, 80, 82, 119, 137, 177-178, 194-195, 216, 341

reasonable disagreement 5, 47, 174, 179, 187, 217, 341

Reed, C. 87

relativism 75, 77, 81, 100-103, 158

relevance, relevant 4-5, 12, 44-45, 59, 71, 76, 81 89, 92-99, 111, 119, 129, 137, 139-143, 150, 156-162, 164, 174-176, 179-186, 192-195, 201, 208, 211-215, 217, 232-234, 236, 280, 282, 284-287, 289-291, 307, 314, 321, 335, 337, 340-341, 343-344

Remer, G. 39

Renaissance 42, 121

Rescher, N. 36, 85, 143, 184

Rhetoric (Aristotle) 36-37, 44, 53-54, 56, 60, 81, 109-110, 124, 251, 350

rhetoric, rhetorical 4-16, 18-24, 26-47, 52-56, 59-64, 68, 71, 75, 77-82, 106, 108, 110-111, 122, 126, 131, 133, 141, 143-144, 148-150, 156, 174-175, 178, 179, 182-183, 185, 190, 198, 203, 209-210, 212, 220, 223, 229, 234-235, 237, 239-241, 244-245, 247, 250-251, 269, 273, 304-307, 310, 313, 315-316, 333, 346, 348-350, 355-357

Rhetorica ad Alexandrum 9, 68, 77, 81, 108, 110-111

Rhetorica ad Herennium 38, 42, 109, 133

rhetorical argumentation 6, 8, 26-47, 79, 134

rhetorical citizenship 209

Rhetoricorum libri quinque (George of Trebizond) 42

Rieke, R. 76

van Eemeren, F. 8, 26, 28-30, 35, 45, 101, 113, 115-116, 129, 171, 198, 244, 319

vice, argumentative 7, 12-13, 208-219

Vico, G. 7

Villadsen, L. 207

Vincent de Beauvais 42

Virtues and Vices (Aristotle) 37

vote-gathering 12-13, 237-239, 244, 248-251, 266

vote-shifting 12-13, 237-238, 244, 248-251, 266

Walker, J. 33

Walton, D. 10, 85-103, 106-108, 114-115, 119, 126, 131-132, 171, 199-200, 230, 244, 251-252

warrant 2, 9-10, 15, 59, 68, 71-82, 103, 126-130, 134-135, 137, 148, 163, 172, 193-195, 197-198, 204, 214-216, 319-329, 336, 340

weight 2-5, 12, 45-46, 69, 73, 75, 78-81, 95-97, 111, 116-124, 139-143, 151, 157-162, 174-176, 180-182, 184-185, 187, 194-195, 213, 215-218, 232-234, 236, 248, 250, 252, 280, 282, 285, 289-290, 340, 344

Wellman, C. 96, 102, 155, 158-160, 163, 181, 197, 286, 340

Wenzel, J. 30

Wilson, T. 42

Wittgenstein, L. 6, 15, 69, 148

Yack, B. 62-64

Zadeh, L.A. 95

Zeno 40

Made in the USA
Coppell, TX
16 September 2021